Movie Talk from the Front Lines

This book is dedicated to the memory of
former Los Angeles Film Critics Association colleagues:

Douglas Edwards
Herbert G. Luft
Dale Munroe

MOVIE TALK
FROM THE
FRONT LINES

*Filmmakers Discuss Their
Works with the Los Angeles
Film Critics Association*

Edited by JERRY ROBERTS
and STEVEN GAYDOS

with a foreword by ROBERT ROSEN

McFarland & Company, Inc., Publishers
Jefferson, North Carolina, and London

Movie talk from the front
lines

British Library Cataloguing-in-Publication data are available

Library of Congress Cataloguing-in-Publication Data

Movie talk from the front lines : filmmakers discuss their works with
   the Los Angeles Film Critics Association / edited by Jerry Roberts
   and Steven Gaydos.
      p. cm.
   Includes index.
   ISBN 0-7864-0005-6 (lib. bdg. : 50# alk. paper) ∞
   1. Motion pictures—United States—Interviews. 2. Motion
pictures—United States.   I. Roberts, Jerry, 1956– . II. Gaydos,
Steven.
PN1993.5.U6M668   1995
791.43′092′273—dc20   94-29998
                                                           CIP

Manufactured in the United States of America

McFarland & Company, Inc., Publishers
   Box 611, Jefferson, North Carolina 28640

CONTENTS

Foreword (by Robert Rosen)   1

Preface   3

The Critics   5

1   Monte Hellman and *Two-Lane Blacktop*
(with Steven Gaydos)   7

2   Ivan Passer and *Cutter's Way*
(with Jerry Roberts)   23

3   Scott Wilson and *A Year of the Quiet Sun*
(with Jim Emerson)   41

4   Joe Dante and *The Howling*
(with David Ehrenstein)   49

5   Richard Rush and *The Stunt Man*
(with Kenneth Turan)   67

6   James Coburn and *Cross of Iron*
(with Steven Gaydos)   85

7   Russ Meyer, Roger Ebert, and
Beyond the Valley of the Dolls
(with Michael Dare)   107

8   Oliver Stone and *Born on the Fourth of July*
(with Michael Wilmington)   133

9   Horton Foote and *Tomorrow*
(with Jerry Roberts)   155

10   Richard Brooks and *The Professionals*
(with Charles Champlin)   173

11   Robert Culp and *Hickey and Boggs*
     (with Steven Gaydos and Charles Champlin)   191

12   Dušan Hanák and *Pictures of the Old World*
     (with Kevin Thomas and Steven Gaydos)   205

13   Charles Burnett and *To Sleep with Anger*
     (with Harriet Robbins)   215

14   William Friedkin and *To Live and Die in L.A.*
     (with Steven Gaydos)   231

15   Robert Altman and *The Long Goodbye*
     (with Michael Wilmington)   253

16   Roy Scheider and *52 Pick-Up*
     (with Kirk Honeycutt)   275

17   Slobodon Šijan and *Who's Singing Over There?*
     (with Harriet Robbins)   287

     Index   297

FOREWORD

Film archivists and film critics share in common an activist stance toward historical memory. For both, an examination of the past is never intended to be an escape from the present, but rather an act of commitment—a form of agenda setting for the future. It was in the spirit of this common affirmation that the Los Angeles Film Critics Association joined together with the UCLA Film and Television Archive to sponsor the film series Critic's Choice.

Critic's Choice screened films from the past, but its organizers deftly avoided falling into the trap of nostalgia—that retrograde form of historical memory that rears its head as film buffery for critics and antiquarianism for archivists. Instead, the agenda for Critic's Choice—both the titles that were selected to be shown and the debates that followed—were consciously intended to provoke rather than sedate.

One key activist goal was to reframe our understanding of past films in response to changing sensibilities. Taking a fresh look at classic titles and a second look at films largely ignored or underappreciated in their time, the series reaffirmed that criticism never comes to final closure. Each new generation brings fresh perspectives to the same work.

A second goal was to build bridges linking critics to filmmakers and filmmakers to audiences, thereby breaking down the splendid isolation within which each characteristically functions. As a result, one-directional communication gave way to interactive discourse: evenings full of questions, arguments, and at times genuine controversy. Rejecting as self-defeating the anti-intellectual assumption that movies should be seen and not talked about, the programs validated informed discussion, critical analysis, and freewheeling debate.

Finally, by creating a theatrical experience of quality prints shown in optimal conditions, Critic's Choice also helped to support the archive's mission of film preservation. The single most eloquent argument for the cause of saving our moving-image heritage is made when audiences in a darkened hall fall in love with images on the big screen and come to realize, viscerally, the tragedy of what might be lost.

Those lucky enough to attend the Critic's Choice evenings in Melnitz Hall had a rare opportunity to meet with an outstanding group of film artists speaking candidly about their work. Both LAFCA and UCLA are pleased that this book will provide an opportunity for this experience to be shared with a broader audience.

ROBERT ROSEN
Director, UCLA Film and
Television Archive

PREFACE

People who write about movies often talk about them with the same passion that they invest in their reviews. People who make movies often rhapsodize about them as if they were their very lives. When a filmmaker is working, his or her daily allotment of complexities, agonies, and small victories often constitutes dramas and occasional comedies and horrors that rival the stories that he or she is attempting to tell on the screen.

When the film critic meets the filmmaker, each often brings out the best in the other through their shared love for motion pictures. A critic may learn why a technique was used for an on-screen effect. And a filmmaker may learn something about the definite ideas that his films elicit. When such dialogues are conducted at a public forum, film fans and students can learn about big and little secrets, unique anecdotes, and workaday methods that had previously remained unsaid or restricted to the remembrances of the cast, crew, or studio figures involved.

When the Los Angeles Film Critics Association initiated the Critic's Choice film/filmmaker series in 1989, it was to celebrate certain films and their makers, investigate the reasons why the final-cut films looked and sounded as they did, and find bridges of understanding between the filmmaking and film-evaluating processes.

The interviews on the following pages illuminate a wide range of subject matter about films that were made for $60,000 or $30 million, adapted from William Faulkner prose or concocted about a promiscuous female rock band, achieved immortality or were in release for a few days before being unceremoniously shelved. Here, you can measure the enduring camaraderie that the late Sam Peckinpah engendered among the cast and crew of *Cross of Iron*; hear testimony by directors Richard Rush and Joe Dante to the virtues and values of making exploitation flicks for B-movie mogul Roger Corman; and find that among the reasons that *Cutter's Way* got made at all had to do with the marketing of the ill-fated *Heaven's Gate* and the ferocity of Jeff Bridges's dog.

The discussions were conducted at public forums arranged under the auspices of the University of California–Los Angeles Film and Television

Archive. The talks were recorded by the archive and transcribed by the Los Angeles Film Critics Association. The Critic's Choice evenings—for which a certain film was chosen by a selecting LAFCA critic, and a maker or makers of that film agreed to talk afterward about its production and his or her techniques and career—provided the filmmaking capital with a unique and ongoing series. Here, at UCLA's Melnitz Hall, filmmakers, critics, and the public shared their ideas. On each evening, the public was afforded the opportunity of an informal question-and-answer session with the filmmaker(s).

The organizers of the series followed the general rule of selecting neglected or "forgotten" movies, such as *Year of the Quiet Sun* and *Two-Lane Blacktop*. Most of the Critic's Choice evenings highlighted the guerrilla remembrances of maverick filmmakers, although such series films as *The Professionals* and *Born on the Fourth of July* were by no means neglected or forgotten. In any case, the views expressed for Critic's Choice by their makers—the late Richard Brooks, in one of his final public appearances, and Oliver Stone, respectively—provided a wealth of illumination.

The initiation and sustenance of the Critic's Choice series is a tribute to the faith and hard work shown by certain members of the Los Angeles Film Critics Association, a confederation of more than 30 print and electronic film journalists. The editors wish to thank past and present UCLA archive staff members, particularly Geoffrey Gilmore, Claire Aguilar, Vivian Mayer, Cheng-Sim Lim, and Andrea Alsberg.

Other particular thanks go to Jacqueline Harris, Charles Champlin, Bill Krohn, Katy Haber, Horton Foote, Tanya Sandoval, Monte Hellman, Roy Scheider, Michael Wilmington, Henry Sheehan, Sam Gnerre, Pavel Cerny and the East European Film Office, Mia Valert of the Czechoslovak Institute, the Typing Company of Hollywood, and the staff of the Margaret Herrick Library at the Academy of Motion Picture Arts and Sciences.

THE EDITORS
Los Angeles

THE CRITICS

Charles Champlin is the author of *George Lucas: The Creative Impulse* (1992), *The Movies Grow Up, 1940–1980* (1981) and other books. He retired in 1991 after serving for 26 years as arts editor of the *Los Angeles Times* and as its film critic from 1967 to 1980. He hosts *Champlin on Film* on the Bravo cable channel. He is a founding member and a past president of the Los Angeles Film Critics Association.

Michael Dare's film and video reviews have been published in dozens of periodicals, from *Billboard* and *Interview* to *Parenting*. He was also an editor for *A Day in the Life of Hollywood*. As a visual artist he has had many public showings, and his Polaroid celebrity caricatures can be seen in *Film Threat* magazine and on *L.A. – The Laser Disc*.

David Ehrenstein has been film critic for the *Advocate* since 1989. He has also written for the *San Francisco Examiner* and the *Los Angeles Herald-Examiner*, as well as for *American Film*, *Film Quarterly*, and *Film Comment*. He is the author of *Film: The Front Line* and coauthor with Bill Reed of *Rock on Film*. He has been active in LAFCA's annual Independent/Experimental Awards, giving initial wide exposure to such filmmakers Gus van Sant, Gregg Araki, Marlon Riggs, and Jon Jost.

Jim Emerson, a former programmer for Seattle's Market Theater and the Seattle International Film Festival, has written about film for the *Orange County Register*, the *Seattle Times*, *Film Comment*, *Premiere*, and other publications. Now a screenwriter, he is based in Los Angeles.

Steven Gaydos has cowritten the screenplays for four films: *Iguana* and *Better Watch Out*, both directed by Monte Hellman, *One Month Later*, directed by Nouchka van Brakel and *All Men Are Mortal*, directed by Ate de Jong. Gaydos, senior editor for special reports for *Variety*, writes extensively about film, and his articles and interviews with filmmakers have appeared in *L.A. Style*, *Hollywood Reporter*, *Movieline*, *L.A. Reader*, *Location Update*, and elsewhere. Gaydos is a member of the Writers Guild of America and is programming chairman of the LAFCA.

Kirk Honeycutt is a film reporter and critic for the *Hollywood Reporter*, a show-business trade paper. Previously, he was a critic for the *Los Angeles Daily News*. A theater arts graduate from the University of California, Los Angeles, Honeycutt appeared in several independent films and plays in the 1970s. He has written one-act plays for Theatre East and has worked as a production assistant on Martin Brest's *Hot Tomorrows* at the American Film Institute. Honeycutt's screenplay, *Final Judgment*, was filmed by Roger Corman's Concorde Pictures.

Harriet Robbins's reviews and articles appear in the main Spanish-language newspaper in Los Angeles, *La Opinion*. She also writes for several other publications, including *Baseline*, *Film Quarterly*, and *Angles*, a quarterly about women in film, for which she is regional editor. In the 1950s, Robbins was a secretary for the Actor's Lab, the experimental Los Angeles theater company that was the West Coast equivalent of the Group Theater. In the 1970s and early 1980s, Robbins served as a film industry acquisitions agent for National American Entertainment.

Jerry Roberts has been film critic for Copley Los Angeles Newspapers since 1985. He is the author of *Robert Mitchum: A Bio-Bibliography*. His reviews, features, and columns are syndicated nationally by the San Diego–based Copley News Service. A free-lance writer and former news reporter for the *Pittsburgh Post-Gazette*, he also served as sports editor for two Pennsylvania newspapers. He was secretary of LAFCA from 1989 to 1991 and vice president from 1993 to 1994.

Kevin Thomas has been reviewing films for the *Los Angeles Times* since 1962. A fourth-generation California newspaperman, he is a Los Angeles native. He has bachelor's and master's degrees in English literature from Gettysburg College and Penn State and has served on the juries of the Tokyo, Chicago, Berlin, Montreal, and Teheran film festivals. He has been named a chevalier in France's Order of Arts and Letters.

Kenneth Turan is film critic for the *Los Angeles Times*. He has been the book review editor for the *Times*, a staff writer for the *Washington Post* and *TV Guide*, and a film critic for *Gentlemen's Quarterly* and National Public Radio's *All Things Considered*. A graduate of Swarthmore College and Columbia University's School of Journalism, he is the coauthor of *Call Me Anna: The Autobiography of Patty Duke* and is on the board of directors of the National Yiddish Book Center.

Michael Wilmington is a film critic for the *Chicago Tribune*. His articles and essays on film have appeared in *Film Comment*, *L.A. Style*, *Isthmus* and the defunct vanguard of underground film study, *The Velvet Light Trap*. A graduate of the University of Wisconsin at Madison, he is coauthor with Joseph McBride of *John Ford* (1975).

1

MONTE HELLMAN

AND

Two-Lane Blacktop

(with Steven Gaydos)

On September 30, 1989, after a screening of *Two-Lane Blacktop*, director Monte Hellman was interviewed by Steven Gaydos and guest panelists Bill Krohn, American correspondent for *Cahiers du Cinéma*; UCLA Film and Television Archive director Geoffrey Gilmore; and Tony Safford, vice president of acquisitions for Miramax Films.

The Film

Two-Lane Blacktop (1971), a Michael S. Laughlin Production. Directed by Monte Hellman. Screenplay by Rudolph Wurlitzer and Will Corry, from a story by Will Corry. Produced by Michael S. Laughlin. Director of photography, Jack Deerson. Edited by Monte Hellman. Music supervised by Billy James. Casting director, Fred Roos. Titles designed by Marion Sampler. Associate producer, Gary Kurtz. Production manager, Walter Coblenz. Costumes, Richard Bruno. Sound, Charles Knight. Filmed on location in California, the South and Southwest United States. (*Editor's note:* Gregory Sandor is credited as "photographic consultant" on the film. It has been widely reported that this ruse was devised in deference to his lack of union credentials, and that Sandor, not Deerson, was the actual director of photography.)

Cast: Warren Oates (GTO), James Taylor (The Driver), Laurie Bird (The Girl), Dennis Wilson (The Mechanic), Harry Dean Stanton (The Hitchhiker), Alan Vint (Roadhouse Patron).

Synopsis: Two young men in a souped-up 1955 Chevrolet make their way through life and America by street racing. Going from one town to the next, they wager that their vehicle can outperform the best hot rods that the street racers in each town can offer. Never given names, these two nomads pick up a teenage female hitchhiker and become involved in a cross-country road race with an aging hipster in a shiny new Pontiac GTO. Whoever reaches Washington, D.C., first wins the loser's car. But along the way, the race places second to the complex and often comic human drama of the four nameless travelers.

Remarks and Reviews

"The surface story of a wager auto race across America is casually denied narrative tension to emphasize the resonance of character and situation.... Hellman seems to have gone out of his way to neutralize the potential of his subject. *Blacktop* could easily have been made as gripping as *Duel*, or as atmospheric as *American Graffiti*. Instead it's elliptical, oblique and equivocal, marred by its own lofty intransigence towards audiences" (David Thomson, *A Biographical Dictionary of Film*).

"[Warren Oates] began in character parts but ultimately moved into leads, most notably in three quirky existential films for Monte Hellman. The short, dark-haired actor could be friendly, ferocious, and funny. In *Two-Lane Blacktop* he talked a blue streak; in *Cockfighter*, he spoke only once. In *The Shooting*, in which he outsmarts and fights sadistic Jack Nicholson, he proved he even was capable of playing a western hero" (Danny Peary, *Cult Movie Stars*).

"The people, the gas pumps, the formica and neon of the drive-ins, the narrow restrooms, the ornaments of road life, half real, half symbols, are given no false glamour, no artificial value of their own. The value is our succinct experience of them" (Bridget Byrne, *Los Angeles Herald-Examiner*).

"Not a single frame in the film is wasted. Even the small touches—the languid tension while refueling at a back-country gas station or the piercing sound of an ignition buzzing—have their own intricate worth.... That the fadeout is strangely chilly and unaffecting does not prevent *Two-Lane Blacktop* from being one of the most ambitious and interesting American films of the year" (Jay Cocks, *Time*).

"*Two-Lane Blacktop* manages to speak compellingly of contemporary alienation without ever tumbling into the usual clichés of sex, drugs, and violence" (Roland Gelatt, *Saturday Review*).

"Monte Hellman's relaxed direction is no looser than is right. When need be he can remind you of the danger—the sudden swerve to avoid the unexpected obstacle—but more often he builds and builds upon the obsessive forward thrusting of the cars, the endless travelling, the awesome, yet ghastly, open spaces that are traversed as the vehicles move through Oklahoma and Arkansas and Tennessee" (Gordon Gow, *Films and Filming*).

"Excellent. Crossing a generation gap with compassion and strength. Big b.o. potential" (*Variety*).

"Perhaps the first racing picture to owe its origins more to the logic of Samuel Beckett than the world of AIP road pictures" (Larry Cohen, *Hollywood Reporter*).

"The America of *Two-Lane Blacktop* is no longer the vast expanse of opportunity and adventure, but instead, as the last scene of the film indicates, it is a vacuum" (Larry Salvatao and Dennis Schaefer, *Millimeter*).

Two-Lane Blacktop

The Filmmaker

Monte Hellman is a uniquely distinguished graduate of the "Roger Corman school" of the 1960s and 1970s "New Hollywood," as it was known, working on Hollywood low-budget units that B-King Corman directed and or produced. His classmates included such now well-known brand names as Coppola, Scorsese, Nicholson, Lucas and Dante, but Hellman never made another studio picture after *Two-Lane Blacktop*, entering an exile from the mainstream that is so severe as to garner Hellman some sort of title as the most respected yet underutilized American director of the last three decades.

David Thomson, in his *Biographical Dictionary of Film*, said of Hellman, "No system could digest the willfull arbitrariness of his best films," and Hellman's career has unfortunately borne out that 1970s pronouncement. Quirky, deadpan, formally severe, austere, philosophical, documentary-like, mythical: his films connect with audiences, but look impossible to market in the blockbuster cookie cutter factory that is modern Hollywood.

Which is not to say the filmmaker has been idle in the two decades since *Two-Lane Blacktop* hit the streets and Hellman's rocketing career skidded to a Hollywood halt. He went from being called "Hollywood's Best Kept Secret" by the *L.A. Times*, and the hot young filmmaker who practically reinvented the Western with his two existential Westerns starring Jack Nicholson, *The Shooting* and *Ride in the Whirlwind*, to struggling for low-budget funding for several little-seen film projects.

Those films include *Cockfighter* (1974), starring Warren Oates, photographed by the Oscar-winning Nestor Almendros and written by cult detective novelist Charles Willeford; *China 9, Liberty 37*, an Italian-Spanish Western starring Oates, Jenny Agutter and Fabio Testi, photographed by Fellini associate Giuseppe Rotunno and featuring a cameo by director Sam Peckinpah; *Iguana*, a strange pirate/Beauty and the Beast romantic adventure starring Everett McGill ("Twin Peaks"), photographed by Spanish cinematographer Josep M. Civit and based on the novel by Alberto Vasquez Figueroa; and *Silent Night, Deadly Night III: Better Watch Out*, the third installment in a cheapie horror series starring Richard Beymer (*West Side Story*) and Robert Culp of "I Spy" fame.

Though all of the films recouped their modest budgets through television and video sales, Hellman's reputation has been established as the ultimate outsider, an ironic fate for a filmmaker that many critics appreciate not only as a maverick, but also as an American traditionalist and a true original. The above four films have screened to acclaim at festivals in Venice, Seattle, Amiens, Paris, Moscow, Torino, Hof, Pesaro and many more cities around the world.

Hellman continues to work, if sporadically, with foreign producers and on shoestring budgets, but his body of work and his reputation as an unapologetic "auteur" is now reaching a New New Hollywood, and there are signs of fresh opportunity in his hometown. He secured the film financing for and served as executive producer on Palme d'Or–winner Quentin Tarantino's breakthrough debut film, *Reservoir Dogs*, and now Tarantino has announced plans to executive produce Monte Hellman's first real Hollywood film in almost 25 years, *Red Rain*. If Hellman was Hollywood's best kept secret 25 years ago, he must also rank as Hollywood's longest kept secret by now.

Monte Hellman's Filmography

As director unless noted: *Beast from Haunted Cave* (1959); *Creature from the Haunted Sea* (1960); *The Last Woman on Earth* (1960, 2nd unit director); *Ski Troop Attack* (1960, 2nd unit director); *The Terror* (1963, 2nd unit director); *Back Door to Hell* (1964); *Bus Riley's Back in Town* (1965, assistant editor); *Flight to Fury* (1966, also wrote the story); *Ride in the Whirlwind* (1966, also editor and producer); *The Wild Angels* (1966, editor); *The Long Ride Home* (1967, editor); *The Shooting* (1967, also editor and producer); *The St. Valentine's Day Massacre* (1967, dialogue director); *How to Make It* (1969, editor); *The Christian Licorice Store* (1971, actor); *Two-Lane Blacktop* (1971, also editor); *Cockfighter* (1974); *Call Him Mr. Shatter* (1975); *The Killer Elite* (1975, editor); *China 9, Liberty 37* (1978, also producer and screenplay);

Iguana (1988, also screenplay and editor); *Silent Night, Deadly Night III: Better Watch Out!* (1989, also story); *Reservoir Dogs* (1992, executive producer).

Reasons for Selection

Hollywood studio films of the late sixties and early seventies tell us a great deal about how our film culture has changed. For one brief, shining moment, while Vietnam raged overseas and race war threatened to engulf the country, young filmmakers and their accomplices in the studio executive corridors took the studio filmmaking apparatus and focused its resources on daring, socially critical, and often politically explosive material.

Paul Joyce's brilliant BBC documentary *Out of the Blue and into the Black* compellingly chronicles the restless mavericks and iconoclastic auteurs of the period. Dennis Hopper, Peter Fonda, Robert Downey, Paul Morrissey, Robert Altman, and others comprised a loose group whose only common denominator was the desire to make their own films according to their own creative compass.

Monte Hellman is perhaps not only the most emblematic filmmaker of this group and time, but also one of its most gifted. *Two-Lane Blacktop* is his only studio film, and his masterpiece. It was created at the intersection of art and commerce, and its blend of sharp social dissection and European existentialism was no match for the commercial juggernauts of Coppola, Spielberg, and Lucas that were about to push this free-spirited brand of filmmaking far from the center of the Hollywood studio system.

—S.G.

The Interview

Steven Gaydos: You said in an interview that we did the other day that this film couldn't be made today and that most films that interest you could not be made. What kinds of films interest you?

Monte Hellman: Start with the easy questions first. Well, I don't know what kinds of films. I'll tell you some films I like. I think my favorite films — sound films, let's say — are *Spirit of the Beehive*, a Spanish film by Victor Erice; *Slave of Love* by Nikita Mikhalkov; any film by Ivan Passer such as *Intimate Lighting* and *Cutter's Way*, which you're going to see here next month.

Gaydos: I think I would agree with you that it might not be possible to make the film now, but why was it possible in 1971? Maybe you can say something about the moment in which the film was made.

Hellman: Well, what happened was *Easy Rider*, and the success of *Easy Rider* made a lot of people at the studios think that somebody knew something that they didn't know, and maybe they should just give some young film-makers a hand and see what they could do. And so originally we had a deal on this picture at Cinema Center, and about three or four weeks before we were to start shooting they decided not to make the film. We went around to different studios trying to set it up, and we'd already cast it. We'd done screen tests on James Taylor and Laurie Bird. We had a package ready to go, and nobody believed we could make it for the budget at that time, which was $1.1 million, and Columbia thought it would cost at least $1.4 million, and MGM thought it would cost at least $1.6 or $1.7 million. Universal wanted to make it, and we told them we had a budget of $1.1 million, and they weren't fazed by it at all. They said, "Well, if you can make it for $900,000, you got a deal." [*Audience responds.*] And so we made it for $850,000. But the reason they were so interested was *Easy Rider*. Ned Tanen at Universal had convinced Lew Wasserman to make this program of five films that was like a special depart-ment: Milos Forman's *Taking Off*, *Diary of a Mad Housewife*, *The Hired Hand*, *The Last Movie*, and *Two-Lane Blacktop*. Ned liked the films and liked *Two-Lane Blacktop* very much. But Lew Wasserman saw the films and was shocked that his studio was making these pictures and did nothing to help any of them. He felt what life they had was an accident.

Gaydos: Why do you think he was shocked?

Hellman: Well, I don't know. But my theory is that it was really the religious statement, if you will, of the films. The political statement. The point of view of the films was counter to middle-class American ideals, and he felt uncomfortable.

Gaydos: Do you know anybody who was at that screening where Lew Wasserman saw the movie?

Hellman: No, I don't. But the amazing thing is that the sales department liked the picture, and they had it booked in something like eight hundred or nine hundred theaters—which was a lot at that time. And, it didn't matter. You know. He had his opinions, and...

Gaydos: You're saying that it did not open in eight hundred theaters?

Hellman: No, I don't think it did. And if it did, it still opened in a lot of theaters, but it was not supported. Well, for instance, in New York, the picture opened on a Fourth of July weekend. Or just after—the Wednes-day after the Fourth of July weekend. And I was in New York promoting the picture, and I looked in the papers on the weekend for some kind of adver-tisement telling people the picture was going to play. And there was nothing. And I asked why they didn't advertise in the newspapers the weekend before the picture was going to open. They said, "Well, it's the Fourth of July weekend, and nobody's home." I guess they don't read papers, wherever they are.

Bill Krohn: It's not hard to see why he was shocked. I'm shocked today. It's just a direction American film didn't go in after that. It looks very modern, and when I saw it in Paris last year, the first comment that a French director made was, "It would be impossible to do this film in America today. It's a time capsule from a period when things were being tried, and with very few exceptions, people don't get to try things anymore."

Gaydos: Someone in the audience already asked me this question: "What happened at that moment?" There've been articles and a documentary by Paul Joyce about it being a kind of crossroads for American film in the late sixties, early seventies. In looking back, do you see that as a crossroads, or that there were different directions that could have been taken?

Hellman: Well, I mean, there were a lot of people who were trying to make personal films and did. BBS was responsible for a number of films that were very interesting: *Five Easy Pieces*, *King of Marvin Gardens*, and, you know, a lot of other films.

Gaydos: Also *Easy Rider*, was that theirs too?

Hellman: Well, *Easy Rider* was theirs too. I personally don't think *Easy Rider* is that interesting a movie. But it didn't matter. What it was saying to the people, that's what's really important, I guess. And, I think in a funny way, *Two-Lane Blacktop* is similar to that because at least in Europe a part of the appeal of the picture, I think, is the fact that it represents for them, rightly or wrongly, a realistic view of what they imagine America is like.

Tony Safford: It's a film that is, I think, difficult to talk about and yet compels one to talk about it. I've seen the film a number of times, but this was, by far, the best audience I've seen it with. And that has to do with, I think, the way you responded to the humor in the film. There are obviously strong elements of absurdism in the film. And it's difficult to see the film with an audience where that doesn't play. And this was, I thought, really a great context to see the film.

Hellman: At the time it was first made and played, audiences laughed a lot. And I happened to arrive in Tokyo at the time *Two-Lane Blacktop* was playing, and I actually got off the train and walked two blocks and saw the theater where it was playing. And the next day I went to see the film with a Japanese audience. It had side-titles, not subtitles, and the audience did not laugh once. I was shocked, and I said, "Well, we really laid an egg here in Tokyo." And after the film they rushed up, and they were crying and emotional, and they loved the picture. But they didn't need to laugh in order to enjoy it. I mean, it's a different culture.

Audience Question: I was wondering how you happened to cast James Taylor and Dennis Wilson in those two parts? And I was also wondering what kind of strategy you took as a director in coaxing along their performances, since they weren't professional actors.

Hellman: Well, first of all, I'll start at the end of the question: They were professional performers, and there's really not a big difference, I don't think. I didn't have to spend any more effort with them than I do with people who've been acting for thirty years. The first role we tried to cast was the girl because we recognized that that was going to be a crucial role and difficult to cast. And I saw a hundred girls or so in New York, and I went up to San Francisco, and I saw fifty girls or so. I saw every teenage girl in Los Angeles, and it was soon apparent that there was nobody who had this special quality, except for one girl early on in New York, Laurie Bird, who was a model. She'd been recommended by somebody. We were struck by the fact that, you know, how similar she was to this character that we at that time just had an idea about because the script hadn't even been written.

We interviewed her for three hours on tape and used a lot of that interview as a basis for the character. I kept saying, "God, we've just got to find somebody like Laurie Bird." After a while somebody said, I don't know who, maybe it was Gary Kurtz, "Well, why don't we test Laurie Bird?" You know. Or maybe it was Fred Roos. So we flew her out to Los Angeles, and we screen-tested her, and I didn't have to sell her to anybody. I mean, they just looked at the test, and they said, "Wow, that's the girl."

I saw a lot of the people for the driver. I saw Al Pacino, I saw Robert De Niro, and I saw Michael Sarrazin, and I saw Jon Voight. You can't think of a young actor at that time that I didn't interview. I just didn't think anybody was right for this character. Fred Roos, the casting director, was getting frustrated and finally he said, "Well, what about composers? What about singers? What about this?" You know. He was suggesting all kinds of people.

And I said, "Well, I saw a face on Sunset Boulevard the other day. And I've never heard of him, and he has a really interesting face. What do you think?" And it was James Taylor. His album had just come out, and they were advertising it. He came in, and I knew it the minute I met him that he was the Driver. He was not really a big star at that time. While we were on the road "Fire and Rain" started hitting the charts and became a huge success. But that didn't happen until we were shooting.

I tested James with a bunch of young actors and didn't find anybody. Fred suggested Dennis Wilson. Dennis Wilson really had lived this kind of life and was a car nut, and I just thought he was right.

You know, the idea of casting two singers — I mean that was not an idea we had in front. It just happened.

Gaydos: You didn't find yourself working with those guys differently than you work with actors normally?

Hellman: Well, I don't think so. I know that James was very frustrated because he was used to running the show and producing his own records. He was very impatient with the other actors if they didn't know their lines perfectly. He knew everybody's lines. He was just there every minute and very good. But Dennis, I thought, had really a quality of being able to surprise me all the time. He was the only actor I think I've ever worked with who could be in front of the camera and be totally unaware that he was performing in front of the camera. I mean, his face would take on expressions that were completely the result of being totally within the scene. He was unselfconscious. I guess that's the expression. And I've never known an actor to be as unselfconscious as he was.

AQ: I was going to say one thing about this movie that seems very different from *Easy Rider*. It's that your people seem to be — the movie as a whole — seems to be very much at home in the redneck cafés and gas stations that you travel to across the country. What kind of reaction did you get from the people as you traveled along making the movie?

Hellman: The people everywhere were very cooperative. We had those police officers in Texas — they were real police officers. The gas station owners were gas station owners. The guy that sold the parts actually sold parts in that store. I used people doing the jobs that they normally do. And they all had a ball being in the film. People everywhere were just terrific. We spent a lot of time in Little Rock, and I just thought that Little Rock was a super place.

Gaydos: We talked about people's perceptions of this as a sixties movie, possibly, the end of the sixties or the beginning of the seventies. How do you see the picture? Which era do you relate it to?

Hellman: Well, I think it's sixties. I mean, there's a feeling. It's not in the film, but I get a feeling of psychedelic, you know, the drug scene. Nobody takes drugs in the film, but I think it's really the end of the sixties.

Safford: I don't find it dated at all. It's profoundly modernist and profoundly contemporary. I'll ask you my one patented question so you can refute it again. I've said that all your films are remakes of *Waiting for Godot*, and this film especially is a remake of *Waiting for Godot* in the sense that nothing happens, and it happens very quickly. You were the first theater director to direct *Godot* in Los Angeles, and I notice this had a seminal impact on your work.

Hellman: Well there are two coincidences in the last couple of days which relate to both parts of your question: Today, in the hardware store, I ran into Jack Albertson's widow, Wally Albertson, who actually ran for public office a few years ago, I guess, and lost. And we were talking about *Godot*, and about Jack [who starred in Hellman's production of *Godot*]. And last night I was coming out of a builder's discount store out in the Valley. It's on a kind of a dead end street, and I was the last customer to leave at about nine o'clock. There was a group of street racers preparing to race on this dead end street in North Hollywood. So everything's changed and nothing's changed.

AQ: How long did it take to write? And how many days of principal photography? Did this get the green light because of Hellman or because of something you pitched to Ned Tanen? And if you did pitch it, what did you say?

Hellman: No. I had been in Europe preparing a film — which didn't get made, as many of my films don't — and when I came back, a producer named

Michael Laughlin had been talking to my agent about me and he had two pictures that he wanted me to direct: *Two-Lane Blacktop* and *The Christian Licorice Store*. I told him I didn't much like *The Christian Licorice Store*, but the idea of *Two-Lane Blacktop* really appealed to me. But I thought it needed some rewriting. He had a deal for both pictures at Cinema Center at that time, and he just went in and told them he wanted me to direct the picture. They said, that's fine. Then when we switched over to Universal it was a package, and I didn't have to pitch anybody. Other than I have to gradually do what I always do, which is say, "Well I think we need a few scenes rewritten," and then wind up writing a whole new script. [*Audience responds.*]

AQ: What was it like working with Warren Oates?

Hellman: Warren was one of my closest friends, and I felt he was my alter ego, that I could express myself within the films through his personality. He was the most extraordinary actor that I've ever worked with, and I don't think I'll ever find anybody that replaces him in that regard. He, I think, was a very complex person, and there were a lot of things about him that I never knew until he was dead—such as the fact that he was a poet. But he was very much like my heroes in the sense that he didn't reveal a lot about himself. He was a great friend—a great companion, but you had to dig for a long time to find out who Warren really was. I think this quality of mystery is very important for an actor. It's something that too few actors today have.

Safford: Hellman, you once told me that you like a certain kind of acting which you definitely see carried to extremes in this film. It's one of the things we've been talking about. And the expression you used, I think, was that you like actors who serve the work.

Hellman: That's true. Not only actors, but everybody who's involved in the film I think should be there for the film and not for themselves. And this is something I learned from a great theater director named Arthur Hopkins, who had directed *The Petrified Forest* and *What Price Glory?* He discovered, really, Spencer Tracy, Katharine Hepburn, Humphrey Bogart, and you can just go on and name them. And that was his philosophy of theater.

Safford: I was just wondering if you could elaborate a little bit more about what originally attracted you to the story and what changes you felt necessary, and how you reshaped it.

Hellman: OK, but let me just go on a little bit more about acting, though. The thing I like in actors is the ability to be unpredictable, the ability to surprise me. In fact, what I like in making films in general is to be surprised. I like to shoot on locations because you don't know what you're going to find. It's the accidents that make the film interesting. Anything that I can plan in advance—and I do plan in advance—by the time I'm shooting the film, it's already boring to me. So it's the other things that happen along the way that, ultimately, make the film interesting for me. And it's actors who have that ability to surprise that I like. As far as what attracted me to the story, I think it was, initially, the aspect of gambling. My father was a gambler, and so I have a kind of feeling for films that have that subject. And in this case it's really the frame of the picture, but it's still what attracted me, initially. The original script was just not very interesting. It was a rehashing of a lot of Disney-type Fred MacMurray movies, and I'm not putting those down — I think there's a place for them and I like to watch them — but I wasn't really interested in making that kind of a soppy, farcical romance which was what the original story was: It was four college kids in a convertible racing this Chevy, and the mechanic falls in love with the girl who has a little VW Bug, and she's chasing them across the country, and he keeps dropping his rags out the window to let her know where they are.

Gaydos: You changed the script a little bit.

AQ: Was that before Willy wrote it?

Hellman: No, that was the Will Corry script. That was the one sold to the studio, you see.

AQ: There's the big scene where there's a big accident on the highway with the truck overturned, and the car, and where the man's been killed. Was that his thing — or was something similar to it in the original script?

Hellman: As I said, the movie that you've just seen has nothing to do with the original script. There was a new script written by Rudy Wurlitzer, and all the scenes were in the new script.

Gaydos: You said at one time Rudy never even read the script?

Hellman: Rudy never read the other script. He tried. He read five pages, I think, and he was unable to read it. He was physically unable to read it. [*Audience responds.*]

AQ: What happened to Will Corry?

Hellman: Will Corry got what he wanted. I mean, he's the only one who got paid a decent salary on this picture. He sold his script for $100,000. He bought a yacht. He got custody of his two-year-old daughter for one year, and they sailed around the world. So more power to him.

AQ: You were talking about rewriting the script. A couple of things I notice is that there's a real improvisational feel to the film, and that you then edited the film. You are credited with the editing. I wonder how much rewriting actually took place as you were shooting in terms of improvisation or other thoughts that came to you? And then in the editing, how much did you take liberty in terms of just discovering things or seeing new things?

Hellman: There were only two improvised scenes. And we shot the scripted scene in both cases, as well as the improvised scene. One was the cicada scene, where they're sitting on the fence talking about the cidadas, and the other was the scene where there are just two lines and she says, "I wish we were back in Santa Fe." So it's not much of an improvisation. Otherwise, everything was scripted, but the actors have the quality of doing something as if it's for the first time, which I think is what any good actor should be able to do.

Monte Hellman at work on his 1974 film *Cockfighter* (photo credit: Steven Gaydos).

Geoff Gilmore: I'm curious about what you think of the American independent movement that exists now. Because the discussion that you guys had earlier that this type of film couldn't be made now, that's probably true within the studio system. But there have been films made outside of the studio system, especially over the last five years, which are perhaps the most interesting American films being made. And this, of course, gives you the feel of an independently made film, as you obviously had to cut. I'm interested in whether you see directors in that work of being of interest to you.

Hellman: Yeah. I think it's true. I mean I saw some very interesting independent films at the U.S.A. Film Festival, and we picked a film which I think was extraordinary, which was called *True Love*. And that's one of the best films I've seen in the last few years. But I don't know how those films get made. I think that certainly it's as difficult to get a film like that made as it would be to get *Two-Lane Blacktop* made today. I think, in a sense, those films get made because somebody has to think they're commercial in order to make them. I mean, most of the time I don't know how a film gets made today unless somebody thinks, "Wow, there's going to be an audience for this film — this is really great," which is terrific. And if it's a private financier, that's great. If they happen to like something and they think something is commercial, that isn't necessarily so.

Gaydos: Also, there are art movies and then there are genre pictures. And you seem to have spent the last twenty-five years making sure that those two things got as mixed up as possible. Do you think that's part of the difficulty of a movie like *Two-Lane Blacktop*?

Hellman: Well, nobody thought that *Two-Lane Blacktop* was an art movie, least of all me. And I don't think it is, actually. But it purported to be a kind of movie about racing, and nobody takes the race very seriously. You can't make a movie about racing and not take the race seriously if you want to make a picture in America.

AQ: Would you feel comfortable with the cable and video revolutions making a picture that would go directly to cable or video without having a theatrical release? And do you feel that that would be possibly a way that you could have more smaller films made now or in the future?

Hellman: Well, I just made a film that was for video. And I didn't feel comfortable at all about the fact that they wouldn't make an effort to get it released in theaters. I thought the screening here tonight was terrific and the print looked good — there's something about seeing something on a big screen. I'm also a still photographer, and I have prints that I have different sizes of. There's a right size for every picture. There are some pictures that look great as miniatures, but there are a lot of pictures that need to be big. And *Two-Lane Blacktop* is a picture that the bigger it is, the better. I mean, the best screening I ever saw of it was in a drive-in theater because it was gigantic.

AQ: I seem to recall a cover story in *Esquire* at the time of the film's release which said something like, "*Two-Lane Blacktop*, the most important American film of the year, with portions of the screenplay within." Did that create an immediate critical backlash that hurt the movie at the time?

Hellman: It was the whole screenplay. In fact, it was twice as long as the movie because we had a first cut of three hours and a half, and I cut the picture down to an hour and three-quarters. So, half the movie is, you know, in the vault somewhere. The *Esquire* readers got a chance to read the whole script. Then when the movie came out, everybody was disappointed because they only got half their money's worth.

Safford: I think the *Esquire* story is a famous story, and it makes a lot of points. But they obviously thought this was the next *Easy Rider*, or whatever the next trendy art film or independent film was going to be. And they were very disappointed when they saw it. I think they gave themselves a Dubious Achievement Award for having jumped the gun.

Hellman: That's right.

Safford: The thing about *Two-Lane Blacktop*—this is just a comment—is that it doesn't resemble the way studio filmmaking was going, or had been, and it's not a trendy film. I think it doesn't fit in with the kinds of trends that captured a big audience for *Easy Rider*, and I think that's why it's lasted.

Hellman: Yeah, I would agree. I mean, I think this is the most disciplined, most subversive, most profound, most contemporary film. That I would say.

Gaydos: If you look back over Hollywood between now and 1971, you notice there are different fashions. There are different things that are in vogue. Whenever *Jaws* was making all the money it was making and when *Godfather* was making all that money, it seemed like it was a different atmosphere than '68 to '72.

Hellman: No, I don't think so. I think that they thought we were going to be making *Jaws*, and we didn't make *Jaws*, you know. We didn't deliver what we were hired to do.

I didn't mean to imply that we weren't influenced by the European films of the sixties. I think that everybody that I know who, you know, had a chance to do something at this particular time when they kind of opened the doors for a few years. We were all tremendously impressed and influenced by the European films that we'd seen.

AQ: I'm just curious to know what you thought of the films of John Cassavetes and Paul Morrissey at the time you were making the film—that late sixties, those early seventies, the ones that they were making.

Hellman: I respect their films very much, but they were not particularly films that influenced me. I think that I liked the films that I grew up with in the thirties and forties, and I liked the European films that I was seeing in the fifties and sixties. But I think when I actually had a chance to make films, the films that I wanted to emulate were the films that I had seen as a kid. I think I'm really a reactionary filmmaker.

AQ: Yeah, but you didn't copy them.

Hellman: Well, no, I didn't copy them. I would've if I could've.

AQ: I would like to ask a question of the whole panel if I could, following up on something that Geoff asked before about the independent features that are coming out today. One thing I want to point out as a student here: It was real big news that this film was screening tonight. I mean, people were talking about it all week. I see most of the people that are up there in the editing room down here watching this. I'm a little discouraged to keep hearing from the panel that, "Well, gee, it's too bad we can't make films like this now," because I think if I could speak for the rest of the students here—we'd sure like to. Why are you so discouraged about the possibility? I mean, we do have *Baghdad Café*; we have Jim Jarmusch's films. There are, it seems to me, some examples of things. Perhaps not quite as challenging as this. But along the same lines, do you feel that this situation is just hopeless, or what do you think?

Hellman: I think it's easier to make a film that's perceived as a comedy. That's for sure. When I say you couldn't make *Two-Lane Blacktop* today, I think it's the unrelenting pessimism that would go against it. You really have to make happy films today.

AQ: I really like the way you ended the film by the burning of the frame. I would like to know, was that in the script? Or was it a decision that you made later?

Hellman: No, it was in the script. It was a decision that I made. But Rudy ended his script with the shot of Warren driving away after talking to the two soldiers, and I was always unsure of it, but again I had this kind of feeling that we could always try things. It was a little bit out of the style of the rest of the movie in the sense that I think the movie is a very emotional statement—at least from my point of view—and the ending is intellectual. I felt uncomfortable about that, but I had to do it, you know. The Devil made me do it.

Gaydos: If I could address the fellow's question over here, very briefly—don't stop trying. The pessimism is based on prevailing trends, and you should always rail against those and try to make the pictures. Don't ever give up. If we're sort of revealing our pessimism, I know that Hellman is as resolute about making his kind of films as he ever was. And there's not one second of one day that he isn't pursuing it and making films.

Hellman: Yeah. Let me just clarify too. When we're saying this film could not be made today, we're saying this film could not be made in Hollywood today. There are a lot of other ways to make films, as we were discussing—the independent film and independent films for combinations of different kinds of coproductions and partially foreign-financed films, films financed by cable. There are other routes than just Hollywood.

Krohn: Before we leave, there's a preservationist matter to be dealt with first.

Gilmore: Absolutely.

Krohn: First of all, I'd like to thank the Sundance Institute for seeing to it that this print got made with those beautiful vibrant colors. [*Audience applause.*] And also, just so we don't end on too optimistic a note, Hellman made a film called *Iguana* that was shown to great acclaim at the Venice Film Festival, and at the Paris Cinèmatheque, and at the Amiens Film Festival in '88, and it's never been seen theatrically or even in a context like this in this country. Right now it would be impossible for that to happen because the Italian producer of *Iguana* has cut all the prints to his taste. I understand that the negative hasn't been recut.

Hellman: I don't know. I hope it hasn't been yet.

Krohn: Here we are in the most overworked preservationist institution in the world, probably, but I would like to just go on record that I think it would be a good idea if somebody struck a print of *Iguana* in Hellman's cut, so that if we ever want to see it here, at least we can see it. [*Applause.*]

For   Further   Study

Books

Tatum, Charles, Jr. *Monte Hellman*. Brussels: Yellow Now, 1988.

Thomson, David. *A Biographical Dictionary of Film*. New York: William Morrow and Co., 1975.

Wurlitzer, Rudolph, and Will Corry. *"Two-Lane Blacktop": The Screenplay*. New York: Award Books, 1971.

Periodical

Krohn, Bill. "'Iguana': Le Retour de Monte Hellman." *Cahiers du Cinéma*, November 1988.

2

IVAN PASSER

AND

Cutter's Way

(with Jerry Roberts)

On October 26, 1989, director Ivan Passer was interviewed by Jerry Roberts after a screening of *Cutter's Way*. Also participating in the discussion was Doug List, a copy editor for the *Los Angeles Times*, who was at the time of the interview entertainment editor of the (Riverside, California) *Press-Enterprise*.

The Film

Cutter's Way (1981), a United Artists Classics production. Directed by Ivan Passer. Screenplay by Jeffrey Alan Fiskin. Based on the novel *Cutter and Bone*, by Newton Thornburg. Producer, Paul R. Gurian. Director of photography, Jordan Cronenweth. Music by Jack Nitzsche. Assistant directors, Larry Franco and Jeffrey Chernov. Filmed in Santa Barbara, California.

Cast: Jeff Bridges (Richard Bone), John Heard (Alexander Cutter), Lisa Eichhorn (Maureen "Mo" Cutter), Ann Dusenberry (Valerie Duran), Stephen Elliott (J. J. Cord), Arthur Rosenberg (George Swanson), Nina van Pallandt (Woman in Hotel), Patricia Donahue (Mrs. Cord), Geraldine Baron (Susie Swanson), Katharine Pass (Toyota Woman), Frank McCarthy (Toyota Man), George Planco (Toyota Cop), Jay Fletcher (Security Guard), George Dickerson (Mortician), Jack Murdock (Concession Owner), Essex Smith, Rod Gist, and Leonard Gist (Black Guys), Julia Duffy (Young Girl), Randy Shephard (Young Man), Roy Hollis (Working Stiff), Billy Drago (Garbage Man), Caesar Cordova (Garbage Truck Driver), Jon Terry (Police Captain), William Pelt and Ron Marcroft (Detectives).

Synopsis: In an alley on a rainy night during a community fiesta in Santa Barbara, California, a womanizing marina boat salesman named Richard Bone

From left, John Heard, Jeff Bridges, Frank McCarthy, and Katharine Pass in a scene from Ivan Passer's *Cutter's Way*.

witnesses a vague act that the next day is identified as the disposal of a murdered girl's body. His boozy, crippled, sarcastic, and obsessive pal, Alex Cutter, a Vietnam veteran, becomes fascinated by the case after Bone becomes a suspect. Bone confides to Alex that wealthy industrialist J. J. Cord might have been the man who deposited the body in a garbage can. The murdered girl's sister, Valerie, abets Alex's intensifying, if inconclusive and irresponsible, efforts to nail Cord for the killing. Alex's hard-edged and alcoholic wife, Maureen, believes Alex, Valerie, and the reluctant and generally apathetic Bone are in over their heads. Bone sleeps with Maureen at her and Alex's home, consummating a seemingly inevitable act, then leaves her in the middle of the night. The house burns down, and Maureen is killed in the fire that might have been started by arsonists seeking to kill Bone, the only witness in the murder investigation. Bone is now at least willing to follow Alex's plan to confront Cord, and he and Alex crash a Cord estate party to seek revenge.

Remarks and Reviews

"The thing about [*Cutter's Way*] that hits you right away, before you can possibly guess how rich it's going to be, is what a terrific movie it is. You catch the feeling through the fine hair on your arms.... We can accurately call [*Cutter's Way*] a film of enchantment—few other American movies since *Chinatown* ... have cast and sustained such a spell" (Richard T. Jameson, *Film Comment*).

"A tense, moody vision of life on the California edge. . . . Heard gives his best film performance" (David Ansen, *Newsweek*).

"Hauntingly powerful, it has snap and style. . . . [An] intensely written and acted drama about murder, revenge and the peculiar volatile tensions of intimate friendships" (David Denby, *New York*).

"A bitter neo-noir with an unexpected bonanza of B-movie virtues. . . . Ultimately less a murder mystery than it is a sensual meditation on the mysteries of friendship and fate, power and personal responsibility. . . . The film is characterized by its superb, unostentatious craft" (J. Hoberman, *Village Voice*).

"In this devastatingly grim examination of the Vietnam nightmare which is marked by our insistent belief in the American dream, Passer unearths misconceptions of heroism and success, finding a corrupt mentality behind each while refusing to point the finger of blame in any particular direction" (Doug Tomlinson, *Directors/Filmmakers: International Dictionary of Films and Filmmakers*, vol. 2).

"A fiercely powerful film about heroes, romanticism, and friendship" (*Motion Picture Guide*).

"A film with guts and convictions. . . . One of the few films in recent times to address itself in neo-noirish fashion to the unraveling of the social fabric" (Andrew Sarris, *Village Voice*).

The Filmmaker

Along with Jiří Menzel, Jan Nęmec, and Milos Forman, Ivan Passer was in the forefront of the celebrated New Wave of Czechoslovakian filmmakers who came to prominence in the mid–1960s. This was during the "Prague Spring," a liberal phenomenon in Czech politics. Passer's *Intimate Lighting* (1966), a straightforward account of two musicians who renew their friendship, gained international prominence.

When Soviet tanks rolled into Prague in August 1968, Passer was in Paris with Forman, his great friend and collaborator. Passer and Forman had coauthored the screenplays for the two films that gave Forman an international profile as a director: *Loves of a Blonde* (1965) and *The Firemen's Ball* (1967). Both films were nominated for an Academy Award in the best foreign film category.

Passer and Forman came to the United States and tried their skills in Hollywood rather than return home where they would have been subjected to intensified Communist strictures which were tightening all areas of society, especially the arts and specifically motion pictures. Passer's first American film was *Born to Win* (1971), a depiction of heroin addiction that starred George Segal and featured Robert De Niro in one of his first studio films. Most of Passer's Hollywood films have been received indifferently by critics and audiences, despite their offbeat pleasures. A contemplative man who enjoys the slow approach to conversation, Passer makes films that often feature moments of odd insight and touching expression. Both *Intimate Lighting* and *Cutter's*

Way are extraordinary treatises on the ideas of faith, loyalty, and consistency in friendships.

The exhibition course of *Cutter's Way* followed a strange path. The movie was released under the title of the source novel, *Cutter and Bone*, and was panned by Vincent Canby of the *New York Times*, a circumstance that is discussed in the interview. Passer's map for the mystery in the film did not follow conventional thriller techniques as it wended through the territory of human insight, intuition, and emotional fragility. Some reviewers who were apparently looking for a genre exercise, or at least for familiar territory, also panned the movie. United Artists pulled the film from release, retitled it *Cutter's Way*, and mounted a new advertising campaign under the newly created United Artists Classics division. The film then accrued modest box-office success and some enthusiastic critical acclaim, particularly at the 1981 Houston Film Festival.

Ivan Passer's Filmography

As director unless noted: *Talent Competition* (1963, cowrote screenplay with Milos Forman); *Black Peter* (1963, cowrote screenplay with Milos Forman and was assistant director); *Loves of a Blonde* (1965, cowrote screenplay with Milos Forman and was assistant director); *A Boring Afternoon* (1965); *Intimate Lighting* (1965, also wrote the screenplay); *The Firemen's Ball* (1967, cowrote screenplay with Milos Forman); Born to Win (1971, also wrote the screenplay); *Law and Disorder* (1974, also wrote the screenplay); *Crime and Passion* (1976); *Silver Bears* (1977); *Cutter's Way* (1981); *Creator* (1985); *Haunted Summer* (1988); *Stalin* (1992, for television).

Reasons for Selection

Murder mysteries and films noir often feature a protagonist who cuts straight through a landscape of clues and character types. This hero — whether he is the smart-guy detective or not — often has no doubts about his methods of pursuit or his objective. Two noir mysteries of recent decades have fascinated me simply because their heroes are extraordinarily atypical, doubtful, and out of touch with the worlds they inhabit: Gene Hackman's Harry Moseby in Arthur Penn's *Night Moves* (1975) and especially Jeff Bridges's Richard Bone in Ivan Passer's *Cutter's Way*.

Cutter's Way is more of a communal character study than it is a murder mystery. And it is as much a contemplation on ideas about friendship, self-reckoning, and violence as it is a look at the dysfunctional, chaotic triangle made up of Alex, Mo, and Bone. In a film about two alcoholics and a brooding gigolo, the emotional synapses between the characters are flowing with symbiotic mood as each member of the trio balances life with the other two. The relationships are played with thoughtful delicacy and explore how people relate to each other based on the ways in which they relate to themselves. Passer is a master of communicating the characters' personal knowledge of each other without the need for dialogue.

Cutter's Way is also a magnificent actors' picture. The first time I saw the film, I was amazed at John Heard's performance, a masterpiece of physical interpretation. Alex has one arm, one leg, and one eye, but Heard makes us more aware that the character is one part self-loathing agony, one survival, and one raging vengeance. During the third viewing, I was astounded at the fullness of Lisa Eichhorn's work, a performance of profound melancholy, grit, isolation, and suspended pain.

But it is Jeff Bridges who carries the film, who shoulders the hero's journey. His Bone is finally moved to throw off the constraints of self-absorption and apathy to make a stand for the lives, wishes, and loyalties of his friends and, in the process, make a stand for himself. It is a benchmark performance in Bridges' career, not only for the extraordinary quality and depth of what he communicates to us about Richard Bone, but also as a linchpin between the actor's enjoyable body of work as a boyish maverick during the 1970s and his mature work as a major star in the 1980s.

—J.R.

The Interview

Ivan Passer: What a sad movie, huh?

Jerry Roberts: The gunshot [that ended the film]—was the gun loaded?

Passer: Sometimes I think it was. Sometimes I think it wasn't.

Roberts: How do you feel right now?

Passer: Just today? Yes, I think today it was loaded.

Roberts: Could you tell us a little bit about the genesis of the project?

Passer: I say that usually movies are being made not because somebody wants to, but because the producers and the money people have to make the movies eventually, somehow. They kind of paint themselves in a corner, and the only way out is to finally make the movies. So, yes, this was a similar case. United Artists were not sure they really wanted to make this movie because, finally, their reasoning was that their revenue people—and I didn't know what they meant by that then—didn't know how to sell this kind of a movie.

So they say, "OK, if you cast Richard Dreyfuss for Cutter, then we'll make the movie." And I said, "I'm sorry, I think Richard Dreyfuss is terrific when he's cast right, but this is not the part for Richard Dreyfuss." So they stopped the project. I was gambling that they were too far into it. So at some point, they said, "Listen, why don't you go and talk to Richard Dreyfuss? Maybe you'll like him."

He was in a Shakespeare in the Park production [*Othello*] in New York for Joe Papp, playing Iago. So I went there. And as you know, it's the toughest audience in the world. People are sitting on the grass playing harmonicas, eating potato chips, and necking and everything. And there was Richard Dreyfuss, waving his arms and yelling and screaming, and nobody listened.

And then this guy came out. And suddenly they stopped munching the potato chips, the music stopped, and they listened to the guy. I said, "Who's this?" It was John Heard. I said, "John Heard?" I had seen him in some movies. He was always playing these laid-back intellectuals [*Between the Lines, Chilly Scenes of Winter, Heart Beat*]. So after the play, I spent about ten minutes with Richard Dreyfuss and three days with John Heard. I came back, and I said, "I want John Heard to play this." And they said, "You're crazy," and they stopped the project again.

I like to cast actors according to what I feel they would like to do — not what they did before, which is against the usual way of doing it. I spent these three days with John Heard, and I felt that he was just ready for something like this, that he was just waiting for somebody to say, "Go."

Roberts: I wanted to talk about Heard's performance. I mean, he's got one leg, one arm, one eye, and he's half-drunk all the time. If you invited any actor to play this, first of all, I think they would think, "This is the most incredible, hammiest part I've ever seen in my entire life." And it could be way over the top. I think that's the sort of a part that an actor would recoil from initially.

Passer: There was this strange anger in [Heard] and some mystery to it, and that was the reason I believed that he could do it. So they stopped the movie, and then after a while they said, "Whom would you like for Richard Bone?" And so we gave them a list of about four to six people. Jeff Bridges was one of those people. They said, "Yes! Okay, we are now making the biggest hit of all times — *Heaven's Gate* — and we would like to have a follow-up movie for one of the stars. So, if Jeff agrees he's going to be in the movie — and we are not going to help you get him — we will make it."

So we sent the script to Jeff, and about a week later we were invited to come to see him. He had sort of a half-falling-down ranch house in Malibu. And the producer [Paul Gurian] and myself — we got there — and the producer was very nervous. This was his first movie, and everything really depended on this meeting. We stopped the car, we rang the bell, and the producer was, literally, shaking: He's about six feet four, has a pony tail, and a big mustache. Jeff came out of the house barefooted, with dungarees on and no shirt. And I knew he wanted the part. I was kind of sure about it immediately, but I didn't have time to let Paul Gurian know when Jeff opened the door, and it made a sound like in a horror movie, it was a wooden gate, and it was creaking a long time.

I see these two German shepherds standing behind him. The farthest one looked like he was crossed with a coyote. It was sort of a brownish thing and didn't like us at all. The producer was so nervous he passed Jeff and that first German shepherd and went to the second one and leaned from his six feet four and said to him, "You are a nice doggie. What is your name, nice doggie?" And the nice doggie jumped and bit off his cheek.

And we looked. Jeff turned around, and we saw the blood, and I thought he had lost an eye because he was totally bloody. He looked like somebody slapped a little child. Jeff said, "Oh my God!" And he ran into the house and came out with some towels, and we put him into Jeff's car and drove him down to a Malibu plastic surgeon.

The plastic surgeon—I remember he was building his house—he looked like a bricklayer. He just washed his hands off a little, and then he was working for two hours on Paul, who had like sixty-seven stitches. We are sitting in the waiting room, and Jeff was saying, "Yeah. I know the dog is crazy—I should have locked him up. And he did it before. My wife is going to be so mad at me." And the nurse said, "He's OK." Anyway, we never mentioned the movie.

And then, after we had made the movie, we had dinner someplace. I was telling the story and Jeff was there, and Jeff said, "You know, I often thought about what I would have done if I didn't like the script." And we said, "You would have made the movie." He had no choice, of course, because he really liked the script and felt so bad about Paul. So that's how it was made, really.

Roberts: Jeffrey Alan Fiskin, the screenwriter, based this on Newton Thornburg's novel *Cutter and Bone*, and the film was released as *Cutter and Bone* originally and then rereleased months later as *Cutter's Way*. What was the deal on that?

Passer: It's true. It was withdrawn in three days because the critic of the *New York Times*, Vincent Canby, wrote that the movie was incomprehensible and that you could not see Cutter's face because of the eye patch. So they took it immediately out of theaters. And then all of the other critics, when the reviews came out like on Thursday, were very positive, practically all of them. So there was some kind of a discussion at United Artists about this. And then [some] critics attacked Vincent Canby. They called him noodle-headed and all that.

I found myself in one of the most bizarre situations in all my life. I went to the head of United Artists to sort of defend this movie. It was Andreas Albeck, who happens to be Czech—his father started the film studios in Prague. He was sitting in his huge office, and he insisted that we are going to speak in Czech, although I wanted to talk to him in English because his Czech was very archaic and not too good. I wanted him to understand what I was saying. But he was coming up at me using this old Czech from the Hungarian-Austrain Empire. I said, "You know, Mr. Director"—I'm later retranslating from Czech—"actually this is a bizarre situation because we could have been sitting in Prague in a film studio, and you could be censoring my film because I think that is what you are doing. And the only thing missing here are Russian tanks outside of the window."

He sort of smiled, and he said, "Oh, come on, we don't have to go that far."

He stood up, and he was about four feet eight, and took me arm in arm, and he put in all that stuff about how he gave me this opportunity, you know — they are very good, these guys, and they know how to pacify angry filmmakers — and I never saw him again. And, of course, nothing happened to the movie.

And then they started this Classics Division, and some people really liked it. United Artists liked the film from the second I showed it to them. They changed the name — nothing else, just the name — and rereleased it, and suddenly the movie picked up slowly, and it was amazing. I'm amazed at the number of people who have seen it.

Roberts: Well, I had to write down the amount of themes that I found in this movie, which I think is pretty extraordinary. Here's the list that I came up with: It's a film noir, murder mystery, character study, mood piece, about America's scarred and confused history in the post–Vietnam era. It's about the idea of recapturing heroism. And it's especially about friendship and commitment and the lives of social renegades; it's about personal catharsis and taking a chance. And it's about, peripherally, the arrogance of the corrupted rich, alcoholism, doing the right thing for yourself and your friends. It's also about violence that stays with people — after they have experienced some sort of violent thing in their own life — that they transfer to other people.

Now, I don't know any other film that I've seen — and my life is about watching movies — that has so many things embodied in one picture.

Passer: It certainly is not a high-concept movie.

Roberts: You got that right.

Doug List: The thing that struck me — in seeing it again — was that I can't recall seeing a film in which all the main characters hate themselves so much and are working against themselves on a constant level. You were talking about getting the movie started, but at the very beginning, were you interested in the book, or did you see a script, or how did that get started?

Passer: Well, at first I saw the script, and I got interested when the producer told me everybody's afraid to make this movie. There was Robert Mulligan on it before, and some other director, and they apparently got cold feet — they were smart. And I said, "Well, that interests me." Then I read the script, and I liked the script. And somehow I like to have the choice to make films to which I feel I can contribute something, that I can, in my arrogance, be the best director for that particular script.

And I understood Cutter somehow because I have seen lots of people who got hurt during the war and in Stalinist prisons. I felt, "Yeah, I can sort of understand this guy." And I liked that he was sort of a mystery without mystery. I liked the potential of the script — it needed a rewrite — and I liked the ambiguity that it was leading to: really, nobody knows anything, and yet they are willing to act on [what little information they have]. I liked that it was going to be shot in Santa Barbara, which is very beautiful. That background of beauty against these corruptions—it was visually very tempting. I liked the people who were involved with it. And I was scared to death about doing it—and that's what I like, too.

Roberts: We saw Lisa Eichhorn in *Yanks* and then in your movie. She was in several other things, and she's quite an actress, a tremendous actress. I was just wondering, do you have any line on whatever happened to her? [Eichhorn's films have included *Wildrose* (1984) and *Grim Prairie Tales* (1989)].

Passer: Yep. Well, she had a reputation that she's difficult, which is very dangerous for an actor. And after this film, she was in a film with Gene Hackman—I forgot the name of it—and finally she was fired after two weeks of shooting, and Barbra Streisand finished the movie. Do you remember that?

Roberts: *All Night Long.* Yeah.

Passer: And apparently the husband of Barbra Streisand's agent at that time was directing the movie. And the agent was Sue Mengers, and she tried to help him [Jean-Claude Tramont] to make a successful movie, so she had something to do with it. And she forced, in a sense, Barbra Streisand to do this move. She lost her as a client after that. It didn't help the movie too much. Lisa got fired, and it was really too bad. You know, nobody finds out exactly why things happened. So she got this jinx.

Roberts: One of the things about the movie—that you hardly see in movies at all—is the not knowing. Alex Cutter says, "He killed the bastard." Everything Cutter says is in the absolute positive. But in this movie's reality, nobody knows anything. Nobody knows who killed whom, or why, all the way through to the end. It's sort of like real life to me, like you just never really know for sure. And that's one of the things I liked about it: the not knowing.

Passer: Well, it was one of the reasons why they forced us to write a last scene, when everything is explained, exactly who did what to whom and why. We agreed to it because it was the only way to have it made. Then, three weeks into the shooting, I called them, and they liked the rushes, I must say. And I said, "Gentlemen, I want to change the ending." There was this five-second silence, and they were so busy with *Heaven's Gate* problems, they said, "Okay, go ahead." Nobody bothers us, and they just were cheering us up all the way. Except when it was finished—they [then] didn't do anything with it.

Audience Question: I've seen this film before, and I've always wondered what happened to the character of Valerie. She just sort of disappears. Was that in the original ending?

Passer: Well. It's my fault. Quite a few people asked me that question. We had two scenes which I shot that are not in the film. There was one scene which deals with that, and because the scene only just dealt with that, I just felt that sometimes you have to choose between two bad things. So I chose. We chose not to use it because it was not up to the rest of the movie.

AQ: When Jeff Bridges has the confrontation with Mrs. Cord and he walks through the living room, and in the glass we see the reflection of the fountain and then we do the one-eighty pan around: Is that him — Ahab finding Moby Dick — the big fountain going up?

Passer: Well, you have a good eye. The theme of *Moby Dick* is here and there, either in the dialogue or visually.

AQ: When I see a film that is this beautifully shot, and not just in terms of lighting but in terms of blocking and the way the story is told photographically, I'm often curious about the working relationship between the director and DP [director of photography]. Jordan Cronenweth is a wonderful DP. Could you say something about how that gets worked out in the process of the film?

Passer: When I was going to film school, we had this eighty-year-old director of photography who did some wonderful movies in the twenties, and he used to tell us, "Gentlemen, remember one thing — when the film is good, the camera is always good." And he was right. That aside, I totally believe in it. And that aside, I still like good-looking pictures. I like those films which somehow visually contribute to the story, or help you to watch it, in a sense. I think it's very important.

I couldn't find anybody. One day we were looking for some actors, with some agents, and were watching some cassettes. And there was some little TV movie, and the movie started, we watched it on television. I said, "Take it back, let's see who was the director of photography of this little movie." And there was Jordan. So we met him, and he then told us he had had a motorcycle accident, and he sort of moves peculiar in a sense. Physically he's very slow — that was the reason he was not too popular with the studios. I think he's the best director of photography in this country.

He learned everything from Conrad Hall. He was Hall's assistant. He takes his time, you know — quality always takes time, always. So they were putting pressure on him. And I said to the producer that if he ever talks to Jordan ever again, I'm going to walk out of the set. So the producer, always behind Jordan's back, would comment on how slow he was, and it got back to Jordan. I learned that when there was that pressure on him, it wasn't that good for the movie. And I thought what he was doing was really something very special.

So we had a system. I would rehearse with actors and do the blockings and all that, and he was there watching. Then he would look at it through his viewer, and he would talk about it. And sometimes he would say, "You know, it would be better if instead of here, he would be there. I would get a better this or that." I would adjust to it, and it was very smooth. Very smooth. And after this movie, suddenly he was discovered. He did *Blade Runner*, as you know. I think that's a spectacular film from the cinema-photographic point of view. And then he did two films with Francis Coppola [Cronenweth was nominated for an Academy Award for his work on Coppola's *Peggy Sue Got Married* (1986). His films include *Zandy's Bride* (1974), *Gardens of Stone*

(1987), and *State of Grace* (1990)]. It was just a pleasure to work with somebody who was a real artist.

AQ: How do you work with your actors? What methods do you have?

Passer: Well, I don't think I have one or any kind of system. I try to get to know an actor, or whomever I'm working with, and try to find a key to communicate with that actor. I believe that language is sort of the last resort, that you use it only when you have no other tools to communicate. Also, it's the slowest tool to communicate with — language — and with my accent on top of it.

I believe that the director, in a sense, is an actor, too. He's behind the camera. He's acting the part of a director, and each actor needs a different character behind the camera. I have so few guidelines. I don't know how effective they are. But since some of you might be studying movies, I'll tell you.

I try to find out about people. I learned that actors, like all of us, their attitudes toward authority are formed usually in a very early age. Usually the father represents the authority. And in a sense, the director does represent kind of a father figure. I learned that they usually repeat their relationship with whoever was their authority figure with the director. It really doesn't make too much sense to try to change it. You don't have the time for it, and all that. So I sort of adjust to it, and I'll give you an example.

John Heard — his father left when he was three years old, and he doesn't really know him very well. He's very, very jumpy with any kind of authority. Jeff Bridges, who comes from an extremely warm family, is always very friendly. So that's what he requires on the set.

I don't really subscribe to the notion that "you are an actor, so act." I think the director's job is to help the actor to do something very difficult, especially if it's something like this character, especially in a span of ten, eleven weeks. So when I realized that John gets very nervous with any kind of authority, I was playing a tough guy. And he knew that I was playing it. But we kept it that way on the set, also. And when it was over, we hugged and kissed and we are very good friends.

It was fun when you had both of them in front of camera. You have to be very friendly and nice with the one, and so I used it. I would not talk to John too much, and I would spend a lot of time with Jeff. John was really jealous, and really his eyes were shining, and the lightnings were, you know, coming out. And that's how I liked it, so that's what we did.

Roberts: You got quite a performance.

Passer: Lisa is a Method actress. And so she was always locked in a camper and always looked very unhappy. I would go to visit her once in a while and say, "So, how are you doing, Lisa?" She was crying. I said, "Lisa, what's wrong?" And she said, "Well, I'm always very unhappy." I said, "Really? Why? What happened?" She said, "'Well, you know it's such a blizzard outside." And it was like today, you know, blue sky and sunshine. "And it's raining and it's cold." I said, "OK." And so I went to the makeup man, Ben Nye, who was a wonderful makeup artist. And I said, "Ben, you know when you do all your job and then you have a few minutes here and there, why don't you keep her company?" And he said, "OK, I'll do it." And then they got married after the movie.

AQ: I was wondering if there were many problems creating Cutter's physical disability. There are some impressive scenes in there where, really, they bring the audience into it. You really believe that he doesn't have those limbs.

Passer: We had to do lots of tests. And I like to do an open call. When I cast a movie, I like to let actors know that anybody who's interested will be seen. Sometimes it really pays off and you find somebody terrific, or somebody will tell you something which you can use for the movie. And this happened. The man came in and he read the book and he came in with one arm. And I talked to him. He was an actor from New Jersey. He had a very thick New Jersey accent. And I said, "Well, you know, I understand you are interested in this part. You don't have the arm." You see, normally they pin it back behind themselves. And it was his idea to have it here. And he had a coat made, and it was filled up, and you couldn't really tell if there was an arm in it or not. That gave us the idea to shoot both ways, from the front and the back. So when you see him sitting on the bed to take off his shirt, his arm is like this. There was a little appliance made by the makeup artist. And then he gets up and walks away from the camera. And his arm is here [*gesticulating*] and, you see, the appliance is down there. And you don't stay on that shot too long, so people have no time, really, to see it.

Roberts: Wasn't the leg through the bed in that [bedroom] shot? Or how was it done?

Passer: With the leg there was a real problem. We were trying to figure out. And then I think it was Jordan who said, "Listen if we give him a black sock, and I shoot it under the lamp against this night table, nobody will see it." And, sure enough, he did it, and it looked like John had no leg. And you cut at the right moment before anybody can really have time to look too close, and it works. It's all tricks.

Roberts: Did you get any calls from Toyota about this at all? [In one scene, Cutter denigrates this make of car.]

Passer: No.

Roberts: The vodka bottles, too. I always think about advertising in movies these days. You see different things about it. Mo's bottles—you never see the label on the vodka. Was that purposeful?

Passer: Yeah. You don't really want to make it look like you are advertising something. So we did it that you know it's vodka, but you don't know what kind.

AQ: What advice do you have for a young producer/director team with a movie on this order who is in the Catch-22 of the talent not wanting to talk to you because you don't have the major studio backing and the studios not wanting to talk to you because you don't have the talent locked in with the project?

Passer: Well, listen, if I knew the answer to that, I probably would have made more movies.

Same Questioner: Would you just keep banging on doors and screaming at them?

Passer: I'll give you one piece of advice, for whatever it's worth, but I do believe that it makes a difference. There is one commodity lacking, and that's a good script. If you get your hands on a good script, or you write it yourself, or some book, play, whatever, which really could make into an exciting movie, they will listen to you. But that's really what it comes down to.

AQ: How did you pick Jack Nitzsche to do the score? And how did the whole bit of using the unusual instrumentation come about?

Passer: I always have liked his music. And I met him when he was doing [*One Flew over the*] *Cuckoo's Nest* for Milos Forman. And you remember, he had this sort of publicity problem because he was accused of rape, and it was said that he did it with a gun or something. [Jack Nitzsche was sentenced to three years probation and fined $3,500 for assault for an incident that occurred in June 1979. The charge of "rape by instrumentation" was dropped. The victim was actress Carrie Snodgress.] And I really don't know what the truth was, but I know United Artists said, "You want Jack Nitzsche, who raped this woman with a gun?"

I said, "Well, what has it to do with music?" I still don't understand. Well, anyway, he's the nicest man I've ever met. Very shy. He really wants to give you the best. And he has this passion for unusual sounds.

He would say, "Well, I know there is this violin gumba in Mexico which is two hundred fifty years old. We have to get this instrument." And he would fly there to get it. And he said, "There are six guys in Toronto who play electric violins like nobody else." And, "There's these guys who play music with glasses." And I think he did the best music, really, for the movie. It's really terrific.

Roberts: It's mood enhancing.

Passer: It's very difficult to do music which would help the film, and at the same time, you shouldn't hear it too much. It should blend the whole thing together. It should lead you in the emotional part, and I think he understands it very well.

AQ: The speech that Cutter gives at the tennis court—about the war and so on—was that basically from the book? Or did Fiskin do that?

Passer: I really don't know right now because the film ignored the second half of the book totally. I always say that when you make a film based on a book, you have to decide if you are going to betray the book or the film. The book is already there, and you have all the examples of movies that were not terribly good [but were] made out of great books—*War and Peace* and all of that. But you should try to make a good movie. And so we used the book. I always preserved the soul of the book. But we changed things. And it was very strange.

I had the book with me all the time. Between shots, I would go and read the book again, even the sequences which are not in the movie, passages from the second part of the book. I had my notes in English and in Czech. I got extremely sort of friendly with the book. And somebody stole it the last day of shooting. I still miss it.

Roberts: Newton Thornburg—didn't you mention to me that he visited the set once? What was that like?

Passer: Yes. He came to the bar you see at the very beginning. He's a very shy man and didn't say too much. We asked him, "What do you think?" And he never told anybody. He was just sort of nodding at us. He lives in Seattle, and the movie was very popular in Seattle. First I heard that he was not sure if he liked the movie. But then, when everybody told him that they liked it, he apparently liked it. And I know it, because his agent is trying to sell me his new book.

List: Well, actually, by ending it where you did, the film is almost more upbeat than the book is.

Passer: The ending of the book was very similar to *Easy Rider*. I didn't care for it too much.

Roberts: I never read the book. What—

List: Well, what happened at the end is after a lot of things out of Santa Barbara, they finally catch up to Bone, and in the last scene of the book, Bone is killed.

Passer: Yeah, and Cutter ends up in an insane asylum.

AQ: Cutter wants to be a hero, and you even put him on a white horse at the end. He dies. Bone then shoots Cord, but he's holding Cutter's hand, so it's not even his own finger, really, pulling the trigger. And to top it all off, we don't know whether or not Cord is guilty. I mean, we know that the world's gone horribly awry, somehow. And we know someone's responsible, but we don't know it's him. So ultimatley, what is the potential for heroism in our world?

Passer: [Laughs.] You know, it's a really fascinating problem: If two guys do the same thing—it's not the same thing. It depends where he came from. I think if a person who grows up in a protective environment does something heroic, it's not the same thing as somebody from, let's say the Bronx, who grew up on the street, doing something heroic because it means two different things.

The guy from the city knows he can get killed. The one from the protective environment knows that God is on his side. And so, it's not the same thing. And heroism has, I think, different shades. It depends on who does what. Something very minor, which nobody notices, can be a real heroic act for a particular kind of a person. But in this case, Cutter finally made Bone to act.

Roberts: So it's not important who shoots whom, but that Bone finally made a commitment.

AQ: I'm curious about the comment you made about Vincent Canby's [review]. Why was his particular criticism so negative?

Passer: I don't know. He gave some very good reviews to some of my other movies. And one in particular, for *Law and Disorder*, was such a terrific review that I was really embarrassed because I didn't think the film was that good. Maybe it was like a backlash, you know? I don't know.

AQ: What directors of the past most influenced you?

Passer: So many. From the Russian silent period to American silent period. Italian movies, such as [Vittorio] De Sica's, of course. Japanese Cinema: [Yasojiru] Ozu, [Akira] Kurosawa, [Kenji] Mizoguchi, all those old guys. I don't know. I'm a sucker for movies. I like everything. You know, there's a great period in Hungarian cinema which nobody knows of, just before the revolution in 1956. If we are influenced — and I mean like the Czech New Wave — by anything, that was it, that period of Hungarian cinema.

AQ: I just wanted to thank you for *Intimate Lighting*. It's not often that you can thank someone for a film that truly inspired you. That film did really inspire me. I just wanted to thank you for giving it to us.

Passer: Thank you very much. I got lucky there.

AQ: What project are you working on now? And what actors will you be working with?

Passer: That's such a difficult question to answer, because every director is involved in several different projects, and you never know really what will happen. I was lately offered a film with Charles Bronson and Sean Young. In this one, Charles Bronson doesn't kill anybody, believe it or not. Then, with Jimmy Caan, a movie in Africa about saving elephants, which is a pretty good script. And then I was also involved with some other projects which I don't know how they're going to turn out. But one is totally different than what I did before. This is a really traditional American genre which everybody's called a gangster movie.

Roberts: Thanks, Ivan.

Passer: Thank you.

For Further Study

Videocassette

Cutter's Way is available on videocassette from MGM/UA Home Video.

Ivan Passer

Book

Thornburg, Newton. *Cutter and Bone*. Boston and Toronto: Little, Brown and Company, 1976.

Periodicals

Chase, Chris. "At the Movies." *New York Times*, May 29, 1981.

Gery, John. "*Cutter's Way* and the American Way: Heroic Alienations." *Literature/Film Quarterly* (Salisbury, Md.) 16, no. 1 (1988).

Grant, Lee. "A New Life For Both Bridges and *Cutter's Way*." *Los Angeles Times*, August 27, 1981.

Hoberman, J. "Passer's Way," *Village Voice*, July 8, 1981.

"Interview with Ivan Passer." *Time Out* (London), January 1982.

Jameson, Richard T. "Passer's Way." *Film Comment*, July/August 1981.

3

SCOTT WILSON
AND
A Year of the Quiet Sun
(with Jim Emerson)

On February 15, 1990, actor Scott Wilson was interviewed by Jim Emerson after a screening of *A Year of the Quiet Sun*.

The Film

A Year of the Quiet Sun (*Rok Spokojnego Slonca*) (1984), a production of the Tor Film Unit (Warsaw), Teleculture (New York), and Regina Ziegler (West Berlin). Written and directed by Krzysztof Zanussi. Director of photography, Slawomir Idziak. Music by Wojciech Kilar. Winner of the Golden Lion for best film at the 1984 Venice Film Festival. Filmed on location in Poland and in the Monument Valley.

Cast: Maja Komorowska (Emili), Scott Wilson (Norman), Hanna Skarzanka (Mother), Ewa Dalkowska (Stella), Vadim Glowna (Hermann), Daniel Webb (David), Zbigniew Zapasiewicz (Szary), Jerzy Nowak (Doctor), Jerzy Stuhr (Adzio).

Synopsis: In Poland, 1946, an American soldier and a Polish widow strike up a relationship, even though neither of them speaks the other's language. The film details the bitter aftermath of World War II and charts a terrain filled with fears and doubts and venal profiteers as it chronicles the course of the couple's unfulfilled quest for love.

Remarks and Reviews

"Our motives and emotions aren't always wrapped in a tidy package, and one of the beauties of Krzysztof Zanussi's *A Year of the Quiet Sun* is that it preserves some of the mystery of why we do what we do. Set in post–World War II Poland, *Quiet Sun* is a magnificently crafted essay on love and hopelessness, rich with history, alive with the struggle of beauty" (Paul Attanasio, *Washington Post*).

"Whatever you do, don't leave this film until its last breathtaking scene, which—like the image of Giulietta Masina's face in Fellini's *Ginger and Fred*—is one of the most moving in film history" (Gene Siskel, *Chicago Tribune*).

"*A Year of the Quiet Sun* is a great, beautiful and humbling work, a film of majestic compassion. Its conception and execution are thrilling; its actors magnificent. This is the work of a brilliant filmmaker who sees no reason to flaunt his brilliance—who submerges it in the story's texture, makes it breathe and pulse with life" (Michael Wilmington, *Los Angeles Times*).

"*A Year of the Quiet Sun* has never played in Poland, and the government has withdrawn it from Oscar consideration in this country. I think the Poles are right—if I were in power, I'd bury the damned thing. It says that love and transcendence and happiness are, in that part of the world, beyond the powers of ordinary mortals" (David Edelstein, *Village Voice*).

"Wilson, who looks like a softer, more frightened Roy Scheider, has a few near-impossible lines to say, such as 'I was an empty man until I met you.' Then you look into his wounded eyes and believe him.... This is a very sad story set in a very grim world, yet it leaves you invigorated (David Ansen, *Newsweek*).

The Filmmakers

Born in Warsaw in 1939, Krzysztof Zanussi (the main subject of the interview with Scott Wilson) has been labeled "the moralist of the Second Wave of contemporary Polish filmmakers," and critic Roger Ebert has called him "the best living maker of films about ideas." He was trained in physics and philosophy before he attended the prestigious film school at Lodz. Many critics have noted the broad-ranging roots of Zanussi's world vision. Scott Wilson was one of the most impressive newcomers to American movies in the late 1960s. He starred to wide acclaim in Richard Brooks' "In Cold Blood" (1967) and that same year co-starred in "In the Heat of the Night." His other films include Sydney Pollack's "Castle Keep" (1969), John Frankenheimer's "They Gypsy Moths" (1969), Jack Clayton's "The Great Gatsby" (1974), Philip Kaufman's "The Right Stuff" (1983), Walter Hill's "Johnny Handsome" (1989) and Steven Kloves' "Flesh and Bone" (1993).

Krzysztof Zanussi's Filmography

All films as director and either writer or cowriter: *Death of a Provincial* (1966); *Face to Face* (1967); *The Structure of Crystals* (1969); *Mountains at Duck* (telefeature, 1970); *Die Rolle* (telefeature, 1971; *Family Life* (1971); *Hypothesis* (telefeature, 1972); *Illumination* (1973); *The Catamount Killing* (1974); *Night Duty* (telefeature, 1975); *A Woman's Decision* (1975); *Camouflage* (1977); *The Spiral* (1978); *Ways in the Night* (1980); *The Constant Factor* (1980); *From a Far Country, Pope John Paul II* (telefeature, 1981); *Imperativ* (telefeature, 1982); *The Unapproachable* (1982); *Blaubart* (telefeature, 1984); *A Year of the Quiet Sun* (1984); *Le Pouvoir du Mal* (1985); *Wherever She Is* (1988); *Stan Posiadania* (1989); *Life for a Life: Maximilian Kolbe* (1990); *The Touch* (1992).

R e a s o n s   f o r   S e l e c t i o n

The finales of physicist/philosopher/filmmaker Krzysztof Zanussi's movies are often miraculous moments of spiritual transcendence: the appearance of the magnificent deer in *Contract*, the snowy omen in *Imperativ*, and the Monument Valley scene in *A Year of the Quiet Sun*. Although virtually unknown in the United States, primarily due to distribution problems, Zanussi has been influential on the work of filmmakers as diverse as Krzysztof Kieslowski (*Camera Buff*, *The Decalogue*, *The Double Life of Veronique*) and Woody Allen (*Crimes and Misdemeanors*).

A Year of the Quiet Sun, a muted, heartbreaking postwar romance that transcends the barriers of language and finally, death itself, is a great film that far too few Americans have seen (although it is available on videocassette in this country). The movie is told through the limpid eyes, even more than the hushed voices, of its extraordinary leading actors, Scott Wilson and Poland's legendary Maja Komorowska. This film has meant a great deal to me ever since I booked it into the 1985 Seattle Film Festival and its American premiere engagement at Seattle's Market Theater—not too long before its U.S. distributor, Sandstar, folded. Its effect on audiences was so deep that after each showing, we would have to gently usher emotionally overwhelmed patrons out into the lobby, where it sometimes took a half hour or more for them to collect themselves. To watch *A Year of the Quiet Sun* is to undergo something akin to a religious experience, a reminder that Mystery and Awe and Love are still possible, in life and in movies, even in a "ruined" world.

J.E.

The Interview

Jim Emerson: This film came out in—I think it was in 1985. And as has been the case for a lot of Krzystof Zanussi's films, it did not get widely distributed in America. The distributor went bankrupt before the film could get nationwide distribution. And the print that we have tonight is Scott Wilson's, the star's personal print.

I don't know if you know anything about Zanussi, but he's a former physicist, and he also had a background in philosophy. His movies like *Camouflage* and *The Constant Factor* and *Imperative* often deal with the scientific community and the sort of rigid structures that people have used to try to order their lives, and sometimes how life itself was sort of bigger than those rigid structures. But the thing that's different about *Year of the Quiet Sun* is that it's a much more emotional film, and Scott had a lot to do with that. Can you just talk a little bit about, how this film came about and how you came to work in it?

Scott Wilson: Well, I met Krzysztof in 1975, I believe. And I didn't know

Scott Wilson in *A Year of the Quiet Sun*.

that he had seen any of my films, but he had. I didn't know that he knew I was an actor. And we got to talking, and he wanted to work with me. I think it was nine years later we got to make the film. About three years before that we were going to make it, and the pope asked him to direct a film on the pope's life. And we got an interesting letter from him saying that — how did he phrase it? — while he would rather do our film, he felt it would be immodest to turn the pope down. Something like that.

So over the years we would meet at airports. Or he would be here, and we would meet at my place, and we would talk and discuss what the film would be about. And it was quite an interesting nine years. Not that it happened every weekend. But it was over a period of time. We tried to decide. We decided that he would be a private, rather than an officer, in the Army, so that he would be more of the Everyman, a more average American, I guess.

Emerson: You talked about admiring Zanussi. He's got an incredible mind, and he speaks all these languages.

Wilson: He's fluent in seven languages.

Emerson: You were also arguing for making the film more emotional.

Wilson: Well, we had a number of discussions. I don't know if they were arguments. But most of his films are very, very bright. And a lot of them are very cerebral. It taxes your brain, and it drifts down to your heart. I love his films. I mean, that's why I wanted to work with him. And I'm happy that he wanted to work with me. But on this one, I think we finally decided we would try to hit them in the heart and let it go up to the head.

Emerson: Also, Maja Komorowska has worked with Zanussi—she's in a lot of his films. Can you give us a little background on her? I know that she was more than just an actress.

Wilson: When Solidarity was imposed in Poland, for one thing, all of the actors over there went on strike and refused to work on television. That was their main source of income. Maja was the first person to do this. She talked her way past the lower-echelon prison officials and got in to see the prisoners. She brought food and clothing and read poetry to them. And between the lines she was sending messages. So she became quite a heroine there. She's like a national heroine.

One day we were on location, and someone had picked my room key out of my pocket without my knowing it. I was waiting for her to go to dinner. I was in the lobby, and she got off the elevator, and the pickpocket saw who I was with and came over and gave me my key back. She's very well thought of there.

It'll be interesting to see what happens in all of Eastern Europe and Russia too, I guess, now that it looks like they're trying to go for free enterprise.

Emerson: Yeah, that was one thing when Zanussi was over here. I think it was '86. We got into a discussion about the free enterprise system and making films in Poland. He was saying that for him he couldn't imagine having to compete at the box office. But he felt that he could make the films that he wanted to make over there and get government money because he could always sneak things past the censors. But he didn't know what he would do if he had to make a movie that would make money or had to compete.

Wilson: You know, the first part of the film where Maja was painting the sun in the car, that was shot on a Russian military base. For a long time I wouldn't tell anyone about that because it would have, I thought, gotten Krzysztof and everyone in trouble because Americans are not allowed on a Russian military base, and Krzysztof had given the colonel of the military base a fifth of cognac or something under the table. So, unofficially, I was on the base. Officially no one knew I was there. But we were. Krzysztof came to my room one night and said that they were going to confiscate our film. I asked him why, and he said because the American was on the military base. And I said, "Well, they knew that."

He said it was the same guy coming to him, asking him, and telling him he's going to confiscate the film. I said, "Maybe he wants a case of cognac or something." But it wasn't that. I had gone on the base another time when they weren't expecting it, really. When I was singing that song there. And he had heard of that, and they weren't really prepared for me to be there. But the spy on the picture is the one that carried me onto the base, so I guess he thought it would be all right. I don't know. I said, "Why don't you tell them that I was on the base when we were shooting the sound track, and then give him the sound track, and that way you'll have the film?" And I believe he eventually suggested that to him, and we ended up keeping both of them. But it was interesting.

Emerson: Also the ending here. I remember that a couple of years before he made the film, Zanussi and the late Russian director Andrei Tarkovsky were going up to the Telluride Film Festival and had driven through Monument Valley on their way up to Telluride, which is in Colorado, up in the mountains. And I guess that's part of what planted that seed in his head. And also what Monument Valley means in the films of John Ford and how that stands as an image of America. There's kind of an interesting story about how you got those shots, right?

Wilson: Well, we stole the shots. I mean, we had just the camera. Krzysztof was pulling focus on the camera, and the cameraman was shooting. But when we were going there, nobody knew exactly what we were going to do when we got there. And we drove, and every fifty miles or so, someone would say, "What do you think we're going to do?" No one knew. So when we got there, somehow or other, it evolved into what we did.

Emerson: There's one other thing that you told me recently that just struck me as real interesting. We were talking about Woody Allen's movie *Crimes and Misdemeanors*. Have you seen that yet?

Wilson: No.

Emerson: Oh. I was telling Scott that he should go see this movie because I swear Woody Allen has been watching Zanussi movies. And Scott goes, "Oh, yeah, he has." He had seen a retrospective of Zanussi's films at the Museum of Modern Art in 1987, and you can really see the influence of Zanussi in Woody Allen's last two pictures, *Another Woman* and *Crimes and Misdemeanors*. What was the story about the letter?

Wilson: When this film opened in Paris last year, Woody Allen wrote a letter to Krzysztof saying how much he loved his work, and he particularly singled out this film. Krzysztof used that in Paris for part of the promo.

Emerson: When you see Martin Landau's character questioning whether there's a moral character to the universe in *Crimes and Misdemeanors*, that's such a Zanussi-like concern.

Audience Question: In the scene of the graves that we were just talking about, I thought that was kind of the turning point for the character of Amelia. I wondered what you felt happened in her, in the character? When she saw that scene, what was she thinking of? Was she thinking of her dead husband? Or that, Norman, it could have happened to him? It made her want to live. I mean, it's just theoretical, but what do you feel is happening?

Wilson: Well, I guess right along with you. But I would think that you touched on it when you said she was probably coming to grips with the fact that her husband, though she may have thought he was dead before, she was probably coming to terms with that. With dealing with him being dead, but that's just my estimation.

AQ: Were the actors trained before as theater actors? What kind of work do they do more—theater or film?

Wilson: That was one of the first questions I asked Krzysztof when I met him. I asked him, how does one become an actor in Poland? It's quite a rigorous process. You prepare a scene, and you go before a committee, and they can pass on you right there. And you're pretty much out. You can do it again. But you get past that and it's like becoming a professional here—I mean, a doctor, a lawyer, an engineer, or something. They go through university and a huge training process. At the end of it, every little town has a theater. The theater directors come to scene night where all the actors do scenes. They end up, in essence, with their fate being determined. But they have a job the rest of their lives as actors. And of course Warsaw is the mecca. That's the place where everyone would like to be. I'm curious as to what will happen now as a result of what's going on over there. Because all of the performing arts are subsidized, in essence. So I imagine there'll be a lot more films made there, but I'm wondering what the training process will be and what will happen with the actors because they'll have to start carrying their own freight, I think.

AQ: What is Zanussi doing now?

Wilson: I'm not sure. I know I got a card from him from Israel the other day. He's planning on doing something there, and I know there are a couple of other films that he's planning on directing. I think he's planning on doing one with Baryshnikov that should be interesting. He's directing operas, and he's all over.

Emerson: He also made a film with Rene Soutendijk and Julian Sands, along with Krzysztof Kieslowski, that was supposed to be shown at the AFI [American Film Institute] festival last year, a film called *A Short Film about Killing*, I think it was. It was sort of this typical thing for some reason with Zanussi's films. At the last minute the American rights got picked up by this person in Canada who is notorious for buying the rights to films and then never doing anything with them. And that's exactly what happened. So the movie hasn't been seen, but it exists.

Wilson: Yeah. Like this film. We won the Golden Lion at the Venice Film Festival, and it hasn't played in Italy yet. It just opened in Paris last year. Two distributors have gone belly up with the film—not because of the film, either, I might add.

Emerson: You may have seen the logo at the beginning, Sandstar. That was a company that existed for a few months. This was supposed to be their first release, and they had one other film called *Out of Order*, which starred Rene Soutendijk. It was a German film about an elevator, and they thought that maybe the elevator movie was a little more commercial than *A Year of the Quiet Sun*, so they poured some money into releasing the elevator movie. And it was a real tight little thriller. They thought that maybe they would make some money on that one, and then they could afford to go for their prestige picture. Only it just didn't work out that way.

Wilson: I met Jim in Seattle at the Seattle Film Festival when this film was in it. Jim at that time owned a movie house in Seattle and ended up showing the film there. I went up to Seattle to try to help promote it. As you can tell, I'm not all that good at it. But I went up, and I think the film did pretty well there.

Emerson: Yeah it did really well. It was a hit in Seattle. I think that was the only place.

AQ: What are your future plans?

Wilson: I'm playing Governor Lew Wallace — the guy that wrote *Ben Hur*. He was the governor of New Mexico in like 1870. It's in a Western called *Young Guns II*.

Emerson: And you did something on *Exorcist III*?

Scott: Yeah, I played a psychiatrist on *Exorcist III*. That will be coming out. I'm waiting for Krzysztof's visit. He says he's writing another script for me, so we'll see if we ever get it made.

For   Further   Study

Videocassette

A Year of the Quiet Sun. In Polish with English subtitles. 107 minutes.

Books

Georgakas, Dan, and Lenny Rubenstein. *The Cineaste Interviews on the Art and Politics of the Cinema*. Chicago: Lake View Press, 1983.

Oumano, Ellen. *Film Forum: Thirty-Five Top Filmmakers Discuss Their Craft*. New York: St. Martin's Press, 1985.

Racleva, Maria. *The Cinema of Ideas: Krzysztof Zanussi*. Boston: Museum of Fine Arts, 1985.

Periodicals

Boleslaw, M. "The Cinema of Krzysztof Zanussi. *Film Quarterly*, spring 1973.

Cowie, Peter. "Made in Poland: The Metaphysical Cinema of Krzysztof Zanussi." *Film Comment*, September/October 1980.

4

JOE DANTE

AND

The Howling

(with David Ehrenstein)

On March 15, 1990, director Joe Dante was interviewed by David Ehrenstein after a screening of *The Howling*.

The Film

The Howling (1980, an Avco Embassy release. Directed by Joe Dante. Screenplay by John Sayles and Terence H. Winkless. Based on the novel by Gary Brandner. Director of photography, John Hora. Producers, Michael Finnell and Jack Conrad. Executive producers, Daniel H. Blatt and Stephen A. Lane. Editors, Mark Goldblatt and Joe Dante. Music by Pino Donaggio. Special effects by Roger George. Makeup effects by Rob Bottin. Filmed in California.

Cast: Dee Wallace (Karen), Patrick Macnee (Dr. George Waggner), Dennis Dugan (Chris), Christopher Stone (Neill), Belinda Balaski (Terry), Kevin McCarthy (Fred), John Carradine (Erle Kenton), Slim Pickens (Sam), Elisabeth Brooks (Marsha), Robert Picardo (Eddie), Margie Impert (Donna), John Sayles (Morgue Attendant), and Noble Willingham, Kenneth Tobey, Dick Miller, James Murtaugh, Jim McKrell, Don McLeod, Steve Nevil, Herb Braha, Joe Bratcher.

Synopsis: A television news anchorwoman named Karen, accompanied by her husband, seeks to exorcize her sexual trauma with a transcendental meditation encounter group at a rural and exclusive California psychotherapy clinic. She discovers that most of the clients at the spa are werewolves, and that they convert to their beastly states when sexually aroused.

Remarks and Reviews

"*The Howling* doesn't take itself seriously.... It's consciously trashy. The picture isn't afraid to be silly—which is its chief charm." (Pauline Kael, *New Yorker*).

"A superior entertainment—as creepy, witty and suggestive as its disreputable genre would warrant" (J. Hoberman, *Village Voice*).

"Dante takes full advantage of some of the inherent silliness that goes on behind the [television] cameras. ... There are good one-liners throughout. ... In a large part the picture works because of the make-up effects created by Rob Bottin" (Har, *Variety*).

"Who knows how much laughter can lurk in a horror film's heart of darkness? *The Howling* knows" (Kenneth Turan, *New West*).

"It's probably safe to bet that *The Howling* is the funniest *intentionally* funny werewolf movie ever made" (Jim Tamulis, *Film Journal*).

"An excellent little werewolf film ... whose witty script is packed with references to earlier werewolf films. ... The makeup effects include an astonishing real-time transformation of man into wolf (using no camera tricks...) that lasts for minutes.... A good, breezy film" (Peter Nicholls, *World of Fantastic Films: An Illustrated Survey*).

"*The Howling* is a brisk chiller that effortlessly revives the prowling-through-misty-forests genre with enough zip and spectacle to play to a general audience and plenty of in-jokes to pander to genre cognoscenti" (Kim Newman, *Nightmare Movies*).

"Wonderful combination of horror, laughs and state-of-the-art special effects. ... A must-see for horror fans, with more than one viewing recommended" (*Motion Picture Guide*).

The Filmmaker

Joe Dante's career has spanned the financial and quality gamuts of Hollywood motion pictures through two decades. He is an anomaly in that he has worked extensively at what might be considered the bottom rung of the business—under the auspices of B filmmaker Roger Corman—and in the fold of the big time, for the king of modern-day high-concept movies, Steven Spielberg.

A Morristown, New Jersey, native who trained at art school in Philadelphia, Dante began in the film business by doing various editing chores for Corman's New World Pictures. He edited several significant B movies through the 1970s, including Steve Carver's *The Arena* (1974) and Ron Howard's *Grand Theft Auto* (1977). Meanwhile, he and fellow Corman alumnus Allan Arkush made their joint directorial debut with *Hollywood Boulevard* (1976), the epitome of the Corman cheapie, which is discussed in the interview.

After *Piranha* (1978), his solo debut as a director, Dante provided a major hit from minimum resources with *The Howling*. It was a film significant to the horror genre in terms of integrating humor with frights, in its werewolf transformation effects, and in its sly references to previous horror films and their makers. Dante has since directed big-budget pictures, including the blockbuster hit *Gremlins* (1984) and the special-effects comedy *Innerspace* (1987).

Joe Dante's Filmography

As director unless noted: *The Arena* (1974, editor only); *Hollywood Boulevard* (1976, codirector with Allan Arkush, also editor); *Grand Theft Auto* (1977, editor only); *Piranha* (1978, also editor); *Roger Corman: Hollywood's Wild Angel* (1978, interviewee only); *Rock 'n' Roll High School* (1979, story only, cowritten with Allan Arkush); *The Howling* (1980, also editor); *The Slumber Party Massacre* (1981, actor only); *Twilight Zone — The Movie* (1982, codirector with John Landis, Steven Spielberg, and George Miller); *Gremlins* (1984); *Explorers* (1985); *The Fantasy Film World of George Pal* (1986, interviewee and assistance only); *The Puppetoon Movie* (1986, assistance only); *Amazon Women on the Moon* (1987, codirector with Carl Gottlieb, Peter Horton, John Landis, and Robert K. Weiss); *Innerspace* (1987); *The 'Burbs* (1989); *Gremlins 2: The New Batch* (1990); *Matinee* (1993).

Reasons for Selection

The Howling remains one of the wittiest and most innovative horror films of recent years. It contains unique and original integrations of humor with horror and was the first major movie of its time to contain many horror-genre references. Since its release and success, many horror films have contained biting humor and been genre-referential. Joe Dante remains a promising talent, and his full range as a filmmaker has yet to be tapped by the industry.

—D.E.

The Interview

David Ehrenstein: It's my pleasure to introduce to you Joe Dante.

Joe Dante: Would you believe we had only one suit for that picture? I was sitting there thinking, you know we only had this one suit to wear. And, boy, we put it all together, and it looks like we had a lot of suits.

Ehrenstein: You passed it around?

Dante: Yeah. It was a chintzy picture.

Ehrenstein: I thought we might start by talking a little about this being the point you reached after coming out of the Roger Corman school of B filmmaking. But still, I think, you'd think to yourself mentally as having one foot in the Corman school. Describe the school for us.

Dante: I'll always have one foot in the Corman school. Everybody knows what the Corman school is: a place where they pay you very little money to do things that you're not qualified to do because you don't know what you're doing. And if it wasn't for Roger's sort of plucky greed in hiring people who really desperately want to make movies, a lot of people in this town wouldn't have careers. And since Roger defies you to make a movie and throws every possible stumbling block in your path, you really learn how to roll with the punches.

And when it came time to do this picture, which was made in some twenty-four days or something like that, you sort of learn how to set up your camera dolly so that you can shoot off in one direction, and then you can turn the dolly around and shoot off another scene that looks like it's in another location. But actually it's off the same dolly. And then, as you get on, and you do bigger-budget pictures, you come up with ideas like that, and people look at you like you're nuts. This is the whole concept of: "Well, why would you want to do that? Why not just take the time and move it and do another shot?" It's kind of hard to shake that sort of economical thinking about the way to do movies.

Ehrenstein: Thinking through this mixture of humor and fantasy and horror in *The Howling* — how did that sort of evolve in your own mind when you started to make movies?

Dante: It just happened. It was just something I felt that audiences at this particular time might like. This is in 1980, and there hadn't been any werewolf pictures in quite a while. And the ones that had been made in the seventies were very tired. A basic werewolf plot is actually, you know, pretty simple: A guy has a problem, and he turns into a wolf and then dies for it.

In an effort to make the picture and to make the concept a little more appealing and get away from the villagers-with-torches-running-around-the-castle concept, John Sayles and I wanted to make a kind of a modern, more urban, and somewhat more sophisticated werewolf picture. I don't know that it seems all that sophisticated today, but at the time —

Ehrenstein: Today, the werewolves would be appearing on *Donahue* and everywhere else.

Dante: Well, yeah. And, luckily, since this is a continuing series — they keep fairly grinding out these *Howling* movies like sausages — we'll be able to cover all of those bases, eventually.

Ehrenstein: How many *Howlings* have there been?

Dante: Well, there have been actually five that I know of [*Howling II: Your Sister Is a Werewolf* (1985); *Howling III* (1987); *Howling IV: The Original Nightmare* (1988); and *Howling V: The Rebirth* (1989)]. And, finally, I think they've had to go back to the original book, which we sort of didn't use.

Ehrenstein: You didn't?

Dante: Well, at the beginning, the book was kind of corny, and so we didn't use much of it. But it's become a real cottage industry. I mean they keep making these pictures. They never seem to play anywhere, but they make them. And I think they make a lot of money in Europe, or cable TV, or something.

Ehrenstein: And also there was the *Piranha* sequel [*Piranha II: The Spawning* (1981)].

Dante: Yeah, directed by Jim Cameron, which was his first feature. He was forced to make it in Italy, where the Italian producer more or less tried to kick him out of the editing room and make the picture himself. But it was good enough to get him *Terminator*.

Ehrenstein: You are involved in a sequel at the moment, right?

Dante: I am. I used to be able to say, "Yeah, well I just make the originals, and the other people make the sequels." And then, finally, I made a picture that they tried for years to make a sequel to. And Warner Brothers just couldn't figure out a way to make a sequel to *Gremlins* that was worth making because there really isn't any reason to make a sequel. It's a self-contained story. It has a beginning, a middle, and an end, and when it's over, it's over. And we all know why they're making a sequel. And so they finally came to me, and they said, "We can't figure out what to do with this. And if you'll do it . . ." I guess they finally came to the realization that I must have had something to do with the original picture.

I think they were under the impression that, really, Steven Spielberg had sprinkled pixie dust on it and it had become wonderful. But then, when it came time to actually make it again, they really kind of were at a loss. So they came back, and they said, "Well would you do it?" And I said, "If you'll let me do anything that I want with it, then I would like to do it." And they said — at that time it was in their interest to say — "Sure. Great. Fine. Do whatever you want." And so I hired a writer, Charlie Haas, and we came up with a concept. And we took it to them and they said, "Oh, yeah. Fine. Great. Oh boy, we love this!" And we made the picture. Once they saw the picture, I think their idea about letting me do whatever I wanted was maybe not quite as paramount in their minds.

But it is unusual to try to do a sequel that is different than the first picture. I think the problem with sequels has been that people just want to repeat the success of the first picture by doing exactly the same thing over again. And it's like you can just take the *Beverly Hills Cop II* title and put it on *Beverly Hills Cop* and reissue it and save yourself a lot of money. And so we didn't want to do that. So this picture [*Gremlins 2: The New Batch*], I think, is a better picture than *Gremlins*. And it's certainly funnier.

Ehrenstein: One other aspect that I find in all of your movies — and it's very apparent in this one — is that you're hooked up to a linear plot.

Dante: They won't let you make pictures without those.

Ehrenstein: You seem to be undercutting it a whole lot. This movie is incredibly [genre-] referential.

Dante: Well, I think that was partly because of when this picture was made. In genre pictures, the audience tends to be one step ahead of the plot anyway because we've all seen the plot. And one of the fun things about going to see certain kinds of movies is to see the story unfold because we've proven to ourselves that we like to see that kind of thing unfold. But that doesn't mean you have to just sort of reverentially go through all the clichés that are always used.

Usually in werewolf movies, people would say, "A werewolf — oh my God, Doctor, what's that?" Then they'd go to a library, and they'd read about it. And it's just not very interesting. So we wanted to have a movie that took place in a world where people did know what werewolves were and took them for granted. And that later became a kid of staple. That's the cliché now in itself, and in vampire movies that have been made since. In other supernatural pictures, generally the same tone is taken. It's a modern world, and everybody scoffs at these things because they're part of pop culture.

At the time this picture was made, I don't think that was quite as apparent. We were sort of trying to make it part of pop culture. The year this picture came out *An American Werewolf in London* came out, which was the picture that John Landis had been trying to make for a number of years. And when he finally found out that we were making our picture, he said, "Well, I better make my picture quick." And he did. Rick Baker — who was supposed to do the effects for *The Howling* — actually worked on it for about a month. And then John called him up and said, "You said you'd do my picture." So Rick left, and Rob Bottin inherited the job. And it was a good, big break for him.

Ehrenstein: In terms of plot — in *Gremlins* it starts out as this picture does, about people, and then you sort of get rid of them. And then it becomes the Gremlins' movie.

Dante: The idea was that the Gremlins were supposed to take over the movie and sort of destroy it while it was on. So it has to start out as a prosaic kind of regular movie in order for it to be subverted. That's even more true, I think, in the case of the sequel, where they really take over. They get up in the projection booth, and they stop the movie. It's not a sort of a standard narrative form, which I think is one of the reasons the studio was a little nervous about it — until we had our preview.

Ehrenstein: That actually goes back to *Hellzapoppin* [the 1941 Ole Olson/Chic Johnson comedy classic].

Dante: Well, it does. But you know, *Hellzapoppin,* which is one of my favorite movies, is such a cold kind of a movie. It doesn't have a lot of warmth to it that people in high places tend to like. They think that, "Well, that's not a real audience-grabbing kind of a movie because it's so intellectual." That's the way they think of it. It's like, "Whom do I identify with? Where's the narrative line? Where's the third act and the first act?"

I'm not positive that that kind of thing has to apply when you're making a movie like *Gremlins* or *Gremlins 2*, which is supposed to be a summer-fun movie. It's not supposed to, you know, move the earth. It's not supposed to have huge messages and stuff. It's just supposed to be entertaining.

Ehrenstein: At this point, we'd like to show a little bit of *Hollywood Boulevard.* And to set that up —

Dante: Oh, boy. I have to set up *Hollywood Boulevard?* Allan Arkush was the codirector with me. We were working in the trailer department, making trailers for pictures. And we were cutting down Filipino movies and trying to make them look like American movies and taking Japanese movies and trying to make them look American and making up stories for pictures that didn't have stories and lying through our teeth about what the pictures were about.

And then we finally sort of thought, "Well, gee, even we could make a picture as good as some of these pictures." That is the main value of *Hollywood Boulevard* itself. It then became one of those pictures that people watched and said, "Well, if they can make that, then I can make a picture." And so, it's sort of nice to think that you're contributing something.

Anyway, we wanted to make a picture, and Roger [Corman] didn't want us to do it because it would take us away from the trailer department, and he would have to find someone else, and God forbid, maybe he'd have to pay them or something. So he said, "Well, I'll let you make the picture, but only if you continue to make trailers while you're making the picture. And you don't get paid for directing the picture, you just get your trailer salary." Then he later reneged and gave us both five hundred dollars for directing the movie.

He said, "It'll have to be the cheapest movie we ever made here at New World." And that was no mean feat. We got our heads together and decided that the only way we could make a cheap movie was to make it around a lot of the footage that we were very familiar with from these other movies that we'd been doing trailers for. So we wrote a story about Miracle Pictures, which is a movie company: "If it's a good picture, it's a miracle." It's not even our joke—it's stolen from a 1933 Jack Oakie movie [*Sitting Pretty*]—but it's still good. Roger was making a series of three-girl movies at the time. He had nurses and teachers. They were like night-call nurses, and student teachers, and there'd be three girls, and they would get in trouble, and they would, you know, take their clothes off. And there'd be drugs and shooting and killing and then at the end they'd all be happy and be OK. And later that became *Charlies' Angels*, and Roger didn't get any credit at at all.

But we said, well, we'll take that formula and call our picture *The Starlets*. And it'll be about girls trying to make it in Hollywood and taking their clothes off and having drugs and getting shot and stuff, and then they'll be all happy at the end. That sounded good to Roger, especially since it was going to be so cheap. And we said, "Well, what we'll do is we'll use our crew as the movie crew in the movie. We'll use our cameras as the background. We'll use our lights, and all that kind of stuff, so we won't have to buy anything. And we'll dress our actors and actresses like the people in the stock footage that we've got, and we'll stretch the budget," because we couldn't afford action scenes. We didn't have enough money for that, because it was a $60,000 movie and was made in ten days.

So what we did is, we found all this great footage of people falling out of trees and stuff. And we would shoot shots of our heroines shooting machine guns, and then we would cut to the people falling out of the trees, which you'll see in this scene. And in this scene, the cheap agent, played by Dick Miller, sends the three girls to the Philippines to make a Filipino war picture. And, actually, when the movie was finished, we had only used about thirteen minutes of stock footage. But this scene is composed almost entirely of stock footage. I think you'll easily be able to see where our stuff goes and where the stock footage goes. Paul Bartel is in it giving one of his more restrained performances.

Ehrenstein: We'll take a look at that, and then we'll be back and open the floor to questions.

Dante: I may not be back. It looks too much like a New World picture to me.

[*Clip.*]

Ehrenstein: It certainly does.

Dante: What can you say? We had to start somewhere. It's a job. You have to do it.

Ehrenstein: Well, we're opening up whole new areas of montage theory, I think, here.

Dante: Yes. Dialectical montage. Semiotics.

Ehrenstein: Yeah. With Mary Woronov enjoying herself, too.

Dante: Oh, Mary is a wonderful actress. I haven't seen this in a long time, you can imagine. To see that scene where she gives biscuits to the dog — which is like, you know, we had a shot of a dog, so we shot this stupid scene to go with it, so we could make the picture longer. It's incredible what you do.

Ehrenstein: Any question for Mr. Dante?

Dante: What questions could there be after seeing that? I mean that says it all, doesn't it?

Audience Question: What was the name of that movie?

Dante: *Hollywood Boulevard* — "The street where starlets are made." That was the ad line for that picture. Roger wanted to call it *Hollywood Hookers*. But I didn't want my first picture to be called *Hollywood Hookers*. And it didn't make a dime.

Ehrenstein: You said to me that there was a point that you reached after getting through the Corman school when you said, "I think this is really it."

Dante: Well, when you're making pictures for Roger, all you want to do is get these pictures out of the way so that you can then make real movies. You know, somehow these aren't real movies. And you don't feel like they're real movies because it's like film school, except your movie is going to open in theaters instead of be seen by the faculty. So there's not a real feeling. And also there was no feeling of anybody ever seeing any of these movies because most of the time they weren't reviewed. They played drive-ins. They never opened in New York unless there was a newspaper strike, so there was never anything written about them. They really were sort of nonmovies. But the funny thing is that you find that after you start to work for the studios, it isn't any different than working for Roger. The pressure is the same. You have just as much time, practically, to shoot the shots as you did when you were thinking fast on your feet and had no time between the shots.

The great thing about Roger is that he knew what he wanted. He let us make *Hollywood Boulevard* because it was going to have tits in it. And it was going to have guns in it, and it was going to have what his audience wanted. As long as you gave him what his audience wanted, he really didn't care what you did. I mean, you could have arty shots. You could do whatever you wanted as long as you told the story.

Ehrenstein: And you had a reasonable amount of nudity at the interval.

Dante: Like when I did *Piranha*, there had to be a piranha attack in every reel. That was the formula. And it was pretty hard to do because once people know there are piranhas in the water, they're not going to want to go in the water. So, it's a little hard to get them in the water for the next reel. But that was the formula. As long as you adhered to the formula, you could make whatever you wanted.

And Roger had made movies himself. He directed and produced movies for years. And you're talking to somebody who, even though he had strange tastes, was somebody who'd made a picture. You find, I think, that's often not the case when you work for major studios because you're dealing frequently with people who really don't have a good idea about the nuts and bolts of filmmaking, and why things are like they are, and how hard it is to do this as opposed to that. And why something will work and why it won't.

And it makes making B pictures seem pretty attractive in a way. You're so limited in that field by the topics that you can deal with. But when we did *The Howling*, nobody came and told us not to make it funny. Although, the first day, the head of the company said when he saw the dailies, "Well, I thought this was supposed to be a horror picture," and he started grumbling. But as long as the audience liked the movie, they really didn't care. They didn't have a lot of egos to impose on the picture. It's not quite the same way when you're working with a little more money and, you know, bigger studios.

Ehrenstein: I was thinking about something like *Innerspace*, which is basically a comedy.

Dante: *Innerspace* is a picture that, when I read articles about me, they always used to say, "Well, gee, you know, he made these quirky movies, and then he sold out. And he made this sort of impersonal factory movie."

Ehrenstein: But it has [cult actor] Dick Miller in it.

Dante: Yeah, but he has a pretty small part. But I think it's the best picture I ever did because it had a good story, and it's actually pretty wacky. It's not like a regular movie. I mean, it's got a lot of weird stuff in it. It's just a bigger package. I just thought it was a good picture.

Ehrenstein: You traded off all these elements where you have your two heroes shot entirely separately.

Dante: But that's part of the fun of it: the challenge of how to have two people interact who aren't really ever together on the screen. That's one of the things I think that makes it unusual.

Ehrenstein: Even though it's an adequatley budgeted movie, obviously, it could have conceivably been a B movie.

Dante: Well, actually, it's based on a Martin and Lewis movie. I mean the concept behind *Innerspace* was, what if Dean Martin were shrunk and put inside Jerry Lewis? And that's what the writer told me. And I said, "I want to make that picture. That sounds great." I might have preferred if it was Lou Costello inside Bud Abbott, but it's a little late for that.

AQ: Where did you go to film school?

Dante: I really didn't go to film school. I went to art school in Philadelphia, and we had a film class: one camera and forty students. Everybody used all their time to go to movies. We didn't make our movie, we just went to movies. Then, toward the end, everybody would say: "Oh shit! My film is due. Holy shit. What am I going to do? Where's the camera?" And so, everybody was like cutting and pasting and putting their picture together at the very last minute. But this was in 1966 or '68. And it was all in black and white. And it was all cheesy looking and bad sound, if any.

When I came to California in 1974, I went to the [American Film Institute] and saw student films from California. I was astounded. I mean, they were in CinemaScope. They had actors in them. They were in stereo. It was unbelievable. I had never seen anything like this. I couldn't figure it out. Why aren't these people working at studios now? I mean, all these pictures looked like studio pictures. It was quite a jolt. It was a big difference between the kind of stuff you could do in Philadelphia and all the things that are available here.

A lot of times, you make—in this business—what people let you make. And when you make a picture that's been successful, that's a certain type of movie, that's kind of what they want you to do. In fact, I remember my partner was on the phone with some guy who had submitted me a script—I think it was called *Vampire with a Badge*. And I decided that I didn't want to do a picture with that title. So he told the guy, "Well, Joe is actually looking to do something away from that now."

And the guy said, "Jesus Christ. I don't understand what the hell's wrong with these guys. They finally find something they can do, and then they don't want to fucking do it. I mean, what's the story here?" And I think there's a lot of that feeling. It's sort of like, "Well, he does that well, and you can bank on something that this guy does in that field." But if he decided to do a love story—"Hmm, boy, I don't know, that's pretty risky. Maybe we don't want him." And so, you know that you get made only what you can get made.

Ehrenstein: Well, *The 'Burbs* was a little bit—

Dante: *The 'Burbs* really wasn't a departure, except in the sense that there were no special effects in it. And the thing about *The 'Burbs* was that I had a picture called *Little Man Tate*, which became Jodie Foster's directorial debut [in 1991], that was about a child genius. I had been developing it. And it fell apart just about a month before we started shooting. Then there was a writers' strike coming up, and it looked like nobody was going to be working for a year. And I figured, you know, if I don't work this year, it's going to be, like, two years, three years, before I have another picture.

And Imagine [Entertainment] offered me this script, which was then called *Bay Window*. And it was sort of like *Rear Window* — they thought. I didn't, but they did. And I liked the characters. But the script ended with the hero being killed and driven away in an ambulance by a guy that he's been persecuting through the movie, the guy who then turns out to really be guilty. And the fact that the guy is guilty turns out to be sort of a *Twilight Zone* surprise, an O. Henry twist ending. And I thought, "Well, that's OK." But then they decided that we wanted to hire Tom Hanks. And suddenly, it was like, "Well, you know we can't kill Tom Hanks. What are we going to do? We'll have to change it."

It became like another current Tom Hanks movie, a picture where the buildup becomes everything. And when the buildup gets to be so good past a certain point, you have to pay it off better than the buildup. And there was no payoff that we could think of that was as good as the buildup. And we shot, in fact, three endings for the picture. None of them, I think, really worked. But also, because of the writers' strike, we had to sort of make it up as we were going along. Then at the very end, we tried to go back to fit in all of the stuff that we had shot to the ending, but then there were all sorts of clues and stuff that had been dropped that had to be explained.

I mean, why is this scene in the picture if it doesn't pay off in the end? So when you go back to pay off all those things, almost any explanation you come up with isn't as good as what the audience has been imagining, which is, "Boy, this is going to be great. I wonder what it's going to be." And then, when it turns out to be something comparatively mundane, it's disappointing. I also had kind of a problem with the fact that the lead characters in the picture act very irresponsibly and boorishly and stupidly through the whole movie. And I thought they shouldn't be rewarded for it. I thought that it was like condoning this behavior.

But when we took it to the preview audience, we had the first ending: [the characters] were all sort of chastised for what they had done. And the audience just didn't like that. They wanted these guys to be heroes. You know, "We sat and watched the whole movie with these guys — you mean now you're going to tell us they weren't doing good stuff?" So even though I had final cut on that movie, it was like, "What am I going to do? Sit there and insist on an ending that the audience doesn't like, and that's going to kill the picture?" I can't do

Joe Dante on the set of *The Howling*.

that. So we went back and shot a whole bunch of endings, and I don't know that the one on the picture is better than the one we had before.

AQ: What was the budget on *The Howling*?

Dante: We had two budgets. The first budget was under a million, like $850,000 or something like that. And we put the picture together, and it was two-and-a-half hours long, as movies tend to be in rough cut. And there didn't seem to be any werewolves anywhere. I mean, we would look high and low, and we just couldn't seem to see any. It was a very cheap picture and a very ambitious picture for such a low budget. And Rob Bottin, special effects expert, had made a lot of werewolves that sort of stopped at the frame line. So he would make a werewolf head, and he would hold it back here like this, but it would cut off like that. And if it was going to attack somebody, the camera would have to move over or else it would show the person holding the werewolf head. By the time we had shot a lot of that stuff, it started to look pretty claustrophobic. So we decided, well, we better go back and get some more werewolves.

We had to go back to Embassy Pictures and ask for more money, which is a really horrible thing to have to do. You have to grovel, and it's just awful. You have to beg. And they said fine. But actually, we got it from some other company, and they said, "Well, what we'll do is we'll give them the cassette rights." Now, this is 1980. I mean, cassettes—what was that? Nothing [*mock-*

spits]! So they gave away the cassette rights to get another couple thousand dollars, which we went back and shot all the special effects with. And the picture made so much money for this company that invested in it—Wescom—that every year they send me a little paperweight that says, "Thank you for the contribution you've made to our company." Now, in the meantime, the picture actually made some money, but I never saw any of it. And Embassy still owes me my editing deferment, because I edited it for free.

AQ: [Inaudible, something about low-budget filmmaking.]

Dante: I think it makes you think faster. And I think the energy level on a set of a picture that's made quickly and cheaply is different than that of a big studio. When you go on a set of a big studio picture, you tend to see, sometimes, people sort of sitting around. You never see anybody sitting around on a low-budget picture because they can't. If they're sitting around, they could be going to get a truck or something, you know, or to get coffee for somebody. It's a different environment. But it's very stimulating.

In fact, in between all these big movies that I was doing, I went back and did some segments of a comedy movie called *Amazon Women on the Moon*, which was a nonunion picture. It was real cheap and fast and dirty. And it was really a lot of fun. I mean it. There's something really nice about being able to work quickly and to not have to think in any way except a sort of a visceral something that just comes to you: "OK, well, let's do this." You know? If you're making a studio picture and you want to change something—in the contracts it actually says that you have to get it in writing. I mean, nobody does this. But it's an example of how restrictive it really is because you know time is money and minutes are money, and the more minutes there are, the more money it is.

On my set of *Hollywood Boulevard*, I remember thinking, "Sixty thousand dollars is a lot of money." If I thought about how much money it was, I couldn't go to work because the pressure was so great. And now I make pictures for many, many, many, many, many times that, and you just don't think about it. It's just sort of a given that that's what movies cost now.

Ehrenstein: You were talking about taking on *The 'Burbs* because you wouldn't be working—

Dante: Well, everybody in this business. I mean no matter how successful they are, there is a thing in the back of your mind about not working again, ever.

Ehrenstein: Well, I was also thinking about the fact of getting to do any kind of work. Because, I remember, you did several *Twilight Zone* [television] episodes.

Dante: TV is a fun thing to do because it's short. And it reminds you of doing low-budget pictures in a way. There's a real appeal, as I found, in doing this *Twilight Zone* episode, in doing something that you know isn't going to take the rest of your life and isn't going to have to sustain ninety minutes of somebody's time. To sit down and watch a movie is giving away your time. There is a responsibility that you feel when you're making a movie to not waste people's time. I mean, you really do want to make a good movie, and you do want to make the audience happy. On the other hand, you want to also make yourself happy. And sometimes that can create quite a conflict.

It's less so, I think, in a [segment of a multistory] movie. Although they're almost never successful — movies that have more than one story in them — because there's always one story that's better than the others. Or, you know, one that sort of just sits there, and they never get good reviews, as *New York Stories* will show you. People just say, "Ah, that middle one wasn't any good." So, to them, the movie was no good. But there's really something liberating about not being responsible for the entire movie and knowing that you actually do have some freedom to take some risks. If they don't work, it isn't going to sink the movie by itself because there are other things around it —

Ehrenstein: To sink it.

Dante: To sink it.

AQ: [Inaudible. A question about Dante directing episodes of *Police Squad*.]

Dante: I did two *Police Squads* — *Naked Gun I*, as we call it. *Police Squad* was a great show to do, except the Zuckers — these three guys, I don't know if you know about the Zuckers [filmmaking brothers Jerry Zucker and David Zucker] — but they're not all Zuckers. One of them isn't a Zucker [Jim Abrahams]. But there are these three guys, and they work together.

They did *Airplane!* and *Top Secret!* and *Ruthless People*. They are really crazy, these guys. And they are friends of mine. They directed the first episode of this show, which was a parody of 1960s cop shows, which wasn't successful. It was such an accurate parody of the sixties cop shows — and it didn't have a laugh track — that people would turn the thing on and say, "Oh, there's Leslie Nielsen in some old cop show." Also you had to really pay attention to that show. You couldn't have the lights on, and you couldn't be on the phone. You had to turn the lights off and sit and watch the screen because there were all sorts of great jokes in it. People felt exhausted after it. They'd say, "Geez, this is a lot of work for television."

The thing is, I was the first director they asked to do an episode that they were producing. And they treated me the way they treat each other, which is that you'd start to shoot the scene, and you'd shoot the angle this way, and then you'd relight and start to shoot the scene this way. And they came in and said to me, "Oh, geez, we just thought of a great joke." And I said, "Well, yeah but I already. . ." "But you got to get it. You got to do it." And I said, "Well, yeah, but I'm done shooting this scene." "No, no, you gotta do it." And I said, "This is television. You can't do this." And they were always saying, "Oh, no, no, no. Do us a favor."

They had a joke where Leslie Nielsen is sitting at a bar and the barstool is like going down or something, and he asks the bartender for a screwdriver, and the bartender gives him a screwdriver, and he fixes the thing. That was their joke. I said, "I don't know if this is funny enough." "Oh, it'll be great. It's going to be so good." It was really a lot of fun to work on that show. It was great. And it was way ahead of its time. The rear-projection jokes in it were just amazing. So I did the second episode and the last episode.

It was on Tuesdays. Then, the next Tuesday, they didn't advertise, because the first Tuesday had such terrible ratings. By the third Tuesday you couldn't even find it. They had moved it. And they [didn't] run the last one until two months later, as a filler when the ball game was rained out or something. It was a very funny show.

AQ: [Inaudible: A question about Dante's producers.]

Dante: Well, I have a producer that I work with all the time, Mike Finnell, who started with me with Roger [Corman]. In fact, he worked on *Hollywood Boulevard* as the prop guy. He was the only guy who would wade into the swamp to get the one wooden hand grenade that we had. Jonathan Kaplan — who was in that clip — plays Scottie, the guy who's giving Paul Bartel all the guns and stuff [Kaplan is the director of many exploitation films as well as *White Line Fever* (1975), *Heart Like a Wheel* (1983), *The Accused* (1988), *Unlawful Entry* (1992), and others]. He gave me a good piece of advice: "Gotta get a close-up because this'll never cut." He'd come over and help a lot.

He saw Mike standing in the swamp looking for the hand grenade, and he said, "What are you doing? Get out of there. Look, give her a rock. Nobody's going to know the difference." And with that piece of advice, Mike Finnell managed to parlay himself into being a producer of major movies. So you see, anybody can do it.

AQ: [Inaudible: A question about Dante's inspiration.]

Dante: Well, part of everything I do is based on some 1950s Universal picture that I saw. Well, actually, it's the same set, even. The Universal back lot is the same one they used to make monster and tarantula movies and a whole bunch of that stuff. My movies are like *It's a Wonderful Life* meets a fifties kind of our movie. I don't think you can remake them. I mean they tried with *The Blob* [in 1988]. But there's something very innocent and sincere about those pictures. And as soon as you try to say, "Boy, you know, we know how this goes," and "Boy, we're aware," it just doesn't seem to work.

A lot of my favorite fifties pictures have been remade. Look at what they did to *The Incredible Shrinking Man* [remade as *The Incredible Shrinking Woman* with Lily Tomlin in 1981]. It just doesn't work when you try to be above the material. You have to have affection for it, but as soon as you try to do *knowing* kinds of gags, you have to be careful. That's one of the things I think that *Gremlins* did OK. It managed to be like those pictures without really being like them, and [managed to] recall them without making real terrible fun of them, like they were no good. I think those pictures that I saw when I was a kid—they had a wonderful sort of liberating effect on me. And I still like them. In fact, we're missing *This Island Earth* as we speak. It's on TNT tonight.

Ehrenstein: Your *Twilight Zone* film episode is, I think, one of the best things you've ever done in that it's so concentrated.

Dante: The studio was a little concerned with the dailies on this. *The Twilight Zone*, as you may remember, was a very troubled movie because of the accident [actor Vic Morrow and two children were killed in a helicopter accident], which happened before any of the rest of us did our episodes. And we frankly didn't think there would be a movie. We figured that's going to be it for the movie—we just won't make it. And then, several months later, for reasons of their own, Warner Brothers decided to go ahead with the movie. But because of the kind of situation they found themselves in, nobody really wanted to claim it as their own. There weren't a lot of production executives on it.

George Miller and I were—it was for both of us our first major studio experience. It was a little misleading in that we were left completely alone. We got to do everything exactly the way we wanted to. Then when George made *The Witches of Eastwick* and I made *Gremlins*, we discovered that it really isn't the way it usually works at all. In fact, it's quite the opposite. In fact, whatever is wrong with this *Twilight Zone* is entirely due to whatever mistakes I made. The only thing I really regret is that at the very end of the eipsode there used to be the thunder from George Miller's episode used to start over the end of my episode, which made what looked like a happy ending not a happy ending—which it wasn't supposed to be. But ever since then, people have said, "Boy, you know, it's OK except for that happy ending." But it really isn't a happy ending. Or at least it wasn't supposed to be.

Ehrenstein: And like all the episodes in *Twilight Zone—The Movie*, they're remakes.

Dante: Yes. The concept was that they would remake the show. As it turned out, Rod Serling had tried to remake *The Twilight Zone* himself as a feature. Interestingly, he had chosen the episode that I did as the subject of his script. He did a ninety-minute script of a story called "It's a Good Life," by Jerome Bixby. And for some reason, it didn't get made.

John Landis and Steven Spielberg were stuck on remaking stories from *The Twilight Zone*, which I really didn't think was such a hot idea because everybody knew them. And they were so dependent on O. Henry twists that the only reason people keep watching *The Twilight Zone* reruns is because of how well done they are. It's not because they are going to be surprised by the ending. Nonetheless, they said, "Yeah, pick one. And it's gotta be one that's already been done." And I picked this one—not because it wasn't done well on TV, because it actually was done quite well—but because the original short story that it was based on was considerably different than the TV adaptation.

And so [screenwriter] Richard Matheson and I worked on changing the concept of the story to a point where people who might have seen the original episodes still wouldn't recognize this one until maybe the middle of it.

Ehrenstein: We're ready to show the episode from *Twilight Zone — The Movie*.

Dante: Gee, I don't see anybody up there. Is [the projectionist] still up there?

For Further Study

Videocassette

The Howling is available on videocassette from Embassy Home Entertainment, Inc.

Books

Kawin, Bruce. "*The Funhouse* and *The Howling*." In *American Horrors*, edited by Gregory A. Waller. Urbana and Chicago: University of Illinois Press, 1987.

Newman, Kim. *Nightmare Movies*. New York: Proteus Books, 1984.

Singer, Michael. *Film Directors: A Complete Guide*. Beverly Hills, Calif.: Lone Eagle Publishing, 1986.

Twitchell, James B. *Dreadful Pleasures: An Anatomy of Modern Horror*. New York and Oxford: Oxford University Press, 1985.

Periodicals

Applebaum, R. "Techniques of the Horror Film: *The Howling*." *Film-makers Monthly*, September 1980.

Fox, J. R., and A. Eisenberg. "*The Howling*." *Cinefantastique*, 1980.

McCarthy, Todd, "A Sanitorium for Werewolves: All Try to Live with the Problem." *Variety*, October 15, 1980.

Sayles, John. "Filmmaker." *New Yorker*, March 23, 1981.

Stanley, John. "They Dare Me to Shock Them." *San Francisco Sunday Examiner and Chronicle*, April 5, 1981.

Turan, Kenneth. "The Wolf Man of El Monte: Rob Bottin's Special Effects Are a Howling Success." *New West*, March 1981.

5

RICHARD RUSH

AND

The Stunt Man

(with Kenneth Turan)

On April 26, 1990, screenwriter, director and producer Richard Rush was interviewed by Kenneth Turan after a screening of *The Stunt Man*.

The Film

The Stunt Man (1980), a Twentieth Century–Fox release. Directed and produced by Richard Rush. Screenplay by Lawrence B. Marcus. Adaptation by Richard Rush. Based on the novel by Paul Brodeur. Executive producer, Melvin Simon. Director of photography, Mario Tosi. Editors, Jack Hofstra and Caroline Ferriol. Music by Dominic Frontiere. Filmed on Coronado Island, San Diego County, California, and in Los Angeles and other California locations.

Cast: Peter O'Toole (Eli Cross), Steve Railsback (Cameron), Barbara Hershey (Nina Franklin), Allen Goorwitz (Sam), Alex Rocco (Jake), Sharon Farrell (Denise), Adam Roarke (Raymond Bailey), Philip Burns (Ace), Chuck Bail (Chuck Barton), John Garwood (Gabe/Eli's Cameraman), Jim Hess (Henry/Eli's Cameraman), John B. Pearce (Garage Guard), Michael Railsback (Burt), George D. Wallace (Father), Dee Carroll (Mother), Leslie Winograde (Sister), Don Kennedy (Lineman), Whitey Hughes and Walter Robles (Assistant Directors) and A. J. Bakunas, Gregg Berger, Ross Reynolds, Robert Caruso, Frank Avila, Stafford Morgan, John Alderman, James Avery, Leigh Webb, Frank Beetson, Jack Palinkas, Garrett McPherson, Nelson Tyler, Larry Dunn, Deanna Dae Coleman, Louie Gartner, Gordon Ross, Marion Wayne, William Joseph Arno.

Synopsis: A fugitive named Cameron stumbles onto a movie location and is offered a way to conceal his identify: He is disguised as a stunt man—who doubles for an actor, who plays an American flying ace in World War I, who poses as a German soldier, who, like the actual fugitive, is also a fugitive. In his new role, the stunt man performs increasingly dangerous and death-defying feats as the cameras roll. His biggest stunt is staying alive in a world of make-believe. Allies turn into enemies, safety becomes danger, and his sanctuary becomes a death trap when it appears as if the autocratic director, Eli Cross, plans to shoot the stunt man's actual death. During the filming of the final stunt, the stunt man makes his bid to escape both the obsessive Eli Cross and his past identity as a fugitive. With the film's lead actress, Nina Franklin, hidden in the trunk of a Duesenberg, he drives the car off a bridge into a river as the cameras roll, then fights to escape what might be his watery grave.

Remarks and Reviews

"Rush is well named, a kinetic action director to the bone. He isn't afraid to hook you and keep hooking you. There is a furious aliveness to this picture. A vituoso piece of filmmaking" (Pauline Kael, *New Yorker*).

"Rush has gambled and won. He is exalting in his craft as only a master craftsman can, with action and ideas in glittering cinematic style" (Judith Crist, *Saturday Review*).

"A stunning feat of moviemaking by a truly daring director. Savage, sharp-witted, furiously fast, gleeful, impudent, remarkably skillful" (Kathleen Carroll, *New York Daily News*).

"Strikingly well-made and considerably ambitious, *The Stunt Man* is one of the most unusual domestic pictures to come along in some time. . . . From the opening virtuoso scene, helmer Richard Rush puts the audience on its toes and through a dazzling display of kinetic direction which he manages to sustain. . . . Fascinates with an impressive cinematic juggling act" (Cart, *Variety*).

"Chock full of slam-bang action and hair-raising stunts. . . . Rush has done an extraordinary job of making all this work, walking the fine edge between madness and melodramatics" (Arthur Knight, *Hollywood Reporter*).

"One of the most interesting American pictures of the year — an exciting, offbeat phantasmagoria" (Peter Rainer, *Mademoiselle*).

"It may be the most original American movie of the year. . . . *The Stunt Man* is at once an exhilarating exercise in pop Pirandello, a bitchily funny satire of filmmakers and a touching moral tale about the perils of paranoia. . . . Rush keeps the audience in a state of almost hallucinatory suspense. It's a sensory, mind-twisting trip that leaves one happily sated" (David Ansen, *Newsweek*).

"*The Stunt Man* is a popular work of modernist art. Richard Rush's whirligig virtuosity has created an alternate reality bigger and better than life" (Michael Sragow, *Los Angeles Herald-Examiner*).

"One of those rare, superior films . . . that will take many years to find an audience. . . . A magnificent mystery. . . . Filmmaking as it's practiced in America, with its emphasis on competition and commercial success, creates the conditions necessary to drive a film crew to the point of lunacy. Movie people can understand this madness, but possibly their executives do not believe the public can share the joke, so *The Stunt Man* remains little seen" (Stephen L. Hanson, *Magill's Survey of Cinema*).

"I've learned more from Mr. Rush than I have learned from anyone since David Lean. . . . He does what poets do" (Peter O'Toole, 1980).

The Filmmaker

Richard Rush won Academy Award nominations for writing and directing *The Stunt Man*. He turned down many studio assignments until he agreed to direct *Color of Night*, starring Bruce Willis. His only project to be realized between *The Stunt Man* and *The Color of Night* was *Air America*, which was directed by Roger Spottiswoode and starred Mel Gibson, years after Rush had a falling out with the producer and walked off the picture along with his star, Sean Connery.

The New York–born Rush studied at UCLA's cinema school in the 1950s, gained technical experience as a recording engineer, still photographer, and director of commercials before his feature-film debut, *Too Soon to Love* (1960), a daring drama for the times about teenage pregnancy, which featured Jack Nicholson in a small supporting part.

Throughout the 1960s, Rush honed his craft with a variety of low-budget and exploitation films, including various motorcycle and counterculture movies for American International Pictures. He has directed three major-studio films since, including the campus-protest drama *Getting Straight* (1970), with Elliott Gould, and the humorous, edgy, and action-packed box-office hit *Freebie and the Bean* (1974), starring James Caan and Alan Arkin as San Francisco police detectives.

The Stunt Man was one of the most critically admired movies of the early 1980s but suffered from what can only kindly be called a botched job of promotion. Released in Seattle without a distributor, the film played to record crowds for forty consecutive weeks, which prompted Twentieth Century–Fox to pick up the film for distribution. Fox then released the picture in Canada and New York with no television publicity and subsequently distributed it in other cities with a scaled-back advertising campaign.

During Academy Award voting time—after Rush had been nominated twice and Peter O'Toole had been nominated for best actor—the film played in only three theaters nationwide, won no Oscars, and was relegated, prior to the video age, to revival houses.

Richard Rush's Filmography

As director, except as noted: *Too Soon to Love* (1960, also producer); *Of Love and Desire* (1963, also cowrote screenplay with Laszlo Gorog); *The Fickle Finger of Fate* (1966); *Thunder Alley* (1966); *A Man Called Dagger* (1967); *Hell's Angels on Wheels* (1967); *Psych-Out* (1967); *The Savage Seven* (1968); *Getting Straight* (1970, also producer); *Freebie and the Bean* (1974, also producer); *The Stunt Man* (1980, also producer, and cowrote screenplay with Lawrence B. Marcus); *Air America* (1990, screenplay only, cowrote with John Eskow, based on the book by Christopher Robbins); *Color of Night* (1994).

R e a s o n s   f o r   S e l e c t i o n

As a critic, what you look for after you have seen film after film is something different. You want to see a film in which you can't figure out what's going to happen before the ending credits roll. Films like this are hard to come by in Hollywood, and they are difficult to get made and distributed. *The Stunt Man* was different. It kept its mystery, and it was afflicted with the problems of backing and distribution.

I fell in love with the film when it first came out. And I showed it a year ago to a group of University of Southern California students, which I was nervous about because, like people you haven't seen in a long time — like someone you had a relationship with once — you don't know if you're still going to like them. I think I liked the film more the second time.

This film has excellent ensemble acting. It also has a very intricate structure, a delicate, challenging structure that is unusual, especially for an American film. The thing I like most about it is its unique point of view.

As an audience, we almost always know more than the people on the screen know. Movies pander to the audience at the expense of characters. In monster movies, everyone in the film is saying, "There are no giant ants out there." We in the audience are very smug; we know there are giant ants, and we're waiting for the people in the film to know what we know. Even in a film like *Pretty Woman*, there's a process of having our expectations fulfilled: We know they're going to end up together, even though the characters don't know.

In *The Stunt Man*, we don't know any more than the characters know. And that's disorienting at first. But I think, ultimately, it's really an enormous achievement. And that's why I was happy to be able to show this film.

—K.T.

The Interview

Kenneth Turan: Richard Rush wanted to say a few words beforehand, so I'll introduce him now.

Richard Rush: *The Stunt Man* has a couple of actors in it who, for me, define the outer limits of the art: Peter O'Toole and Steve Railsback — who's sitting back there tonight. Any movie with a title like *The Stunt Man* suggests the kind of flick where you kick back and watch the actors slug it out on the screen. Well, it's certainly true. But that's not all that *The Stunt Man* is about.

It's also about things which are more serious to the human condition, like the panic and paranoia we seem to feel over our inability to understand what's happening around us, and the control over our own lives. This isn't the kind of paranoia they put you in rubber rooms for, but the kind that you feel when you just hear that your boss has had lunch with your assistant. Or your best friend used to date your wife. Or the kind you feel when you're playing poker with strangers who keep winning.

I think we seem to view the events of our lives as though we were peeking through a keyhole. It's a limited view of the truth. And there is something in our nature that makes us want to understand everything that's going on around us. And since we see so little of the truth, we tend to make up the rest as we go along.

We invent arbitrary rules of right, wrong, good, bad. We invent enemies to test our strength against. We invent gods to protect us from the enemies. We insist that the gods are benevolent in the hope that they will be. And we grow more paranoid every day in the fear that they won't. And this seems to be the substance from which our reality is cut, which is why it is sometimes difficult to tell truth from illusion.

Now since we're dealing with such portentous topics in the film, you might suddenly find yourself unsure of how to react, whether to laugh or cry. If that happens, just look at the person on your left. If you can't see their face because they're looking at the person on their left, that means they don't understand it either, and we're all in serious trouble. But we can fight about that after the movie.

[*Movie.*]

Turan: This is based on a novel by a man named Paul Brodeur, which came out in 1970. Did you read it then? I haven't read it. How was it different from this?

Rush: Radically. Actually, Columbia Pictures owned the novel, and I had just done *Getting Straight* for them. They asked me to do this afterward. Peter Guber, who was twenty-four years old or so at the time and running Columbia, gave me the book and said there was something of interest in it, that Truffaut had expressed interest and so had Arthur Penn. As a matter of fact, some of the imagery from this sort of appeared in *Night Moves* [directed by Arthur Penn] and also, of course, in *Day for Night*, Truffaut's picture.

I read the book, and I had a lot of trouble with it. It had a kind of Illusion and Reality in capital letters. It made a lot of esoteric comparisons to art and life, and it had a crutch which bothered me: When in doubt, make the central character crazy. Eli Cross was very crazy, and therefore, you don't have to justify his actions.

But there was something in it that I couldn't forget about: the idea of a fugitive who hides his identity as a stunt man and by posing as a stunt man, starts to believe the director is going to kill him. That seems like a very interesting way to deal with that idea of being unable to understand what's going on around you—the panic, the paranoia, that we all tend to feel from time to time—and still do it as a straight-line action story. So I asked them if they'd let me take it in a different direction. They said yes and we went on with it.

Turan: And what happened? I know it was a long, tortuous road, but—

Rush: Right. They brought Larry Marcus in to do the screenplay with me. And after about nine months I was ecstatic about it. I really loved it. We handed it into Columbia. They had a bad economic turn and couldn't afford to do the picture, and they passed. My agent at the time said, "No problem, I'll have your deal in a week."

Turan: Right. Famous last words.

Rush: Inside of a month it had been turned down by every studio in town, twice. And I managed to buy the rights from Columbia after my turnaround expired. It took about seven or eight years to get the money together for it.

Turan: What were you hearing from the studios when they were saying no? What made them uncomfortable?

Rush: What I was really hearing was: "It's too complex. They can't put their finger on what it's about. Is it a fantasy? Is it an action-adventure? Is it a comedy?" And, of course, the answer to all that is yes.

Turan: All the things that make it good is what they didn't like about it.

Rush: That's what frightened them about it. They hadn't seen it before. And, as a matter of fact, after I did *Freebie and the Bean*, it made a lot of money for Warners and was [a top] grosser that year [the 12th-biggest grosser of 1975]. And so I thought I'd take advantage, and I said, "Hey, let's do *The Stunt Man* now." And they said: "If you'll do it as a straight-line action story, terrific." And I said, "Guys, I haven't waited for five years to do this as a straight-line action story." And they said, "OK."

And about a month later, I got a call saying, "Do you mind if we use the title?" They had put a couple guys on the script and tried to turn it into a straight-line action story. And, as a matter of fact, they did put out that picture. We had a fight over the title, and they called it *Hooper*. It was with Burt Reynolds. Remember it? It even had a few lines left over from *The Stunt Man*.

Turan: Why didn't you give up on this? Why did you persevere for so long with this?

Rush: Truthfully, I was getting a lot of scripts at the time. A lot of offers. And every time I would get tempted, I would go back and read *The Stunt Man* for comparison. I kept saying to myself, "Geez, I can't give this up." You know? The only time I tried to give it up is when I had *One Flew over the Cuckoo's Nest* for a couple of years. There was no way of getting that financed in the business. Finally, when it went back to Michael Douglas, he got it financed in the music business — you know, outside the movies, in San Francisco.

Turan: Now, the Mel Simon organization is no longer a filmmaking entity. How did it come to them to put up the money?

Rush: Mel was a shopping-center tycoon who had just gone into the film business, a man with a lot of money and enthusiasm. And I sort of got in early in the game. I met him in New York, and we pitched him the story. The one or two people he had working for him read the script and liked it. We sat in his jet with me riding backward between Boston and New York and made the deal. And it stuck. Afterward, he started saying yes to a lot of projects and had to hire a staff to cover it, and pretty soon was sort of a studio in his own right.

Unfortunately, he hired the same guys who had sunk two or three other studios with twenty pictures behind. He only ended up with two or three really good ones.

Turan: I want to talk a little bit about getting it cast. The roles seem to suit everyone so well. First of all, let's start with Peter O'Toole. It almost feels like he was in mind when it was written. Was that the case?

Rush: Yes, very much so. It didn't necessarily start that way, but as we were writing it, you know, Peter's face became stronger and stronger. And I had, you know, I adored him as an actor. I had never met him. I didn't have any particular access to him. One day somebody said, "He's coming to a party tonight at a friend's house. He's in Los Angeles. Do you want to come?" And I said, "Sure.'" And I went to the party, and I talked to Peter all evening.

I didn't mention *The Stunt Man* because it seemed so tacky to bring it up at a party that I couldn't force myself to do it. He left, and I was kicking myself, saying, "You asshole." When he came back in the door suddenly, and he said, "Hey. Somebody just told me you're the guy who directed *Freebie and the Bean*. That's my favorite movie." I said, "I've got a script for you." I gave it to him, and he took it to London and called me back a couple of weeks later and said, "I've been throwing it against the wall to see if it would stick. I love it and want to do it."

Turan: Now the character that Steve Railsback plays is very complex. He seems to go through a lot of different kinds of emotions. Did you think that [role] would be really tough to cast? And how did you come down to Steve to do it?

Rush: It's a stunningly difficult role to me because you have to climb into that kid's shoes at the beginning of the movie. You only get to know what he knows. There's no "Meanwhile, back at the ranch." So you're seeing the whole thing through his eyes. We put the audience in a very strange vice by not telling them whether he's a good guy or a bad guy, or what his crime is—until well into the third act.

So you find yourself rooting for him, and worrying about the fact that you're rooting for him—maybe he's not such a good guy after all. And it takes a remarkable actor to carry off the levels he was going through: that young fugitive, the changes. Always working three things at once. The thing that delighted me and amazed me both about Steve's performance—that not many people seem to tumble to it consciously—is that he's a stunningly good comedian. He does stuff in there like, you know, that goofy kid in the water with the old lady who's just turned into Nina Franklin, where he's laughing, "I seen you on TV." Very tricky stuff to carry off, which he does like magic.

Turan: One thing that struck me while I was watching the film: The plot has kind of an animosity or a strangeness between some members of the cast. The director has tried to—literally, during the shooting—keep them apart. I wonder if you did anything like that to emphasize Steve's character's apartness from the rest of the film.

Rush: No. This was one of those fortunate casts where it was like a commando guerrilla team fighting behind the lines, where everybody was crazy about everybody else and would kill to make sure that the picture worked. So everybody was working very hard and very tightly, and they were all such accomplished actors that tricks weren't [necessary].

Turan: I think there's never been scenes as sympathetic to a writer in Hollywood as some of the scenes that Allen Garfield did. I guess he was Allen Goorwitz in this.

Rush: Right. It's interesting you should single him out. I've always loved Allen's work. And I adore his work in this movie. But he was the one who felt slightly challenged by Peter, in the sense that if Peter arrived by helicopter, he would have to rent a limousine.

Turan: Really?

Rush: That kind of thing. One day, it was during that big banquet scene where the smoke rings are floating around and the cop comes. That scene took several days to shoot. There's lot of coverage in it. And it's a delicate scene — every time you take another take, the food has to be replaced. Most of the actors are wise enough not to eat it, but Allen kept eating his. And it was making Peter sick. After a couple of days of Allen eating, you know, twenty to thirty meals a day, he couldn't handle it anymore. But neither could Allen. And at one point, in the middle of a take, he fell asleep.

We saw him sleeping there when the take was over, and we all got up quietly, tiptoed out of the room, turned off the lights, and watched at a distance when Allen woke up and found himself in those strange circumstances.

Turan: Now, is there anything about Barbara Hershey that comes to mind when you see the film again?

Rush: Yes. How much I like her. Most people don't know because of Barbara's strange, checkered past, that she's an extremely bright, extremely well read, very articulate lady. She's not the dummy that she's cunningly playing here. That girl can throw her IQ into whatever level she wants it to be.

Turan: I noticed. I recognized one of the ADs [assistant directors] on the set — Whitey. One of the ADs whom I know is a real AD. I wonder who else in the film are real crew people, real stunt people, that are like, basically, acting their own occupation?

Rush: At this point, it's difficult for me to say. It was a problem on the picture. You look through the lens, and you see reflectors and crew people. You look behind you, and you see reflectors and crew people. You're wondering which way to point the camera, which one looks better.

I did happen to notice — and I haven't seen the picture in a while — that we had one accident on the picture. It was a stunt man who was the high-fall specialist in the world at that time [A. J. Bakunas]. And it was that long tumble down the side of the tower, which was a free-fall tumble, much harder than a high fall. And he broke his leg on it, to his delight, because we gave him a speaking part for the rest of the picture. So, instead of him getting a week, he ended up with twelve weeks or something. But he was the kid in the striped T-shirt who came up to Eli at one point playing an AD.

Turan: Because the film is so complex, was there a lot of preproduction? Was there intricate storyboarding? Or did it just work like another film?

Rush: Having come from low-budget pictures, which is a kind of guerrilla warfare, I had sort of been trained from an early stage not to tell anybody what you're doing so they can't argue with you. So storyboards became taboo. I had a lot of time, frankly, to work out screenplay material because after seven years you end up doing ten rewrites. Time was eroding the story. The Vietnam story was receding in history. And we were getting into more and more trouble with the screenplay, until one day it occurred to me what the solution was.

And it's what Sam says in the picture. He says, "You want to do this great big antiwar story, and your problem is you haven't got a war. You've lost relevance." And Eli says, "This picture isn't about shooting wars. It's not about wars. It's not about fighting wars. It's about fighting windmills." You know — name the disease, and maybe you've got it. So actually naming the disease the polemics of the piece sort of almost became another added suspense line rather than a detraction from the story. And I was almost glad we had to wait. Because that was a fortunate addition to the texture.

Turan: It definitely was. Whose idea? Where did it come from? The crime is this — the guy falling asleep in the ice cream?

Rush: That was early in the game when Larry and I were constructing the story. We sort of worked as collaborators work, improvising by standing up and shouting at each other and then getting the good stuff on tape. I'm relatively sure that one will happen to be mine.

Turan: Now, compared to your other films, was it a tough shoot? Was it an easy shoot?

Rush: It was a very tough shoot because it was a very physically demanding picture with the big stunts playing against heavy dramatic scenes. But it was a delightful shoot because, like I said, everybody really liked it and liked each other, and we were all getting what we wanted. You know, we saw the dailies. That's the shot in the arm that keeps you going for the next day. I've usually had that kind of luck.

On *Freebie and the Bean* I didn't. For the first time in my life I had some genuine problems on that one: Two actors [James Caan, Alan Arkin] who were afraid of each other at the beginning and I had to unite them somehow. And nothing unites them like a common enemy. I miscalculated. I didn't expect to turn out to be the enemy, but I did.

Turan: What about editing a film like this, where there's just a lot going on? Did you take more time than usual? Or was it something that you were used to doing?

Rush: I tend to take a fairly long time in postproduction. This one was demanding. I had two good editors on it: Jack Hofstra and Caroline Ferriol. Both very fast.

Turan: Even though the people in the studios had a lot of trouble understanding why this would work, you didn't have any trouble with the cast. Everyone understood what the film was trying to do?

Rush: Yes, I think so—to the extent that they were really supposed to. I've never really met a good actor who, let's say, is playing the doorman, who doesn't believe that the picture is about this doorman who opens the door for this couple who happens to be the leading couple. And so everybody does have their own view of the film. Privately, you work individually with the actor because if two people are going to have a fight on the screen—an argument—they better both believe they're right. So, you don't want to talk about who's right and wrong in general. You want to talk to each one about why they're right. And I think it's important that those separations are kept.

Turan: One of the things I find myself looking forward to when I see the film again is the score. I really get attached to that score, and I wonder if that was an easy one to come up with?

Rush: We did have some problems. Dominic Frontiere worked with me once before, on *Freebie and the Bean*. And he's a marvelous man for a lay musician—like me—to work with because he's very articulate and verbal. You can describe to him what you want in complicated terms, and he can sit down at the piano and start working it and translate it into music. We actually made one mistake. We started off in the wrong direction. He did half a dozen compositions which weren't working. Then we changed directions totally to where we went with these kind of sad little waltzes played by inept musicians, which suggest the feelings of the people in the movie.

Turan: It's amazing [the film is] here because of all the problems it went through. But once it was finished, you had trouble getting it distributed.

Rush: I think the genesis of the problem was probably the fact that the head of the company and I were cast as enemies. He had done a great number of films while I was doing this one. They had a heavy production schedule. And a lot of their films weren't releasable. He had taken a pretty strong stand against this film. And it sort of became apparent that if this went out and made a lot of money, then—

Turan: He would look pretty foolish.

Rush: He would look foolish. And, you know, probably would cut my cost in the company. And so, finally, when he made a deal for distribution with Twentieth Century-Fox for a Mel Simon product, this was the one picture left out of that distribution deal. So I had to go out and, you know, trick the studio and everything. And he had put it in the trades that this picture was having a problem. Which, in our business, makes things very difficult because studio executives are men who have to protect themselves first and worry about the product second. If the head of a company is having a problem with one particular piece of material out of twenty, then it's really not such a great idea to take a chance on it and add to your burdens. I think that's what slowed it down to begin with.

So I started previewing the picture and cheating on the previews. You know, I'm not stupid. I may be crazy, but I'm not totally stupid. Like, I would go into a town and say to the head reviewer, "I'd like you to do me a favor. Look at the movie. If you love it, review it. And if you don't, hold your review until we're released."

Generally, they'd say, "OK." They'd realize it was somebody trying to do a good thing. And fortunately our reviews, when we went into those towns, were super-raves, and we'd have incredible survey numbers and get standing ovations, and so on. So I'd bring back these. Well, we did it in Seattle. That was the first preview, and it brought back these great results. They said, "Well, Seattle isn't really, you know, it's a strange town, go do it someplace else." So we went and did it in Phoenix, and we did it, you know, in a few other places, and came back with the same stuff. They all said, "OK. The audiences seemed to like it, the critics seemed to like it, but that doesn't mean we can get an audience to come and see it."

Turan: They always have something to say.

Rush: Right. Fortunately, there was a guy up in Seattle who was a theater-chain owner who loved the picture and wanted to test it. And so against some heavy objections, we worked out a test with the man, and we worked out a campaign for the test, and we opened there. And he ended up breaking the house records and making a million dollars in that one theater. It was a four-hundred-seat house in a campus. It took a year, you know, to do that.

Turan: No kidding.

Rush: But, you know, phenomenal results came, which I brought back, triumphantly, to which the studios said, "Seattle's a nonmarket. It doesn't really count." And we had a chance to get into the Avco [Theater] for six weeks. There was a fallout in the summer, and it looked right, and we grabbed it. And then we expanded right after it opened, and we became the number one grosser in L.A., and Fox had to pay attention. So they added it to their list, and that's how we got the distribution, finally.

Turan: That's amazing.

Rush: It was a tough road to realize, strange.

Turan: What kind of an afterlife has the film had? Is it one people keep saying to you that they like?

Rush: Yes. I must say, it's the most satisfying, I think, thing in my life to hear that continually. It's been quite a while now. It seems to be a picture that has lasted in people's memories, and [for] those who like it, it's become one of their favorites. So, it's one of the things that doesn't leave you by the time you reach the curb outside.

Turan: How does it feel seeing it again? What crosses your mind when you see it again?

Rush: Strange things. At one point I was looking at Peter O'Toole's costume. He was wearing a little leather pouch on his waist. I remembered that I walked in that day, and he came up to me. He said, "How do you like the costume?" He'd usually check it out with me in the morning before we started. I said, "God, Peter, that's exactly what I've been after. That's the Americanization of Peter O'Toole." This was his first American picture. Everybody started snickering, and I couldn't figure out what they were laughing at until lunchtime when I suddenly realized he was dressed exactly like I was. He had even had the little leather pouch made that I kept my wallet in and my cigarettes. It was things like that that occurred.

Turan: That's funny. I know that this is the sixty-four-thousand-dollar question, but when will we see another picture from you?

Rush: God, you almost did. I spent three or four years developing what was my favorite and most exciting piece of material. I really liked the screenplay as well as *The Stunt Man*. And I had got Sean Connery locked in the key role and set all the locations in Southeast Asia and had gotten the generals of the various countries to promise to napalm anything I wanted. We were all set to go. Unfortunately, somebody with a lot of power and a lot of strength bought into the company and liked the screenplay very much and decided he wanted it for himself. So the player paid me. I didn't get to shoot the picture. We'll see how it came out.

They, of course, did a heavy rewrite afterward. It's an absolute industry obligation to territorially urinate on a piece of material once you take it over — for better or worse. You know, sometimes that works out fine. It's a different show. It's not going to be the particular love affair that I had. But it's *Air America*, with Mel Gibson [1990, directed by Roger Spottiswoode].

I've just signed to do a picture that I've been researching for about a year, that I'm very excited about, called *The Fat Lady*. And *The Fat Lady* is an airplane. It's a C-123 cargo ship. The story really deals with the kind of bizarre events that surrounded the death of a man named Barry Seal, who was a dope smuggler who turned informant, and did it with such a vengeance that he was called by the U.S. Attorney's office "the most important witness in the history of American jurisprudence."

Strangely enough, he got sunk by some Cold War zealots who had their eye on the wrong ball. We actually had [this drug] cartel in our pocket, and the wrong decision was made, and our friend Barry got machine-gunned to death. But it was a fascinating story and far more reaching than the dope aspects of the story or the solid action-adventure which happens to carry it in the foreground.

Turan: What is it with you and airplanes? Are you a pilot?

Rush: I am a pilot. And I have an airplane that I'm very fond of, and I fly often. It's a great way for getting away from — if you're a coward — your problems because it keeps your attention while you're up there.

Turan: It's years between projects, and things that you work on for years kind of disintegrate. What keeps you going, really? What makes you not say, "This is just a ridiculous business, and I'm getting out of it"?

Rush: Because there is always something that is very exciting almost within your grasp. It's very hard to get off the merry-go-round when you see the gold ring is still there.

Audience Question: [A man asks about a long monologue in the film.]

Rush: You're quite right. It was the old lady sequence, which was [originally] three times as long as it was. One of the major axioms for aspiring filmmakers who might be in the audience is that your film can't be over two hours because if it is, they can't run it at two, four, six, eight, and ten [o'clock]. People won't know when it's running, and theater owners — it isn't just a myth — they really are sort of adamant about it.

And I'm long-winded on film. It was a terrific, tight, fast-running two hours and thirty minutes, then two hours and twenty minutes, then two hours and ten minutes. No, pardon me. We put it out at two-ten, which is very daring, which is over. But I had to get it down to that contractually. And I found — with other pictures that I've done — that studio executives are usually very bright men who can come up with stunningly good reasons as to why a scene should be out of a picture. Once you get it down to size, suddenly there's no more argument. It doesn't matter. You might not have taken out the scenes that they suggested. It's not a problem anymore. So that's what happened to that monologue.

Turan: You have a background of shooting exploitation-type films. Was that a good training ground for you? Was that helpful when you wanted to do other kinds of films?

Rush: Oh, I think it was a very exciting training ground because that's where you learn to make films, where you have a chance to work. And I sort of developed a reputation in those days as being the best of the two-dollar hookers. If you had only two bucks, get Rush. If you had three, get somebody else. The trade-off put me somewhat in demand. And my trade-off was: Give me a chance to experiment on this film, and I'll give you all the exploitable action stuff you want to make up for it. And that bond usually held, and everybody ended up happy.

Turan: Did you enjoy shooting the stunt stuff in this film?

Rish: I did. Strangely enough, *Freebie and the Bean*, which was an enormous car-stunt picture, was the one that started the business of two cops and a police car. I always found myself standing on the top of a forty-story building and saying: "God, it's strange the things adults will do for a living." On [*The Stunt Man*] I didn't have that problem. I sort of knew why I was doing them. There was more behind what was going on.

Turan: Were they difficult to film? I mean, like the one very complex scene where he ends up falling through the plate-glass window?

Rush: Great fun. Of course, doing them in pieces makes it all possible, by having a good cutting sequence in mind. But each one of the pieces is difficult. Going through the plate glass wasn't too bad because it's not real glass. And the falls aren't too difficult. And it was hard to persuade Steve to keep his head buried between those two bras. But, you know, we do a lot for our art.

Turan: Was that a tough jump?

Rush: It was a tough jump. But even on something like that, one practices on the ground beforehand. And gets the distances gauged. It's strange. Things are really almost the opposite of the way they seemed in the movie in the sense that it would seem that Eli was pushing the stunt man to more and more dangerous stunts. It's really just the reverse. Stunt men get very pumped up. And they make their reputations and their money by doing more and more dangerous things. They're always trying to kill themselves, and it's the director's job to stop them, to figure out what's going to go wrong and keep it from happening.

Turan: I assume you did that OK.

Rush: Reasonably. I think one of the more challenging things we did on that film were those airplanes, those WWI airplanes that were flying over the Coronado Hotel [Coronado Island, San Diego, California]—in pretty close proximity. When we tried to get permission to do this, the FAA laughed. We really did need those connections. There were three of us on the picture who were pilots: Chuck Bail, myself, and another guy. We sort of drew straws for who would fly the mission and who would stay home and marry Jane, you know. There was a naval base just down the road. We got the name of the commander and called him and got permission to land at the air base in one of these planes, which is not unreasonable. The only thing is that, in order to land at the air base, you have to fly over the hotel. While over the hotel, you lose radio contact for about five minutes and make some difficult and close passes.

Chuck won the draw, and I had nightmares for two nights preceding the sequence because I kept dreaming of a headline that read "Rush Destroys National Monument." The hotel is a national monument. But it all worked out. And then I expected the sky to fall on us afterward. After we had the stuff in the can, nobody ever mentioned it. It worked fine.

Turan: Was the hotel happy to be used that way? I know it's still a lovely place.

Rush: They were wonderful. They were delighted. The people, the patrons, seemed to love it. We rented the top floor and housed the crew and cast there so we could keep the noise on the roof and at least isolate the population, by one story, from our people. And the young lady who played the hairdresser had a very fortunate habit of mooning people. Her finest moment came when she saw the crane, and she went up on the crane and mooned several hundred people who were around. So, you could see that the patrons of the hotel had a good time.

AQ: Just a comment: I was reading about the film for a year before it came out. I was living in Cleveland, Ohio, at the time, and I remember reading about it in *Film Comment* and was thinking I'd like to see it. The film opened on a Friday with no advance publicity except, on the day before, there was an ad which showed Peter flying. And that's all they ever did on it. I went to it on opening night, and the place was packed. When the film was over with, there was a huge round of applause. So, there was something going on with this movie so that even in [Cleveland] it was just unbelievable. And even the manager couldn't believe what was going on. He didn't expect it to be that crowded. And [the] box office was growing and growing.

Rush: That's spectacular. A strange, sour note goes with all the good stuff—I found out afterward—and that was Fox's print deal with the company. By the way, I never had trouble with Mel Simon. He was a great guy, and he kept saving my ass every time I would get into really serious trouble with the head of his company. They went to grammar school together. They had made a deal. They had ordered only two-hundred prints. That was the total print order on *The Stunt Man*. So it's remarkable that it did what it did—break records in L.A. and then in New York—because it was always out. It never had that 1,000- or 1,500-theater release at one time, that kind of wide release you need in order to get the huge grosses.

Turan: Why do you think that happened? One of the things that seems to be a recurring theme in Hollywood is that executives really seem to underestimate the tastes of the audience. Everyone who saw this film liked it, but everyone in the studio would say something like, "No, this is going to be too much for people." What's going on there?

Rush: Those are very difficult jobs to work your way up to—a lot of responsibility and ferocious competition. And the way those jobs are guarded is by not making mistakes. It's funny: You can have a flop picture as a studio executive, but if that flop was a flop—

Turan: Like every other film.

Rush: —that hired two top stars and had a name writer and dealt with a subject that had been successfully dealt with six months before, that person is going to survive because he didn't take chances. He used proven elements. It was a conservative, strong approach, according to the system. It tends to kill the excitement and invention and continuing progress of where film can go. On the other hand, we're seeing bigger grosses than we've ever seen before in history. And I can't say that you can't argue with them because you certainly can. I do. But you can see why it's a struggle.

Turan: No one says you can't make *Batman*. But there's got to be room for something else.

Rush: Exactly. The strange thing is that it always has seemed to be the breakthrough picture that really gets out there and grosses well and unfortunately these days, is ending up with two or three or four sequels. But it's still the breakthrough picture, the one that dares to deviate, that somehow gets through that way.

Turan: The story that's always taught me is *Star Wars*.

Rush: Right. Everybody had turned it down.

Turan: And then *E.T., the Extra-Terrestrial* was put in theaters. I mean, everything that's a little different unnerves people. Yet it's often what an audience is looking for.

Rush: We get the rest of it on fifty to ninety-six channels for free. And you know, if you can't really do something that's different from that stuff, then I don't think we can continue to drag them out there.

Turan: Well, I think that's a good note to end on. And we look forward to your next film.

Rush: Thank you.

For Further Study

Videocassette

The Stunt Man is available on videocassette from Fox Video.

Books

Brodeur, Paul. *The Stunt Man*. New York: Atheneum Publishers, 1970.

Freedland, Michael. *Peter O'Toole*. London: W. H. Allen, 1983.

Periodicals

Champlin, Charles. *"Stunt Man —* Real, or. . .?" *Los Angeles Times*, August 17, 1980.

"Dialogue on Film: Richard Rush." *American Film*, June 1981.

Ehrenstein, David. "The Greatest Stunt in Filmdom: Making *The Stunt Man*." *Los Angeles Herald-Examiner*, August 22, 1980.

Fleming, Charles. "Lost and Found: Richard Rush." *Variety*, July 27, 1992.

Grant, Lee. *"The Stunt Man* in the Act at Last." *Los Angeles Times*, August 15, 1980.

Klemsrud, Judy. "At the Movies: Peter O'Toole and a Film They Tried to Ignore." *New York Times*, January 9, 1981.

McBride, Joseph. "O'Toole Ascending." *Film Comment*, March/April 1981.

Mann, Roderick. "Barbara Hershey: Color Her Orange." *Los Angeles Times*, August 19, 1980.

Moss, R. F. "Peter O'Toole's Devastating Comeback." *Saturday Review*, April 1980.

Sragow, Michael. "Will *The Stunt Man* Survive? Richard Rush Is Paranoid. You Would Be, Too." *Rolling Stone*, March 5, 1981.

Wolf, William. "The Filmmaker as Houdini." *New York*, November 17, 1980.

Yakir, Dan. "Hollywood Film-Flam." *After Dark*, November 1980.

6

JAMES COBURN
AND
Cross of Iron
(with Steven Gaydos)

On May 17, 1990, a panel discussion took place after a screening of *Cross of Iron*. The panel included James Coburn, Robert Culp, David Warner, Robert Visciglia, and Katy Haber. Steven Gaydos was the moderator.

The Film

Cross of Iron (1977), directed by Sam Peckinpah. Screenplay by Julius J. Epstein and Herbert Asmodi, from the book *The Willing Flesh* by Willi Heinrich. Produced by Wolf Hartwig for Anglo-EMI, Rapid Film, and Terra Filmkunst. Director of photography, John Coquillon. Editors, Tony Lawson and Mike Ellis. Assistant director, Bert Batt. Production designers, Ted Haworth and Brian Ackland Snow. Music, Ernest Gold. Technicolor. Distributed by EMI. Running time: 133 minutes.

Cast: James Coburn (Sergeant Steiner), Maximilian Schell (Captain Stransky), James Mason (Colonel), David Warner (Captain Kiesel), Klaus Lowitsch (Kruger), Roger Fritz (Lieutenant Triebig), Vadim Glowna (Kern), Fred Stillkraut (Schnurrbart), Senta Berger (Eva), with Burkhardt Driest, Dieter Schidor, Michael Nowka, Veronique Vendell, Arthur Brauss, Slavco Stimac.

Synopsis: A German battalion is decimated by fighting on the Russian front in 1943. Sergeant Steiner's men are worn to the edge and must deal with the fierce enemy and with their own morally bankrupt senior officers.

Remarks and Reviews

"*Cross of Iron* is Sam Peckinpah's idea of an anti-war tract, but more than anything else it affirms the director's prowess as an action filmmaker of graphic mayhem . . . production is well, but conventionally, cast, technically impressive, but ultimately violence-fixated to its putative philosophic cost. . . . *Cross of Iron*'s overwhelming image is not of disillusion, even less war's absurdity, but the war itself. The battle sequences, shot on Yugoslavian terrain, are bountiful, with bodies wheeling and flying about amid the grotesqueries" (*Daily Variety*).

"When *Cross of Iron* was released in Europe in the spring of 1977, it received rave reviews. It became the biggest-grossing picture in Germany and Austria since *The Sound of Music* and won a Bambi, one of Germany's most prestigious performing-arts awards (David Weddle, *If They Move ... Kill 'Em!: The Life and Times of Sam Peckinpah*).

"Peckinpah's only war film ... displays his familiar preoccupation with the individual confronted by events beyond his control.... The film reveals a special feeling for the universalities of war: lives in the balance, the single-mindedness of daily survival, and the suppression of emotion. Sombre and claustrophobic photography, an intelligent script, and Peckinpah's clear understanding of a working platoon of men, are all far removed from the monotonous simplicity of most big-budget war films" (*The Time Out Film Guide*).

"Painful to follow, occasionally beautiful to watch, this quite horrid film offers too much opportunity for its director to wallow in unpleasant physical details, and its main plot of bitter rivalry offers no relief" (*Halliwell's Film Guide*).

"Compelling without being particularly distinguished. The standard Peckinpah action scenes are excitingly done" (*Leonard Maltin's Movie and Video Guide*).

"Peckinpah did make one solidly intelligent and engrossing film during this period of decline, (the 70s), *Cross of Iron*, but it received little attention at the box office" (Scott & Barbara Siegel, *Encyclopedia of Hollywood*).

"*Cross of Iron*, Peckinpah's largest production, is a fiercely edited view of World War II slaughter where the Wehrmacht wear the patented scars of his [Peckinpah's] honorable killers" (James Monaco, *Encyclopedia of Film*).

The Filmmaker

One of the great renegades of film directing, Sam Peckinpah became a legendary figure for his fierce and uncompromising approach to his craft and his lyrical depiction of violence and moral ambiguity on the screen. He was born in 1925 in Fresno, California, educated at the University of Southern California, and made his first important inroads to filmmaking as a dialogue director and assistant to Don Siegel. He began writing scripts for television Westerns, and also directed episodes of *The Rifleman*, *The Westerner*, and other series. He carried his expertise at Westerns over to the big screen and created two classics of the genre in *Ride the High Country* (1962) and *The Wild Bunch* (1969).

Sam Peckinpah's Filmography

The Deadly Companion (1961); *Ride the High Country* (1961); *Major Dundee* (1964); *The Wild Bunch* (1969); *The Ballad of Cable Hogue* (1969); *Straw Dogs* (1970); *Junior Bonner* (1971); *The Getaway* (1972); *Pat Garrett and Billy the Kid* (1973); *Bring Me the Head of Alfredo Garcia* (1974); *The Killer Elite* (1975); *Cross of Iron* (1977); *Convoy* (1978); and *The Osterman Weekend*.

The Panel

James Coburn, star of the film; Robert Culp, longtime friend and Peckinpah collaborator; David Warner, costar of the film; Robert Visciglia, prop master on seven Peckinpah films, including *Cross of Iron*; and Katy Haber, longtime Peckinpah associate, script supervisor on *Cross of Iron*.

Reasons for Selecting

Some years ago, a Los Angeles film critic who shall remain nameless wrote an article on Sam Peckinpah which defamed Peckinpah's *Cross of Iron*, calling it "a picture that was so bad that nobody in the world could possibly defend it."

I wrote a letter to the publication that had printed the critical attack on *Cross*, pointing out that Orson Welles had called *Cross* the "finest anti-war picture ever made," and that one of Peckinpah's biographers, Terence Butler, called it "one of Peckinpah's finest works." They published my letter, but still I wasn't satisfied. Peckinpah devotees tend to be as irascible as the subject of their admiration.

I decided to present the film to the public, to see what a contemporary audience would make of it. I felt that most of its negative reputation was based on its sympathetic portrayal of the German army and its distributor's fainthearted promotion of the film. Also, at the time it was made, Peckinpah was fair game. He had gone from cause cèlébre to aging enfant terrible in less than a decade. Now, a dozen years after its release, perhaps the film could be judged on its merits.

We had a beautiful print for our screening, used by Vestron strictly for making tape copies, so it had been through a projector only a few times. It was also the longer, European cut of the film.

The response was fantastic. The most common observation was that this truly was one of Peckinpah's best and least appreciated films. And my own appreciation of the film also increased. I knew it was not as bad as its reputation, but I must admit, having seen it only once during its original release in 1977, I did not remember how special the film really was.

It is perhaps the most truly poetic film Peckinpah ever made, with a unique, strangely hypnotic beauty, considering the grim subject matter. It is a film filled with strong performances, richly drawn portraits of men at war, and bitter, ironic humor at the folly and wastefulness of violence.

The discussion afterward pointed out how Peckinpah crafted the film out of logistical difficulties, endless script rewrites, and seat-of-the-pants inspiration. It's a hell of a testament to his fierce, chaotic creative process. You can understand why he drove producers crazy, but you can also see the artistic vision he was after.

The end result of our revival? *Cross of Iron* is easier than ever to defend. And our evening was a vivid illustration of one rule that film critics should break at their own peril—never bet against Orson Welles.

—S.G.

The Interview

Steven Gaydos: One thing I want to mention before we get started with our discussion is the incredible difficulty there is to try to even show a movie like this. This is not a lost movie from the 1920s or 1930s. This is a lost movie from the late seventies. After AVCO's collapse—the company that distributed this—there have been eleven company collapses after that of companies that owned the rights to this. Currently no one owns the rights in America for videos or nontheatrical or theatrical release. It's truly a lost movie, already.

So at screenings like this, the purpose of them, as other evenings we've had here on Critic's Choice, is to show films that are critical favorites and that are already in danger of being completely lost.

As for Sam Peckinpah and *Cross of Iron*: There seems to be a perception among many critics and film aficionados that Sam Peckinpah's career ended sometime shortly after *The Wild Bunch*, which is when—for the general public—it began. And most of his later films have been sort of dismissed and tossed away. But everyone seems to agree that he was an incredibly important American filmmaker.

So many books to be written about him. So much journalism to be expended on the man. What was it that he brought to the cinema? What was it that made him special, that made people talk about him, aside from the sensationalism? You know. How well does *Cross of Iron*—which is dismissed as one of his worst films by so many—express it?

By the way, here in Los Angeles one critic wrote recently, "There's no one in the world that can appreciate this film." [*Audience chortles.*]

Any thoughts about what Sam was trying to do with his films and whether or not this film was representative of what he was up to?

James Coburn: I don't think Sam really made any intellectual judgments or any kind of preconceptions about any of his films. He created them as we went along. We worked from a script, generally. But, the things that evolved from that script were a lot of accidents. A lot of planned accidents.

A lot of things would happen while we were makng the film. We'd be shooting a scene. He would say, "Say that line again" in the middle of the scene. And it would cause something to change in you. You know, first you would be infuriated that somebody would say that. And then he would say, "Say the line again."

Something would happen. It would be—it would be—a—it would be tense. He would create a tension that wasn't there. Because, you know, you

James Coburn in *Cross of Iron*

learn your lines, and you know what you're doing. You have your action. You're playing it. And you want to get a certain response.

And he would break that down. He would throw it off balance. Everything was a little off balance. He was very enigmatic that way. And I think that probably one of the things that infuriates so many people was his enigmatic nature. All of his films have that quality, this one to a greater extent because of our producer, I think. [*Loud chuckles.*]

We had a guy named Wolf—Wolf Hartwig—who produced the film. He was a German porno filmmaker. Yeah. And his old lady, his wife, was the lady in the scene with—well, how do you describe that scene, Katy?

Katy Haber: The penilectomy. He was proud of that scene. He thought his wife was superb.

Gaydos: And wanted a close-up, I read. Do you feel, James, that this film stands with Sam's other work?

Coburn: It's not for me to say that. I mean, I don't know. I'm very proud of the film. I think it's a document that people have missed. It's certainly an antiwar film. And it's a film about the heroism of men who fight war. I think that's one of the things that Sam was concerned with, that all soldiers are going out there to fight for something. It's their own personal heroism of getting through that awful, awful thing called war.

Gaydos: Robert, you and I talked a couple of days ago about your involvement in this film. Since you weren't in *Cross*, people might wonder why you're joining us on this panel.

Robert Culp: My involvement in this picture didn't begin until after it was over with. I happened to be in England coincident with the very, very end of the editing process. I think within a day of my arrival, Katy—Miss Haber—and Sam found out that I was in town and said, "Why don't you come over and take a look at this because we have very close to an answer print here." I did, and I was blown into the middle of next week. Mind you, I'd been working for Sam off and on for twenty years. I wrote for him the first ten years of our relationship, and not a word of that ever got on the screen. It's all buried someplace in somebody's archives.

He used to call it his annuities, which were, you know, stuff that was not produced, unfinished, undone. One of the pieces, a full-length piece, came within an ace of getting on, and rests with Warner Brothers, sitting gathering dust someplace, as they still own it.

What I have felt about this film from the very beginning—and I've seen it now three times—is unchanged. I felt then, and I still do, seeing it now the third time, that it's the best, most definitive picture of men in war ever made.

If you go back and challenge your own memory of the Kubrick picture, going all the way back to the very beginning of meaningful war films: *All Quiet on the Western Front* as a picture about men in war, down in the trenches, quite literally in this situation, this is the best definition I've ever seen.

I tried very hard to get a couple of jobs writing reviews for this picture. Because I knew—seeing the movie—that it was, as all of Sam's pictures were, with the conceivable exception of *Ride the High Country*—and before that doesn't count—they were all, every single one of them was ten years ahead of its time.

Ten years ahead of its time in this business is monumental. It might as well be in another century, as far as its success is concerned because people don't understand it, don't relate to it. Because in Sam's case of his special concept of irony—which no director, not even Ford, ever possessed.

I did not succeed in getting those jobs. One was with *Playboy*. I had the job one day, and their regular critic screamed his head off, and I got fired the next day. This picture needed to be trumpeted, and I felt very strongly then that no one would do so, and indeed, that's what happened. And that's how I came to be involved.

Gaydos: Maybe it was fifteen years ahead of its time because we're still running into the same problems with the critics in terms of even publicizing this event tonight. We didn't get any coverage at all by the critics. They still don't like the film.

Culp: Sam's shooting from the hip in terms of that curse that was placed upon him by the god of nature—the term *poet*. Sam's the only real poet we've had in a long, long time. And it killed him, of course.

Gaydos: Since all of you knew Sam and worked with him for such a long time, what do you think of the perception of Peckinpah, and perhaps the reality, as an artist in decline as early in his career as, maybe, after *Straw Dogs*?

I don't think anything had the critical reception, again, after *Straw Dogs*. *Alfredo Garcia* certainly didn't. *Killer Elite* certainly didn't. Even *The Getaway*, which was a big commercial, success didn't. Why do you think this is?

Culp: To tell you the truth. I think you're operating from a fallacy, to start with. Sam's incessant phrase, and everybody on this table will back me up on this, was "Let's get it on." To "get it on. Get it on." The phrase "Get it on."— he found that from the very beginning way back in the days of TV, when I first knew him, when we were all struggling in the fields of the Lord, trying to do television and get anything on that would tell a story.

Anybody wants to tell a story that's about something, and Sam, unless he was starving to death, wouldn't even consider doing anything else but. He found it more and more difficult as time went on simply because his reputation, of course, began to precede him in terms of what could be expected from him in terms of his relationships with executives.

I will never forget the day we put together the deal at Warner Brothers with the picture that never got made: He came into the room with his blank glasses on. He was clearly afraid to open his mouth in front of these guys, hoping that somebody would carry the day and get this picture green-lighted— which is what it's all about, it's not about anything else.

He sat there and stared at the floor and mumbled. One had to lean very close to him to hear what he was saying, and he said very, very little. I shouted my mouth off a hell of a lot, and the picture got a green light. We were on. And then a mistake happened, and it was off again.

Sam was an extremely difficult man, as all of you know. No matter what.

But, that's what everybody who cared about making pictures rather liked about him. He was right more often than he was wrong. And he was almost always right about making a picture. But any other guy—outside of Sam—would have had the bat handed to him, and been shown the way to the plate more often, had he been able to play the politic.

First thing the man ever said to me when we first knew each other—Jesus, this is pushing thirty years ago—he said, "You have to learn to beat the bastards at their own game."

And he never did.

Gaydos: Katy, Robert—what kinds of examples could you give me on this particular picture? I listened to some of the script meetings, story meetings, on this. What kinds of technical battles and creative battles did Sam fall on in *Cross of Iron?* What were the difficulties in Sam realizing his vision on this picture?

Haber: One of the prime things was that there wasn't enough money. We had to stop shooting about three-quarters of the way through because there was no money left. We all stopped while Wolf Hartwig went to London to pick up some extra money, and we just hung around and waited.

Also, there was the problem of shooting with a Yugoslavian crew who were still all basically in the Resistance. Their relatives were in the Resistance. And having a German producer walking around saying that he was in the panzer division and had a bullet in his ass to prove it created a lot of animosity and, therefore, a lot of difficulty in getting things done.

We also had a very mixed crew. We had Americans. We had English, Yugoslavians, and Germans. And trying to keep them all together working was quite hard, as Robert Visciglia knows.

Gaydos: Robert, any examples of the kinds of problems you were encountering on this shoot—as opposed to other shoots with Sam?

Robert Visciglia: Well, as Katy said, we had German, English, American, and Yugoslavian people that fought in the war as partisans. As a matter of fact, four men that worked with me on the guns—they were the gunsmiths and handled all the German guns and the Russian guns—all fought for the partisans.

My assistant, a Yugoslavian, Peter, was shot—both of his ankles were shot—so he kind of walked like this when he was twelve years old. So, we had constant bickering back and forth between us—I'd say, "Where are the machine guns?"

[*mock-Yugoslavian.*] "The Germans got 'em."

I'd say, "Yes, but we need them in the trenches."

"We take our own machine guns."

I said, "They're all our machine guns."

"No, the Germans take care of their machine guns. We take care of ours."

But they all worked great together. They were all very good, excellent people. It's funny. That was my first picture in Europe. And you talk to a Yugoslavian grip, or a German grip, or anybody else in the foreign moviemaking business, and it's like going down across the street from Warner Brothers and talking to a grip from Warner Brothers or Paramount. They have all the same knowledge. They have all the same slang expressions. And they're all very good.

David Warner: Bob, you must tell everybody about the tank battle.

Coburn: You tell them.

Warner: OK, I will. There was only one tank available for the whole sequence. And if you ever see this movie again, I think you'll notice that in every shot there's only one moving tank at any given time. And the reason for that — apart from financial things — was that Richard Attenborough had them for a movie called *A Bridge Too Far*. So Mr. Peckinpah couldn't get hold of the tanks that he needed, but I think Tony Lawson, the editor, did a pretty good job with that.

Haber: The other thing is on the first day of shooting Sam set up the camera, and he said to one of the grips, "Would you mark the actors?" And they all stood there, and Sam said, "Mark the actor." And about four Yugoslavian crew people shuffled around on the ground trying to find a bit of wood and a nail. Sam said, "What are they doing?" And Stevie Goodman, who played the general in the hospital sequence, said, "In the specific order from Rapid Film to Yadran Film, you didn't order any nails. If you'd like nails, then we can put them on the budget."

Gaydos: What was the budget on that film?

Haber: I was hoping you wouldn't ask me. I can't remember.

Gaydos: [*Turning to Coburn.*] James?

Coburn: Yeah, they said they'd promise us everything, and gave us half, and charged us double.

Warner: They gave us his wife.

Coburn: Yeah.

Visciglia: And it's kind of funny if you watch that sequence. That sequence was supposed to have been shot very early in the film. But Sam kept it as a carrot in front of the pig's nose as he led Wolf, the producer, along.

And Wolf said, "Well, when are we going to shoot my wife's big scene?" Sam said, "Well, we're going to get that, but we need more tires for smoke, and we need more gasoline to burn fields, and more ammunition to fire the guns." And, so, Wolf would run all over Europe and come back with a bag full of money to keep us going. And Sam kept pushing that last sequence with his wife clear to the end of the picture.

Coburn: It was the next to the last day.

Visciglia: It was the next to the last day that we shot that thing.

Coburn: And we shot so much film on it, we ran out of film. And, yeah, we had to come back and shoot the rest of it the following day. And it was the last day of the film. We didn't have an ending. We shot that whole ending in half a day.

Haber: But Sam didn't even direct it. He left it for Walter Kelley to do it. He went off and did something else.

Coburn: He went up and cried. He went up in that thing and cried, "They're taking my picture away from me."

Visciglia: We sat on the railroad tracks you saw at the end of the picture where all the trains were burning. And Wolf, our producer, was loading the cameras. Physically loading—himself—the cameras on trucks. He was loading them on, and Sam and I were sitting there with a bottle on the railroad tracks, smoke burning, people moving out, everybody saying good-bye. And Sam looked at me, and he said, "Now, tomorrow, this is what we're going to do." And I said, "Sam, we don't have any cameras, no actors."

"I don't care. This is what we're going to do tomorrow."

That's the kind of a guy he was.

Gaydos: Katy, you mentioned something before that I found interesting. You said that the producer was very proud that he was the commander, or something, of a panzer division in North Africa?

Haber: Well, he told Sam that he was a panzer division general, but actually, the truth was that he ran the brothels in Paris for the German generals.

Gaydos: Which someone pointed out made him uniquely qualified to become a producer.

Coburn: But Sam really loved producers in a very strange way. He loved to antagonize them and loved to be antagonized by them. And Sam kept saying about Wolf [*sotto voce*], "If he wasn't who he was, we would have to invent him."

Haber: There's also a wonderful scene missing. I don't know why it's not in this cut. But Wolf also wanted to play a part in the movie, so Sam made him the general that Brandt speaks to on the other line, and, you know, he says, "General we have to move out."

And Sam did this shot of Wolf sitting at the table. And in the middle of him on the telephone, the entire ceiling caved in with everything that the special effects department had to pour on his head, and he was left in a pile of rubble with a telephone still in his hands saying, "Vee vill evacuate! Vee vill evacuate!?"

Gaydos: Bob, were you involved in that episode?

Visciglia: You mean when Wolf was in the bunker? Yes, I was part of the − − −. [Drowned out.]

Coburn: He loaded it.

Gaydos: What was above his head, by the way? What was dumped on him?

Visciglia: Well, it was a conglomeration of a lot of stuff that we'd gotten from the various pigsties that we'd had out in the field. That part with

Sam Pekinpah and Maximilian Schell fooling around on the set of *Cross of Iron*.

Maximilian Schell in the picture that you see where we blow all the buildings up right after Mr. Steiner's crew has been mutilated and shot, that used to be a place where they made the greatest prosciutto in Yugoslavia.

And, actually, on the other side of what was covered up with the smoke was where all the hams hung. Well, of course, the hogs were in the fields. And that's what hit Wolf's head from out of the bucket.

Gaydos: I have some people here that are going to help take the mikes around to the audience, and we'll start asking some folks here to join in.

Audience Question: Since Sam made a good many films that had quite a bit of violence in them, what was his personality really like?

Coburn: He called himself a working alcoholic.

Visciglia: That's a profession—not a personality.

Coburn: Ah, well, yes. But it affected his personality. No, his personality was erratic. He was filled with a great deal of love for humanity, of all people. We all loved him, too. I mean, he was the hardest working man I ever met.

And the hardest drinking man I've ever met, too. For three hours a day, he was an absolute genius. It generally took him like, you know, like a few drinks to get *there*. But, when he was *there*, it was brilliant.

There was nothing like working with Sam Peckinpah. He was a genius. He was a poet, as Bob said, but he was that *thing*. It was like playing in a jazz orchestra where everybody is swinging, you know. Like when everybody is right there on top of it.

And that's the kind of feeling that you loved. Right Katy? I mean everybody was there. He would generate a kind of attention that would just be invigorating. It would be. It was sensational. Did you find that?

Warner: Yeah. Absolutely. I was going to talk about the violence and the violence in the movies. I was fortunate enough to be in three of his movies. This was the last one I was in. The first one was a movie called *The Ballad of Cable Hogue*, in which, if anybody has seen, I think there were three gunshots in the whole movie, but lots of music, and lots of laughs, and things like that.

We were in the desert outside Las Vegas, and at the same time we were shooting during the day. Sam was editing, for those of you who have seen *The Wild Bunch*, the last reel.

And, if you remember the last reel, or the last fifteen minutes. And he would come into the bar, of course at night, and he would say, "I'm having great difficulty in editing and finishing the picture."

He did have trouble finishing pictures, which I may say something about later. However, he would come in and he would actually sit down while we were making *Cable Hogue*, and one evening when we'd done some musical numbers or really some light stuff, he said, "You know, I think I've made my statement on violence with this picture that I'm cutting now."

And the point to me was that this was—and I hadn't seen that movie, but I saw a very long, rough cut—and, of course, it was a masterpiece even then—for four-and-a-half or five hours. The point was that *The Ballad of Cable Hogue*, as far as I was concerned, was the next in his canon of work. And it was totally different.

Coburn: Yeah. I'll say.

Warner: Yeah. It was totally different. It was just an absolute reverse of *The Wild Bunch* and, of course, the smaller-budget pictures done before—*Ride The High Country* and the others—weren't overly violent. They were Westerns, but there was some quality about them.

So *Cable Hogue* was made. And it didn't have violence. It didn't have slow motion. It didn't have exploding blood. It didn't have anything like that. It had music and laughter and all that sort of stuff. And of course the studios, or whoever, just weren't really interested in it.

Straw Dogs was the next picture after that because of the reception for *Cable Hogue*. And so I've deviated from the question about what he was like, but I think you've got a clue to something to do with his work and the way that he thought.

Gaydos: If I could just throw in a question to augment hers: One thing I've discovered in the years of being a Peckinpah fan—and meeting the people that have worked with Sam—I don't know if I've known of anyone in Hollywood that has the kind of loyalty and love that this guy had. What was the key to that?

Coburn: Because he brought the best out in you. He brought the thing out in you that you didn't know existed. He would take you over to the edge of the abyss, push you off, and then jump in after you.

Warner: Right. I think he was easier on his colleagues than, maybe, on his family. And I say that only because one of the members of his family is here tonight. I mean, I know that the family didn't quite get the same kind of care and consideration, as far as I can think, that we may have got. And I think that's sad and unfortunate. And I can't explain that or say anything.

Except that on a personal level I had—after I'd done *Cable Hogue*—I was ill, and I jumped out of a window, and I had an accident. There were rumors that I was on drugs, and this and that and the other. Well, I wasn't, but I was having a very nervous time, and I was out of action for about two years. I had to learn to walk again. And Sam, and Katy [*turning to her*] were around at that time when I was in the hospital.

Sam said, "I'm going to make a movie called *Straw Dogs*, and I think you should be in it." And I said, "Sam, but I can't walk. I'm trying to learn to walk." He said, "That doesn't matter. You need to be in front of a camera." And I said, "But I've got to try and learn to walk."

"You'll learn to walk." And he said, "And if you can't, then you'll have to play him as an invalid, won't you?" And all that sort of stuff.

Well, that was all fine, and I did a heroic bit, and I learned to walk again—or learned to hobble a little bit.

But the main point here was that I was uninsurable. On the train down to the location in England for *Straw Dogs*, Sam and I had a glass of whiskey or whatever, and he said, "Listen, you are not insurable. Lloyds of London will not insure you, but—fuck 'em." He said, "I'll be personally responsible for you, and, of course, you will be responsible to me." I said, "Of course." And so he went ahead with the picture, and I wasn't insured. Everybody fell ill except for me. Basically, that's the kind of thing that Sam would do in his loyalty to the people whom he worked with and the people whom he liked.

But also on the picture, members of the crew would be arriving on one plane, and members of the crew would be leaving on the next. The airport was a constant arrival and departure of various members of the crew who didn't live up to Sam's perfection, I suppose.

Coburn: Yes.

Gaydos: I heard one time that Sam didn't really love you unless he'd fired you at least once. Does everyone here feel that they were loved by Sam?

Haber: I was fired eleven times.

Culp: He never got a chance to fire me. I fired him—the son of a bitch. I said I'd never talk to him again. And then I got to England. And then five years later—we hadn't spoken in five years—there was *Cross of Iron*, and I changed my mind. Damn quick.

That's the essence, really, of what we're talking about here. Somehow the people who related to Sam as strongly as they did, did so because of three factors, I think. One, they sensed things, as we do in this business, very damn quickly. He was a savage perfectionist.

And he knew the difference between right and wrong. On every level, he chose to ignore some [people] on a social or a moral level. And in his own personal life, sometimes. But, as far as the work was concerned—never at any time. Never, at no time. That was one part of him that we instantly, all of us, related to.

Arthur Conan Doyle had a great quote, and it applies to Sam and probably to the relationships of most of the people that knew him: "Mediocrity recognizes nothing above itself. Talent recognizes genius instantly."

And that's how we all recognized Sam from the very first moment.

Later, he redefined himself for some folks. There was a mean son of a bitch in there, too. On the other hand, he would turn around, directly, and there was this little boy that you just adored. And you'd follow him any place. That may sound a little bit pointless—it's so far after the fact—but nevertheless I think most folks will bear me out.

Gaydos: Mr. Visciglia?

Coburn: You've been fired a few times, too, as I recall.

Visciglia: He'd fire me at the bar the night before, and I'd go back to work the next morning.

Coburn: It's because you owned all the props, man. How many medals do you have?

Visciglia: Ahh—six, seven.

Coburn: Sam always gave medals to anyone that finished the film.

Visciglia: They needed it.

Coburn: And you deserved it.

Visciglia: Yep. On the *Battle*—we called it *The Battle of Cable Hogue*, but it was really *Ballad*—there were thirty-four people fired on that picture. The unions here in Los Angeles refused to send any more people to the crew of Peckinpah in *The Valley of Fire*. They said, "If he fires anybody else, he's going to have to do with what he's got." And nobody would go near us.

I went to him one day, and I said, "Sam, we have to get out of here and get to Tucson," because that's where the picture was finished. And I said, "We've got two weeks to shoot there. We're not going to have anybody left to get to Tucson to finish this thing if you keep firing them."

And the only reason he fired them is because they weren't moviemakers; they weren't interested in the picture. He didn't just go up and say, "You're fired." Not Sam. But I said, "Anybody that gets to Tucson deserves a medal." And lo and behold, that's when the medals started.

Coburn: Was it?

Visciglia: That's right. That's how it started. He gave, I think, five medals out on that picture that were in gold with the inscription "*The Ballad of Cable Hogue.*" And the other people on the crew got silver.

Years later, when I was doing *Junior Bonner*, one of our very good sound mixers right now, Charles Wilborn, had done some great stuff. It was his second picture—on *Junior Bonner*—and he said, "Bobby I got a silver one on the last picture. Do you think I'll get a gold one on this one?" And Chuck, who was exceptionally good and has gone on to great things, I looked at him, kiddingly of course, and I said: "Chuck, some people never get gold." [*Pause.*]

I saw Sam cry one time when an electrician on the crew of *Ballad of Cable Hogue* came up to him after two weeks and said, "Sam, I've been on this picture for two weeks, and I don't know what it's all about. I'm just an electrician pushing a lamp around. I'd like to get a script and read it."

And Sam had a script sent out to the middle of the desert from the office and gave it to him. And going back in that night after having a couple of drinks, Sam really got choked up about the fact that this guy was interested in the picture and wanted to know what he was doing on that set.

And that's what Sam did to everybody. Involved us all to the limit.

Coburn: Yeah. I'll say to the limit. Beyond what you're capable of doing. And if you didn't go beyond what you were capable of doing—[*gesturing a mock slitting of his throat*]—out!

Culp: You must remember that nobody in this business starts out to do it for money. Nobody. Except, you know, executives. But the people in front of the camera or immediately around do not start out to do it for money. They start out because they desperately love it.

How many actors have come up to you guys and asked, "How do I become an actor?" And how in hell do you answer them? The only answer is, "*If you don't have to,* forget it." Well, the same thing applies to the writers. The same thing applies to the cameraman—he has to because he loves it.

Now, Sam knew that. That's the secret. That's the secret to getting a team that works. So it really isn't terribly complicated. He involved you on the level that you were there because of pride. Pride in what you did for a living.

AQ: With this film, obviously, it wasn't shot in sequence. Can somebody please describe what it was like to follow his direction, because you were there trying to follow the emotions of the different segments of the film, and there was so much going on in each part. Can anybody answer that one?

Coburn: Well that's generally the way films are made. But, you have a script—you know what's going on. And the thing you have to be aware of all the time is the dynamic of which [segment] you're playing. You remember that.

Sam remembers that—or the director remembers that—and it's up to him to really kind of guide that one way or the other. But as you're putting it together, it's kind of a mosaic you put together in your head. You justify everything from the last scene you did, and it builds kind of like that.

Does that more or less answer the question? Or is it some specific thing about this one?

AQ: It was because this film had more action, more cuts, more going on in the full length of the movie, I was wondering if it was hard to follow him through it? I mean, you're talking about a small budget, you know, all the problems that go along with making it. Did it affect, also, the comprehension of the script?

Coburn: Well, no, it wasn't really following. I think it was an evolution. Because he's right there. You know, we were all right there together. And what was happening was what he was paying attention to. He wasn't trying to make something happen that he had in his mind. He would watch, and he would just guide it, as it was happening. He was shaping it every scene. He would shoot with three cameras. [*Turning to Visciglia.*] Or just about all the time?

Visciglia: Yep.

Coburn: And that's a little difficult because the editor probably had a hell of a time with that.

Gaydos: David?

Warner: No, no, obviously James was there for the whole of the movie, which was how many weeks—how long?

Coburn: Geez, I don't know. Six months, I think.

Warner: Six months. James Mason and myself for those scenes were there for two weeks. And you know, that's how movies are made. But I mean where part of being in a movie is something that is just instinctive after a while. You don't think about how we fit into the jigsaw. You become part of the whole without thinking about that.

AQ: I was just amazed at all the cuts.

Visciglia: The man who put that thing together and all those cuts is Tony Lawson.

Gaydos: About the role of Steiner, James, it seems like a tough role to pull off because it doesn't have a line to it like a lot of roles. How did you work out Sam's ideas and your ideas to get that extraordinary performance?

Coburn: We did a lot of research. We went to the war archives in Kassel, in Germany. Saw films there. We went to the British Museum, the War Museum. Saw films there. There were some wonderful shots there. But what we were trying to do was to find out what it was about — not only the Germans, but the war itself. What was it like on the inside to be right there inside all of this chaos? It wasn't anything we really decided. It was something that we evolved.

The script was constantly being redone. Redone according to what we did the next day, or the day after, or the day before. It was in constant change. And we discovered things of the moment. Sometimes there'd be a question, like, with Max. There was one scene that we rewrote. We rewrote it, and it was a big l-o-n-g scene where Max and I — we were talking.

And Sam said, "Ahh, maybe you should just, ahh, listen? Yeah?" So the scene was Stransy talking to Steiner. And Steiner was listening. He listened to this guy. And that was far more significant than having any kind of an answer or a question and answer like in a philosophical conversation.

I think the only philosophy in there was, actually, from the book. And that's what we tried to do. We tried to be true to the essence of the book rather than to do the book itself.

Gaydos: In an interview I read, Sam refers to a James Jones book that he says he stole outrageously from for this. Are you aware of that piece at all?

Haber: Yeah. Walter Kelly, just before we started shooting, showed him the James Jones book with all the photographs. And he literally took it to the art department, and the wardrobe department, and then to special effects, and he said, "I want some of this reproduced."

Gaydos: One thing that struck me with the film was that all Steiner had was the loyalty to his platoon. And I think that might be part of the problem for audiences, that it's very austere in that way.

Coburn: Oh, yeah, it is very austere. The character is a very strange, enigmatic character. That whole scene in the hospital sequence was a very strange scene. I don't even think Sam knew what was going on.

I really don't because, you know, we'd say, "Well, what about this?" And I cut my hand really badly when I was breaking the bottles. And a friend of mine was over and he said, "Just put some cayenne pepper on it." And we poured cayenne pepper on it, and we finished the scene. My hand healed in a very short period of time, too. I was amazed by that.

Gaydos: More questions?

AQ: You brought up a point a minute ago about the philosophy in the book, and I notice there are a couple of different scenes where you quoted Kant, and I think Heidegger, and then there was a scene where you were standing in front of the bunker there, and you were swapping quotes with one of the other soldiers?

I was wondering if that was drawing attention to later, when you let the

Russian boy go. And you said something really interesting, and almost spacey/philosophical about what you thought about war to the kid before you sent him off. And I was wondering—was that a quote from someone else? Or was that the philosopher of the soldier speaking?

Coburn: That was the philosopher of the soldier speaking. All those quotes came out of a kind of a bantering that Sam had. There was a book. I mean, there were several books. He was fascinated by the austerity of these quotes from the German-Prussian military—and he had to have a scene with those quotes in it. And that's what that was basically about. It was, really, setting down what that military philosophy was from the German point of view.

AQ: The Russian boy at the beginning of the film comes back in the last scene with dyed hair. Was that something that came up—spur of the moment—during the shooting?

Haber: Yes.

Coburn: Yeah, it really was. Sam would get these visions. Kind of a vision that he would, ahh, he would say. Like, well, we didn't know who was shooting at us—and he says, "The kid's shooting at you."

Visciglia: That's right. That's what he said.

Haber: But he also had his hair dyed. So it was a dark-haired kid rather than a blond kid.

Coburn: Yeah. Yeah.

[*Continuing sotto voce, mock-Sam.*] "The kid, the kid's shooting at you." The kid's dead, Sam. What do you mean the kid's shooting at me?"

"The kid, the kid's shooting at you."

"OK" [Laughs.]

Haber: Bring back the kid!

Coburn: Bring him back.

We were shooting *Pat Garrett and Billy the Kid*, and we were just about finished with it. He was in love with Billy the Kid. And he said, "You know, God damn it, let's not kill him!" I said, "Well, Sam, I mean that's the legend. That's the myth." And he said, "Let's create a new myth."

When you think about it, it might have been fun to see it that way.

AQ: The follow-up movie [sequel] called [*Breakthrough*], starring Richard Burton—I was wondering if there was any creative input from any of you, or did Sam even discuss it?

Haber: None of us had anything to do with that movie at all. That was Wolf Hartwig cashing in on this movie. And nobody had anything to do with it.

Gaydos: I had read that they offered it to Sam, but he didn't consider it for a second. I don't know if most people know that this movie did have a sequel.

Coburn: They offered it to a lot of us, and we all said, "Not a chance unless Sam directs it."

Gaydos: Robert, you said you sort of came back into the fold with Sam on this picture. Do you remember the circumstances of AVCO and this picture being released here? What the situation was, in terms of its response? And I mean in general.

Culp: When Sam said, "Help me," I'd jump right in. And he did. And I did.

He said, "They're going to bury this thing. It's going to die." I said, "Then say no more. Let me go to work." And I simply picked up the phone and started calling people.

The last person in the world you want to do is call somebody at a studio because they have already—when you've reached that point of no return—they've written it off.

Coburn: They just didn't know what to do with the film. That was it. They didn't know how to sell it. They hated it.

AQ: I think I read that you shot a second ending? Or, not a second ending, but you reshot the ending? Is there anything on that?

Coburn: No, no. We didn't have an ending. We had a half-day to shoot what we shot. And it was all totally improvised. I mean, Max dropping the gun, tripping over it, and the barrel fell off the gun. And all of that laughter was—why, it was very funny to watch Max fumbling around with the thing. And we were looking for an ending. We didn't have one. And that, actually, [is] all that happened and the laughter comes.

[*Mock-Sam.*] And Sam said, "That's it! That's it! The Kid is shooting at you!"

AQ (cont'd.): Were there any other impromptu bits in this thing?

Coburn: Sass Betty was our special effects man. He worked for three days planning this battle. And when it went off, it was like you were in a battle, and we were coming right down right in the middle of this, and you didn't know what was happening.

Well, you know, you're dodging, you're falling down, standing up, running, talking. There was a conversation, and something had to happen. You had your microphone on. And, well, if you didn't know the lines, you made some up really rapidly.

Warner: No, I was just going to say something about the ending that you improvised and like in the end of *The Wild Bunch*. I mean, really, he did say that he couldn't end it, but he did.

And *Straw Dogs* he "couldn't end." So he put Hoffman and myself in this car, and we had to turn on the stuff and improvise the end.

Well, Hoffman, of course, being of the Method School [of acting] could improvise, but me being English—not so hot at the improvisation—had to really fake it, and it didn't work at all.

But that was at the very end of something like where he'd say, "Well, where are we going?" And I'd say, "I don't know my way home." And he'd say, "Neither do I." That was improvised. Turned on the thing and went and did it.

The thing there was Sam who, like all great directors, sometimes trusts his actors' instincts.

Coburn: He trusted actors a lot. He loved actors. I mean, he gave them, you know, really gave them their head.

Visciglia: Even on *The Getaway*, the ending of *The Getaway*, if you remember the picture. Slim is running off with the money.

And then we see the bus, and the kid is in the bus. He was on the train with the gun that goes "bang." That came out of the sky. Sam thought about that, but we almost finished the picture and put it out.

Well, he alerted the highway patrol because the little kid had left the El Paso area with his mother to go on vacation, and we didn't know where he went. So, we got the highway patrol, and they were out looking for the family driving in a private car. The kid had left the picture.

Sam found him, got him back, and we stuck him in the bus. And the bus went over the hill, and the little kid looked out the back of the bus with the gun and went "bang."

And that ending came out of the blue.

AQ: I wanted to know what you were thinking about when you were laughing at the end. Did Maximilian Schell make up a little joke about his buddy, J.J.? That got a big laugh, and I was wondering, where did that come from?

Visciglia: Who was J.J.?

Coburn: That was the scene that we wrote together. You know, where I listened most of the time. That was the scene with his little buddy, J.J. Yeah.

Visciglia: No one's telling who J.J. was.

Coburn: No. Max was very prolific. He would write these l-o-n-g speeches. I mean he would write really *l-o-n-g* speeches for himself. Little answers for me, and then these *l-o-n-g* speeches.

So that was a lot of fun. And then Sam, naturally, would trim them down a bit and get down to the essence of things.

One thing I'd like to say about Sam. Sam, when you were preparing a film, you would prepare it and prepare it, and he would keep on preparing it until it was absolutely necessary to start shooting. And he would just hold it.

And then he would start shooting, and he would never want to finish shooting. Never, I mean, right to the very end. Until all the cameras were broken, or the film would run out, and everybody was on their way home—so he had to stop shooting.

And then the editorial process began, and then he never wanted to *quit editing*. The only way you could get him to quit editing was to get him another job.

And then he would go to work on that *preparing*. And he'd prepare and prepare. And the same process would go on over and over again. But I think that's probably why he never liked to end anything: *"Let's not kill him."*

You know? It's the same thing.

Haber: He also did most of this film on a stretcher 'cause he had a septic leg. He had to be carried on the set on a stretcher. And if it was a moving shot or something, Cliff Coleman put him on his motorbike and drove him around on his motorbike.

AQ: What miracle would it take to get this film rereleased? It's the most potent antiwar film I have ever seen.

Coburn: I think it's probably because it was about German soldiers instead of American soldiers, or English, or French, or something. There haven't been many films made about that other point of view. The soldier's point of view — from that war. Because it really has an insidious nature to it. But we say it. We say it in there: "Do you suppose they'll forget?"

In an interview in '79, Sam was talking about the fact that the *New York Times'* Penelope Gilliatt said: "You can't tell the uniforms apart." You know, she hated the movie and said, "You can't tell the uniforms apart."

And this was in public, and Sam said, "That's the fucking point!"

Haber: I want to say that this, actually, was the film that Sam wanted to make. The same day that he was offered this movie, he was offered *King Kong* and *Superman*, and he turned them both down.

AQ: Could you talk about how Sam enjoyed using children to contrast the violence around the adults who were creating it? He used it in many of his films. And he did it in this film, that is, the children dancing and the little boy.

Haber: They're not contrasted; they're seen as the viewers. It's from their point of view — how adults react and how children view them.

Culp: That's exactly it. Katy put her finger on it. It's not terribly complex.

Much of human behavior, that is to say, adult human behavior that Sam observed, he saw with the eyes of a child — which most poets do. There isn't any other way to express it on film, other than to have a child see it or experience it. It's that simple.

The opening sequence in *The Wild Bunch:* the main title sequence in *The Wild Bunch* with the kids is the exact, perfect metaphor for the picture itself, which is not revealed until the guys have gone by on horseback.

And he's using that incredible technique of the eye blinking in the sunlight, to get from cut to cut, so he can lay in the credits over the frozen frames, which are the inside of the eyelid.

Then you go into the kids, and there's the scorpion and the ants.

Yeah, they are there, because Sam related very, very strongly — as some people do — to children. I never saw him not relate to kids, of all ages. He also related to the child in other adults very strongly.

And that portion of the story that he would, forever and always, see as the ultimate irony: Let the audience discover it. The child can see it, but won't know what it is. The audience will, therefore, be able to discover it on their own; you're not shoving it down their throats.

Coburn: Sam never said what anything was. I mean you'd ask him a question about something, and he would say, "Well it's kind of a— Well, maybe a little bit of a— You know, kind of—yeah." And somehow you'd understand.

It got to be when you worked with Sam over a period of years, it would be kind of a shorthand. Bobby would come up with a gun, and he would say, "I thought you had something that's ahh, I don't know."

And he probably would have three other ones, right there, saying, "Here, here, here."

"Yeah, yeah, yeah." And he'd take the funkiest gun out and hand it to you and say, "You use this one. Yeah."

Warner: And that's the way he would squeeze a performance out of James Coburn.

For Further Study

Books

Seydor, Paul. *Peckinpah: The Western Films*. Urbana: University of Illinois Press, 1980.

Simmons, Garner. *Peckinpah: A Portrait in Montage*. Austin: University of Texas Press, 1982.

Weddle, David. *If They Move . . . Kill 'Em: The Life and Times of Sam Peckinpah*. New York: Grove Press, 1994.

7

RUSS MEYER, ROGER EBERT

AND

Beyond the Valley of the Dolls

(with Michael Dare)

On July 12, 1990, writer and director Russ Meyer and film critic and screenwriter Roger Ebert were interviewed by critic Michael Dare after a screening of *Beyond the Valley of the Dolls*. They were joined in the discussion by members of the film's cast, including Edy Williams, Charles Napier, Dolly Read, David Gurian, John LaZar, Haji, and Michael Blodgett. Robert Rosen, director of the UCLA Film and Television Archive, introduced the participants.

The Film

> *Beyond the Valley of the Dolls* (1970), Twentieth Century–Fox. Written, directed, and produced by Russ Meyer. Screenplay and story, Roger Ebert. Director of photography, Fred J. Koenecamp. Film editors, Dan Cahn and Dick Wornell. Art direction, Jack Martin Smith and Arthur Lonergan. Set decoration, Walter M. Scott and Stuart A. Reiss. Sound, Richard Overton and Don Minkler. Music, Stu Phillips. Associate producers, Red Hershon and Eve Meyer.
>
> *Cast:* Dolly Read, Cynthia Myers, Marcia McBroom, John LaZar, Edy Williams, Michael Blodgett, Charles Napier, Pamela Grier, the Strawberry Alarm Clock.

Synopsis: A female rock trio attempts to make it in Hollywood. In the classic pulp / soap opera tradition, they encounter all the temptations of the flesh and mammon, and their foray through the hippie / love / rock / Hollywood excesses of the day ends up on a downward path of disaster and misfortune.

Remarks and Reviews

"The folks down at Fox must have been on mushrooms to back this one; it's like a bad acid trip, man" (Mick Martin and Marsha Porter, *Video Movie Guide* 1988).

"[Russ Meyer] gave her [Erica Gavin] a minor part in *Beyond the Valley of the Dolls* only because he knew she could do a lesbian scene. At the end, he kills off her character by shooting her in the mouth. It was nevertheless a major studio film and a major improvement on films Gavin had done after *Vixen*.... Big-breasted and shapely, she [Edy Williams] married Russ Meyer, who then put her in *Beyond the Valley of the Dolls* as porno star Ashley St. Ives, a sexual vulture who likes to make love anywhere but a bed" (Danny Peary, *Cult Movie Stars*).

"Russ Meyer's *Beyond the Valley of the Dolls* is a film of amazingly intense hatred.... Picture Meyer ... given a campy script by Roger Ebert about three girl rock musicians and their manager coming to L.A. and trouble. Meyer loathes these people; their type (hippie-drug-rock) is alien to him. Look at his brilliant montage of LA—inside and out it is a grotesque and menacing chaos to him.... The movie is not, of course, gloomy or embittered; it is ebulliently, zestfully savage" (Donald Lyons, *Interview*).

"It's strange to watch all the perversions and aberrations in 20th Century–Fox De Luxe color. They look so glamorous compared to other porno films—and don't kid yourself—20th has entered into the porno business with this film and *Myra Breckinridge*. But at least this film is constantly funny and absurd, while *Myra* is an offense" (Robert Weiner, *Interview*).

The Filmmaker

In a 1973 article in *Film Comment* magazine, Roger Ebert described writer-director-producer Russ Meyer as possessing "an instinctively satirical sense of the ridiculous that comes from something of the same 1950s sensibility that produced Bob and Ray, Lenny Bruce, Stan Freberg and *Mad* magazine." Ebert goes on to describe his collaboration with Meyer when he wrote the screenplay for Meyer's *Beyond the Valley of the Dolls*, how the duo conspired to "create characters ... and situations to cover the exploitable content we wanted in the film." Recalls Ebert, "Meyer wanted the film to appeal, in some way, to almost anyone who was under 30 and went to the movies."

That sense of adventurousness and hustling has characterized the long and legendary career of Russ Meyer. From his first no-budget soft-core classic, *The Immoral Mr. Teas* in 1959, Meyer has made 20-plus films almost entirely in the realm of the beyond-independent auteur. They have been mostly self-financed, written, photographed, and directed. He has earned the praise and attention of loyal fans and legions of critics who see Meyer as a director who, as Ebert observed two decades ago in *Film Comment*, "is an original, who developed his own style during a decade of independent productions he totally controlled."

Russ Meyer's Filmography

The Immoral Mr. Teas (1959); *Eroticon, Eve and the Handyman, Naked Gals of the Golden West* (1961); *Europe in the Raw, Heavenly Bodies* (1963);

(1963); *Lorna* (1964); *Mudhoney!, Motor Psycho! Fanny Hill* (1965); *Faster, Pussycat! Kill! Kill!, Mondo Topless* (1966); *Good Morning—and Goodbye, Common Law Cabin* (1967); *Finders Keepers, Lovers Weepers, Russ Meyer's Vixen* (1968); *Cherry, Harry and Raquel* (1969); *Beyond the Valley of the Dolls* (1970); *The Seven Minutes* (1971); *Blacksnake!* aka *Sweet Suzy* (1973); *The Supervixens* (1974), and more.

Reasons for Selection

It was 1970, and I had just moved to New York City to be an actor when someone in my class at the Lee Strasberg Institute invited me to a preview of a new movie. It was the first time I had ever been to an advance screening, and the theater was large and packed. When the film began, the audience started laughing, and they never stopped until the film ended, whereupon they immediately jumped to their feet in hysterical applause. But then it turned out the film was not really over, and they all went back to their seats for the first of innumerable codas, whooping and hollering in the most outrageous reaction to a film I had ever seen.

It was a most baffling encounter, and I could not figure it out for years afterward. I knew I was laughing too, but I could not tell if we were laughing at the picture or with it. To this day, I'm not really sure if it's a comedy, but it unquestionably cracks me up. It is simultaneously the best and the worst movie ever made, and that screening is still one of the most exhilarating experiences I've ever had in a movie theater. The film was Russ Meyer's *Beyond the Valley of the Dolls*.

Ten years later, through a twist of fate, I accidentally became a film critic for the *L.A. Weekly*, where my assignments were invariably B movies. After seeing thousands of B's, I kept coming back to Russ Meyer's films as the epitome of exploitation. I concluded that *Beyond the Valley of the Dolls* was unquestionably the best B movie ever made, the one against which all others must be compared. Some classic B's, such as *Plan 9 From Outer Space*, are fun because they are clearly the work of an idiot who thinks he's a genius. Others, like *Amazon Women on the Moon*, are fun because they are deliberately camp. What puts *Beyond the Valley of the Dolls* in a league of its own is the way it miraculously straddles the line. There's no way to tell whether the film is serious or not until you meet Russ Meyer and see the twinkle in his eye.

When I was voted in as a member of the Los Angeles Film Critics Association, it was not that I had any particular desire to hang out in a small room with a gaggle of hatchet men and women. But you take what you can get. Actually, they're a fun bunch; I was attracted to a series of screenings that the association was doing in conjunction with the UCLA Film and Television Archive, in which a member critic showed a film with the movie makers present and then discussed the film afterward with the filmmaker and audience.

While other critics salivated over the prospect of getting Scorsese to discuss *The Last Temptation of Christ*, I daydreamed about seeing *Beyond the Valley of the Dolls* on a big screen again. I called Russ Meyer, and he bragged about a perfect 35 mm print he had. He agreed to let us show it and to personally attend the discussion. I called Edy Williams, and she also agreed to attend.

I had no idea if screenwriter Roger Ebert considered *Beyond the Valley of the Dolls* a highlight or an embarrassment in his career, so I was delighted when he agreed to fly in from Chicago to attend the screening. My cup ranneth over when I was miraculously able to gather the entire living cast as well. It was a fun reunion, since many of them had not seen each other in 20 years.

This turned out to be one of the most popular screenings in the Critic's Choice series. More than two hundred people were turned away at the door. The Voyager Company shot the discussion as a documentary to be included on the letter boxed laser disc of their prestigious Criterion Collection. So far, Twentieth Century–Fox has refused to let them release it, despite Mr. Meyer's approval, despite the fact that it is not available in any other format, and despite the fact they have no plans to release it themselves. Are they embarrassed about it? I can't imagine why, unless they've got something against transsexual superheroes who run around beheading Nazi manservants and guys dressed like Tarzan.

—M.D.

The Interview

Robert Rosen: Good evening. I'm Bob Rosen, director of the UCLA Film and Television Archive. And I'm also a member of the Los Angeles Film Critics Association. On behalf of both organizations, who are sponsoring this event, I'd like to welcome you.

We'd like to see the archive as more than a place where movies are shown, but a place where directors and critics, even, can feel at home and maybe even talk to one another. You know, in Los Angeles the critics have really taken the work of the archive, particularly, in preservation as if it were their own. I'd also like to publicly thank Roger Ebert for his support for preservation and particularly that program that was recently done about Martin Scorsese, Spielberg, and Lucas and their involvement with the cause of preservation. We need that kind of support.

I also worked this room — as a teacher. And for a number of years one of the high points of the courses I gave was a screening of *Beyond the Valley of the Dolls*. The course was dealing with films that were commercial that were intended for a general audience, but they took risks that broke boundaries that did something different that dared, in some sense, to be provocative. The aim of a course like that is, of course, to inspire filmmakers.

Ten, fifteen years later academic critics discovered postmodernism, postmodernist irony, pastiche, and all kinds of other fancy things. And way back when, Russ Meyer was already doing it.

Michael Dare: I can't possibly explain why this is one of my favorite movies of all time. There's almost no excuse for it. I can't say it's the best movie ever made, but I can honestly say it's one of my favorites.

For the Los Angeles Film Critics Association to pay tribute to this film is sort of like the National Wine Critics Association paying tribute to Boone's Farm. First of all, I'd like to ask Russ Meyer how on earth he convinced Twentieth Century–Fox to let him make this movie.

Russ Meyer: Well, I think Roger said it. He said they put two nuts in charge of the asylum. The man that gave us our shot—or there were two men—Abe Burrows, an Obie playwright, and Darryl Zanuck. And they'd seen an earlier film that was making a few bucks in New York, and they couldn't get a print because we were booked into about one hundred ninety theaters. And at that time that was a lot of theaters for an independent film.

So they had to go to a theater that was local to them, and it happened to be a stroke house down on Forty-second Street. So the two big people went there and saw the film and supposedly, Burrows said, "Well, if a klutz like that can make a film that successful and that attractive for $69,000, you ought to throw him a bone." So that's how it really began.

I went over to Fox and met the son, Richard Zanuck, and he gave me five thousand bucks. And by that time I had become quite friendly with Roger. We thought a lot about the same kind of ladies, anyway. We had a little bit in common. I respected the fact that he was much younger than myself and could put a certain amount of input into the picture that I couldn't by myself.

Fortunately, not for some people, but the Manson murders had come along at that time, so I was able to incorporate that as a basis for the ending of the film. Zanuck himself in a long cablegram that he sent me from Cannes after Roger finished this marvelous treatment said, "I think it's a little tough, that whole aspect of utilizing the Manson killings, but I'm sure you'll use good taste when you do present it."

Roger then completed the script, and it was one of the most fulfilling experiences of my life to work under circumstances where, heretofore, I'd only worked with a crew of five, and now I had about fifty-five. A lot of Indians to do your bidding. And I shall never forget it. It was an experience that was probably the most rewarding period of my life. That's a long speech for me.

Dare: Mr. Ebert, what was the specific assignment that you were given here? Did you have guidelines?

Robert Ebert: A camp, rock 'n' roll, horror, exploitation musical. I had been a fan of Russ's work since *The Immoral Mr. Teas*, which played for two and a half years at the Illini Theater in my hometown—providing people with someplace to go during final exam week and in between, too. It was a long run.

And I had seen all of Russ's movies subsequent to that, including *Motor Psycho!*; *Faster, Pussy Cat! Kill! Kill!*; *Mud Honey!*; *Lorna*, *Mondo Topless*; even *Eve and the Handy Man*, and the others.

And so when the *Wall Street Journal* ran a front-page article about him, "A Tribute to King Lear," written by the reporter with a marvelous name of Stephen Lovelady, I wrote a letter to the editor of the *Wall Street Journal* saying that I thought it was about time that Russ Meyer was acknowledged as an original filmmaker. And as a very good filmmaker.

In times to come, and years to come, and into the next century, Russ Meyer's films will be seen as art in the same sense as Andy Warhol's work and Al Capp's work—popular art of a very particular and original and unique nature.

Just recently I put myself way out on a limb. I saw *Wild at Heart*—David Lynch's new film—at the Cannes Film Festival, where it won the Palm d'Or, the grand prize of the Cannes Film Festival. And it sounded a little bit strange to be writing these words, but I felt to be honest to myself that I had to say that "there was nothing in *Wild At Heart* that *Beyond the Valley of the Dolls* didn't do much better twenty years earlier."

When it was mentioned earlier that this movie was part of postmodernism, it seems to me that the only true postmodernist works are those which were made before anybody knew that they were postmodernist—because, you see, once you know what you're doing, you're not doing it anymore. How can you set out to be postmodernist? At that point it's too late. You're premodernist again.

And this movie is exactly what it is, an extremely original and unique film. There's not another movie like it, as far as I know. I wish there were.

So, after I wrote the letter to the *Wall Street Journal*, Russ wrote me a letter. And the next time he was in Chicago we had dinner, and then when I came out here we had dinner again. And we became friendly.

And when Twentieth Century–Fox offered him the opportunity to produce *Beyond the Valley of the Dolls*, which at that point was only a title, he called me up and offered me the job, and I took it. I came out here.

He tried to get me to stay at the Sunset Retirement Home. He felt it would be very quiet there, and I'd get more work done. I wound up at the Sunset Marquis, but I quickly became aware of Russ's theories about writing, which was that it was much the same activity as typing.

We were supplied with a suite of offices at Twentieth Century–Fox. We had a secretary named June in the middle, and at the left was Russ, and on the right was me. He insisted that the doors be kept open so that he could hear if the typewriter was going. And if there was ever a moment when there wasn't any typing going on, I would hear [*Shouts.*] "What's the matter?"

And so the remarkable thing under these circumstances is that it took as long as six weeks to write the screenplay. His system was that we would talk through things with long yellow legal pads. We started the process by screening *Valley of the Dolls*. We had, neither one of us, ever read the novel, and I hope never to read the novel.

And we thought, well, *Beyond the Valley of the Dolls*. *Valley of the Dolls* is about three young women who come to Hollywood hoping to find stardom and success, and they find their way down to the bottom through abuses in terms of drugs, and alcohol, and sex.

This seemed like a good place to start for us and so we, essentially, took the same thing. And instead of making them actresses, we made them rock singers. And then we just made it up as we went along.

I remember the day that we found out that Ronnie Zeemambarzo was a woman. He was not written as a woman until the moment that he opened up his shirt. Up until that moment he was a man.

And I said, "Russ, you're not going to believe this. We've just had a startling development in the plot here." He said, "That's fabulous. That's great."

And so we did a treatment, another treatment, and a couple of screenplays. And then Russ went to work and shot the film and casting these wonderful people who all look exactly the same today. I think we could do a sequel, you know, and set it in 1971.

Dare: I have sort of a generic question for all of the actors who are here today, which is, basically, what was your life like in 1969 when you got cast in this movie? And how did this film change your life? Let's start with Michael Blodgett.

Michael Blodgett: I'll tell you, I haven't seen this film in a long time. I'll tell you something: Watching it knocked me down. I'm not kidding. Honestly, I have seen it maybe once in fifteen years.

I'm not an actor anymore. I stopped doing anything on camera about 1976, and I've been a writer ever since. I've written some novels, and I've written several movies. But back then I was heavily into acting, and it was my career. As a matter fact, I was going to law school at the same time. I was like putting myself through law school by working movies.

I had taken some time off to do a picture for Joseph L. Mankiewicz at Warner Brothers called *There Was a Crooked Man* which was written by David Newman and Robert Benton, the people that did *Bonnie and Clyde*. It starred Kirk Douglas and Henry Fonda and Burgess Meredith. It was a huge, big movie that I had the third lead in.

So it had not been released at the time that my agent called me and said, there's something real interesting going on at Fox. And there's a guy over there that has made several films, and they made a lot of dough. And the people at Fox would love to have him come and make some of that dough for them. His name is Russ Meyer. I had loved his other pictures, like *The Immoral Mr. Teas*, and I knew who he was.

I went over, and I sat down with him, and he was unlike anybody I'd ever met in this business before. He was candid, not full of bullshit, at least as I read it.

And you know he said, "You know what I'd like to do? You've done a lot of work and a lot of the other people who are going to be in this film haven't. And I'd like you to come in here and sort of be a linchpin in this."

I said, "Jesus!" That was a great stroke for my ego, right? And I thought about the Warner Brothers picture coming out. And I thought about a lot of things. And I said, "I don't know."

He said, "I'll tell you something. We are going to have a lot of fun. That I can promise you."

And we really did. I'll tell you, the kinds of things that happened during and after, the relationships that came from this picture. I mean, it's . . . Russ was married to Edy after the picture. I went out with Cynthia Myers, I don't know, three or four years. . .

Ebert: You're kidding! [*Everyone cracks up*.]

Blodgett: Dolly married Dick Martin, and he would come down on the set down at Fox. I mean, it was a time. You got to understand, also, that in 1969–70 that this town was just sizzling. I mean, it was a drug culture. Sex was wide open. There weren't any diseases or problems. And I'll tell you, he was a man of his word. We really had a lot of fun. Thank you for inviting me this evening. It just blew me away. Thanks.

Dare: Who's next in line? Haji. Yes.

Haji: Hi guys. Nice to see all you people here today. Thanks for coming. What was the question? What did the film do?

Dare: Well I just, ah. What was your life like in 1969 before this movie? And how did the film change that?

Haji: Well it's always been a pleasure working for Russ. I was away at the time when Russ was committed to doing this film for Twentieth. But you know when I was working with him on *Faster, Pussy Cat! Kill! Kill!* I used to always tell Russ, "Oh you're going to go to the big time. Don't worry, Russ, you're going to be working at the big time." And he used to be very modest and say, "Oh, sure, sure," you know.

When I came back into town someone told me, "Did you hear about your friend Russ Meyer? He's working over at Twentieth." And I said, "Oh, I can't believe it." Immediately, I got in my car and I went to Twentieth Century–Fox. I didn't even call him to say I was coming. I just went to the gate. And they said, "Yes?"

I said, "Oh, I'd like to see Russ Meyer. Could you please tell him Haji is here?" And he greeted me very nicely. I went upstairs, and it was so exciting to walk into the office and see him there.

I said, "I told you, baby. You're going to make it to be big time." You know.

And he says, "Where have you been, anyway? Listen, everybody's been cast." He was very nice. He said, "I'm just going to put you in somewhere. You'll work for a couple of weeks. Make some money. And we'll find something for you to do."

He let me figure out some of the dancing I did, which I enjoyed doing. And then from there, after the film was over, I had such a small part in the film, but I got a lot of publicity from it. I don't know why, but I had a nice spread in *Show* magazine and a few others. So I figure, well maybe I can make a little money from this. So I took the publicity, and I went to an agent and I said, "Look." I was a dancer at the time. So I said, "Why don't you send me on the road and make some money?"

And he said, "Better yet, I'll book you in Vegas."

And that was with Circus Circus. I worked there for a while and made some good money. And it was a nice place to work. Really was. And that was my reward from *Beyond the Valley of the Dolls*.

Dare: Edy Williams.

Edy Williams: [*Reenacting a line from the film.*] "Oooh, I'd like to strap you on sometime." [*Big laughs.*] Roger, I get more fan letters. They really like the lines you wrote. . . .

Ebert: You know. I can't take credit for that line. That line is Russ's line. And I think he got it from someone else: "I'd like to strap you on sometime."

Meyer: Oh, no, I'm sure that's Edy's line. [*More big laughs.*]

Williams: Well, let's see, I met Russ at Twentieth Century–Fox, and he showed me the script, and I said, "Oh my God, you're going to film this in six weeks? This script needs three months." And I remember I said, "I really would like to be able to rehearse on the set in order for it to be really good" in what I was doing. And it was wonderful because most directors, they don't stop and get real involved with what they're doing. They do it very, very fast.

And he said, "OK, if you want to rehearse. Then you have to be on the sound stage before the crew arrives at five in the morning."

And I thought, "Wow, he is game. He is—this is incredible, this is fantastic." And I thought, "OK, you're on." And we did. We met very early in the morning. And we mapped out the scenes on the set using the props and everything we were going to do. He planned it all out. And then his crew came. And I really felt like the scenes went much better than other films I've done because he had that rapport. He communicated with everybody.

And he invited *everybody* to come to his apartment and rehearse the scenes. And he fixed dinner for *everyone*. [*Everyone responds to the inference.*] You know it was. . . [*Big laughs. Her voice rises to a crescendo*]. And then we got married! [*She cracks up.*]

And I had a wonderful time with him because we got to go promote the picture. It was great. Me and him and *Beyond the Valley of the Dolls*. The three of us. We went to all these exciting places. We went to London, and then we went to Chicago.

And I did something else. And he did something else. But it's incredible, because it's like, you know, everywhere, it's like part of my life, and I'm real proud of it. And everywhere I go, people ask me about him.

And I say, "Well we don't really see each other," because actually we haven't been next to each other closely in about, what, twelve years? So right in front of everybody, right now, I have to shake Russ's hand, because he got us all here tonight. [*Applause/laughter.*]

Meyer: I'd like to bring up one point when we did the Rolls-Royce sequence.

Ebert: It was a Bentley, Russ.

Meyer: OK, with the Bentley, whatever. I showed it to Edy. I was a little concerned because I had met her family, and I was afraid maybe it might have been a little too strong. And she chastised me for saying, "It's got to be stronger than this." And one shot that was in the film was because of her criticism. She said, "I at least should take off my pants." And that really...

Williams: I did?

Meyer: Yeah, you really chewed my ass out there.

Williams: [*Defiantly, with her teeth gritted.*] I said, "I can't do this scene with all these people around watching." And I said, you know, "You're going to have to have everybody leave because otherwise there's no way I can do it. I've never done nudity in a picture before." And so.

[*Softening.*] Actually he was very nice because he said, "OK, I'll have the crew leave, and everybody will leave the set, and I'll turn the camera on and you can do the scene yourself." [*An aside through giggles.*] Something like that... Anyway, we should have kept the goddamn Rolls-Royce.

Meyer: Who ... who...? [owned it?] [*Cutting it off short.*] Well, anyway. Also, I think she had come up with some really good stuff, particularly that thing ... you know ... "strap you on with." That line with when we had the Princess Livingston and the guy by the name of Ross and so forth?

Williams: Yeah. Ken Ross.

Meyer: It was a marvelous piece of acting. Together with the fact, too, about driving along in the Rolls-Royce. That was—I mean, I think you contributed so big to that motion picture. There's no question about it. Just as everybody else that worked on it. You had a special something that came very much to bear. I do appreciate that. Your contribution was very, very large.

Dare: Well, thank you Edy. John, why don't you tell us what you'd done before *Z Man*.

John LaZar: Well, I was in Hawaii doing a picture and the late Bill Benjamin—he was a casting agent for Fox, and he discovered me, and brought me out to Fox. I met Russ. Russ handed me *The Burple Blade Goes Snicker-Snack*. I looked at it, and I said, "OK." And I did it. And he seemed to like it. I was so new to the film business that for the first six weeks I thought I was shooting a Western.

And you know, to placate me they said, "You know, really you're doing *Richard III.*" So they treated me very well. But, but. . . what else do you want to know? Oh, I sired my first son during the shooting of that film. He's now a policeman in San Francisco, which is really weird. I'm from San Francisco. My father was a gambler. I'm an actor. He's a cop. I don't know where we went wrong. [*More laughs.*] That's about it. I'll tell you honestly, it's the best role I ever had in films. And Russ is beyond a shadow of a doubt the best director I've ever worked with. I'd kill to get a role like that, again. Literally. [*More laughs and applause.*]

Meyer: It just so happens that we've got one role coming up that probably you'd be very well suited for.

LaZar: I don't have to kill anybody?

Ebert: He didn't say that.

Dare: So, David, what was your life like in 1969?

David Gurian: What was my life like? I don't know what it was like. But this was my first and last role in the moving picture business. But I still feel like a star. No, it was a big opportunity for me at the time. I mean, this was one of those things where you sit down, and you read for somebody, and you've studied acting in college, and you've done teenage drama workshops, you know, *Cinderella*, *Rumplestiltskin*, and stuff like that. And you sit down in front of somebody who's professional, you know, producers—Roger and Russ. And they go, "Gawd, that was a great reading." And you go, "Really?"

And they go, "You know, you're kind of up for this part." And you go, "Oh, OK." I knew that. And you take your little portfolio with your little eight by tens and you walk out on the platform, and you jump downstairs, you know, like this. But no, seriously, Michael and John and Dolly and Chuck and a few other people that aren't here helped me out immensely on this. I mean, I was out in the ozone. And they befriended me. And we had a great time. These people are really, really wonderful. And it's tough to be an actor. Real tough. And to stay in the business like they have, and to contribute like they have, is commendable, seriously.

Dare: It's your turn, Dolly.

Dolly Read Martin: Oh, God. Oh, thank you. [*Responding to an enthusiastic audience and some whistles.*] I'm from England, and I was a Playmate in 1966 for *Playboy* magazine, and I came to America, and in 1969 I was broke. I'm talking broke. I couldn't work over here. And I remember going to the International House of Pancakes to get a job as a waitress, and they turned me down. And to this day I've never been in an International House of Pancakes—that'll show 'em. And I was really, really broke.

My agent sent me for the role. And in fact, not this role, a different role. As I went up to Twentieth Century–Fox there was a big sign up. They had made *Hello, Dolly* then. And it said, "Hello, Dolly" and I said, "Yeah! Yeah!" And I got the job.

And Russ was fabulous. Is fabulous. But tough. Wow. I mean he was. He's got a heart of mush. He's just the most wonderful, warmhearted, super guy. But, he's like Poppa. Poppa Bear. And between threatening you every five minutes and loving you every five minutes, he was a total gentleman and a super guy.

And Roger was a staple. Every time Russ was going to make me cry, Roger was there. Right, Roger? Remember that?

Ebert: Right.

Read: He doesn't remember that! [*Everyone cracks up.*] But then I remember after the movie was over, and we all had a super time. After the movie was over, and I was in the hospital for one thing or another. And when I woke up from the operation, there was Russ with a big bouquet of red roses, and he was the first person I saw. He's always been there for me. He was there when my parents came over from England. He took them to San Francisco. I mean he's a super, super guy. And I loved doing the movie. It took a lot of guts for me to come here twenty years later. [*More laughs.*] Lower that light a bit!

Dare: Charles, you've made several films with Russ. How was this one a different experience from the others?

Charles Napier: Yeah, they keep saying all these wonderful things. How come you never did that for me?

[*Laughs.*] Shit. We made them out of the back of a pickup truck. (Very funny.) No. I was just watching this. This was a strange twist for me, this character, because he had already trained me, you know. I was an actor trained in that which I wouldn't advocate—sex, violence, and drugs—but I was already burned out when I got to this.

And we used to bludgeon them all over the side of the mountain. I can't remember. Live ammunition, believe it or not, man. It's like basic training, you know. Four chicks, one grip, and a campfire, two steaks—that was it for six weeks. [*Raising his voice.*] And by God, we're talking about Death Valley. You were in the movie, and you didn't walk out until you made it or you were dead. I'm not kidding you.

Ask Haji. She was a little distracting. She used to do makeup with only sneakers on. As bad enough as it was. I think the first time I met Russ I was going with a chick with very large melons, and she said she had an audition with this guy and wanted me to go along and make sure she didn't get raped. I think that's how I met Russ, as I recall. She didn't get the job. I wound up playing the sheriff in *Cherry, Harry and Raquel* and then *Super Vixens*, and.... But anyway, it's been fun, and I've gotten a lot out of it.

I'm still working actively, thank God. And I've done OK by Russ and, you know, the career is still going. By the way, how would you guys like to see another one? It's called *Up the Valley of the Beyond.* Would you like that? [*Audience response is "Yeah."*] Well, he and Roger are trying to put something

Russ Meyer's *Beyond the Valley of the Dolls* (back row, left to right: John LaZar, David Gurian, Charles Napier, Michael Blodgett; front row, left to right: Dolly Read Martin, Roger Ebert, Edy Williams, Russ Meyer).

together. I hope they can bring it off. But anyway, thank you for coming and everything else. That's all.

Dare: I'd like to open this up with questions from the audience.

Audience Question: What ever happened to Cynthia Myers?

Meyer: Cynthia, I believe, lives near — what the hell is the name of that town? — Palmdale? Yeah, Palmdale. Yeah. I've spoken to her a couple of times. She's married, I think, to an Air Force colonel and has a little boy. She and I were supposed to meet in Las Vegas, but she didn't show up for the trade show for video. Beautiful lady. Probably the most famous centerfold that *Playboy* ever published.

Read: Bullshit. [*Raucous laughter breaks out.*]

Meyer: I'm sorry, I forgot.

AQ: Did she ever do any movies after *Beyond the Valley of the Dolls?*

Meyer: I think she did a Western after *Beyond the Valley of the Dolls.* But I didn't see her. I haven't seen her in years, of course. I have a great admiration for her. Her contribution was exceptional to the film.

Dare: This is a question for Russ. I understand you did a lot of combat photography in World War II? Is is true that you actually photographed Patton coming onto the Normandy Beach? I heard you photographed Patton landing on Omaha Beach.

Meyer: Well, that wasn't any great achievement until the First Army had secured everything. And I can't come up with any kind of imposing speech here because I have two close confederates who were in the same one hundred sixth Signal Photo Comapny; Paul Fox is one, and the other is Jim Ryan. I made a shot at Patton at the end of the war. Garson Kanin was making a picture called *True Glory*. It ended up winning the Academy Award for the best documentary, 1945.

I had the occasion to get this assignment to photograph Patton in a circumstance that might have resembled Normandy, whereas we were really outside Munich. And I recall, the officer, who was a close friend of mine, was terrified of anyone with a rank that exceeded his. Of course Patton was a three-star general.

He said, "I just haven't got the balls to go up and report to the General." He says, "You're going to have to."

I said, "Hell I'm just a staff sergeant. That's your job." He said, "I'm sorry. You're just going to have to do it. You'll have to do it."

So I went up. He was an imposing figure to present yourself to. And very accommodating. I had seen him in other circumstances when he was pretty raucous and straightforward.

But he said to me, "Officer, was that your officer?" I said, "Yeah." He said, "Why didn't he report?" I said, "Aw well, he was a little nervous."

He said, "Well I would probably have made him a little more nervous."

Anyway, we made the shots. But I must say when I was in his presence, I felt in the presence of greatness.

I had an opportunity once before to photograph something that had been brought about by Patton himself. It was through the Sixth Armored Division, toward the end of the war, and we were advancing about one hundred miles a day. I was with one of the armored regiments, and I was awakened in the middle of the night and asked to come to S2, which is Intelligence.

There was a colonel in charge of the regiment. And there was Patton by himself. He had discovered, or learned, that Hitler and Goebbels were going to be in Weimar, which was about one hundred kilometers from where we were, and he gave specific orders to the colonel.

He turned to me and said, "Sergeant, you'd better be very damn careful what you shoot. And make sure you do your job right."

Of course, my knees had turned to jelly by that time. We left and they routed everybody out of their sacks, and the armored regiment mounted up. He also mentioned the fact that there would be no stopping for any kind of casualties. All of a sudden, both myself and Slick, a guy from Alabama, here we were sitting on top of the greatest news scoop of the war. And there was no competition. Usually the GIs were always second-best to the press that were, you know, certified news cameramen before the war.

But anyway, we drove those hundred miles sandwiched in between a couple of tanks. We did get to Weimar. And Hitler indeed had been there, along with Goebbels. They literally had beat the life out of the town.

But here we were sitting on something. I figured that I had the "news of the day job" just absolutely, actually iced if I could have gotten that footage. I was thinking of my future more than anything else. So of my times with Patton, that's probably the most memorable of all. There were two shots in the picture *Patton*. They were made outside of Paris in a small town where Ernest Hemingway was hanging out and involved with the FFE, which was a French underground group.

One side item to this. I'd been working on an autobiographical film, along with a book, for a number of years. And I found out that Patton was not without heart. When he was in a town called Nutsford before the invasion, he carried on some sort of very poignant affair with a lady that owned a pub by the name of the Golden Stocks Inn. And I went there. Jim Ryan and I went there, and we photographed it.

And in the lobby every week a bowl of white carnations has been set up, delivered, and installed there. The woman's dead. But it bears a message that this was a gift on the part of General Patton, on behalf of this lady and so forth.

So I was glad to see another side to this tough old rascal that so many feel so very strongly about, pro and con.

Not a long question, but a long answer.

Dare: How did those experiences lead to your other film career?

Meyer: Well, I liked the war and didn't want it to end. I had found a home in the Army, you know; it's just that I was afraid I had to come back and get a job, you see. Well, it was not an easy transition.

I tried to get a job when I came to Hollywood, and there was no opportunity. But I was fortunate to get a job with an industrial filmmaker, and that was the greatest training ground of all. You go out with two guys and work for a year and do a film on the Southern Pacific Railroad, and that had more influence.

And then I got involved, thanks to a marvelous photojournalist by the name of Donald Arnitz, who's no longer among the living, and he approached me. He came up there, and I was dissatisfied with the income I was receiving. And he said, "Why don't you get into this titty-boom game?"

And I said, "Well, Don, I don't know anything about that." You know. "I'm doing industrial movies on railroads and things of that nature."

And he said, "What you lack in ability, you'll make up in enthusiasm."

So it came that way. You would combine an industrial movie with so-called nudity or glamour or things of that nature. And that's why most of my films do resemble industrial movies. Better to see my product, my dear. There's always a sermon at the end or a sermon at the beginning. Pointing out the shortcomings and the frailties of the people that you've been dealing with. Borrowing heavily from your own personal existence. It works fine, you know.

I'm ready to do another one. Been on a book for three and a half years, and I think it's time. Roger's come up with a great script. And if God wills it, we'll make another *Dolls*. We won't dare use the title, though.

AQ: In John Waters' *Shock Value*, he talked about you already writing a sequel and that it had something to do with Elvis?

Meyer: Yes.

Ebert: This is a film called . . . is it called *Up the Valley of the Beyond*, or . . . ?

Meyer: Yes. I sometimes confuse my titles.

Ebert: It is also called *Beneath the Valley of the Altar Vixen, Son of Beyond the Valley of the Dolls*, and my personal favorite, *Into the Chasm of the Hyper Vixens*. This is a screenplay that was originally part of a two-picture deal at AIP, and *Super Vixens* was the other part of that deal, and AIP bailed out.

And Russ made and released *Super Vixens* himself to enormous success. The movie involves characters that might make you think of Elvis and Howard Hughes. There's Dr. Pretorius down in his dungeon, trying to give people the secret of eternal life through injections of the pituitary glands from pregnant beavers. Marilyn Rueters, correspondent for *Rolling Stone* magazine, Moisha Sabra, the crack agent for Israeli Intelligence; Krakow, the loyal assistant; Elmo Trimblor, the strongest man in the world. I don't know who I left out.

I think my favorite scene comes when Marilyn Reuters is shackled above a twenty-two-foot high Waring blender. And Dr. Pretorius is about to pulverize her so that he can inject her into Elvis, while Elmo Trimblor and Moisha Sabra are trying to break their way through the stout oaken doors of his underground dungeon. And they're able to save her just in the nick of time because Dr. Pretorius' finger wavers for a second between blend and puree. Sorry, I didn't want to sound like I was pitching anything.

AQ: I'd just like to say that a lot of people might think your movies are sexist, but I think they've done a lot for the feminist movement. But I do have a question. Now, in a lot of your movies, lesbianism is a very beautiful thing, and the women are gorgeous, and there's music, and it's very beautiful. And very natural.

But why is it in *Beyond the Valley of the Ultra Vixens* the lead character really, really wants anal sex? He loves anal sex with women, but when he has the opportunity to have anal sex with a man, he runs in fear. And also like in *Z Man* and *Lance Rock*, why that couldn't have worked out either? What was wrong with that?

Someone: [*Off mike*.] Everybody's going to want to meet this girl.

Meyer: I don't know what the answers are.

Ebert: That movie is called *Beneath the Valley of the Altar Vixens*. [*More raucous laughter erupting*.]

Meyer: A woman called me today from Holyoke, Massachusetts. And her name was Asplindin. That was her last name. And she wanted to know if she could order a copy of *Beneath the Valley of the Altar Vixens*. She said, "It's the funniest film I've ever seen." And of course I agreed with her. The book-keeper sent her a copy. It's probably the most popular film I have.

It was interrupted. Roger and I were going to do a film on the Sex Pistols. I had shot the film beforehand, and then this opportunity came along for us to work on a picture in Britain, and Roger wrote a brilliant script called *Anarchy in the U.K* and then *Who Killed Bambi?* and so on. And unfortunately the man who was their manager didn't have sufficient funds to make the picture. I earned a lot of money and had a good time and one thing or another. But regrettably the film wasn't made. We shot some three days, and then they folded the whole thing.

Ebert: You know, I wish that they had made a documentary called *The Making of "Who Killed Bambi?"* If only so it could have had the scene in it where you silenced Johnny Rotten, who was protesting his wages of five pounds a week, a can of baked beans, and a six-pack of beer daily. And that was what Malcolm McClaren was paying him, that wasn't what you were paying him.

And I remember once you met with Johnny and Sid Vicious, and Johnny was getting a little bit out of line, and you turned to him and said, "Listen you little whippersnapper, we fought the Battle of Britain for you and we'll fight it all over again, and this time you'll go into the drink." [*Everyone cracks up.*]

What amazed me is this completely silenced Johnny Rotten, who for the next several days of our relationship listened to everything Russ said and agreed with him and obeyed all of his orders. Johnny Rotten apparently didn't know that (a) America didn't fight the Battle of Britain and (b) that he was Irish. [*More cracking up.*]

Meyer: I regret I didn't answer all those points the young lady made. You were comparing the fact that probably presented the so-called, for want of a better expression, the girl-girl sequence in *Beyond the Valley of the Dolls*, which I thought was a very attractive and a very sexy presentation of two women that handled themselves exceedingly well and projected the point very well.

But by and large when I show a confrontation between the sexes, it's generally a contest. It's generally kind of—it's more combat than something that's soft. It's meant to be outrageous and spoofy and bigger than life. Or at least a little bit bigger than life.

In the case of Lamar Shed, who was the young man who spurned the affections of Asa Lavender, who was both the dentist and a marriage counselor—hardly equipped, I think, for either job. And it was never made clear as to who would do it to whom. But I thought to myself, always that Lamar Shed, meaning the young hero, was to be the recipient. Whereas Dr. Asa Lavender was the perpetrator.

I don't know if I am helping you at all there. Lamar had one problem with his affliction, and it was summed up beautifully by a lady that I so much admired—June Mack—regrettably she's gone. And she had the name of Junk Yard Sal. And in one of her lines to Lamar, she said after she had tried to win him over to make changes [in his] errant ways, to make love to her in a conventional manner, she said: "One thing's wrong with you, Lamar, you can't look a good fuck straight in the eye."

AQ: If this movie we just saw took out all the references to the times as they were then—you know, late sixties, early seventies—but left the sex and violence intact, do you think a major studio would release it today?

Meyer: Well, most of them are horrors to begin with. Make a buck, then release it. This film was very successful.

This is the twentieth anniversary of the picture. Some people think the film was not a success. But I'm proud to say that owning ten percent of it—I got my check last month. Twenty years. Not too many films pay off that long. And I don't want to put it necessarily on a monetary level. But, yes, I have every reason to believe that the film would be just as successful today as it was then. Fox was very much in need of a monetary transfusion. They were shocked by the fact that it did get an X rating. One thing—I pleaded the case, but it was unsuccessful. I recall the puzzlement on the part of Richard Zanuck and Brown and so on and so forth, and the distribution arm when they saw a rough cut of it.

And no one really understood it like Roger and I did, and Zanuck said to the head of distribution, Peter Meyers, he said, "What do you think we ought to do?"

And Peter said, "Well I think what we have to do is take this and put it in fifty theaters and hope to make some money with it because we're very much in need of a cash flow."

I had to rise to the fore then. Because this was my baby. I had worked with it, you know, for a long, long time. As with any of the films I've made, it's always a very personal issue. Well, any filmmaker of any kind of content would feel much the same way as I did.

And I got up, of course, and I offended the distribution arm, and I said, "No, this is not the way to do it. What you have to do is get one theater on the boulevard and let the film build. There'll be a lot of talk about it. Get some good reviews, hopefully, even bad ones—they work just as well sometimes as the good ones."

So Zanuck said, "Well, that sounds like a good idea." And he turned to Peter and said, "Is there anything available on the boulevard?"

Peter jumped up and said, "No, there's nothing available."

Zanuck had his brightest hour. He stood up and says, "Go out and buy one, Peter."

So we ended up at the Pantages, and the rest is history.

The film—it still plays to this day. I had the good fortune of going to Moscow and showing it together with *Super Vixens* and *Mudhoney!* Now,

Mudhoney! I was conned into taking, which is looked upon by some people as an interesting gothic presentation on my part.

The Russians didn't go for it. It was just too damn depressing, but they loved *Super Vixens*, which starred Charles Napier as Harry Sledge, and they loved *Beyond the Valley of the Dolls*. And instead of one screening, we had six screenings with each of these. We even went out into the neighborhood theaters and showed the films. Always packed.

And I had a marvelous lady who was one of those United Nations types of translators, and she was able to take down every part and translate it. And the audience just hung in there with that. And if she got a little bit behind, they'd start clapping.

Yeah, my reaction to the Soviets changed enormously after having visited the country and noticing what people saw in something I had produced many, many years before, in each instance, and embraced it so warmly. And enjoyed it just like us folks do.

Dare: May I ask what the critics of the time thought of this movie?

Ebert: I want to just add something to what was just said, if I could. If you look in the official corporate history of Twentieth Century–Fox, published by the occasion of its corporate anniversary, you won't find any mention of *Beyond the Valley of the Dolls*. If you read David Brown's recent autobiography, he lumps it in with *Myra Breckinridge*, another picture made at the same time, and dismisses them in less than a paragraph as flops.

The movie grossed in 1970 $47 million. And it cost $900,000 to make. A large percentage of that was paid to Jacqueline Susann for two screenplays that were not used. So by any terms imaginable, it was an enormous hit. It is still on the *Variety* list of all-time top-grossing films.

What has annoyed me over the years is the willingness of various managements at the studio to pretend that they never made this movie. They have not — despite the fact that it has been constantly in repertory for twenty years, that it plays at the Electric Cinema on Portobello Road in London every Saturday at midnight — that's where the Sex Pistols saw it more than a decade ago — despite the fact that it plays in Paris, and in Germany, and all over the world.

They won't make new prints. They don't like to keep it in stock in 35 mm. They released it briefly in video and then withdrew it. And to this day it is not available in any video format. Although I'm happy to say that, apparently, the Criterion Collection, which is the most prestigious organization connected with Home Video, is going to bring out a letter-box version of *Beyond the Valley of the Dolls* [*interrupted with applause*], but Fox has not supported it.

And I submit to you that they didn't make any other movies in 1970 that are as widely seen today, and that would include *Patton, M*A*S*H*, and *Butch Cassidy*, their other releases that year.

It sounds a little bit like I'm blowing my own horn, but I'm quite a soloist, actually.

AQ: Did Tom Wolfe ever write a screenplay for you?

Meyer: No, that's a guy that I knew in the army. His name was Thomas J. McGowan. And I warned him, I said, "You should not use that pseudonym." It was in *Cherry, Harry and Raquel* that Charles Napier first starred and the first opportunity I had to work with the gentleman. So, gratefully, Thomas Wolfe never said a thing. Or Tom Wolfe. But it's on the credits there.

AQ: The other question I have is for Mr. Ebert. One of the things that seem that you really pride yourself on, at least on your show many times during arguments, is your Pulitzer Prize. I read an interview with Mr. Meyer some time ago in a publication where you said, and I'm not going to claim that this is a direct quote, but he said, "I really love Roger because he's really into tits."

Do you think your affiliation with Mr. Meyer in any way endangered a second Pulitzer Prize?

Meyer: I've been accused of ruining a lot of careers... [*drowned out by Roger.*]

Ebert: Yeah I won the Pulitzer Prize after my association with Russ Meyer. I won it in 1975. I don't really bring it up on the show very frequently; I don't feel that's necessary since I'm sure it's constantly in Gene's mind.

But I'll answer your question fairly seriously because ... [*pregnant pause*] ... there might be the feeling that it would be disreputable to be associated with Russ Meyer. In other words I wrote this movie, but then I went on to win the Pulitzer Prize and get a national television show and publish books, and so now I might want to just dismiss this as a youthful indiscretion that, ah, you know, the hotheaded adolescent that I was at that time, and I know better and am wiser now...

One thing that I have learned from Russ Meyer, and I try to practice in my own life, is a lot of people have their lives divided up into compartments. And this compartment is open for some people, and this compartment is open for other people. And you can know this, but you can't know that. And if I'm with this group, I'll say one thing, and if I'm with this group, I'll say something else, so that I can be all things to all people.

Russ Meyer—I think everybody at this table will agree with this—Russ Meyer's life is all inside one big embracing compartment. Everybody who knows Russ Meyer knows everybody else who knows Russ Meyer.

I can remember going out to dinner with Russ and his pulchritudinous lady of the moment and also with an old army sergeant who was on the edge of senility, probably, and this was his one night a week to get some barbecued ribs and the chance to get a look at pretty girl. Russ was loyal to this man because this man had been loyal to him during the war.

Russ has stood by his family. He has stood by his friends. He has flown across the country to visit people in need of him. He came halfway across America in order to attend my mother's funeral and flew back the same day because he wanted to be there. And Dolly spoke about him being at her bedside.

Russ doesn't have the girls snuck off in the bedroom and the Army buddies in the living room and the critics up in the library and the producers down waiting for him at the bank. Everybody is always part of the same thing.

There is no hypocrisy in Russ's behavior. He will tell you exactly what he thinks. He will not try to put a different light on his behavior on one occasion than he will on another occasion. He is one of the most honest people I ever met.

And there might be a tendency or a temptation for me to think that it might not be wise at this point in my career to be on a panel like this or to be associated with Russ. I don't want to do that. Just because I've had success in other areas doesn't mean that I haven't certainly enjoyed and learned from the work that I've done with Russ.

AQ: There was something that I heard about from a friend of mine called *The Seven Minutes* that Edy starred in and was written by John O'Hara. I was wondering if you could tell me a little bit about it.

Meyer: Irving Wallace wrote the book *Seven Minutes*, and it was a second film I made at Fox, and it was my swan song there. But I accompanied Zanuck and Brown over to Warner Brothers with my associate, Jim Ryan, who's here taking pictures. I think they did an interesting kind of horror film, and this was called *Choice Cuts*. Regrettably, there was another vice-president in charge of production, who had done *Klute*, and you know, Zanuck had left, and they paint your name out in the parking space, and so on.

Seven Minutes was a film I shouldn't have taken, but I had such a fat head. I figured that after the great success I had experienced with *Dolls* that I should ignore the projects that I was better suited to and do Wallace's film.

Some people think of it a lot more than I do, as to its content and ability to perform. But it was not a success. Of course a lot of it, I think, had to do with the fact that the studio was pretty well through at that time. Certainly the regime that was in control. Zanuck had been kicked out. Elmo Williams was put in as president.

But, regrettably, even though the film was not successful, it does play a lot on television, but severely hacked, unfortunately.

AQ: Tell us about some of the people you've worked with.

Meyer: I had an opportunity to cast some really interesting actors. Berry Kroeger. I don't know if you would recognize that name. He played a lot of Communist parts and spies, and he came off as being gay. And I had him play the part of a critic on the stand.

And I read the part to him and he said to me, "What am I? The Fox fag?"

And that made an impression on me. But he did a beautiful job. And Ansen. What is his name? David Ansen? Who is now the critic for what, *Newsweek*? And he made reference to some of the characterizations, one of which got me a condemned rating the way I portrayed a Catholic bishop. And he made reference to Berry Kroeger's performance. And how did he put it? He said he would have stopped traffic in a gay bar on a Saturday night. And that was a great tribute to the guy's acting. But there were a number of other people. I had John Carradine, as Edy pointed out, wonderful people. Wayne Maunder, who had been Kit Carson. We had Yvonne De Carlo. And, oh, yeah, Tom Selleck. Yeah, he had his first role. He never makes reference to it. It's amazing how sometimes I'm a little irritated about the fact that he should have made reference every now and then, but then...

Ebert: [*Something inaudible.*] But even the cameramen I can say, one who I admire enormously, Fred J. Koenekamp, who did the camera work on *Dolls* and was a great contributor. I was saddened when he was interviewed recently in the *International Photographer*. I'm a member of that union as well as the Directors Guild and Writers Guild, in which he listed all of the films that he had done, and one film was pointedly absent. And that was *Beyond the Valley of the Dolls*.

Williams: That was because of his wife. His wife was very jealous of all the good-looking women.

Meyer: Well, that might have been true, but he had developed migraine headaches, as I understand it, and he was replaced by another cameraman. It hurt me, naturally, because I'm very proud of the film. And I can say to him in spite of the fact that he ignored it, his contribution was huge.

And he told me the last day of shooting, we were running down the beach, it was when we were done, and Martin Boorman was in the surf — there's a man I pay homage to.

He said, "Would you ever hire me again if you had another film?"

I said, "You bet your life." And he says, "Well, I am very honored to have you tell me that."

But anyway, this is the business. One guy can be a certain character on a given day, and six months later, he's totally different, regrettably. But his contribution cannot be ignored. When you see his name up on the screen and the work he did, particularly with that Sorcerer's Apprentice sequence. The lighting was marvelous. We did something like eighty setups in one day there. It was a nice moment that we experienced.

Dare: Roger, considering the fact that this film has an X rating, how do you differentiate Russ Meyer's films from pornography?

Ebert: Russ doesn't ordinarily direct sex scenes in a way intended to arouse anyone. In my way of thinking, or in terms of the way I look at his films, the lesbian sequence in *Vixens* is the only erotic scene in all of Russ Meyer's work.

And what — the point that people have missed is that Russ is a comic director operating in a pop art context. He will almost invariably cut away from a sex scene in such a way as to frustrate the anticipations of what he cheerfully refers to as the "one-arm viewers."

He likes to cut away to the demolition derbies, oil wells, various other aspects from his industrial filmmaking past. He also frequently seems to be very reluctant to locate a sex scene in bed. He'd much rather have it in a treetop, or in a barnyard, or in the back seat of a Rolls-Royce.

When he does shoot it in bed he invariably likes to use an angle that has not been exploited by other directors: from directly beneath the action, shooting up through naked steel bed springs.

The notion that one could be comfortable having sex in this position is one that I have never wanted to put into practice by trying out for myself. I don't think it's possible. I think you need a mattress at the very least.

And then he will cut away to details. He is the master of the insert shot. The little wheel at the bottom of the bed jerking back and forth. Or an exterior and the whole house is shaking. It's a comic attitude toward sex that he's dealing with here.

When he talks about sex as being about confrontations, I think that is the way that sex is presented. It's an Olympic event in his films in which there are hardly any winners. So that because they, to me at least, they're not erotic, and they're not arousing, they don't qualify as pornographic, if I understand the Supreme Court's definition. You see, now, I have never discussed this with Russ, or at least if I have, I don't know if he's agreed with me or not. I've always felt that the role that sex plays in Russ Meyer's cinema is that it allows him to make his own films and make money doing it.

He can make any film he wants. He has financed most of his own films and released them himself—produced them, directed them himself, written most of them himself, photographed some of them himself, edited some of them himself. He can do physically every job that you need to do on a film, from photographing to sound to editing to casting to direction to promotion to advertising. There are certain kinds of film that you can make at a certain budget level, and he has won that freedom by using sex as his nominal subject. Every beginning filmmaker at UCLA knows that you can get a horror film made that doesn't need to have stars in it. And a sex film doesn't need to have stars in it because the subject matter is the star.

And to me that's the way Russ uses sex. Not as his obsession, not as his interest, but as the ticket that he buys in order to be able to enjoy the rest of the ride. But I don't know if Russ would agree with that or not.

Meyer: Well, as I said before, they were confrontations. You know, it's qualifying for the pentathlon. Six prodigious events. One critic once said that when my characters experience an orgasm, their eyes cross. It's like the mating of the wildebeest and the water buffalo, enormously noisy.

The women, of course, are the aggressors. I like that idea, yeah. They're the ones in charge. They're the smart ones. That's why I rarely have any difficulty with any kind of feminist organization. They realize that the men are all klutzy, you know, the willing tools of the women.

I hung in there, and I was influenced very strongly by Al Capp, if you will recall, and any of his work, Daisy Mae, they were the smart people. The men, they were the willing klutzes that conformed to their wishes. I followed that pattern, and I think it will continue as I make films, that the women will always be the superior personage in any one of my films.

Before we leave, can I say something, once? I am sitting here at this table with a number of people that I admire so much that contributed so much to this picture. Without any one of their participation in *Beyond the Valley of the Dolls*, the picture would be of far less value. I mean, Mike Blodgett—what an incredible job you did in that film. I mean, there couldn't have been anybody else that could have played that role nearly as well as you did. Without a doubt. Physically, mentally. His humor, his satire.

And of course, Edy Williams, probably one of the most interesting sequences I ever shot. The one with the Rolls-Royce, because here was the industrial film. Here I had the motor car, and the emblems and the hubcaps, the beautiful girl, the willing tool at her disposal.

Now here's Charles Napier. Where is Charles? [*He responds*, "Right here."] Charles and I have done some real struggles together. And without his help I wouldn't have been able to dredge myself up after having made a couple of losers: *Blacksnake!* and *The Seven Minutes*. We made a film together, and without his aid it wouldn't have worked. I must work again with him, and we plan to do so. It won't be the Elvis Presley. It'll be more like [*turning to Roger*] what were we thinking now in terms of country and Western, you know?

All right, now Dolly. [*She responds*, "Yes darling."] Do you remember I said something to you in one of the reviews? I've completed a book and I've got a tremendous wealth of good and bad reviews, and I choose to use them all. One person made a reference to you with your "wide-eyed look" in the beginning when you said "groovy," which always gets a laugh, and someone said she resembled a "Mouseketeer at a gang bang."

There was only one person who could have played superwoman. This man [John LaZar] right here. There was no one else that we had, no one that we found, you know? This man, I mean he had the ability to play it so straight. And he had this great background, this Shakespearean background, there's no question about it. I've often felt a little unhappy by the fact that I may have ruined his career. But you see, the man has not decomposed. He looks as good today, and this is twenty years later. What is his secret? And I'd damn well use him again. I'll tell you I admire you so very, very much.

Now, this man here, over here, who played Harrison. Roger's managing editor made reference to—and I noticed, I picked up on the audience when the girl said, Cynthia said, "What you need is a downer." I mean, this guy was so down, and you played it so expertly, and she was ignoring him by the fact. She even told me, actually told me I was a lousy lay. I made an ass of myself. And she said, "What you need is a downer." And this guy couldn't be any further down. I think he did a marvelous job. Marvelous job and such a pleasure to see. I was concerned that you weren't coming.

And your secretary called, and then I put her in touch with Mike [Blodgett], and there's a man now. I have to say thank you so much. He said something to me. He said, "You know, what do I do? I've never done this sort of thing." I said, "Just get on the phone and call all the people you can possibly call and make sure they got down there." And I think you delivered everybody [*He responds*, "Yeah."] except Duncan McCloud who, regrettably, I tried to reach him. Yeah. Yeah. And I think everybody else we tried.

I regret John Harmon, Jack Harmon, isn't here, who did the marvelous montage. I had an opportunity to work off the lot.

And a great sound man who did the mixing, Don Minkler, who regrettably is gone. I toast him.

Henry Roland who played Martin Boorman in so many of my films — a dear, lovable man.

Yes, yes, I owe so much to everybody here. Very much so.

And then, Roger. What can I say? I mean he's so honest, this man. He gets on a show and they grill him and they say, "Well, what about this guy Meyer, this pornographer? What do you say about working on his films?"

And he comes right straight on, head-on, says it like it is. He's not kissing anybody's ass. He's just simply saying he's a friend of mine, I like his films, I was pleased to have been part of them, and hopefully again. There's the true measure of the guy.

Now, he said I went to see him when his mother passed away. He sat with me three days when my mother died. He gave up his time to be with me. Now, there's a kind of friend you can't ever forget. He's a dear friend, and I thank you so much.

For Further Study

Books

Frasier, David K. *Russ Meyer: The Life and Films*. Jefferson, N.C.: McFarland and Company, 1990.

McCarthy, Todd, and Charles Flynn. *Kings of the Bs*. New York: E. P. Dutton, 1975.

Turan, Kenneth, and Stephen F. Zito. *Sinema: Pornographic Films and the People Who Made Them*. New York: Praeger, 1974.

8

OLIVER STONE
AND
Born on the Fourth of July
(with Michael Wilmington)

On August 16, 1990, screenwriter and director Oliver Stone was interviewed by Michael Wilmington after a screening of *Born on the Fourth of July*.

The Film

Born on the Fourth of July (1989), an A. Kitman Ho and Ixtlan Production. Directed by Oliver Stone. Screenplay by Oliver Stone and Ron Kovic. Based on the book *Born on the Fourth of July*, by Ron Kovic. Produced by A. Kitman Ho and Oliver Stone. Director of photography, Robert Richardson. Editors, David Brenner and Joe Hutshing. Music by John Williams. Filmed in and around Dallas, Texas, and in the Republic of the Philippines.

Cast: Tom Cruise (Ron Kovic), Kyra Sedgwick (Donna), Willem Dafoe (Charlie), Raymond J. Barry (Mr. Kovic), Caroline Kava (Mrs. Kovic), Frank Whaley (Timmy), Jerry Levine (Steve Boyer), Tom Berenger (Recruiting Sergeant), Ed Lauter (Legion Commander), John Getz (Marine Major), Jason Gedrick (Martinez), Abbie Hoffman (Strike Organizer), Tom Sizemore (Veteran), Cordelia Gonzalez (Maria Elena), Michael Wincott (Veteran), Tony Frank (Mr. Wilson), Jayne Haynes (Mrs. Wilson), Lili Taylor (Jamie Wilson), Bryan Larkin (Young Ron), Stephen Baldwin (Billy Vorsovich), Oliver Stone (News Reporter), Dale Dye (Infantry Colonel), William Baldwin (Platoon Member), James LeGros (Platoon Member), R. D. Call (Chaplain), Rocky Carroll (Willie), Corkey Ford (Marvin), David Neidorf (Patient), Billie Neal (Nurse Washington), Josh Evans (Tommy Kovic), Seth Allen (Young Tommy), John C. McGinley (Official no. 1), Wayne Knight (Official no. 2), Daniel Baldwin (Veteran), Mel Allen (Mel Allen), Alan Toy (Paraplegic), Annie McEnroe (Passerby), and Ron Kovic, Jamie Talisman, Sean Stone, Anne Bobby, Jenna von Oy, Samantha Larkin, Erika Geminder, Amanda Davis, Kevin Harvey Morse, Jessica Prunell, Jason Klein, Lane R. Davis, Richard Panebianco, John

Pinto, Rob Camilletti, J. R. Nutt, Philip Amelio, Michael McTighe, Cody Beard, Ryan Beadle, Harold Woloschin, Richard Grusin, Richard Haus, Liz Moore, Sean McGraw, Norma Moore, Stacey Moseley, Mike Miller, Ellen Pasternack, Joy Zapata, Bob Tillotson, David Warshofsky, Michael Campotaro, Paul Abbott, Bill Allen, Claude Brooks, Michael Smith Guess, William R. Mapother, Christopher W. Mills, Byron Minns, Ben Wright, Markus Flanagan, John Falch, Dan Furnad, Fred Geise, Greg Hackbarth, Don Wilson, SaMi Chester, Chris Pedersen, Chris Walker, Willie Minor, David Herman, Bruce MacVittie, Damien Leake, Paul Sanchez, Richard Lubin, Norm Wilson, Peter Benson, Sergio Scognamiglio, Richard Poe, Bob Gunton, Vivica Fox, Mark Moses, Jake Weber, Reg. E. Cathey, Edie Brickell, Keri Roebuck, Geoff Garza, Joseph Reidy, Holly Marie Combs, Mike Starr, Beau Starr, Rick Masters, John Del Regno, Gale Mayron, Lisa Barnes, Melinda Ramos Renna, Andrew Lauer, Ivan Kane, Ed Jupp Jr., Michael Sulsona, Karen Newman, Begonia Plaza, Edith Diaz, Anthony Pena, Eduardo Ricardo, Elbert Lewis, Peter Crombie, Kevin McGuire, Ken Osborne, Chuck Pfeiffer, Frank Girardeau, William Wallace, Chip Moody, Eagle Eye Cherry, Frank Cavestani, Jimmy L. Parker, William Knight, David Carriere, John Galt, Jack McGee, Kristel Otney, Pamela S. Neill, Jodi Long, Michelle Hurst, Elizabeth Hoffman, Lucinda Jenney, Lorraine Morin-Torre, Brian Tarantina, Real Andrews.

Synopsis: In suburban Massapequa, Long Island, a young boy named Ron Kovic grows up in an all-American environment. As a high school senior he becomes a wrestling champion and is infatuated with a girl named Donna. But he is fascinated by a U.S. Marine Corps recruitment presentation, joins the corps, and is shipped to Vietnam. On his second tour of duty in 1968, Sergeant Kovic accidentally shoots and kills an American soldier during a confusing firefight, and later, a bullet shatters his spine. He spends much of 1968 rehabilitating in a filthy and understaffed Veterans Administration hospital in the Bronx. Upon his release, he learns that life in a wheelchair back in his parents' home is not conducive to his needs and his changing sensibilities. Turning points include an ugly confrontation with his mother and a visit to see Donna at Syracuse University, where she has become a war protester. He leaves for Mexico, where he goes on a liquor binge, then tries a reconciliation with his conscience by visiting the Georgia parents of the youth he killed in Vietnam. Eventually, he becomes a war protester at the 1972 Democratic National Convention in Miami.

Remarks and Reviews

"Oliver Stone has made what is, in effect, a bitter, seething postscript to his Oscar-winning *Platoon*. It is a film of enormous visceral power with, in the central role, a performance by Tom Cruise that defines everything that is best about the movie. . . . Watching the evolution of Ron Kovic . . . is both harrowing and inspiring" (Vincent Canby, *New York Times*).

"I have been anything but a fan of this director, but the new film . . . is a gripping, unrelenting but extremely powerful work, whose shortcomings evaporate from memory, but whose strengths are indelible. . . . The Vietnam sequences may be more frightening than anything in *Platoon*" (John Simon, *National Review*).

"This is perhaps the first I-was-there picture (including Stone's own *Platoon*) to vent full-blast the self-doubt and self-pity and justifiable rage so many veterans have felt. . . . It gives you more of one man's reality than you can easily handle, combined with more political honesty than anyone could expect from Hollywood" (Stuart Klawans, *Nation*).

"Much of what Cruise accomplishes here, his open-throttle fullness without actory display, must in some measure be due to Stone's direction. Stone's talent for helping actors . . . is underscored here by the performances of the whole cast. . . . As persuasive a picture of the day-to-day life of man in a combat zone as I know. . . . [Stone] treats everything in the film with immediacy and force. . . . The heat of the film is almost palpable as we sit before it. Stone, Kovic, Cruise . . . reach deep inside to make this picture, and it earns something more than respect" (Stanley Kauffmann, *New Republic*).

"Oliver Stone again has shown America to itself in a way it won't forget. . . . The most gripping, devastating, telling and understanding film about the Vietnam era ever. . . . Typically, Stone drenches the picture in visceral reality. . . . Cruise is stunning" (Daws, *Variety*).

"Images are piercing blasts. . . . It's an overpowering movie. . . . Cruise is sensational" (Duane Byrge, *Hollywood Reporter*).

The Filmmaker

Oliver Stone won Academy Awards for directing the Oscar-winning best pictures, *Platoon* (1986), as well as *Born on the Fourth of July*. He also won an Oscar for the screenplay of *Midnight Express* (1978). Wide recognition as a total filmmaker came to Stone in 1986 when he wrote and directed both *Platoon* and *Salvador*. Stone then became a dynamic force in Hollywood, where he continued to make provocative movies based on politically turbulent issues, including *JFK* (1991), a brash revisionist version of the assassination of President John F. Kennedy.

Both *Platoon* and *Born on the Fourth of July* reflect Stone's personal views on the terror and travesties of the Vietnam War. Although the latter film is based on the actual combat experiences of former U.S. Marine Ron Kovic, both films are infused with Stone's own intensely personal view of the war. Stone served in Vietnam with the U.S. Army's Twenty-fifth Infantry Division and First Cavalry Division. He was wounded twice, receiving the Purple Heart as well as the Bronze Star.

Stone's films — both early in his career as a screenwriter for hire, and later as a screenwriter/director and occasional producer — are imbued with an uncompromising sense of total, unflinching commitment. For a generation of American moviegoers, he is the ultimate interpreter of both the Vietnam experience and the decade of the 1960s.

Stone's muscular style and liberal interpretations of ostensibly fact-based stories have not been embraced by some critics. But for a filmmaker of his unswerving passions and maverick sensibilities, Stone has managed to gain a high place at center stage in the filmmaking capital, where safe procedures, status quo politics, and replications of previous successes are standard.

Oliver Stone's Filmography

As director, except as noted: *Street Scenes 1970* (1970, also photography); *Seizure* (1974, also screenplay and editing); *Midnight Express* (1978, screenplay only, adapted from the memoir by Billy Hayes); *The Hand* (1981, also actor and screenplay, adapted from *The Lizard's Tail*, by Marc Brandel); *Conan the Barbarian* (1982, screenplay only, cowritten with John Milius); *Scarface* (1983, screenplay only, adapted from the 1932 film *Scarface*, written by Ben Hecht); *Year of the Dragon* (1985), screenplay only, cowritten with Michael Cimino, adapted from the novel by Robert Daley); *8 Million Ways to Die* (1986, screenplay only, cowritten with David Lee Henry, adapted from novels by Lawrence Block); *Platoon* (1986, also coproducer with Gerald Green, and screenplay); *Salvador* (1986, also producer and screenplay, cowritten with Richard Boyle); *Wall Street* (1987, also actor and screenplay, cowritten with Stanley Weiser); *Talk Radio* (1988, also screenplay, cowritten with Eric Bogosian, adapted from the play by Bogosian and Tad Savinar and the book *Talked to Death: The Life and Murder of Alan Berg*, by Stephen Singular); *Blue Steel* (1989, producer only); *Born on the Fourth of July* (1989), also actor, producer, and screenplay, cowritten with Ron Kovic, based on the book by Kovic); *Reversal of Fortune* (1990, producer only); *The Doors* (1991, also screenplay, cowritten with J. Randal Johnson and partly based on *Riders on the Storm*, by John Densmore); *JFK* (1991, also coproducer and screenplay, cowritten with Zachary Sklar, based on the books *On the Trail of the Assassins*, by Jim Garrison, and *Crossfire: The Plot that Killed Kennedy*, by Jim Marrs); *South Central* (1992, executive producer only); *Wild Palms* (1992, producer only, television); *Heaven and Earth* (1993, also coproducer with A. Kitman Ho and Robert Kline, and screenplay, based on the books *Child of War* and *Women of Peace*); *Natural Born Killers* (1994, also screenplay, cowritten with David Veloz and Richard Rutkowski).

Reasons for Selection

This film is not considered obscure or neglected, and my obvious choice from Oliver Stone's filmography for a series on neglected films would have been *Salvador*. But it is actually my second-favorite Stone film after *Born on the Fourth of July*. The reason I feel as strongly as I do about this movie is very personal. When I was going to college, the protest experiences seen in film were the experiences that I went through.

There is no film that I know of that brings back that era like this one does, with the immediacy, the impact, the emotion. I violently disagree with some critics who say that this film is too exaggerated and that Ron Kovic's antiwar education is not properly handled. To me, the film mirrors the emotions that I experienced. It was overpowering to see it again. And it is the only movie that I have seen in the past several years that has really made me cry. And that happened the second time I saw it.

Since Oliver Stone became a very visible director, I think that he has shown that he is the successor to all of those filmmakers in America and abroad who try to grapple with reality and bring it to us with the emotion that lies under it. And, in that, I think he's in a great tradition.

— M.W.

The Interview

Michael Wilmington: I want to start it off by referring to some of the complaints about the film, specifically the complaints that it's unrealistic. That bastion of critical tastes, the *New Yorker*, suggested that it was unrealistic for a character like Ron Kovic to be gung-ho. It was suggested that kids at this time read *Mad* magazine, *Catch-22*, *The Catcher in the Rye*, and they were more irreverent. When I read that, it struck me as a kind of a gross misunderstanding of what working-class kids in a town like this really do go through.

Stone: You're probably talking about Pauline [Kael].

Wilmington: Well, I'm talking about not just Pauline Kael, but about what's a kind of upper-class elitism among American film criticism in general. That tendency to kind of look down your nose at characters like this.

Stone: She's always quoted. And it's amazing because I only read her because people see my films through her, and that's the only refraction I have of her. I gave up reading her when I was in film school when she said that *The Killer Elite* was the best of the Peckinpah movies. So I've always mistrusted her judgment. I don't think she has a sense of reality.

She said in the review that this film — I did read the review — looks like the Middle West. Well, this is wrong because it was shot in the Middle West, but we went to great details to get that early Long Island look of the 1950s, when there was not as much development, when the trees were planted right after World War II. There was a lot of sky. That's what always struck me about Long Island, the size of the sky. The potato fields.

But, yeah, people like me and Ron Kovic went to Vietnam because we believed. We did read *Mad* magazine. And I asked Ron about that, and he said, "I read that magazine, and I still went." You could have a sense of irony, but at the same time you have to keep in mind that Ron is very much a working-class boy, and he's proud of it. And he says it very much in your face. I mean, he makes no bones about his simplicity and his view of life.

His father was an A & P manager, and his mother was this, and he had these brothers and sisters, and this is the way he wanted to portray himself. He's very direct. He's one of the most honest people that I know. All his thought processes, to a certain degree, are working on the surface. He lets you see his thought processes as he thinks it. That is to say that often his thoughts are also confused with his emotions, as they are with many of us. Our lives are not as clear-cut as some people sitting on the side lines. So I think that a lot of people had a problem with Ron's lack of cerebral attitude. After the war, it's hard for a person to read a book. And he did read. Possibly, I didn't show it enough. I do have shots of books throughout the movie. He was very influenced by both Martin Luther King, Jr. and Gandhi.

But, ultimately, I got to tell you, I think he turned against the war because it was in his heart. It was a visceral reaction to his paralysis. Many years ago, when I wrote the script for Billy Friedkin, he said to me, "If he goes against the war because he's in a wheelchair, you will lose the audience because they expect him to turn against the war."

And I wrestled with that for many years as a writer. And, you know, I tried to suit Billy's point of view. But what occurred to me ten years later is that, yes, he did turn against the war because he was in the wheelchair — it's that simple. It wasn't out of thought. I couldn't do a scene where he discussed Vietnam politically. I just didn't feel right. It felt false to that character. And for that I was [criticized].

I think the film was criticized because it did not show the reeducation of Ron Kovic. But the reeducation is there in the sense of going to the demonstrations in Syracuse and in fighting the fight at home with his brother, fighting with his mother, seeing the indifference of the country, seeing Steve and the way he treated him at the hamburger stand, going to that ex-girlfriend and, through her, seeing that there was another way.

The seed was sown in Ron's mind that protest against our system could be valid and could be a good thing, as opposed to a bad thing. And those seeds are primitive, but they were laid there in that Syracuse scene. And, in reality, the real Ron Kovic? He did a lot of reading. He traversed the country many times to California and back to New York. He was exposed to the political movement over a longer period of time than in this movie. We could have shown that. But I don't think it would have been as effective a movie. It probably would have been more realistic to the political conversion of somebody. But we chose to go, I think, in a more dramatic fashion with a Georgia exegesis that, as you know, has been much written about but did not really occur. He never went to Georgia. But he did write about it in his book, and he confessed to the crime.

Wilmington: Well, what about that scene? A number of people wrote about that scene. I, by the way, loved that scene. It's one of my favorite moments in the film. But being the devil's advocate for a second, I'll throw the

Tom Cruise as Ron Kovic in *Born on the Fourth of July*.

criticism of it toward you: number one, the character in the film, Tom Cruise's
Ron Kovic, is being insensitive and callous in revealing what really happened
to the family's son in the scene and thereby destroying the cherished illusions
of the parents; and number two, the direction is boorish somehow because it's
standing behind this insensitive action.

Stone: I thought a lot about that after I read that, and I think it's a very
valid point. I think it's a good criticism. I don't agree with it. I think that when

Ron goes to Georgia, he has to go. He has no choice. He's reached a point of such pain that he cannot carry it anymore. He has to rid himself of that pain. He goes and he tells the parents who happened. He puts pain on the parents, yes, that's true. But measure that pain against his. What's going to happen in two months or a year? What difference does it make that their son was killed by an NVA [North Vietnamese Army] or by Ron Kovic? And they know deep inside themselves that it really is no different. The boy was killed in the war. He died, whatever. People die in war because often, as we all know, that fifteen, twenty percent of the boys and girls killed in war are from friendly fire.

So, it's not as big a revelation for his parents as it is something for Ron to get it off his chest. His release is more important than theirs. They will adjust in time. I'm trying to work that out so that you understand. If it's a question of guilt, then the release that Ron felt is more important than what happened to the parents. I'd like to hear from the audience if you can elaborate on that or disagree with me.

Wilmington: One reason I think that that scene is crucial is because the whole film is about the stripping away of illusions and being able to confront what's really going on in the war and in your life and in everything else. I think, ultimately, it's just as important for the parents to know the reality of what happened to their son as it is for Ron to reveal it. We tend to live with too many lies. For most of the people who demonstrated at that time, they felt they were demonstrating against a monstrous lie that had to be overcome and had to be overturned.

That's another thing that I like in your work because I think that—in a decade where a lot of the movies, even some of the best, reinforce a number of lies and dubious statements about our society—you're devoted to pulling down the mask or questioning things.

Stone: Well, the interesting thing is, when the film was released, I got about a thousand letters. They were almost exactly the same from all parts of the country. I mean, I constituted them as hate mail, and they told me to get out of the country, and that I desecrated the flag. And it was all pretty organized stuff. And when Dornan [Republican U.S. Congressman Bob K. Dornan of California] came out with his statements, and they were reiterated by Pat Buchanan in his syndicated column; the essence of that argument was that Ron Kovic had never shot his own man. Now, that went to the crux of the political issue of Vietnam: He never killed his own man. That's what these people were saying, because the Marine records do not show that he killed his own man.

The Marine records show—as the colonel in the movie shows you—that it was "investigated," yet nothing was. The record shows there was no murder. There was no accidental killing. I was there, in Vietnam. This happened constantly. There was just a lack of investigation in all these episodes. But on that basis, they went on to say that because he did not kill his own man, everything was falsified in the movie. But if you read the [Kovic] book, you know. And if you hung out with Ron, after ten years, you know that that's a central theme of his life, that he killed that man.

He faced up to it, in a sense, by writing the book because he confesses to it in the book. But in a movie you cannot show somebody writing a book, or you can, but I did not choose to take that path. That is a form of confession: writing. I chose to do it by having him go to this family in Georgia—which he never did. He never went. And I showed it in this way because I believed that, as you said, he could not enter the public arena of demonstrating against the war until he had exorcized his private demons.

Wilmington: That's another key thing about the war, and about the movie, too, I think. I can remember very clearly all the times that we would all sit around at the student union at the University of Wisconsin at Madison and listen to [President Lyndon Johnson's] speeches and look at him, and people would all roar with laughter because we all knew that he was lying. And we were right. And that's essentially what the war was, and that's essentially what a lot of history shows us, that a lot of wars come from lying public policy.

Audience Question: I think for many people, like me, who were basically educated during the antiwar movement, the idea of a mainstream political film is a contradiction in terms. And why did you choose to end it the way that you did? And let me just elaborate on that a little bit. I think this also touches on your explanation of Ron Kovic's [political] change based on his own paralysis, or his own body.

I think one of the most important things that happened during that period was this complete dropout of idealism and the idea that you were being lied to and you had been all your life. And what I find really curious about the structure of the film is that at the end you come back to that idealism in the '76 convention. So, to my mind, the ending kind of obfuscated [the story]. I mean, I think you could have done something much more interesting with this kind of return to idealism at the end. Because, obviously, he wants to believe in his country. He wants that, according to the film. But that's kind of glossed over. And, instead, you have this "hail the conquering hero" kind of ending.

Stone: I think I could have ended the movie at the '72 convention. It would have been a darker ending. Ron shifts alternately from the light to the dark and back to the light again. It's a subjective ending in that sense. I wanted to show that he may have been thrown out of the convention in '72, but he was accepted in '76, that there was a home for him.

And he is an idealist, and he believes, very much, in America. That's why he alternately wants to run for office, and sometimes does and sometimes pulls out. He certainly believes in a Frank Capra ideal for this country, which I think is a good thing because I've seen his darkness, and I've seen where he can go in it and never come out. And I think he needs that idealism. He also needs to be photographed and applauded. He needs applause and he needs to be wanted. He happens to be a great speaker. Possibly, I think, maybe I should have him speaking. I did have him speaking, and I cut it out because it was a very specific speech that he actually gave at the 1976 convention.

Same Questioner: Not to be too didactic, I mean his life is one thing, but the film is something else. So, in certain respects, you departed from his real life, decided to do something for dramatic effect that you thought would be important [reference to the Georgia scene, discussed above]. So, to me, obviously, it's a dramatic choice that you made to end it the way that you did. So, I don't think you can really say, well, he's like this way in real life. For me it's not enough.

Stone: Well, we tried to reflect his spirit.

Same Questioner: Yeah, but the ending goes back to glorifying. To me, the ending comes dangerously close to saying he's co-opted, and also very close to saying everything's OK.

Stone: Uh-hum. Why co-opted?

Same Questioner: In the film you make a point out of allowing him to say during the earlier convention that the people of the United States are one thing, and it's the government and the politicians who are corrupt. In the second convention it's like, well—what?—the politicians are not corrupt anymore?

Stone: I understand what you're saying, but the Democratic Convention of '76 was on all accounts a little more popular than the Republican Convention of '72. I mean, it was supposed to be a return to a more democratic spirit, which gave us Jimmy Carter. It was hope, I thought, in '76. At least I was there at that time, and I felt there was a surge of spirit. The Vietnam War was over, and it was supposed to be sort of a new beginning. I don't feel like he was co-opted. I think that he had a message to give. He was a Socialist Party member, and he made a very strong speech for veterans and veterans' rights. He had something to say. It wasn't like he was just being photographed.

Possibly I made a mistake of showing just that aspect, and you think that that was just what he's interested in. But he did have something to say, and he went out there. Here's a boy from Massapequa whose father was an A & P manager, who is getting up there to speak to the American nation on national television. For him, that's a huge moment. But maybe I overdid it with the adulation part because I was trying to end a two and a half hour movie. Maybe the music was too much. And you saw the glitzy aspect, as opposed to the content.

Wilmington: [*To audience questioner.*] I'm not trying to question any of the very intelligent points that you're making. I disagree with that analysis of the ending, because I think, again, mainstream movies work in a certain way. But what I would like to question is the idea that a mainstream political film is a contradiction in terms. I think that's a little dangerous attitude. I suppose, to a certain extent, it comes from the idea that maybe the only pure radical films that you can see are films by Godard or somebody like that. But the effect of it is to say that mainstream films can't be political, that you can't try to communicate either complex or simple political ideas in a mainstream film.

And I think if you look at the history of American film, you see that's not true. Sometimes films can be very, very daring in their time, daring to a point that it's difficult to conceive how they were made. Examples are *I Am a Fugitive from a Chain Gang* in 1932 or *The Grapes of Wrath*, without the last scene, in 1940. For their times, these are kind of astonishing films. So, the alternative is to say that the only decent political or radical films that can be made are only going to be seen by a few people at a university and that they shouldn't be seen by the masses. And that becomes a form of elitism itself, and something that I'd really strongly disagree with.

AQ: I'd like to point out two things about the film. The scene where Ron comes back from the hospital, and he's in his room with his father—for anyone who's had an estranged relationship with their dad and lack of communication and then a reunion, that was a very powerful scene, very effective. And secondly, I grew up a few miles from Massapequa, and the scenes in the summer at nights with the crickets and the humidity, you know, it was right on there.

My question is, with all the criticism you received about this film, about it not being one hundred percent the truth, how, in your opinion, does a director take the story of one's life, or a historical document, and apply that to a two-hour feature film? And did any of the criticism affect the way that you directed the Jim Morrison story [*The Doors*, 1991]?

Stone: Boy, this is a good question, and there's no answer except in doing it. Michael can tell you better than I can that the biographical film has been a stock-in-trade for movies since Darryl Zanuck and before.

Wilmington: They're almost never accurate. In fact, most historical plays aren't particularly accurate. It's called dramatic license.

Stone: Dramatic license—right.

Wilmington: Escape hatch.

Stone: My feeling is that you shouldn't violate the spirit of that time or the character. If you do, that's wrong. But you have the right to use metaphors, to condense events, to cut events, as long as you stay true to what you perceive to be the spirit of that character and that time. If *Mississippi Burning* says that the FBI agents were the heroes of a murder investigation when they were not, when, in fact, they opposed it, I think that's wrong to the spirit of that time. But I think we have to take those liberties to make it work for ourselves. I mean, we make the film for ourselves, and if we didn't, we would be like most [documentarians]—I just don't think we'd attract a paying audience. I don't know why. It's a good psychological question.

Wilmington: What about the difficulties of making political films by trying to keep both a perception of reality and a philosophical perception fine and true while at the same time trying to make a film that's an emotion machine that's going to work very viscerally and directly on a great number of people? You're one of the few people, I think, who really is able to do it.

Stone: Well, a lot of people say that's my problem. With the Morrison film, all the purists are going to be outraged because it's obviously an approximation of a reality. It's my vision of what it was like, or could have been like, or should have been like in the sixties. I never lived that life, but I took liberties with it. I can't answer your question, Michael, it's just too difficult a question.

Wilmington: Do you perceive a conflict developing between telling the truth and telling an effective story? Does it ever bother you?

Stone: Where would I have done that most egregiously? I mean, just give me an example.

Wilmington: Well, inventing the scene in Georgia in *Born on the Fourth of July*, or maybe having Richard Boyle go over the edge too much in *Salvador*.

Stone: Oh, yeah, where Richard Boyle would show up at every major event in *Salvador* and recent Salvadoran history and be there when he wasn't there? You know, it's a good question. I think that I took more liberties years ago than I do now because I caught so much flak. You know, you get a little weary. And you probably are a little more sensitive about it because you know what the consequences are of it. When I did *Salvador*, I said, "Why can't he be at Archbishop Romero's murder? You know? Right in the front row," because I liked that idea, because it's a great visual. And, as you go along, you become more and more like Alan Pakula [director of the painstakingly accurate *All the President's Men*, 1976].

Wilmington: Well, the film just has to be around for a while because of course, *Young Mr. Lincoln* is full of historical distortions and stuff that never happened, but if it's around for forty years and people still love it, then there'll be a twenty-page analysis of it in *Cayuga Cinema*. . . .

AQ: What are your principles of selection? How do you decide what you're going to show and what you're not going to show, or how you're going to dramatize something in a slightly different way or not? And how's that related to your view of what politics is and how the film relates to politics?

Stone: Boy, this is harder than I thought it would be. As I said, I think the criteria is not to violate the spirit of the person or the time. That's what I have to judge it by. Inside those parameters, I try to make it as exciting and energy-ridden as I would like it to be, as a kind of movie I want to see. I want to make it dramatic, I want to hit the points. I want to see the developments. I want to move on. I want to see the life, the arc of the life, the energy flowing. But as long as I don't violate it. That's the criterion I've used. I guess it's a not-to line. You know, a line that I don't want to cross because I don't want to violate the sense of truth.

Politics? You're asking if politics are like movies, I guess. I begin to wonder because the more you get involved in movies, the more surreal life seems when you see all the actors in Washington. You go to Washington, and you meet these politicians, and they're very good actors. And I think they have a good sense of what plays and what doesn't play. And that's what keeps them afloat.

So, I think that *Iraq* is a good movie of the week, in a sense that it makes the cover of *People* magazine. It's an event. It's exciting to the human theater. And we all are interested in politics, which has become really our interest in theater. A war is coming, we get all excited. The whole nation stands up. And all the newscasters get on. They're like critics at the feast, you know. And I wonder if politics and movies are not really the same thing.

Wilmington: Well, hasn't TV sort of made them the same thing? I mean, was Ronald Reagan really our president, or did he just hang around the White House and then hit his marks when he had a speech? . . . I suspect that were we to discover what Ronald Reagan really did during his eight years in the White House, we'd be astonished—we'd want the job, too. I think he probably did very little. What about that phenomenon where politics have become show business, where, to a certain extent, we're kind of ruled by TV images that sway us one way or another?

Stone: Well, not only images, but we're ruled by dramatic ideas that George Bush is really a screenwriter the way he gets it out. He just says the line, and he makes the point: "Read my lips" or "I'm going to make him into garbage, I'm going to eat him." And that's the way we all talk. We become actors in this scenario.

Wilmington: I was reading about the savings and loan scandal recently. And I remember about the flak you caught on *Wall Street*, when people said you're going too far and being too exaggerated. And now do you feel that maybe you didn't go far enough? It seems that these people were far more preposterous and really swinish than we could imagine.

Stone: No, I think I did the right thing at that time. I have a few qualms about that movie, still, but not about that nature. No, I saw that going on. And when we were doing the research, it was very clear that huge fortunes were being made. It reminded me very much of the movie I'd written called *Scarface* When I was down in Miami and I saw the same phenomena in *Wall Street* as I saw in Miami—one group was getting rich on coke and the other group was getting rich on stocks. And the principles were the same: make money.

AQ: There seem to be two schools of war films in Hollywood. On one hand, we have John Milius, who makes films that glorify war, and I believe that's his intent. And on the other hand, we have your films, and I think of *Platoon* in particular. I'm sure you intended it as an antiwar film, but any film with the Dolby sound and the bright lights does glorify war, does send young men into wanting to be in war. And now we have a war they can go fight [Operation Desert Storm]. How do you deal with this in trying to make a film that you know is going to encourage people into war, even though that's the exact opposite of your intent?

Stone: I don't think I'm as noble as you think in the sense as I set out to make an antiwar film. That's a very dull-sounding principle. I think I set out in *Platoon* to show an approximation of the truth as I remembered it because it bothered me that there was a big amnesia hole in our memory, our national memory, about Vietnam.

So I said, "Look, I was there. I saw certain things. I've never seen them dealt with. And I want to put it out there before I forget." It was ten years after, and I was already beginning to forget. So I wrote the script in '76, and it finally got made in '86, and so it was eighteen years or so afterward. You know, I really wasn't weighing the consequences of whether it was prowar or antiwar. I think my approach is much more barbaric. I was just trying to remember, on film, just as I was trying to show you what Wall Street was, the way I perceived it, just as I tried to show you *Born* and its barbarism. When I'm making a film, I'm not that aware of the message. I really am not. I hear about it later, but I'm not aware of it.

Wilmington: So, you're saying that there were good sergeants and bad sergeants? This was not a parable, this was your memory of the war?

Stone: Oh, yeah, definitely. It's also a parable, it can be both. It can be the truth and a parable, you know? The fact was that I was in three different combat platoons in Vietnam over a fifteen-month period. And I noticed in each platoon that I was in was fairly fractured, for want of a better word, between what I would call rednecks on one side and kind of hippie types on the other. You know, there were guys doing dope, and there were guys that were drinking beer; guys listening to country music, guys listening to soul music. Now that's a crude distinction because sometimes people would be in different camps. But I would say that one element was fairly racist about the Vietnamese.

The other element, which included a lot of blacks, it was not their war; they didn't have a beef with the Vietnamese—they just wanted to make it through the day. They counted their days, they'd smoke dope, drink, or whatever it would take to get through. So, I felt like each platoon I was in was fractured. When I went back to the United States, I felt the same thing was true in our country. Three parties in our country: those against the war, those for the war, and a larger element that was totally indifferent, the neutral people. But we couldn't be neutral in Vietnam because you were there. But, no, it wasn't a parable; it became a parable.

AQ: I know you're a Vietnam veteran because it says so, but in looking at you, looking at your career, you seem a very well adjusted person, a successful filmmaker. Was your experience in Vietnam somehow less traumatic than those we've seen on the screen, or is it just a miracle you recovered?

Stone: I think writing *Platoon* helped me a lot and *Born on the Fourth of July*. I think they exorcized certain things. I think I identified real closely with Charlie Sheen when he came out of *Platoon*. I think there's a lot of well-adjusted vets. Probably more than the ones you read about. I meet them all the time because I go around, and they come up out of the woodwork, and they introduce themselves, and they've done very well in life. I think it's a shame that a lot of people perceive Vietnam vets only as people who have problems, although a lot of them do. A lot of them have not come home.

Same Questioner: Maybe you should do a film about a well-adjusted vet so that the rest of us know this?

Stone: I've been told that by some well-adjusted vets.

Wilmington: In light of what you said, it reminds me that François Truffaut once said that the only true antiwar film would focus on the effects of war rather than the action. In other words, a film that showed the devastation and the aftermath, rather than the heat and the pitch of battle.

AQ: I've noticed in your films a great deal of camera movement, and I wanted to know whether the desire to go from one subject to another within a shot just comes from the gut, or is there a great deal of thought or deliberate contemplation that determines what you're going to go from and how it's going to interrelate with everything else in a scene?

Stone: I think I've got a screw loose upstairs. I hate rigidity. I could never shoot the Ozu style [the celebrated simple techniques of Japanese filmmaker Yasujiro Ozu]. I always saw life as moving. My perception of things is always on the move. There's very little time to stop and think. I appreciate calm, and I will probably practice more of it as I get older.

Often, the camera is a subjective point of view. In *Wall Street* it's always moving because we sort of wanted the camera to be a shark, you know, the predator mentality that never stops. It always has to move to eat to survive.

In *Born*, it was more fixed, but we would alternate. When his world became looser and looser, all the things that he knew, the camera was zinging around like mad. And then there would be moments when it would quiet down. He would be able to get a grasp on things in the second part. But then they start to come undone again. And then we tried to match the lighting and the movements to his inner state. But essentially the moves of the camera are dictated by the character of Tom, of Ron Kovic. I've always felt that the camera is a player. I've never had a feeling that the camera is watching as the audience is watching. I've always felt that the camera was a participant in the drama and, in fact, a character in the scene. If I'm here, he's here, you're there. It's a triangle right now. But when the camera is there, there's a fourth player, and all our thinking has to adjust to there being four people in the room.

AQ: Do you find it difficult to decide what the camera movements are going to be?

Stone: Sometimes I do, but often it just feels right. Often I may not know exactly what I want to do, but I know what's wrong. It's like I have a do-not-do-this kind of signal that goes off. And with some thought, or feeling, it does fall in. But sometimes I get right up on the day, and I change the movements because the rehearsal leads me in another direction. And then we shoot it that way, and it wasn't planned that way. So often me and my DP [director of photography] have some fights about that. But he's pretty loose, and he's been able to swing with spontaneous decisions.

AQ: Relating to what he's talking about—the camera movements. How many times have you worked with the same DP? And how aligned are your minds in shooting the film? That's one question. I have two others: Ron Kovic's reactions to some of your dramatic license—did he argue with you at times? Was he happy? Did he adjust his feelings about it? And the last question is: Did you see *Full Metal Jacket*? And what were your feelings about that concept of a war movie?

Stone: I did the smart thing. I hired Ron as a cowriter so I would avoid exactly those problems later on. I made him part of the crime in that he was involved from day one with me. I would sit with him, and I would talk through these things, and by the time we shot, he was one hundred ten percent there. He was a Marine again. As far as I know, he has never objected to the licenses taken. He knew about them. I think his biggest fear was always his mom, you know, "Gee, what's she gonna do when she sees this?"

Wilmington: What did she do?

Stone: She was furious. And it hurt him. But he didn't back down. I mean, we had it out a couple of times, but you see, he felt—he didn't get along with his mom after the war, for those reasons, and we had to show it. So, Ron alternates. He goes from confession to holding back to confession.

In answer to your other question, my DP has been Bob Richardson for six movies. I found him in documentary. He had done a documentary in [El] Salvador, and I hired him. And he's a great hand-held cameraman. He was thirty-two at that time, and we've sort of grown together. We've learned about films together, which is wonderful because he's like a younger brother to me. I hope we can continue our relationship like [director Bernardo] Bertolucci did with [cinematographer Vittorio] Storaro. I'd like to work with him for another fifteen movies, if I can. We fight, though. And there's always that sense on some movies that it does get pushed to the limit where, you know, you think the relationship is over. But we manage to continue.

Full Metal Jacket? I liked that first half very much. Thought it was great, the training section. I think the second half is metaphor. But for me as a veteran, it's away from reality, and I had a problem with reality things, so many I wouldn't have had as a civilian. But it didn't look like Hue, didn't feel like Hue. A sniper could never do that to a patrol, as far as I know. They wouldn't philosophize over the corpse of a sniper like that. These are realism things that bothered me, but I admire Mr. [Stanley] Kubrick. He's a great filmmaker. He was my hero when I was twelve years old and I saw *Paths of Glory* and [*Dr.*] *Strangelove*. I thought they were the greatest films. And he's always been a great influence in my life.

Ron Kovic and director Oliver Stone.

AQ: I'd like to reply to the gentleman who commented that he thought that *Platoon* was a glorification of war instead of just a realistic statement or maybe your experience condensed into a two-hour movie. I saw that movie for the first time while I was stationed at Fort Benning. We'd just come back from a long exercise, and my whole platoon went and saw this thing. And we just came away totally blown away from the whole movie and felt it was really realistic. It really shows that grunts will be grunts forever, you know. We're basically the same now as they were back then—it's just different circumstances. So I thought that the realism part was on. Maybe some of the events, some of the personalities, were condensed. But I felt it was really on. Also, can you express your feelings about the current situation in the Middle East and if it has any similarities with maybe the onset of Vietnam?

Stone: Oh, boy. Thank you for your comments. You're an infantryman, right? You asked me about the Middle East. It's a very tricky question. I've moved away from the beliefs that countries are fighting. I feel it's an issue about economics, and it's really about oil. You know, what is the United States, ultimately? I'm beginning to wonder. Is it a nation-state? Or are really big corporations running the world? I mean, the oil really does belong to the oil companies, their seven sisters. They are multinationals.

I would be concerned if Japan, France, England were not willing to defend that oil. Then something is askew. I would say to you, look beyond the country. Your president is a puppet, really, he's a figure. The American flag is a figure, a metaphor. But the old meaning of nations is changing, and it's been changing all this century. And I think that people like us can get smarter about this thing, and see the world in the terms almost of what Buckminster Fuller in *Critical Path* was talking about. That would be a worthwhile book to study. It really talks about the world the way it is, as opposed to all these little nations that are supposed to be fighting each other.

Wilmington: I'd like to jump in here and talk about the whole idea of politics into films. I'm thinking back to 1986, and how startling both *Salvador* and *Platoon* seemed back then, given the climate of the times, which was not only apolitical but empty of ideas. And it was a time in which most movies were sort of big emotion machines.

You were sort of swimming against the tide at that time, maybe not so much now. You have a number of people also swimming with you. But what about the whole problem of doing films like that within a huge monolithic industry that, during the 1980s, seemed to have become progressively more conservative? Was it less conservative than we thought? How were you able to do it?

Stone: No, those two films were very flukey, in a sense that they were financed, really, by an English company—a very small English company [Hemdale Film Corporation]. And they were financed off the back of the videocassette revolution, which came into full force in '85. So it was really a fluke. No American company would make *Salvador*. No American company would distribute *Salvador* when it was finished. They said it was anti–American and that it was a downer. And *Platoon* was made right after *Salvador*, again, by the British company. It was partly financed this time Orion Pictures, which is an American company. Orion put a very little amount of money in it. I mean we're talking a $6 million movie here. And they hedged their bet in various ways so that they were not at risk.

It was a very horribly conservative time in '85. It was interesting the break came. Reagan was riding high up until October, November, of '86, when the Oliver North scandal broke. That's when I sensed a shift in the mood, and *Platoon* came out the next month and was a huge international success. I felt that was the wind shifting, and Reagan was not going to invade Nicaragua after

December '86 although up until then, I really did believe that was going to happen. There would be another Vietnam in Nicaragua. Because I was down in Honduras, and these places, Costa Rica, and you saw the American reserves that were there. They were there ready to go into Nicaragua.

I was talking to the kids, too. They were exactly like me when I was nineteen years old in Vietnam. They were fighting the Commies in Nicaragua. So something happened in '86. But the film climate was terrible from '80 to '86. If you remember correctly, I think the only two dramas I remember from that period were *Missing* and *Raging Bull*, and they both died at the box office.

The big money was *Ghostbusters*, *Beverly Hills Cop*, the big-budget comedies. The Saturday night gang was in power, and they still are, [Dan] Aykroyd and [Eddie] Murphy. The big bucks were all into that kind of movie. They did not want to touch controversy. They did not want to see it. It changed, thank God, because of videocassette profits. Pictures like *Sid and Nancy* got made, *A Room with a View*. There were some hard-hitting films in that period from '86 on. And then it's still going because of Spike Lee and a few others. The videocassettes make the difference. But now, it's going the other way, because they figure the earning margins on the videocassettes will dip because all the salaries have jumped up. And the majors have basically usurped the independent position. People like me, that used to work for the independents in '85, are now working for the majors.

Wilmington: That's kind of a bad development in certain ways. Independents [brought] us this great source of vitality throughout a dull decade.

Stone: Well, it depends. I might have crossed over, and Spike Lee may have crossed over, in working for major studios, but we have final cut. We are making films of our choice, and will, until the time when we change or we lose our energy.

Wilmington: Well, what about the future? What about the Jim Jarmusches or the Spike Lees of the future? Not that Jim Jarmusch has been co-opted, because he maintains his independent position, but is there going to be that kind of feed in the future, do you think? Or is that door closed?

Stone: Well, it's a far better market than when I came out of film school in '71, when it was like six or seven major films being made a year by each studio, and that was it. It's a much better market. I mean, you can still make a movie cheap. I saw a picture the other day that blew me away. It was made for $130,000, which proves that it can still be done. It was called *Henry: Portrait of a Serial Killer*. It's an amazing film, and it was done by young director [John McNaughton], who's not so young anymore. He lost six years of his life making it. And it's just an amazing movie. And it shows you that you can still make a movie cheap with just an idea and a few faces, a room, and a car. [Steven] Soderbergh did it with *sex, lies, and videotape*. You don't need that much to get a new idea across. So, I'm hopeful. And I think that there's more money around to make those kinds of movies than ever.

AQ: There were quite a few references to *Yankee Doodle Dandy* in the movie, and George M. Cohan, and the movie ends with [Cohan's song] "Grand Old Flag." I mean, was that conscious on your part, or was it just coincidence? George M. Cohan was born on the fourth of July.

Stone: Ron was called that by his mom. That was in the book. "He's my little Yankee Doodle Dandy." That was sort of his nickname in the house. That's why we used it. It's also because I like it.

AQ: You don't make antiwar movies, but when I saw *Platoon*, I thought of *All Quiet on the Western Front*. And I noticed the book [*All Quiet*] was shown in this movie. I was wondering if you have any thoughts about why such great works of art that have shown the truth about war somehow don't work and don't prevent us from getting into war after war.

Stone: Well, *Grand Illusion* was made on the eve of World War II, was it not?

Wilmington: Jean Renoir specifically made *Grand Illusion* to try to stop a conflict between France and Germany because he was trying to reawaken the camaraderie on both sides that he's witnessed at the end of World War I. He made the movie and it was a worldwide hit. It happened to be the favorite movie of [German field marshal and Nazi Party leader Hermann] Goering, and did nothing to stop the war. It just shows us a lesson about human nature, and about art, and about what survives and what doesn't.

AQ: Even though it's important to tell the truth about these things, the truth is somewhat ambiguous. What happened in Vietnam and Cambodia after we left—that wasn't so great, either. The antiwar movement tended to be black and white. And the government tended to be black and white. And the truth was somewhere in between.

Stone: I think you're right. But, you know, I know the argument. I went back to Vietnam. And I know the argument about the boat people and this and that. But the fact is, we did escalate the situation insanely from the 1950s on. We did move into a position which the French abandoned. In fact, we supported the French financially in their colonial war against Ho Chi Minh. I still say we could have made a good deal with Ho Chi Minh back in 1946. That goes back to, I think, a very good intelligence in our foreign policy. George Washington did say we must only make treaties with countries that are in our national interest. Well, what is in our national interest? Is the war against Communism in our national interest? That hard question was never asked in the 1960s when I was growing up. It was never asked. It was assumed. As a result of that we paid the price, which I don't think makes sense considering what happened in Vietnam. And what were we fighting in Vietnam for? Was it oil? Rice? I don't still know. I think Adolf Hitler would sit through a film and say, "I'm against war." But if he feels he needs Czechoslovakia, he's going to grab it, because in his thinking, you can only think subjectively.

And there are certain wars, let's face it, that have to be fought. I would not like to go against the Blitzkrieg or Hermann Goering or Adolf Hitler in their prime. I'd be scared of them. But who's going to take them on? There are certain people that have to fight people like Hitler; otherwise, they'll conquer the world. So, I think certain wars are justified. That's why I can't say, point blank, I'm antiwar. That's a simplification. That's an idiotic statement, in my opinion. We're all antiwar.

AQ: I was curious just to see, visually, whom do you like as painters?

Stone: Millet, Van Gogh, Pollock. I like Julian Schnabel. I like Picasso. There are dozens. But I really don't know if that correlates to film. I mean, I do it the best I can. I do throw colors on. I like to mix contrasts in varied styles and go to extremes.

Wilmington: I guess we have to end on a question that can't be answered, which is sort of typical of life. Thanks.

Stone: Thank you, Michael.

For Further Study

Videocassette

Born on the Fourth of July is available on videocassette from MCA Home Video.

Books

Hickenlooper, George. *Reel Conversations: Candid Conversations with Films' Foremost Directors and Critics*. New York: Citadel Press, 1991.

Kovic, Ron. *Born on the Fourth of July*. New York: Pocket Books, 1976.

Worrell, Denise. *Icons: Intimate Portraits*. New York: Atlantic Monthly Press, 1989.

Periodicals

Biskind, Peter. "Cutter's Way: Film Editing Isn't the World's Most Exciting Job, But Oliver Stone's Movies Add a Certain . . . Pizzazz." *Premiere*, February 1990.

Canby, Vincent. "At Close Range: The Human Face of War." *New York Times*, January 21, 1990.

Chutkow, Paul. "The Private War of Tom Cruise." *New York Times*, December 17, 1989.

Collins, Glenn. "Oliver Stone Is Ready to Move on from Vietnam." *New York Times*, January 2, 1990.

Corliss, Richard. "Tom Terrific: In His Fiery New Film, Hollywood's Top Gun Aims for Best-Actor Status." *Time*, December 25, 1989.

Dutka, Elaine. "The Latest Exorcism of Oliver Stone." *Los Angeles Times*, December 17, 1989.

Fisher, B. *"Born on the Fourth of July." American Cinematographer*, February 1990.

Goldman, Ari L. "Ron Kovic Today: Warrior at Peace." *New York Times*, December 17, 1989.

Maslin, Janet. "Film View: Oliver Stone Takes Aim at the Viewer's Viscera." *New York Times*, December 31, 1989.

Scheer, Robert. "Born on the Third of July." *Premiere*, February 1990.

Seligmann, Jean, and Larry Wilson. "Lifestyle: Heroes with Handicaps." *Newsweek*, January 15, 1990.

Sharbutt, Jay. "New Film Brings the Old War Home Again." *Los Angeles Times*, December 17, 1989.

9

HORTON FOOTE
AND
Tomorrow
(with Jerry Roberts)

On November 1, 1990, screenwriter and playwright Horton Foote was interviewed by Jerry Roberts after a screening of *Tomorrow*.

The Film

Tomorrow (1972), a Filmgroup Production. Directed by Joseph Anthony. Screenplay by Horton Foote. Based on the play *Tomorrow*, by Horton Foote, from a story by William Faulkner. Produced by Gilbert Pearlman and Paul Roebling. Director of photography, Alan Green. Editor, Reva Schlesinger. Music by Irwin Stahl. Filmed in Tupelo, Lee County, Mississippi, and Itawamba County, Mississippi.

Cast: Robert Duvall (Jackson Fentry), Olga Bellin (Sarah Eubanks), Sudie Bond (Mrs. Hulie), Richard McConnell (Isham Russell), Peter Masterson (Lawyer Douglas), William Hawley (Papa Fentry), James Franks (Preacher Whitehead), Johnny Mask (Jackson and Longstreet), Effie Green (Storekeeper), Ken Lindley (Judge), R. M. Weaver (Jury Foreman), Dick Dougherty (Buck Thorpe), Jeff Williams (H. T. Bookwright), and Jack Smiley, Billy Summerford, and Thomas C. Coggin (Thorpe Brothers).

Synopsis: In the early part of the century in Yoknapatawpha County, Mississippi, a laconic cotton farmer named Jackson Fentry is the lone juror who refuses to vote to acquit a man named H. T. Bookwright of the charge of murder. Bookwright shot and killed the notorious Buck Thorpe. Through the narration of Bookwright's lawyer and via flashback, we learn that 20 years earlier, young Fentry ran a sawmill at rural Frenchman's Bend, and there, in winter, took in a sick, pregnant woman named Sarah Eubanks. After a time, he married her. Sarah died after childbirth. Fentry raised the boy as his own and named him Jackson and Longstreet after two Civil War generals. A few years later, Sarah's brothers, the Thorpes, took the boy forcibly from Fentry. Back in updated time, after Fentry's stern and terse refusal to vote for Bookwright's acquittal results in a hung jury, the judge declares a mistrial. The lawyer narrates: "Somewhere in Buck Thorpe, the adult, the man that Bookwright slew, there still remained at least the memory of that little boy, Jackson and Longstreet."

Remarks   and   Reviews

"One can hardly fail to praise the film on its own terms. *Tomorrow* is simply one of the best independent productions in the recent history of American narrative film" (Bruce F. Kawin, *Faulkner and Film*).

"The special beloveds are the unexpected films, the 'sleepers' that arrive without fanfare, are viewed without expectations, and make an indelible mark on memory and heart. *Tomorrow* is such a film" (Judith Crist, foreword, *Tomorrow & Tomorrow & Tomorrow*).

"This type of film, sensitive, quiet and truthful, is almost impossible to sell; it suffers because of its integrity and fragility. . . . Probably the best two-character drama since *Midnight Cowboy*" (James Delson, *Show*).

"Every once in a while a film comes along of such rare beauty and compassion that it makes other films look like empty celluloid exercises. *Tomorrow* is that kind of film" (Louise Sweeney, *Christian Science Monitor*).

"Warm with human compassion and finely acted . . . humanity registers profoundly, thanks to the finely honed dialog provided by Foote and the trick-free direction of Anthony" (Land, *Variety*).

"[Duvall] shows almost no surface emotion, yet projects the torment and tenderness of a man who bends to misfortune the way a tree does" (*Playboy*).

"Bellin is brilliant . . . best ever screen presentation of [Faulkner's] work." (*Leonard Maltin's TV Movies and Video Guide*).

"Duvall turns in one of his many virtuoso performances. . . . Beautifully scripted by Horton Foote, who creates a realistic atmosphere of the era" (*The Motion Picture Guide*).

"The movie explores loneliness, love, devotion and dignity with notable artistry and integrity" (William Wolf, *Cue*).

"I still point to Fentry as my favorite part." (Robert Duvall, 1985).

The   Filmmaker

Horton Foote won Academy Awards for the screenplays of *To Kill a Mockingbird* (1962) and *Tender Mercies* (1983). He was nominated for another Oscar for his screenplay of *The Trip to Bountiful* (1985). As the author of the ambitious and honored play series called the *The Orphans Home Cycle* and as one of the best-remembered teleplay writers of television's early years, Foote is among America's most distinguished, versatile, and prolific dramatists.

Many of Foote's plays are autobiographical, often reflecting his familial roots in his native Wharton, Texas. His illuminations of the rural southern past and of family matters in Texas have some parallels to the usually more rustic and explosive entanglements afflicting Faulkner's characters in Mississippi. Aside from the film of *Tomorrow*, Foote adapted Faulkner's prose on three occasions for television: *Old Man* for a 1958 *Playhouse 90* production directed by John Frankenheimer and starring Sterling Hayden and Geraldine Page; *Tomorrow* in 1960, also for *Playhouse 90*, starring Richard Boone, Kim Stanley, and Charles Bickford; and *Barn Burning*, starring Tommy Lee Jones in 1980 for the PBS series *American Short Story*.

Foote is also a stage director and former actor. He studied acting at the Pasadena Community Playhouse and with the American Actors Company in New York. At age 28 in 1944, he saw his first play produced on Broadway, *Only the Heart*. His plays include *Texas Town*, *The Trip to Bountiful*, *Tomorrow* (based on the teleplay), *The Traveling Lady*, *The Road to the Graveyard*, *In a Coffin in Egypt*, and *The Habitation of Dragons*. *The Orphans Home Cycle* is comprised of *Roots in a Parched Ground*, *Convicts*, *Lily Dale*, *The Widow Claire*, *Courtship*, *Valentine's Day*, *1918*, *Cousins*, and *The Death of Pape*. Foote's only novel is *The Chase*, which was adapted by Lillian Hellman for the 1966 Arthur Penn film of the same name, starring Marlon Brando, Jane Fonda, and Robert Redford.

Foote's many teleplays include *The Roads to Home* for *The United States Steel Hour*; *The Shape of the River* for *Playhouse 90*; *Expectant Relations*; *The Trip to Bountiful*; *The Midnight Caller*, *The Dancers*, and *A Young Lady of Property* for *The Philco Television Playhouse*; *Nights of the Storm* for *The Dupont Show of the Month*; an adaptation of Flannery O'Connor's *The Displaced Person* for *American Short Story*; and *The Habitation of Dragons* for TNT's *Screenworks*.

Foote performs the voice of Jefferson Davis in Ken Burns's documentary, *The Civil War*. Foote's late wife, Lillian Foote, was a film producer. Their children, Hallie Foote and Horton Foote, Jr., are both actors. Hallie Foote stars in three of the films that have been made form *The Orphans Home Cycle*, which are *1918* (1985), *Courtship* (1986), and *On Valentine's Day* (1986). She also starred with Brad Davis and Frederic Forrest in the teleplay *The Habitation of Dragons*.

Horton Foote's Filmography

Storm Fear (1955); *To Kill a Mockingbird* (1962, from the Harper Lee novel); *Baby, the Rain Must Fall* (1965, from his play *The Traveling Lady*); *The Chase* (1966, from his novel, adapted by Lillian Hellman); *Hurry Sundown* (1967, cowritten with Thomas C. Ryan); *Tomorrow* (1972); *Tender Mercies* (1983); *The Trip to Bountiful* (1985, from his play); *1918* (1985, from his play);

Courtship (1986, from his play); *On Valentine's Day* (1986, from his play *Valentine's Day*); *Convicts* (1991, from his play); *Of Mice and Men* (1992, from his play adapted from the John Steinbeck novel).

Reasons for Selection

Not the least of my reasons for showing and discussing *Tomorrow* has been my abiding appreciation for the writing of Horton Foote. I also have fascinations for southern culture, in particular for William Faulkner and Mississippi, and for the dramatic anthology programs of early television, where Foote's first version of *Tomorrow* was seen.

I was impressed by the movie's fidelity to the spirit of Faulkner, particularly with regard to rural southern penury and that breed of men that Faulkner calls "the lowly and invincible of the earth," a phrase preserved by Foote in the screenplay. The film has a beautifully evocative pictorial simplicity and an austerity that accommodates both stark reality and Faulkner's peculiar literary portraiture of Yoknapatawpha County. The performances by Robert Duvall and Olga Bellin are brilliant.

Although the obscurity in which *Tomorrow* dwelled for years has been chipped away by critical championing, and another book has been written about it, it remains one of the "lost" classics of the recent American cinema as well as one of the most precise and reverential movies ever made from the works of any of the American literary masters.

—J.R.

The Interview

Jerry Roberts: "Tomorrow" was originally published in the *Saturday Evening Post* in 1940, and it was later published in *Knight's Gambit*, which was a volume of the Gavin Stevens mystery stories which William Faulkner wrote about the fictional territory he created, Yoknapatawpha County, Mississippi. Bruce F. Kawin, who wrote the book *Faulkner and Film*, made a case that Faulkner was the most cinematic of novelists. But Joseph Anthony, who directed this movie, said that Faulkner was practically impossible to transfer to film. And, my first question for Mr. Foote—who first adapted *Tomorrow* for television on *Playhouse 90*—is, how did you address the specifics of transferring William Faulkner's literature into drama?

Horton Foote: Well, I had done one other Faulkner work for *Playhouse 90*, *Old Man*, and it had a great success in the sense that it repeated three times and everybody was very pleased with it. And, so, I thought, that's about all the Faulkner I was going to do. And then Herbert Brodkin, who was the producer, sent me this story. And I thought, well, this is kind of typical, you know, we struck oil once, and now they want to try it again. And I was very skeptical.

I read the story, and I couldn't connect with it, really. I liked the story, but I didn't know how to get into it. I was taking a walk—I was living down by the Hudson River—and I was taking a walk after reading the story. And in the story—which is essentially about the relationship between Jackson Fentry and the boy—there's about two paragraphs about a woman, whom he describes as black complected and doesn't name her.

We hear through narration that she was the mother of this child, and that she appeared and disappeared. I began thinking about her, to tell you the truth, and I just became fascinated with her. I became nervous about this because usually in adapting, I'm not that bold. I kind of reconstruct certain things. But I gave her a name, Sarah Eubanks, and I became kind of obsessed with her. Really, that's how I got into the story, by trying to figure out who she was and how she got there. Then I started writing from that point of view.

Of course, it was first on television, live television. It has, essentially, never changed too much. Of course, there are things that we were able to do in film that we couldn't do then. Live television was much like the theater in that we were restricted. For instance, we couldn't move people because the camera restricted us. We had to cut from scene to scene and have them in the scenes. In other words, we had not the fluidity that you see here.

And then some years passed, and Herbert Berghoff, who has a theater in New York, a small theater—I've always loved it—he asked me if I would like to do it with him as a play. And we did it as a play with Olga [Bellin] and Bob Duvall. And it was a limited run, but very successful and moving. Duvall and Olga, both of them were very moving. And so Gilbert Pearlman, who's one of the producers—and is here tonight—and Paul Roebling came to me about doing it as a film. And I thought, well, I've done it twice now—what else can I do?

But I was so moved by those two performances, and I was so anxious to see them recorded, really, that I began to rethink it. I really think I've found the form I like best of the three forms it's taken, which is the film form. And I don't quite agree with Joseph Anthony. I think Faulkner is very cinematic. I think you have to find his world and not try to exaggerate that world or to goose it up, as so many, I think, of his adapters have done. You have to respect the dignity of the people, no matter how inarticulate they are or how taciturn they are in their responses. And I, of course, was greatly helped by Anthony in his feeling for the lives of these people.

Roberts: The genesis of the film *Tomorrow*, then, was through Mr. Roebling and Mr. Pearlman?

Foote: He's right there. Stand up and let him see you, Gilbert.

Roberts: Mr. Pearlman, good evening. Mr. Roebling and Mr. Pearlman gave you the opportunity—

Foote: They gave me more than that. They really introduced me to independent filmmaking. Because up until then, I didn't think—I didn't realize

Johnny Mask and Robert Duvall in *Tomorrow*.

—that one could make a film outside of the studio, which was an enormous revelation for me. And it changed my whole life because I've never stopped trying to do that with all its difficulties. We made the film—I think this is right, Gilbert—for $400,000. It took a lot of sacrifice and a lot of love on everybody's part. But, of course, I think that's how films should be made. And there was enormous dedication from every level.

The other thing which interested me in seeing the film, again—I haven't seen it for a while—was there was an enormous pressure put on us to not do it in black and white. And I didn't have the pressure so much, but the producers did have it. And they were told by distributors that it would limit them terribly, and if they would only use color, that it would have a much wider audience. But they felt, and I think myself in seeing it again, that it was a very wise decision. They wanted it to have a certain look, and they decided to go ahead and shoot it in black and white.

Roberts: Well, I hope Ted Turner never gets a hold of it to broadcast it on television. You were involved through much of the production, obviously in the preparation and on the set during the making of the film and in postproduction. And this is extremely rare in moviemaking for a screenwriter. What were the contributions [throughout these processes] that you made personally on this picture by this allowance?

Foote: Well, I had worked with Anthony, the director, a lot before, when we were training. I was an actor at one time, and we were trained by the same teachers, so we spoke a common language. I was on the set all the time, and you know, I put in my two cents if I didn't think things were right. But mostly I really was nodding approval.

As far as the editing was concerned, I was there. And always welcome. But at that time, I'd had very little experience in editing. So, really, I just kept my mouth shut and learned and realized how many wonderful things could be done in an editing room. There was a lot of editing and a lot of hard work in the editing room. And it was a great education for me.

Roberts: Olga Bellin gives such a great performance in this movie. And I was just wondering, I looked up her career in various film sources and, basically, *Tomorrow* is what's there. I mean, she's such a tremendous actress.

Foote: Oh, she's dead now.

Roberts: Oh, she is?

Foote: Yes, she died several years ago. She was a tremendous actress, but it's one of those things.

Roberts: Your history with Robert Duvall began way back in the fifties at Sanford Meisner's Neighborhood Playhouse and has continued all the way through with every few years something wonderful coming out of it. And we've been blessed with *To Kill a Mockingbird* and *Tomorrow* and *Tender Mercies*. Could you talk a little bit about how you came to know Duvall?

Foote: Well, I used to take Sandy's classes when he would go off and do a job, directing plays with his advanced students. And he was doing a play of mine and called me up and said that I should come and see this young man who had been in the Korean War and had started rather late for an acting student. But there he was, and he was doing this play of mine. Robert Mulligan, the director of *Mockingbird*, was in town, and Kim Stanley, who was a friend of mine, was here. My wife and Mulligan's wife and Kim and I and Bob went to see this play. And I was rather nervous because, you know, they were students, really. I thought, I hope I'm not getting Mulligan and Kim into something that won't be too interesting for them.

In any case, Sandy had done a wonderful job directing and the whole play was interesting, but this young man who was Robert Duvall, came out and he played an alcoholic, a total alcoholic, an alcoholic that was so devastated that, in the course of the play, he commits suicide. And we were all just thunderstruck by the brilliance of this work. And I said to Sandy afterward, "It's remarkable." And he said, "You want to know something even more remarkable?" And I said, "No." He said, "He doesn't drink or smoke." And I said, "How in the world did he ever find these things?" Well, he went down to the Bowery. And he just observed and watched.

I mention this because, as I work with Bob, he has an enormous capacity for investigating other people and finding a way to project himself into their lives. Now, the accent he uses [in *Tomorrow*], which throws off some people,

I think is wonderful. He heard it when he was a boy in Tennnessee. And he remembered it, and he told me. He said, "This man has this bovine kind of way of talking." But he was insecure about it for the film, but it worked wonderfully in the theater.

So he went down to Mississippi about a month before shooting. Nobody knew who he was. He wasn't a well-known actor at the time, in any case. And he just lived down there talking this way all the time. And he decided that the accent was OK, that people accepted it.

And, then, in *Tender Mercies*, he did the same thing. He went all over Texas and, finally, in East Texas, he told me, "I found a man that I think talks like Mac Sledge." And what he would do was record the man. He would call up the man and send him the lines for the scene that he was going to work on, and ask him to make tapes of them, and the man would send them back. Now, he doesn't literally copy all of this, but it does help him. And he's a master at it, really.

Roberts: I thought it was great, the accent.

Foote: So what happened was, we were casting *Mockingbird*, and we needed somebody for Boo Radley. Mulligan called me and asked me if I had any suggestions. And I said, "Well, not really." Then my wife reminded me, as she often does, that we'd seen this remarkable actor. And, of course, I took all the credit for it. I called up Bob, and I said, "I think I have . . ." And, of course, he'd seen the play with Duvall. That was the beginning of our work together. We've just finished a film together.

Roberts: *Convicts*.

Foote: We've done about nine things together.

Roberts: You have said that this movie [*Tomorrow*] restored your faith in the movie business.

Foote: Well it restored my faith in human beings, I think. Because I realized that everybody in this world isn't motivated by greed. I mean, people were there, really, out of a sense of devotion and love. And I feel that's a very strong motivation too often lacking in our profession. And it just gave me great courage. It made me fall in love with my profession all over again.

Roberts: And we've gotten from that *1918* and *On Valentine's Day* and *The Trip to Bountiful* and now *Convicts*. But in the early days, your first introduction to movies, I believe, was *Storm Fear*.

Foote: That was a long time ago.

Roberts: That was with Cornel Wilde in 1955, and then following that, you were sort of among what was known as the great innovators — writers for television during what has been called the Golden Age of Television — among them Tad Mosel, Robert Alan Aurthur, Paddy Chayefsky, Rod Serling. You were writing for *Playhouse 90* and then —

Foote: *Philco/Goodyear* first [the weekly alternating shows, *The Philco Television Playhouse* and *The Goodyear Theatre*].

Roberts: *Philco/Goodyear*, yes, where *The Trip to Bountiful* was first broadcast with Lillian Gish. Then I believe the next step in movie work was *To Kill a Mockingbird*. How did that come about?

Foote: Well, I'd worked with Mulligan in television, and I'd not worked with [producer] Alan Pakula, but he offered me something to do, and I didn't feel I wanted to do it. And he wanted to do *The Chase* [Foote's only novel]. He wanted to do it badly. And the day he came with his offer, we sold it to Sam Spiegel. But he said, "Could I please tell you my ideas if I was going to produce it?" And my agent and I sat and listened to him, and he was fascinating. And I've often wondered how my life would have been had he done *The Chase* rather than Sam Spiegle. But, in any case, he didn't get it. But I thought he was very bright and again, had a great passion about whatever he was doing.

So *Mockingbird* came along. I don't really like to adapt too much. It's painful in many ways to do. They sent me the book, and I stalled around. Again, my wife read the book, and she said, "You better sit down and read this book." I did and I liked it. So I called him and said I was interested. "But the first thing," I said, "why isn't Harper Lee doing this?"

They said, "Well, she doesn't feel she can and doesn't want to." So they said, "The only thing is for you to meet with Harper Lee, and if you all get along, then it's yours. You're our choice." And so, you know, I hadn't great experiences as a screenwriter in those days. Harper and I met, and we became very close, and are very close friends. And so I was hired, and I worked on it.

And this is another thing, I was very bold. I said, "I don't really want to work on the coast because my family's in the East." And so Alan said, "That's fine with me." So there's this whole new breed of screenwriter starting. When I first started in Hollywood, you had to punch a clock, and you had to sit in this little old office in the studio. They wanted you there where they could watch you.

Roberts: Real creative circumstances.

Foote: Well, a lot of creative things came out of it. But, in any case, I liked it better in my attic in Nyack [New York] with Alan Pakula driving out. And we would work on the script. He's very knowledgeable about film. He'd had much more experience than I had, so I learned a lot from him. We did a number of drafts, really. Then we felt it was right, and we said this was the first draft — really it was about the fourth draft. Gregory Peck read it, and he said to Alan, "Come on now, is this really the first draft?" Well, anyway, it was our first official draft.

I learned a lot because of two things. One thing I got from a review of *Mockingbird* by a very good critic [R. P. Blackmur], called "Scout in the Wilderness." And he compared it in a way to *Huckleberry Finn*, which is a favorite book of mine. And that helped me to solidify some ideas I had.

Then Alan said to me, he said, "You know, you can't be too reverential, because the novel has a long time span." I think it's three or four years. He said, "I think we should just put it into four seasons and make it one year." Which freed me to reconstruct in my own mind and kind of architecturally take it apart and put it back together again. And that was very freeing to me. It was those two things, really, that helped me to get inside the novel. There's that point, you know, where you have to stop being respectful and say: Well, this is really mine now; just make your mistakes, whatever you do, and just go ahead and do it.

Roberts: After that there was *Baby, the Rain Must Fall*, with Steve McQueen. And then, as you wrote in the foreword to [the book] *Three Screenplays*, you became disillusioned with the business.

Foote: I guess they also got disillusioned with me. I think it was a mutual disillusionment. I don't think I was just so pure. The material they wanted me to do sometimes didn't interest me. And I had some interesting experiences. But, for instance, *The Chase* was my original work, and then Lillian Hellman was hired to do the screenplay, which was fine for me. But she said quite openly that she was using it as a departure. And she departed so far that, you know, I didn't know why they bought the work to begin with. It has its merits and a lot of people liked the film, and that's fine.

But I suddenly felt that I was losing control as a writer. I didn't know what was happening. You buy something, then you change it radically, and I just never have been that kind of a team player, I suppose. I recognize this, though, and do, I hope, work well as a team player when I'm in sympathy with what's going on. But I just don't like the title Writer for Hire. It offends me very much. And as you know, the American screenwriter is the only writer that doesn't control his copyright.

Many years ago, before film talked, I suppose, writers didn't care and the studios began to control the films through the copyright. Whoever owns the copyright really owns the film. So, through custom, it's just been taken away from us. I felt, actually, very frustrated and just decided that, until *Tomorrow* came along, I really didn't want to work in film.

Roberts: In a *New York Times Magazine* piece that was published a couple of years ago, a very lovely story by Samuel Freedman—a feature story on you—he points out about screenwriters that there are hardly any cases in the history of American film where a screenwriter has built a filmography in which almost every single one of those films bears the signature of the screenwriter and not of the director, not the star. The outstanding characteristics of the writer are there. Your films are Horton Foote films, and they're [about] Horton Foote's world, as opposed to anybody else who's involved in the film. Now that's a fairly outstanding achievement among screenwriters, and it's evident in almost every frame of your work.

There's a faith in the material by the other filmmakers. Obviously, there is control of your own writing, but how do you go about ensuring this?

Horton Foote (photo credit: David Spagnolo)

Foote: Maybe it's not being too bright, I don't know. You just kind of bow your neck. Well, no, I'm being superficial about this. Thank you, if that's true. I'm not sure. I've had enormous help. I mean, I've been so fortunate in the actors I've worked with, and the directors I've worked with. They've liked my world, whatever this world is, and are very supportive of it. They find a way, I think, to bring it to life. I think whatever success I've had, I owe greatly to them.

But I do think that the time is coming when the film writer finds a way to take the responsibility, to share the responsibility of the films. I think it's too bad that so many writers are divorced from the product—the minute they finish the script. I think they would learn a great deal, and also be very helpful to the film, if they could take part in the whole process. I'm now in the editing room—and actually have asked contractually that I share the final cut, which isn't always easy to come by. You have to trade off things to get that kind of bargain. But I worked for it.

Roberts: At the age of seventy-three—

Foote: Seventy-four.

Roberts: Seventy-four. You are busier than almost at any other time in your life. And just for a few credits, you just did a draft of a television movie. *Dividing the Estate* is on the stage in Cleveland. *Convicts* is in the can, starring Robert Duvall and James Earl Jones. *The Widow Claire* is being prepared for a movie by Joyce Chopra. And *Talking Pictures* is being produced onstage by Peter Masterson in Houston. And you did the voice of Jefferson Davis in Ken Burns's *Civil War*. To what do you attribute this sudden flurry of work?

Foote: I don't attribute it. I just get up in the morning and go to work. First of all, I think I'm nineteen. I don't think I'm seventy-four. I just feel very privileged, and I don't know why this is. You know, I work every day, and I would write if nobody did anything of mine. I would continue to work. Fortunately, some people are interested in the various things—people that I respect and who give me a great deal of support.

I think this is the thing that is so wonderful about the projects that I've been involved with—for instance, *Dividing the Estate*. This was an extraordinary ensemble company of actors. I had been a little disillusioned lately with the theater. Films had been kinder to me than the theater. And I fell in love with the theater all over again. But that's because of what people bring to the work.

Then there's the work itself. It is a collaborative medium, and it's nice to have the plays printed, but you know they don't come alive until your directors and the actors and the producers get in there and make it happen. And I'm very grateful for that.

Roberts: There was a point, though—it was written about and this has been discussed before—back after [your initial Hollywood experiences], in the sixties or seventies, where you were disillusioned.

Foote: *Disillusion* is the wrong word. Sam [Freedman] put that in there [the *New York Times Magazine* piece], and it's nice reading. But actually I wasn't disillusioned. It's just that I didn't really understand the sixties. I mean, I was fascinated by the sixties, and I was interested in the sixties, but, you know, four-letter words and taking off your clothes really weren't my style.

I didn't object to that, and I wasn't horrified by it, but I just decided to go into the country and work on some plays. And it was true. There were maybe five minutes when I said to my wife, "I'm not going to continue this,

I'm going to sell antiques." And she said, "No you're not. You're going to get right back in there and start writing." But that was, really, very momentary. And, you know, I was working on *The Orphans Home Cycle*, and I wrote *Tender Mercies* at that time. And, all of a sudden, they were producing me again.

Roberts: You've done a lot better at the writing than I assume you would have done selling antiques.

Foote: Well...

Roberts: Could you talk a little bit about *The Orphans Home Cycle*?

Foote: It's nine plays that I began to work on after the death of my father, really. I worked on it for about two and a half years, and some of them have been produced in the theater, and some of them are now films. *Convicts* is part of that cycle. It takes place over a span of years. I wrote them out of sequence. And they have been produced as plays out of sequence, and as films out of sequence. So, although I call it a cycle, and someday I hope all nine will be done in the theater as well as on film, it's not in that sense a series. Each of them is an entity that stands on its own.

Roberts: Since *Tender Mercies* in the eighties, there seems to have been a concentration on films.

Foote: Well, theater, too, except that the theater is now all over America, and I've had a lot of productions, two in New York, off Broadway, *The Habitation of Dragons* in Pittsburgh. But film—I have become passionately fond of film. There was a time I would think that theater was my first passion. But now I hate to give up either one. And just the whole idea of achieving a world in film is very exciting to me.

Audience Question: Well, I just wanted to say that it seems to me that your life and work has had a kind of common sense that seems to have eluded most people in the film business, in that you've worked independently so that you could have a sense of control in your work. You've remained true to your voice, even though for a period of time it wasn't popular. You've been loyal. I noticed Peter Masterson—I'd forgotten when I saw this originally that he was an actor in this and, since, a director for you [Masterson directed the films of *The Trip to Bountiful* and *Convicts*]. There's Robert Duvall. Your family has pulled the cable on your shows—this I know. All of that. But even beyond that, you, I know, involved yourself. You've always been in acting classes. And I wondered if there was some place that you're going these days. I know that Peggy is gone.

Foote: Peggy Feury he's talking about, who was a great, great force here in Los Angeles. She had a studio called the Loft Studio, and many of our finest film actors trained with her on an ongoing basis.

Same Questioner: And I just wondered what you're doing these days, to acting class?

Foote: Well, not any place, unfortunately, and it's a great lack for me because ever since I first came to Los Angeles, I'd go up to Peggy's studio. She had a remarkable way of working. She would take one playwright and have everybody in her studio work on scenes. And she did that with the nine plays [*The Orphans Home Cycle*]. It was a marvelous way of working. I learned a great deal from seeing different actors play different parts. I'm not rigid in that sense. I welcome whatever an actor can bring.

And I often think that, with [*The Trip to*] *Bountiful*, if I were rigid, I have long since gotten over it because I can't think of two more different in-struments, or talents, that Lillian Gish and Geraldine Page. And Lillian first did it in the theater and was remarkable and wonderful. And, of course, Geraldine did it in the film, and I thought she was remarkable. But they were so different it was like a cello and a flute. But you realized what an enormous contribution a great talented actor can bring to work.

And this is the gift that I used to get from Peggy. She had a way of exciting people—never asking, but showing you the possibilities, and opening up the craft for you, making you realize what people can contribute. No, I miss her greatly.

AQ: Horton, I know you've directed some of your work in the theater and have considered [directing] on other occasions. What has you kept from direct-ing your own work on film?

Foote: Well, on two films, I have worked with the actors. But it's an enor-mous journey. First of all, to stay with a film from beginning to end as a direc-tor takes an enormous span of time, and I really haven't had the time. And I don't know that I really feel competent to do it. I don't know that I know technically that much because, you know, a director spends his life learning all these various things. I'm really, essentially, a writer. I have worked with ac-tors, and I know a little bit, I think, about the acting process. And I have strong opinions about what is up there in the editing room. I can stomp and holler like the best of them. But, really, as long as there are talented directors like Joe Anthony or Peter Masterson or Bruce Beresford, I'm very happy. That suits me fine.

AQ: Mr. Foote, you had mentioned this evening that you hardly recog-nized Lillian Hellman's screenplay of your story [*The Chase*]. My question is have you ever had any response from Faulkner to the two little paragraphs you spotted that you blew up to create Miss Eubanks?

Foote: Well, actually, what happened was that when I did *Old Man*, I had heard that he liked it. I had never met Faulkner. I was almost afraid to meet him. I admired him so much, I thought it was best to keep my distance. Now, when I did this, I was very nervous because, really, the whole first half is an invention on my part. But he did like it, I was told. And more than that, he did a very generous thing. He allowed me to share the theatrical copyright. In other words, you have to get his estate's permission and my permission ever to do this in the future, which is almost unheard of. So, I felt that shows what an enormously unselfish man he was.

Then I finally did *Barn Burning*, which was just an hour thing for *American Short Story*, but he was gone then. But I have since taken part in a Faulkner seminar that they have each year at the University of Mississippi. And I have to say — this is immodest — but this is their favorite of Faulkner's works. That pleased me. And they said he liked it a lot, too. So, I trust he did.

I'm very fond of [the adaptation of] *Barn Burning*, except for the end, which is just something that takes place in this little boy's mind. And I didn't feel that I was able to solve it. I don't think you can solve it. It's that kind of introspective thinking aloud that's almost impossible to do in film. I think that [John] Huston in [his 1988 adaptation of James Joyce's] *The Dead* came as close to it as anybody that I've ever known.

AQ: I wonder if you would indulge me in a question that's not about you. But could you tell me what Harper Lee's personality is like? And why she never wrote anything else? I mean, that's my favorite novel and movie, too. Then she never wrote anything else, and I wonder why.

Foote: Well, I've never asked her. I see her, and we talk. She's a very private person, and she has a wonderful sense of humor. As a matter of fact, I hadn't seen her for about ten years. I was lecturing in Mississippi, and I just decided to call her up in Alabama. I called, and her sister answered the phone, and she said, "No, she's not here, but she's going to be back." Then I said, "Well, say I'm going to call back." So, when I called I said, "Harper, this is Horton." And she said, "Well, do you still have all your teeth?" And I said, "Yes, do you have yours?" "Yes," she said. I said, "I'm gray as a fox." And she said, "So am I."

Well, we took up our friendship again. And she's a very secure woman and lives very well. She has a little place in New York, and she goes to Alabama. And she probably is writing. I doubt that she's not writing. But I don't think she has this kind of drive that so many of us have, that's really tormenting. But she's just very secure. And, you know, we talked about many things. Everybody asks me about her — every reviewer, everybody — and I just don't know about her writing, and I would never ask her. But I have a hunch something's going to come out one day. I'm sure she's working.

AQ: Mr. Foote, would you comment on any spiritual element that you see in your worldview and [in] the things that you write?

Foote: I'm often asked that question. And whatever is there that people pick up, I'm delighted. But I don't approach it that way. In other words, I try to be faithful to the world that I'm creating. And, for instance, whatever their morals or spiritual or religious values are, I try the best I can to show those. In other words, whatever my own beliefs are, I don't try to proselytize or try to impose them on the characters. My writing comes out of observation. I've grown up in what was mostly the Protestant South. Now, we have all kinds of persuasions, so to speak. But so many of my characters reflect the Protestant South. But I get that from the characters rather than imposing any sense of my own beliefs.

AQ: I just have a quick question for you. I'm wondering are you related to [historian] Shelby Foote [author of the three-volume *The Civil War: A Narrative*]?

Foote: Yes I am. We're third cousins.

Same Questioner: All right. I won a bet.

AQ: Most of the dialogue was fairly brief and sparse through the film tonight. There were a lot of really long scenes that were about subtexts and were very nice mood pieces. How would that translate to today's film industry, where they're after scripts that run exactly one minute to a page? Would that script have been shorter than one hundred twenty pages?

Foote: Was this script shorter than one hundred twenty pages? I can't answer that now because it was done so many years ago. No, I think it was longer. Actually, I think a lot of it was cut in the editing. That's where I learned the power of the editor, and they have great power.

Same Questioner: I have a technical question as well. When you're writing, how much of the scenes that have no dialogue are actually your written scenes? Like the scenes with the rain, the whole opening scene?

Foote: Those I did for the film. They were not in the original. The whole rain sequence was something I did for the film because I very much wanted to get a sense of the seasons and the changing, of these people being in this kind of physical world and being at the mercy of the cold. The cold, always, was the theme that I developed, which was not in the [Faulkner] story because of Sarah Eubanks. And watching it, you see that Joseph Anthony has great security as a director. If I were directing, I don't know that I would have dared to let people deal with this much minutiae that I see he allowed them to deal with. I think it took great courage, and, of course, I think paid off in the end. But those activities I put down. What he did with those activities was something else. He extended them and elaborated on them.

Same Questioner: Well, the sense of the seasons was just ideal. I'm from that part of the world. It was just—I was there all the way, I went through the whole winter. It was just wonderful.

Foote: Yes, it's nice.

AQ: I know that early on in your playwriting career in New York, you worked with Agnes De Mille and you worked on pieces that combined dance, theater, and music. And I just wondered, how did that influence your later work?

Foote: Well, I don't know consciously how it did. It must have because I learned another kind of structure, I think from them because dancers have their own sense of structure. And, of course, I think one of the greatest dramatists we have is Martha Graham, who is an enormously talented storyteller, but she has her own way of structuring. You just have to rethink if you're working with dancers. You just have to accept their world, which is not abstract, although it tends to be thought of in that way—but it's very specific what they do. And I did learn a great deal with them. I worked a long while with dancers. But this kind of work, I just have to let it bleed through. It really doesn't serve me because the whole structure is different here.

AQ: Yes, Horton, in many of your plays the flu epidemic is a recurring thematic catalyst for much of the background for the play. Did you yourself endure that as a child?

Foote: I was here on earth, but I was only a year old, so I have no memory of it. It's one of those oral traditions, you know, that's handed down. It was very vivid to me from my memory of it. It's like I've been through it, but I never really experienced it. That epidemic in 1918 was the second largest disaster in the whole world. I mean, I think the Black Plague may have killed more people, but it killed more people than all the world wars together. It was just devastating. And so, I had very vivid storytellers around me as a child. And they would dramatize it so it was almost better than living through it because I didn't have all the pain or all the drama.

Roberts: Someone was asking about worldview. Just to close, I'd like to say that what your films collectively mean to me is that there are people in the face of heartbreak who can come up with gentleness and grace and faith. I sort of relate it to a lot of the things I've seen you do. I'm happy you're doing it. I just feel no one else is doing the kind of thing you are. I'm happy seeing Horton Foote's world.

Foote: Thank you. Thank you very much.

For Further Study

Videocassette

Tomorrow is available on videocassette from Monterey Movie Company.

Books

Faulkner, William. *Knight's Gambit*. New York: Random House, 1949.

Foote, Horton. *Three Plays "Old Man," "Tomorrow" and "Roots in a Parched Ground."* New York: Harcourt, Brace and World, 1962.

_____. *Three Screenlays: "To Kill a Mockingbird," "Tender Mercies" and "The Trip to Bountiful."* New York: Grove Press, 1989.

_____. *Tomorrow*. New York: Dramatists Play Service, 1963.

Harrington, Evans, and Anne J. Abadie, eds. *Faulkner, Modernism and Film*. Jackson: University Press of Mississippi, 1979.

Kawin, Bruce F. *Faulkner and Film*. New York: Frederick Ungar Publishing Co., 1977.

Yellin, David G., and Marie Connors, eds. *Tomorrow & Tomorrow & Tomorrow*. Jackson: University Press of Mississippi, 1985.

Zinman, David. *Fifty Grand Movies of the 1960s and 1970s*. New York: Crown Publishers, 1986.

Periodicals

Benson, Sheila. "Robert Duvall's Vein of Troubled Loneliness." *Los Angeles Times*, March 6, 1983.

_____. "*Tomorrow* Returns, Still a Jewel." *Los Angeles Times*, September 28, 1983.

Chase, Chris. "Quick—What's This Man's Name?" *New York Times*, April 23, 1972.

Faulkner, William. "Tomorrow." *Saturday Evening Post*, November 23, 1940.

Freedman, Samuel G. "From the Heart of Texas." *New York Times Magazine*, February 9, 1986.

10

RICHARD BROOKS

AND

The Professionals

(with Charles Champlin)

On January 29, 1991, director and screenwriter Richard Brooks was interviewed by Charles Champlin after a screening of *The Professionals*.

T h e   F i l m

The Professionals (1966), a Columbia Pictures and Pax Production. Directed, written, and produced by Richard Brooks. Based on the novel *A Mule for the Marquesa*, by Frank O'Rourke. Director of photography, Conrad Hall. Music by Maurice Jarre.

Cast: Burt Lancaster (Dolworth), Lee Marvin (Fardan), Robert Ryan (Ehrengard), Jack Palance (Raza), Claudia Cardinale (Maria), Woody Strode (Jake), Ralph Bellamy (Grant), Joe De Santis (Ortega).

Synopsis: A wealthy American hires four soldiers-of-fortune to rescue his wife, who has been kidnapped and taken to Mexico.

R e m a r k s   a n d   R e v i e w s

"The title is accurate. This action–Western ... has the expertise of a cold, old whore with practiced hands and no thoughts of love. There's something to be said for this kind of professionalism: the moviemakers know how to provide excitement and they work us over. We're not always in the mood for love or for art, and this film makes no demands, raises no questions, doesn't confuse the emotions. It's as modern a product as a new car; it may be no accident that Ryan, the man in this Western who loves horses, is treated as some sort of weakling" (Pauline Kael, *5,001 Nights at the Movies*).

"Dust storms and Lee Marvin's boozing binges got production of this Western off to a slow start, but it was also Marvin who taught Italian actress Claudia Cardinale the rudiments of riding. All the lead players in this expensive effort had served as enlisted men in the marines or army, causing Marvin to muse on the fact of "all those millions riding on the backs of Pfc's." At age fifty-three, circus acrobat Burt Lancaster performed all his own stunts, including his cliff-scaling sequence" (John Eastman, *Retakes: Behind the Scenes of 500 Classic Movies*).

"Far-fetched story, but real action and taut excitement throughout; beautifully photographed by Conrad Hall" (Leonard Maltin, *Movie and Video Guide 1992*).

"After the *Lord Jim* excursion, it is good to see Brooks back on his own professional form, filming the tight, laconic sort of adventure which usually seems to bring out the best in Hollywood veterans" (Penelope Houston).

The Filmmaker

Richard Brooks won an Academy Award for writing *Elmer Gantry* (1960), but his film career spans five decades, beginning with his screenwriting work in the early forties. He coscripted *Key Largo* (1948) for John Huston and went on to write and direct box-office hits such as *Blackboard Jungle* (1955), *Cat on a Hot Tin Roof* (1958) and *Sweet Bird of Youth* (1962). *The Professionals* earned Brooks two Academy Award nominations, for best director and best screenplay adapted from another medium, and the film was ranked among the top ten Western films at the box office. Brooks's stylistically daring adaptation of Truman Capote's *In Cold Blood* (1967) was a landmark film of the sixties, and Brooks continued to aggressively tackle tough and controversial material with his adaptation of Judith Rossner's best-selling novel *Looking for Mr. Goodbar* (1977) and his vigorous direction of the dark political satire *Wrong Is Right* (1982), based on the novel by Charles McCarry. Brooks's last film is the gambling drama *Fever Pitch* (1985).

Richard Brooks's Filmography

As writer: *White Savage* (1942); *Cobra Woman* (1944); *Brute Force* (1947); and *Crossfire* (1947, John Paxton adapted Brooks's novel, *The Brick Foxhole*).

As director and writer, except where noted: *Crisis* (1950); *The Light Touch* (1951); *Deadline U.S.A.* (1952); *Battle Circus* (1953); *Take the High Ground* (director only, 1953); *The Flame and the Flesh* (director only, 1954); *The Last Time I Saw Paris* (1954); *The Blackboard Jungle* (1955); *The Last Hunt* (1956); *The Catered Affair* (director only, 1956); *Something of Value* (1957); *The Brothers Karamazov* (1958); *Cat on a Hot Tin Roof* (1958); *Elmer Gantry* (1960); *Sweet Bird of Youth* (1962); *Lord Jim* (1964); *The Professionals* (1966); *In Cold Blood* (1967); *The Happy Ending* (1969); *$* (1972); *Bite the Bullet* (1975); *Looking for Mr. Goodbar* (1977); *Wrong Is Right* (1982); *Fever Pitch* (1985).

R e a s o n s   f o r   S e l e c t i o n

Richard Brooks has a long and distinguished filmography: *Elmer Gantry*, the Tennessee Williams adaptations, *Looking for Mr. Goodbar*, and many others, each film about something, each marked by high craftsmanship and an aura of the filmmaker's particular fierce dedication.

I chose *The Professionals* not least because it was one of Brooks's favorites among his own work and because I think it's one of the very best of what we might call the modern Westerns — Westerns which are no longer either literally or philosophically in black and white. It is Brooks at his best, creating a muscular adventure whose plot is full of surprises and whose characters are both varied and remarkably dimensional. As usual, Brooks's strong private sense of right and wrong underscores the story, although where and in whom the right and wrong reside are the questions the story untangles in very dramatic terms indeed.

— C.C.

T h e   I n t e r v i e w

Charles Champlin: Richard, *The Professionals* was based on the novel. How much of the novel did you keep, and how much did you lose?

Richard Brooks: Well, not much of the novel. When I got to Mexico and looked around, I called this guy. He lived up in Washington, somewhere. And I said, "Where's this hacienda?" And he said, "I don't know." I said, "What do you mean, you don't know?" He said, "I've never been to Mexico. I wrote the story in El Paso." I figured I was free, then.

Champlin: I was just kind of curious. It was made in, what, the early sixties, 1964 or something like that?

Brooks: In '64 we shot it, yes. I think it was released in 1965. [Editor's note: It was released in 1966.]

Champlin: I was curious about what it cost.

Brooks: Oh, well, this all was done in about four and a half million. Amazing, isn't it? Of course, I wasn't paid.

Champlin: You weren't paid?

Brooks: No, not much.

Champlin: This was made in which studio?

Brooks: Columbia. And I was lucky. That cast — they were all professionals. They were real pros.

Champlin: It looks like it must have been a hard shoot.

Brooks: Oh, yes, it was. The horses and the wranglers and the whatnot. The fact that we didn't lose any horses — we were lucky. And, of course, there was a lot of good, good work in there.

Champlin: Where were you shooting?

Brooks: We shot in five deserts: outside of Las Vegas, to the southeast in the Red Rock Canyon, Death Valley, Arizona, and Mexico.

Champlin: It looks hot.

Brooks: Oh, it was hot. It was hot. But you realize that in that whole picture there was only one drop of blood, and that was on Robert Ryan's shirt. And I thought that was pretty good.

Champlin: Yeah. It was remarkable. And great music, too, I must say.

Brooks: Oh, yes, Maurice [Jarre] did a marvelous job. He was terrific.

Champlin: Richard, I understand you began as a newspaperman. And you did a radio-writing job? I remember you told me once that you wrote five fifteen minute radio shows a week.

Brooks: News shows, yeah.

Champlin: News shows?

Brooks: News, yes. That was in New York. You see, they were going to pay $30 a week. And what I was making at the *World Telegram* was $17. So I took the job. But the radio station had no wire, so I had to rewrite the papers.

Champlin: Ah. But then you came out here, I guess? And you were writing radio plays out here, weren't you?

Brooks: Yes. Yes. I came out here. And, as usual, I had met a couple of actors in New York from Hollywood. And they said, "When you get out to Hollywood, don't call anybody until you call me." And, of course, when I did, they said, "Well, how long you gonna be in town?" And I never heard from them again. So I decided to go home. I was driving down—in those days there were no freeways—and I was trying to get to Sunset Boulevard, where—that's what you used to follow out to get on the highway [Route 66]. And as I passed on the corner of Vine and Sunset, there was NBC. A long gray-blue building or something. And some guy yelled "Brooks" as I drove by, and I stopped. It was a guy from an advertising agency. He said, "Where you going?" And, I said, "I'm going home," meaning back to New York. And he said, "Well, why don't you stay out here and work?" So we went in to see somebody at NBC. He knew a few people, but they had more than enough newscasters. But there was a guy there—Andrew Love was his name—who said, "Do you think you can write a short story every day?" I said, "Yeah, I can write. You talking about originals?" He said, "Yes." I said, "If I steal, sure." So, I said, "What'll you pay?" He said, "Twenty-five dollars a day." So I took the job. I worked there for one hundred eighty-two stories.

Champlin: Amazing.

Brooks: I began to dream about just doing one story. Finally I heard of some guy over at Universal—a producer by the name of Waggner with two g's—so, I went over there. And he said, "Well, we're doing a terrific story here, starring Maria Montez, Jon Hall, and Sabu. Do you want to work on it?" And I said, "Sounds pretty good to me." He says, "What do you get paid?" Well, I had just read a short story by [James] Farrell called *A Thousand Dollars a*

Week." So, I said, "A thousand dollars a week." He said, "I'll call you." I went back to work for NBC. Two weeks went by, and I called him and I said, "What happened?" He said, "Hey, I'm the producer. I get only two hundred a week." I said, "All right." So I took the job. Anyway, I wrote one more that was called "White Savage." Then I wrote something called "Cobra Woman." Then I went back to writing short stories for NBC. And they called me and said, "C'mon over, I want to talk to you." So I went over. And he said, "Do you want to? We're going to do another one with Maria Montes, Jon Hall, and Sabu. Name me a desert." I said, "There's a lot of deserts." He said, "Yeah, well, name one." I said, "Well, how about the American desert?" He said, "No, the bad guys would be the Indians. I don't want that—cowboys and Indians." I said, 'Well how about the Turkish desert?" "They got one?" I said, "Yes." "What kind of story?" I said, "Hey, I don't even know what kind of story we're working on." Finally, we went out to the Turkish desert, the Australian desert, and finally he didn't want to do the Chinese because they had just made *The Good Earth*. So finally I said—and this is the windup—I said, "Why don't we do the one in North Africa?" He said, "OK." So I went and got some *National Geographics*. And it turns out that there was a pretty good idea in one of them, which was that they sent two ships—mail ships from Calcutta or someplace in India. One was to go around the Horn of Africa to London, and the other one was to go to Suez, where they threw the mail packet on a camel. And then Maria Montes, Jon Hall, and Sabu rode from there to Alexandria, where they put it on another boat. The [Suez] Canal was going to be built there, [and this was] to prove there was a shorter route. You know, a Western in Egypt.

Champlin: Right.

Brooks: So, the guy reads the story and he says, "You let me down, boy." So I go over to see him. And he says, "Where are the Riffs?" I said, "The Riffs had nothing to do with the canal." He said, "No?" And he took me to the projection room, and he showed me a movie called, the title of it was *Suez*, with Tyrone Power and Annabella, I think.

Champlin: Right, yeah.

Brooks: And, sure enough, in the first reel, six guys in white sheets drive up and blow up the canal. Well, it turned out that they were not Indians and they were not Egyptians. It turned out at the end of the picture that they were the British trying to stop the French from building the canal. So he calls his boss—a guy by the name of Jack with a very loud voice. And he said, "Jack, I think we got the Pony Express in Egypt." And he said, "Well, what else is it about?" And he says, "Well, it's about the Suez Canal." And this guy yells back over the phone, "The Suez Canal? When does this story take place?" And he says to me, "Hey, when does this story take place?" I said, "About 1836." "Jack, 1836." Jack yells back, "Well, when the hell was that?" And, so, I went that day, and I got on a trolley car and went downtown, and I joined the Marine Corps. I was away for three years.

Champlin: You were writing screenplays over at MGM. How did you make the break to becoming a director?

Brooks: I was working with John Huston in the [Florida] Keys on a picture called *Key Largo*. John said to me one day, "Ever seen a movie made?" And I said, "No, they don't allow writers on the set." He said, "Well, I think I'm going to have you on the set for this one. They won't pay you, but at least you'll see how a movie is made." So they gave me a little table in the back of the stage, and every time John wanted a rewrite, there I was. And there were a lot of them. Now, one day, I said to John, "What'll I do if I don't have you to direct a movie?" And he said in that voice of his [*mock-Huston*], "Well, kid, you'll have to direct it yourself." That's what I had to do. The next day the cameraman came up to me at the little table. Who was the cameraman? The German cameraman? Marvelous cameraman. And I'll think of his name, maybe. And he said to me—I won't attempt his accent—And he said, "I hear you are becoming a director?" I said, "Karl"—because his name was Karl Freund—I said, "Karl, it would be a good idea, but I don't think it's going to happen that fast." He said, "Tomorrow I give you your first lesson in direction." It seemed he had directed in Germany. And so the next day he came and brought a little brown bag and inside were two 16 mm movies. I took them home, and I ran them on my projector at home, and they were terrific. They were two porno movies. I ran them twice. And next day I brought them back, and I said, "They're terrific, Karl." He said, "I'm producer, I'm not actor. I direct a little bit on this, yes." And, you know, there were the guys who wear the black socks and the sideburns. One had one lady and two men and the other had an animal, a man, and a lady. Well, anyway, he said, "What's the lesson in direction, Karl?" He said, "You watch these very carefully?" And I said, "Yes, Karl, very carefully." "You are sure?" I said, "Yes, Karl! Yes! I watched them very carefully." "It's very important!" he said, "You see, when you get to be a director, you will say to yourself every day, where do I put the camera? Under the table? Up in the ceiling shooting down? Where? You sure you watched these pictures carefully?" I said, "Yes, Karl." He said, "Well, this is the lesson. When you're directing your first picture, just get to the fucking point!" And to this day I think of that whenever I make a setup. Is it extraneous or not? That's how I learned to direct. Then I went to MGM. And then Elly and a bunch of the guys over there brought me over. And they told Mr. Mayer that I would stay there and write if he would let me direct my own movies. He said, "Of course." So the first picture I wrote was for Clark Gable. I didn't know it at the time, but Mr. Mayer called and said, "You know who's going to star in this picture? Clark Gable." I said, "That's great." He said, "But, we've got a little problem. Problem is, he's the biggest star we have. You've never directed a picture. It would be a disaster. So the next one." It took me a year, and I wrote another script. I think it was called *Mystery Street*, about a case that took place on the beach in Boston. Anyway, I got a call from Mr. Mayer. I go to see

Mr. Mayer, and he says, "We've got a problem. Do you know who's going to star in this picture? Montalban." I said, "That's very good. That's good casting." He said, "So you see, he's never been a star, and you've never directed a movie. Next time." Next time I worked about seven months on a script. And somebody brings me over to meet Cary Grant. And he thought I was the guy who had played the detective with the short hair. What was his name? On the radio? "Just the facts, ma'am."

Champlin: Jack Webb.

Brooks: Jack Webb. Because I had a short haircut, he thought I was Jack Webb. I said, "No, no." And he said, "I know your name. Brooks. Brooks something. Are you a real writer?" I said, "Yes." He said, "You just wrote half a script that's not too bad." I said, "We've got a problem, Mr. Grant. If you want to do it or not, I've got to direct it." He says, "How do you get along with people?" I said, "OK." He said, "All right. I'll do it." That hour I became a director. That's how it happened.

Champlin: There's a wonderful story because at one point you were watching a dolly shot, and the dolly ran over your foot?

Brooks: Oh, yes. Yes. That's when we were shooting the picture. I didn't trust the cameraman because he told me the very first day, "I can't stand you. Here you've just come into the studio for three or four years, and they give you a picture to direct. I've been here thirty years, and every year they promise me and nothing happened." Well, so, when I made the shot I would walk along. If it was a dolly shot, I'd put my hand on the camera to see that they didn't change my marvelous composition. This was a shot of Cary Grant and José Ferrer. And in the middle of the shot, suddenly it's over. And, I said to the operator, "OK for camera?" And he said, "No. There was a terrible bump." It seems that the camera had kept going. I stopped and the camera kept going. And it was riding on two planks; two-by-twelve-inch planks—those were the tracks. He said, "No, there was a bump." But the bump was that it ran over my foot. So Cary Grant is running toward the camera. And I said, "Well, OK, let's line up for the next one. Or, let's do it again." And Cary Grant said, "The camera ran over your foot. I saw it." He said to Howard Koch, who was the second assistant, "Take him to the hospital." Now, in those days at MGM on that street there was a funeral parlor on one side and a little hospital on the other. I said, "I'm not leaving the stage." And Cary said, "Why not?" I said, "Cary, if I leave the stage to go to the hospital, in five minutes they'll have another director here, and that'll be the end of me." And he said, "Well if that's the end of you, it'll have to be the end of me because I'll walk off the picture." So they took me to the hospital. They took some stills to make sure nothing was broken. And that's what happened on that dolly shot.

Champlin: [Cary] Grant was a terrific guy.

Brooks: Oh, terrific, yes. As a matter of fact, he was the guy who said, "You know, you've got some Spanish-speaking parts here. There are a lot of fellas who were silent picture stars who can't get a job. Why don't you give them a job?" And I said, "Like who?" He said, "Gaucho. You remember" — what's his name, they used to call him Gaucho. Gilbert Roland was one and the guy who rode the chariot in the first *Ben-Hur*.

Champlin: Ramon Novarro.

Brooks: Ramon Novarro. And then another guy from the silent picture days who did serials. He said, "Give them a job." So I gave them a job. They were marvelous. They were terrific. But that was Cary.

Champlin: That was an interesting film. I don't know if many of you have ever seen it. That was called *Crisis*. And José Ferrer plays a South American — or someplace — dictator who needs brain surgery. And Cary Grant is the brain surgeon who goes down. It's a no-win situation. If the guy dies, he's in trouble. And if he lives, he may be in trouble for kidnapping.

Brooks: Well, that's what they kept telling him: "When you go into operate doctor, if the knife slipped a little, who would know?" Because he was a terrible dictator. And it was, really, the basis of the story was the ethics of a doctor who was called upon to save the life of a man whose politics he cannot stand. And how it works itself out. That was the first movie I ever directed.

Champlin: It's interesting to see your career. I mean that was, I guess, 1950 or something like that? And how you evolved along with the changing...

Brooks: Times ... yeah.

Champlin: Changing times and the things you could do in pictures. I mean, it's amazing to think of *Crisis*, or even *The Professionals*, which was twelve years later than that. And then up to *Mr. Goodbar* and then *In Cold Blood*. I mean, did it feel like a great advantage to you? I should think to finally do these, and then go back and do a couple of those [Tennessee Williams] things, again...

Brooks: And also *Blackboard Jungle*, with that music. It was the first rock music ever used in a movie. Yes. And *In Cold Blood*. I said I would make the picture. Truman [Capote] brought the book to me. I said I would do it, and that I wanted to do it in black and white, not color. And in those days they were trying to get all the pictures in color because they were afraid television wouldn't play them. Well, here I am in Kansas the day before we started shooting, and one of the heads of the studio suddenly appears. I'm in the diner with a cameraman having a cup of coffee in the morning before we went up, the day before to set the locations. And this guy drives up in a limousine with Jeff Chamberlain from Technicolor. And he says, "I want to talk to you. Why can't you make the picture in color?" And they keep calling me from New York, and I don't know what to say to them. And I said, "Well, color would be wrong for this picture because this picture has to do with the nature of fear, and to me, fear is black and white, not color." And he said, "Well, what if I told you that I could get you Paul Newman instead of these two kids? Nobody knows them [Scott Wilson, Robert Blake]. Who the hell knows them?" So, I said, "Well, [you] can't do that, Mike." You got Paul Newman and the doorbell rings at this Kansas farm at three in the morning. And the farmer goes down to open the door to see who it is. And he sees Paul Newman. And he says "Paul, have a cup of coffee." I said, "You can't do it." He said, "Do you mind if I call [Truman] Capote?" I said, "Go ahead." He said, "You got his number?" I said, "Yes." So, he went to the wall phone in the diner, and he called Capote. He told him about the black and white and the color, and why can't we have it in color, it would be a better-looking movie, etcetera. Truman evidently asked to talk to me, so I went to the phone. He said, "Is that what you told him?" And I said, "Yeah, that's what I told him." He said, "Put him on the phone." So I said, "Mike?" He went back to the phone, listened for about thirty seconds, and hung up. What Truman Capote had told him was: "Let the guy alone, or I'm going to the *New York Times*." That settled the issue right then and there.

Champlin: Terrific. Listen there's one story that you told me a while ago that I just loved. And it's the time you directed Winston Churchill, and that whole story.

Brooks: Oh, yeah, yeah. Well, that was the picture in Africa, in Kenya.

Champlin: *Something of Value*.

Brooks: *Something of Value*. And I thought, you see, when I was doing the story the first one who met me was a black fellow who was with the Mau Mau. This was in the hotel in Nairobi. And he said, "Your script is all wrong." I thought, "Jesus, how did he get the script?" I ran into the room, opened the suitcase, and the script was still there. I said, "How did you? Why did you say that?" And he said, "Would you like to talk to Professor [Louis B.] Leakey? Maybe he can convince you." Now, Professor Leakey lived about eight or ten miles outside of Nairobi in a little farmhouse, and this guy drove me out there. And there's Professor Leakey. He said, "Your script is all wrong." I said, "Did you read the script?" And he said, "No." I said, "Well, how would you know?" He said, "Well, if it's like the book, it's going to be wrong." "Oh," I said, "Why is that?" He said, "Well, the guy who wrote it [novelist Robert Ruark] stayed in the bar all day for four months. That's where he was when he wrote the book." He said, "Now, if you want to know the truth, you should meet the Mau Mau." Now the war is on at that time. All the Pangas, and all that beheading, and everything. And I said, "Meet the Mau Mau?" He said, "Yes. I'll arrange it." So I took Sidney Poitier, who was in the movie, and Rock Hudson. We got in a car. And this guy, a Scottish officer, drove us through the hills up to Mount Kenya into a camp. There were the Mau Mau. We talked for a little bit. And what I wanted to know was how they did the sacrificial oath, and so on and so on. They told me to go see Jomo Kenyatta, who was in prison. I said, "I will. I'll go tomorrow. Is it all right if we talk now?" And the guy says to the Scottish interpreter, "He wants to ask you a question." I said, "What's that?" He said, "He wants to know"—this was the chief—"he wants to know how are things in Little Rock, Arkansas?" That was the time that the governor was standing at the doorway of the school and wouldn't allow any blacks to enter the school. Then I went to see Jomo Kenyatta. They allowed me to see him in prison, and we talked about half an hour. And he said, "This story is really a story about Africa. And if you want to get the real story, get a book by Churchill." It was written in 1911 or '12 — something like that. And I did, and I read it. It was a strange place, Nairobi. I was trying to get Sidney Poitier a room in the hotel. And they told me, "Mr. Brooks, we can't do that. They work here, but they can't stay here." I said, "This guy is an actor. Things are different for actors. Besides which, he's a friend of mine, and I'd like him in the hotel. If he doesn't stay in this hotel, I'll have to move to another hotel." And Rock Hudson says, "I'll move with him." "Well," he said, "you know, I don't own the hotel, Mr. Brooks, I just manage it. I'll talk to the owners." And so the next day I came in from location hunting, and there he is waiting — the manager — and I walked down the hallway, and there's a room just like mine — down the hallway — and he says, "How's this?" I said, "Very good." I said, "What changed your mind?" "Well, you told me this black actor is getting $30,000 for this movie." I said, "Yes. What about it?" He said, "Well, you said he's going to work twelve weeks?" I said, "Yes." And he said, "Well, any black man who gets $30,000 for twelve weeks' work is not black." And that's how that one was settled. When I got back to England, I decided that I'd try to get Mr. Churchill to do an opening for the movie. And I kept calling him and couldn't get him on the phone because he was in the South of France at Somerset Maugham's house, painting. One day, I get a call, and I go up the river, the Thames River, to the castle on the river [Blenheim Castle]. And that's Churchill's place. "What do you want me to do?" he said. I said, "I want you to be at the opening of this movie. Say whatever you want to. Talk about your book, whatever." And he said, "Well, how do we do this?" And I said, "Well, we'll have two cameras, and I'll give you a sign, and you talk for as long as you want to talk — thirty seconds or three hours — it's OK with me. That's what we did. We recorded him, and he talked for about forty-five seconds, close to a minute. Well, I get back to America, and we put this piece with Churchill on the front of the movie. And we take it out to Encino to a preview of it. And the next morning, we're supposed to meet in Mr. Mayer's office while all the experts discuss the show. And there they were, and I show up. And one guy jumps up and says — that was [Eddie] Mannix; he was the head bouncer at the studio — and he says, "Before we start talking about this movie as though it were a serious talk, you gotta get that fucking Englishman off the movie. Otherwise people will think it's a British picture and nobody will go and see it." And I said, "Well, you're talking about the greatest statesman in the history..." And he said, "Hey — off." So when the picture opened, Mr. Churchill was gone. I came back to the studio about twenty years later to make a movie, and I asked Roger Mayer, who was the head of the lab at that time,

"Did you ever find a piece of film that ran about forty-five seconds to a minute of Churchill?" He said, "You mean that African picture with the Mau Mau?" I said, "Yeah." He said, "I'll try to find out." And he found it. And so on my 16 mm I have Churchill.

Champlin: Earlier, just before the film started, we were chatting. Can you tell the *Godfather III* story? I guess that's been in print, but I've never seen it.

Brooks: I had just finished making *Looking For Mr. Goodbar* at Paramount. And Barry Diller, whom I liked because at least he's literate, he can read, walked into the office and said, "Here's a ticket to Miami. Go." And I said, "Go to do what?" He said, "Mr. Bluhdorn wants to see you. Don't ask me about what because I don't know." I said, "You're really serious about this?" He said, "Yes." So, I get on a plane, and I fly to Miami. I get off the plane, and I don't see anybody I know, but there's a guy with a sign: Brooks. He gets my bag, he checks me out. I get into his car, and he drives—not away from the airport but around to the other side of the airport, where they have smaller planes. And some guy comes out and he says, "Are you Brooks?" I said, "Yes." He said, "I understand you drink vodka?" I said, "Yes." And so he handed me a glass of vodka. I said, "This is my wife. Who are you?" He said, "Bluhdorn." I said, "You're Bluhdorn?" He was about twenty-seven. Bluhdorn was about fifty-seven. He says, "That's my father." And he puts me on this small plane, a small jet plane, with about six or eight seats, gives me another vodka, and we fly over the water. And it's getting dark. Finally, we land near the jungle. And that's the Dominican Republic—half of which he owns, and the government owns the other half. I said, "Why am I here, Mr. Bluhdorn?" He said, "Tomorrow." I said, "Can't you tell me why I'm here?" "Tomorrow, I'll tell you tomorrow." So he took me to the hotel that night. The next morning that big car calls, and we drive out to Mr. Bluhdorn's house, which is kind of a large ranch house, and he says to everybody there—and he had thirty servants or so, or people who served him—and he said to everybody, "Out, everybody out." And they left, including his wife, his daughter, his grandson, and I don't know. And then he hands me a script. And I said, "What is this?" And he says, "I want you to read it." I said, "You brought me down here? You kidnapped me into this goddamn island? You could have mailed it to Hollywood. I would have read it there." He says, "No, no. I want you to read it here." I said, "Where do you want me to read it?" He said, "Wherever you want to. You want to sit in the sun?" So I sat in the sun at the pool. I'm reading the script, and he's watching me through a pair of binoculars from the second floor. Finally, I finish reading the script, and I'm pretty slow at reading, and he's right by my side right away. He says, "So? What did you think?" Now, Puzo had written the script. And it's *Godfather III*. And I said, "Well, it's very good, very good." You know, that's what they want to hear right away. I said, "But it's not for me. *Godfather II* finished off the story for me, but now maybe there's another story to tell, but this is not it." I said,

"Besides which, why do you want to make three?" He said, "Well, the first two were very successful. So, we'll make a third one." I said, "I see." I said, "Well, why don't you get the man who made the first two? He made two big, successful movies. Get him to make number three." He said, "I can't stand him. I hate him." Meaning Coppola. He says, "When I tell you who I can get you to play the young man in this movie, you'll jump at it and do it immediately." I said, "Who?" What the hell was the guy's name?

Champlin: John Travolta.

Brooks: I said, "John Tavolta?" I said "Well, I hate him even more than you hate Coppola." Anyway, I go back to Hollywood, and, eventually, they made *Godfather III*. Now, I haven't seen it yet. I'm afraid to go see it.

Champlin: That was 1975? Wasn't it? Or something like that?

Brooks: That was '75, yeah.

Champlin: It's been in the works a long time. We have some questions from the audience.

Audience Question: You said these lead actors were all very professional. Define what you mean by being professional.

Brooks: Oh, yes, they were. Well there are a number of things: Number one is that they were always prepared. That's one thing. And they didn't make believe that they were executives or something. They were actors in a movie. And they behaved. They were always on time. They had respect for the other people. And in a case like with Marvin, who's a real expert on guns—God, there isn't anything he doesn't know about a gun. And, if they didn't know something, I told them to ask Marvin about guns. But I didn't want them to kill themselves, which they could easily have done. The only trouble I had—and Marvin himself behaved very well—there was this lawyer who kept coming around on the set when I was about sixty-five miles southeast of Vegas. And it turned out to be that lawyer.

Champlin: Marvin Mitchelson?

Brooks: Yes. So I kicked him in the ass, and threw him off the set. He said, "I'll sue you, I'm a lawyer." I said, "All right, sue me, but get off." And sure enough, he called people at Columbia and wondered if he really had to get off the set. And they said, "What did he say?" He said, "Get off." And then they said, "Well, you better get off." But, even [Lee] Marvin behaved very well there, and he was having a lot of problems with his lady, Michelle [Troila]. But professional, in addition to being on time and knowing your lines and learning your craft, means that you become part of the show. And it's not a matter of always begging off or arguing something about how you feel that day. I don't give a shit how you feel. Get ready for work. And you blend with the other performers so that it becomes a cohesive unit. And you become believable. Unless it's believable, it's no damn good. What good is it if it's not believable? I had that problem with John [Huston] on the first picture I worked on with him. Everything was fine. He would go fishing. I would write all day,

and he would read during lunch hour and then in the evening make his suggestions. Well, we're now coming to the end of the movie in Key Largo, and I
would write a scene. He comes in from fishing. He reads it and he says, "No."
I said, "What's the matter with it, John?" He said, "I don't believe it." I said,
"Well, John what do you want me to do?" "Rewrite it." I said, "You got any
ideas?" He said, "No." He said, "You got the case here where Bogey resists
Robinson the whole movie, and now he's on the boat, and suddenly he decides
to fight Robinson. Why?" Well, there started something like six weeks of
arguments, every day. Every time I wrote a scene, it was not any good. It didn't
work. He didn't believe it. And finally, I had to go back to the beginning of
the script, and the beginning of the movie. And I thought I found something
there that might help. Because it was established in the first twenty pages, and
here it was bearing fruit. And so I wrote another scene, and he said, "I don't
know." Now we really had a fight. Verbal. Verbal. He said, "For what would
you be willing to die? Knowing that you were going to die? What? Your country? A girl? Money? Politics? What? Look, you got a baby. It's in the building.
The building is burning, but you know beforehand that if you go into that
building to try to save that baby, you're dead. Would you do it?" Well, all
those are hard questions. And so I asked John the same questions, and he said,
"I don't know. Might not." Anyway, it went back and forth. No rancor, but
terrible battles such as that. And, finally, I wrote a scene which depended on
the first twenty pages, and he said, "Well, we might be able to make that
work." That was over five weeks on one scene. So, John taught me something
about doing it right. You want to write it, make it believable. Otherwise, it
won't work. It'd be no good. And he wouldn't be able to shoot it. And, then,
the most important thing to John was structure — structure, structure, structure. What happens first, second, third, and fourth, and so on. Not clever
lines. Not the bullshit. You know, I read a couple of scripts within the last
three or four years, one from Southern California Film School. And there was
a heading in there for a scene, E.C.U. I said, "What the hell is that? I've never
heard of an E.C.U." So, finally, I talked to the student, and I said, "What the
hell does that mean? What's an E.C.U.?" He said, "What is it? It's an extreme
closeup." I said, "I see. Well, when you're writing it, do you know what lenses
you're going to use? Do you know who's going to be in the picture? Maybe she
can't take an extreme closeup." Then he had another thing in there, in between scenes, something that was called a "quick cut." How can you make a
cut quicker than it is? "You got to get a faster machine." So, those things you
finally learn that they're not really important, that you dolly down to the guy's
shoelaces and you zoom up to his face, and you show the empty gap in his
mouth of a tooth where it used to be. What's the story? What happens and
why is it happening? That's the important thing, and that's what I learned
from John. He was terrific.

Champlin: *The Professionals* is such a wonderfully structured film.

Richard Brooks

Brooks: Yes, it is. Good structure.

Champlin: It really just moves along like a train. How long did it take you to write the script?

Brooks: Well, it varies. In the case of *The Professionals*, it was about eight months. In the case of *Lord Jim*, it was two and a half years, because you know, with Conrad everything is in the mind, very little dialogue you can use from a Conrad novel.

AQ: You once said that you shouldn't write a script with a particular actor in mind, but how could you have written *Elmer Gantry* without Burt Lancaster in mind?

Brooks: I was still in the war when I wrote my first book, which was reviewed in *Esquire* magazine by Sinclair Lewis. I was in Quantico at the time, and it was a very complimentary review. I wrote him to thank him. And he wrote back on the back of my letter—he didn't even waste a letter—in which he said, "Well, if you're ever in New York, give me a call. This is my number. I'll buy you a drink." So, after about three months, I got a twenty-four-hour pass, and I went into New York. I called him, and he said, "Where are you?" I said, "I'm outside the Astor bar." He said, "That's across the street from where I am. I'll meet you there in a few minutes." He meets me. Takes me into the bar, and he buys us each a drink. Then he asks me, what did I do in the Marine Corps? I said, "I was in the Second Marines, the photographic section." "Oh, great." I said, "As a matter of fact, there's a book you've written, which if I ever get the money, and you ever have the inclination, I'd like to make it as a movie, which is *Elmer Gantry*." And he said, "Oh, that's interesting. I think if you want to help yourself, you should get all the reviews you can when the book came out. Half of them are good. Half of them are terrible. And H. L. Mencken's is the worst of all." He said, "The second thing to do to help yourself when you're making this movie—if you ever do—make a movie, not a book." And that released me and helped me very much. Lancaster came along because I had written a script for Lancaster from before, which was called *Brute Force*. And before that I wrote the story for him based on a Hemingway short story, a ten-page short story, called "The Killers." And that was his first movie. And so I knew him. And we'd go to the fights together at the Hollywood Legion Stadium. And finally I had a script. And said, "You want to read a script?" I gave him the script. And he said yes. That's how it happened. But I didn't visualize him before. But that doesn't mean that you should not. Everyone has his own way of doing something. And when you're ready to write a script, write it. It doesn't make any difference who's in it. Or if you want to write it for somebody, do so.

AQ: If you were going to make *The Professionals* again, today, how would you change it? Because of a different audience? Or because of the ratings that you'd have more freedom to do? And we're dealing with another set of people in the suits and the studios.

Brooks: Well, I don't know that I would change it any other way. I've never wanted to do a picture over, although I know every picture should be done over. But I didn't want to do it over. Some other people have tried to make it. As a matter of fact, there was a TV show that stole this whole idea. And the son of a bitch brought me over to some guy's house, and he ran my copy of the print. And then he made a TV show. He had four characters and a black man. This guy—what's his name—he was the fella who asked me to bring my print over, and he ran it some five or six times. He's the guy who throws his pen away or pulls a paper out of his typewriter in front of him.

AQ: Stephen Cannell.

Brooks: I remember he had this *A Team*.

Champlin: Mr. T. instead of Woody Strode.

AQ: How'd you come to choose Connie [Conrad] Hall to do the shooting?

Brooks: That's a good question. Because he's a good man. Well, my assistant director at that time was Tom Shaw. He said, "Hey, I know a cameraman for you." And we were just preparing to do *The Professionals*. I had him come over, and I said, "All right, let's go." So we went to the desert, to Death Valley. We shot about two thousand feet of film. Then I got a call from somebody at Fox, who said, "Don't use this guy. I'm calling your boss. I don't want him used in this movie of yours." I'd never heard of anything like that. That's the day we hired him. Anyway, Connie Hall was great. And his friend, with whom he had gone to school at USC, asked to be the operator. They tossed a coin or something, I don't know. Fraker.

Champlin: Bill Fraker.

Brooks: Fraker was the operator on that picture.

Champlin: Really?

Brooks: Oh, yeah. Terrific. Both were a great pair. He was a great man, Connie. A lot of bad luck with women...

AQ: How did you come up with Jack Palance's wonderful speech about revolution?

Brooks: Well, he was talking for me. Anyway, inasmuch as it was going to be about the Mexican Revolution, I spent five months in Mexico studying on that revolution. And I thought, how romantic we are about revolution. Half of it's good, and half of it's not. But we still have something that we care about. Because as [Jack] Palance says near the end of the movie, "Without love, without a cause, we are nothing." And that's what I happen to believe. Now, very often, my cause is me.

AQ: One of my favorite films of yours is *Bite the Bullet*.

Brooks: Oh, it is mine, too.

AQ: How tough was that one to make in comparison to this one?

Brooks: How tough? Just as tough. The thing about *Bite the Bullet*, that was really a love letter from me to America. That's how beautiful I thought our country was. And, so, when I did that race — that was a real race that they used to run, from somewhere in Wyoming to the *Denver Post* door. That's where it ended. A seven-hundred-mile race. And I loved that story. Now, [Gene] Hackman is another one of those pros. Disciplined as all get out.

AQ: I wanted to ask you about the book you wrote, *The Producers*. Who was it based on?

Brooks: On several producers. One of them was Mark Hellinger. On a number of them. One of the writers in there was a guy who used to write for Mark Hellinger, and finally we went to Mexico because he was one of the unhappy ten. Maltz. Albert Maltz.

AQ: [*Champlin repeats the question.*] She was complimenting you on the great fire out at the Santa Monica Pier that ends *Elmer Gantry*. Evidently the lady was a witness.

Brooks: That was a helluva fire. We got twelve hundred people on stage.

And set up all the material. We had three cameras going. Among the twelve hundred people, there were over two hundred stunt people to try to help the extras. Well, they weren't extras. We got them from the factories out here to play extras.

AQ: Were the Long Beach retired citizens part of your extras?

Brooks: No, they came from the airplane factories. Well, anyway, the special effects man—I give him the signal, he sets off the fire. No fire. I said, "What happened?" He said, "Mr. Brooks, I don't know what happened, but I guess we didn't do it right." I said, "Well, I guess you didn't." He said, "Well, you see, they soaked all of these drapes, and all of the ribbons, and everything else, so they wouldn't burn the stage down." So I got the firemen, with Tom Shaw, and we went for a walk along the Columbia street. And I said, "You know what you guys did? You just ruined me, soaking all that stuff down. Now, we can't have a fire." They said, "Well, what kind of fire you talking about? A flash fire?" I said, "Yes. When it starts here and goes across the screen. A flash fire." He said, "I don't know how you're going to do that." I said, "Hey, you're a fireman. You ought to know how to start a fire." He said, "I put out fires. I don't start fires." I said, "Well, why don't you become a policeman or something else? What the hell are you masquerading as a fireman for? If you're a fireman, you ought to know how to start a fire, you bastard!" So, we walked for a while longer, and finally he said, "There's only one way you're going to get a flash fire with the way we treated that material." He said, "If I were you, I would go to the studio and order from them some of their old nitrate film. Lay it in. Set a match to it, and run." And that's what we did. We bought three old movies from Columbia and burned them. That's how that fire was done.

For Further Study

Videocassette

The Professionals is available on video from Columbia Home Video.

Books

Clark, Randall. *American Screenwriters*. Detroit: Gale Research Co., 1986.

Crist, Judith. *Take 22; Moviemakers on Moviemaking*. Coedited by Shirley Sealey. New York: Viking, 1984.

Kantor, Bernard R. *Directors at Work: Interviews with American Filmmakers*. New York: Funk and Wagnalls, 1970.

McGilligan, Pat. *Backstory 2: Interviews with Screenwriters of the Forties and Fifties*. Berkeley: University of California Press, 1991.

Marshall, J. D. *Blueprint on Babylon*. New York: Phoenix House, 1978.

11

ROBERT CULP

AND

Hickey and Boggs

(with Steven Gaydos and Charles Champlin)

On February 19, 1991, actor and director Robert Culp was interviewed by Steven Gaydos and Charles Champlin after a screening of *Hickey and Boggs*. Joining the discussion were *Boggs*'s production manager, Elliot Schick, and Culp's son, Jason, who also worked on the film.

The Film

Hickey and Boggs (1972), United Artists, a Film Guarantors Ltd. Production. Directed by Robert Culp. Screenplay by Walter Hill. Director of photography, Wilmer Butler. Music by Ted Ashford. Special effects by Joe Lombardi. Edited by David Berlatsky. Production manager, Elliot Schick. Filmed on location in Los Angeles.

Cast: Robert Culp (Frank Boggs), Bill Cosby (Al Hickey), Rosalind Cash (Nyona Boggs), Vincent Gardenia (Papadakis), James Woods (Lt. Wyatt), Michael Moriarty (Ballard), Isabel Sanford (Nyona's Mother), Robert Mandan (Mr. Brill), Ed Lauter (Ted), Lester Fletcher (Rice).

Synopsis: Two luckless private eyes in Los Angeles get caught up in case involving mobsters, a Chicano street gang, and $400,000 in stolen loot. After gunfights all over Los Angeles, a shootout at the Coliseum, and a helicopter attack, Hickey and Boggs manage to survive and nail the bad guys.

Remarks and Reviews

"To illustrate the disorder of the modern world in *Hickey and Boggs*, all of the mystery sequences take place during broad daylight and the private lives of the detectives are shown at night. Breaking archetypes, these men are not handsome, romanticized loners but are weary, displaced persons. Hickey's arrival home at night scares and angers his wife, who complains that she is not running a boardinghouse. Boggs is an

191

alcoholic who spends most of his spare time in bars watching television commercials and brooding about his ex-wife. His singular enjoyment is watching her striptease act in a seedy night club, where she psychologically castrates him" (Alain Silver, *Film Noir*).

"The city of Los Angeles can be seen in all of its wonderful sleaziness in *Hickey and Boggs*. And besides that, you get plenty of action, a well-crafted mystery, and some outstanding characterizations in the bargain. Much of the credit for the film's success should go to Robert Culp, whose maiden directorial effort shows inventiveness, wit, an obvious understanding of the role of editing in the creation of suspense, and a talent for handling actors" (Stan Berkowitz, *Coast*).

"What, in fact, lifts *Hickey and Boggs* above the ordinary is first off the sardonic naturalism of the Culp and Cosby performances.... The peeling and grimy reality of the Los Angeles we see is admirably enhanced by a large supporting cast of faces and personalities which are unfamiliar, fresh and credible.... Culp has brought off the difficult task of doubling as actor and director with remarkable assurance and control" (Charles Champlin, *Los Angeles Times*).

The Filmmaker

Best known for his role on the hit television series "I Spy" with Bill Cosby, actor Robert Culp has had a long and prosperous career in Hollywood on both the small and large screen. Along the way he costarred in Paul Mazursky's hit movie *Bob and Carol and Ted and Alice* (1969), made a sharp, funny appearance in Monte Hellman's cult horror quickie "Silent Night, Deadly Night III" and starred on the small screen opposite William Katt in the successful adventure series "The Greatest American Hero." Culp garnered rave notices for his performance in the Julia Roberts thriller *The Pelican Brief* for director Alan Pakula.

Though *Hickey and Boggs* drew impressive critical plaudits for a debut feature, Culp has largely abandoned his efforts at writing and directing films. There was a long collaborative friendship between Culp and director Sam Peckinpah, and Peckinpah was heartbreakingly close to shooting Culp's script of *Summer Soldiers* before financing collapsed.

In 1994 Culp returned to the small screen for a reprise of his "I Spy" role alongside Bill Cosby, and he continues to stay busy in Hollywood as he has developed from being one of the many hip leading men of the 1960s into one of the American film industry's most durable character performers.

Robert Culp's Filmography

As actor, except as noted: *P.T. 109* (1962); *The Raiders* (1963); *Sunday in New York* (1964); *Rhino!* (1964); *Bob and Carol and Ted and Alice* (1969); *Hannie Caulder* (1971); *Hickey and Boggs* (also directed, 1972); *The Great Scout and Cathouse Thursday* (1976); *Turk 182* (1984); *The Pelican Brief* (1993). His extensive work as an actor on television includes starring roles in the Western series *Trackdown* (1957); *I Spy* (1965–67); and *The Greatest American Hero* (1981–82).

Reasons   for   Selection

Hickey and Boggs is one of the most underrated detective films of the last 30 years; an important film because it demonstrates the underappreciated talent and creative aspirations of two actors who are best known for their mainstream television work.

Robert Culp and Bill Cosby were inspired to make a film that reflected their own feelings about Los Angeles, about changing American morality, and about the crime-film genre itself. Its artistic success is in great contrast to the complete indifference the film was accorded by the Hollywood establishment. A first-rate directorial debut for Culp, the film is to date his only feature directing credit. And the multitalented Bill Cosby has never made another film as gritty and compelling as Hickey and Boggs.

The   Interview

Charles Champlin: I'm always interested in how a movie ever gets started. I mean, how long did you have to schlepp it around town, or was it an easy sell? — not, I would think, probably.

Robert Culp: It was not an easy sell. Nobody had ever heard of Walter Hill.

Steven Gaydos: This was Walter's first screenplay?

Culp: First screenplay. Warners offered it to Mr. Cosby and myself. And we said to them, "Fine, if Culp directs." And that did not sit well with them. And so then we said to them, "Then sell it to us." And they said, "We will, because the next team of guys costs us twenty million to get out." I remember the phrase. And, at that point, since we had it in what was in effect a kind of turnaround, Bill and I began to try to get the dough. And that really meant, mostly, that I was doing the legwork and stuff here because he was all over the place. But he checked in, and he stuck with me all the way, and of course, the second I turned anything up, he was, you know, ready, and ready to go to work. I had the money three times and lost it three times. And a guy who had been production manager and so forth for *I Spy*, and old, old pal, I ran into on the street and he said, "What are you doing?" And I told him.

And he said, "Why don't you come down and take some offices? You're going to put this together, it's just a matter of moments." And so I did over at Goldwyn, what is now Warner-Hollywood, I guess. And this went on with the business of getting the money and losing it. It went on for six months. And finally, one day, Fouad Said, who had created Cinemobile for *I Spy* and had built it into a huge organization after the show was canceled, walked in and said, "What's the problem?" And I told him.

And he said [*mock-Fouad*], "There's no problem." And he went to the bank and put up all of his stock in Cinemobile, which he owned himself. So he put up the whole company as collateral to make the picture. Unheard of.

The problem still remained of getting a release of a negative pickup. So, finally, I've forgotten how the play came, but in any case, the gentlemen who were then running UA [United Artists] said, "OK." Finally. "We will give the release. You got the dough, we will release the picture, you have a negative pickup."

And I remember how much it costs, down to the penny. Do you remember, Elliot?

Elliot Schick: It was just around a million dollars.

Culp: Yeah, it was $1,104,000 to negative, to answer print. And, I don't know what happened, but it was caught in the middle of the composer's strike.

First of all there was John Barry, who was going to do the score, who was well known to everyone then. He was a superstar already for doing all the James Bond pictures. And he was scared off. I thought I could get an Englishman to do it because they weren't going to go all the way over there, but indeed the Composer's Guild went all the way to England and threatened him, and he backed off the picture. And finally the score, which was very difficult to come by, was done by someone whom no one had ever heard of. It was the only picture he ever did. And I feel. . . . It hurts me, this score, every time I hear it, even though there's a kind of quality to it now, that in retrospect, kind of fits the picture. Strange. Anyway, that's how it all came to pass.

Gaydos: When you and I talked about this before, you mentioned that the problems didn't end with getting the picture made; they continued on to getting the picture released and seen.

Culp: Oh, yes, their release pattern for this infuriated both Bill and myself. You have to realize that a certain amount of the menu for every distribution organization is in what they call pickups. That's what this is, a negative pickup. They guarantee you a certain amount of money if you fulfill a certain number of prerequisites that they contractually insist on. They're fairly general, however; they have to trust you. We did [the requirements], and they take the picture, but that does not mean that it's their favorite picture or that anybody involved in it is their best friend. And as a consequence, in this instance, the picture was released on Labor Day weekend, which historically, at that time, was a dead weekend throughout the country. Not so anymore. It's not so bad anymore. Then it was. And the advertising campaign was minimal. It happened to be on the exact weekend of the Republican National Convention in 1972, when Nixon was coming up for a second term. And, in New York, where we went to do PR, Bill and I, you could have fired a cannon down Fifth Avenue, and all you would have gotten was an echo. The streets of that city were absolutely, desolately empty on that weekend because everybody and all the news people and everybody who cared about anything were all in Florida at the convention. It was an unfortunate weekend. And as you know, that first weekend is crucial in deciding for the studio and the distribution organization what they're going to do the next weekend and those after.

Gaydos: And, as you say, without allies and close friends and people that are really involved in the picture at the studio, it doesn't have the same status at the studio?

Culp: No, certainly not. It did, however, receive a kind of critical notice that on the one hand was wonderful and very satisfying and gratifying to me but, on the other hand, was not the kind of response that you want for this type of picture.

One guy called it "the best dick film since *The Big Sleep*." And "best action picture since *The Wild Bunch*." And stuff like that. And on the ten-best list with *Straw Dogs* and *Godfather* and so forth, that year. But that sort of critical analysis does not jibe with the type of film that it was. It's a genre picture.

Champlin: What did it finally do?

Culp: It made a dollar. I mean, it made a profit. But not a huge profit, no.

Champlin: Is it out on cassette?

Culp: I don't think so.

Champlin: It's one of James Woods's first films, I should think, isn't it?

Culp: It was Jimmy's first or second film. Same thing with [Michael] Moriarity. He had done only *Bang the Drum Slowly* before. Vince Gardenia, same situation. Nobody knew Vince. He'd been around for a while, I mean, I'd known him in New York, but he wasn't known yet. He hadn't developed his, you know, steam.

Gaydos: Talking about the production of the film itself—when you and I chatted about it last time, you mentioned the unusually high number of locations here in L.A. What was the number?

Culp: There were more locations in Los Angeles on that schedule than any picture that had ever been shot. We moved five and six and seven times a day.

Gaydos: Elliott, do you remember the problems inherent in that?

Schick: Fouad Said went to Japan and decided he needed somebody to keep an eye on Bob. And since I came out of Sam Arkoff's AIP [American International Pictures], he figured I would be good. Bob didn't know why he needed a stoolie on his picture. After three days he was rather pissed about it. Afterward we went into Herb Jaffe, and I said we needed $138,000. Now, can any of you picture fighting for $138,000 today? I don't think so. But we fought for that, and Herb finally gave in to it. And then we became friends, and we've been friends ever since. I had three weeks prep on this picture.

Culp: That's all.

Schiff: We were finding locations all day long, while we were sleeping or working at night, shooting at night. I fell asleep occasionally. We literally pushed this thing twenty-four hours a day. Even though we had notified the fire department that we were going to have an explosion at Chavez Ravine, three fire departments came out because people called in scared and said, "They're blowing up Dodger Stadium!"

Culp: The football game was an interesting item in terms of the difference of making a picture then versus making a picture today — an independent film, a small film. We stole the football game. All of it wherein you saw people, you saw, you know, extras. What would be extras today, those weren't extras at all. And those were the two real football teams. The way it happened was, the owners of the two clubs would agree and charge you a certain fee to come down on the field, and then everybody fought you tooth and nail to keep you off the field. But I had a guy who'd been a dear friend, a cameraman, Rex Metz, who bullied his way onto the field and literally stole all the stuff with the teams that they never knew we got, then got the tie-in shot with Bill and me going up the steps with the crowd, and the rest of it he was authorized to get.

But it's impossible to do that today. Absolutely, flatly impossible. You couldn't do it. You'd have to put those people in there as extras, and the price goes up just unbelievably high.

Schick: You would have had to deal with every agent for each player on the field, whether it was at Dodger Stadium, because that was a real game that you saw. That was not staged for us.

Culp: No, that was a real game. We just picked it up.

Schick: We just went in and stole it.

Gaydos: It's called guerrilla filmmaking.

Schick: But that's the way we made the movie. We went in and found places. Bob had gone out on a limb, which upset me. He had his own money in it. He had pulled people in at the promise we were going to start shooting in three weeks — and we were still talking to UA about guarantees, etcetera.

Culp: The one thing I could not tell Elliot, and I couldn't tell it to Fouad — I couldn't tell Elliot because he was bound, honor bound, to tell Fouad about any kind of dangerous stuff that I might reveal. So I just didn't tell him. I was the only person around who knew I was going to lose Bill on the other end of the schedule. I couldn't delay. There was no delay because Bill was going to start *The Electric Company*. And, in point of fact, I did lose him by one day, and he had to come back on a Sunday from New York and finish the last stuff, which was the stuff over the cliff when he finds the house actually did fall off the cliff.

Schick: By the way, we didn't push the house off the cliff. We got very lucky. I'm sure when you drive by you'll see the houses up there supported with steel. We did find an empty lot that the POVs [points of view] down on the Pacific Coast Highway match perfectly. But it was that kind of fun. We went crazy. For example, you were not allowed to land a plane at Cabrillo Beach. And what we did, we took the plane off a low bed, put the wings on it, and we were allowed to taxi it. Then one Sunday morning a friend of ours, Al Nicholson — who was our location manager, also flew a plane and had experience because he had once worked at a morgue—combined all of those skills and he did a touch and go. And that's how we touched down at the beach in the parking lot.

Champlin: Jason, how old were you when this was all happening?

Jason Culp: Ten.

Champlin: Had you been around or been watching *I Spy* being shot or anything?

J. Culp: No, actually, what's special about the making of this film for me is that through a series of circumstances, personal ones, our family was reunited during the summer of '71. And we actually all came together on the very day he got the green light for the last time to make the movie.

So the whole summer became, you know, making the movie for the whole family. And all of us kind of had our heart in it in one way or another. My older brother was there every step of the way, and he learned the craft that he now practices himself.

Champlin: Oh, really? What is that? Is he an actor now?

J. Culp: No, art directing. But he was everyone's gofer at the time, at age thirteen.

Champlin: It must have been a gas to do it at age ten, I should think?

J. Culp: It was great. I mean, I don't know if it had been stated that I was going to become an actor, but, you know, it was something that I could do. And it didn't require too much. I could lay out in the sun and get a tan so I'd look Chicano.

Gaydos: What's the timetable on this film in relation to the end of *I Spy*? *I Spy* ended in what year?

Culp: *I Spy* ended in January of '68. And this is all of '68, '69, '70, and half of '71. So, it's four and a half years later.

Gaydos: And two questions that may be a little related. I've seen this picture. It is so purposely downbeat and sleazy and seedy and nonglamorous. Did people tell you that they thought this was sort of an odd choice for Cosby and Culp to do a picture like this?

Culp: We deliberately chose the material because it was that. I did more than Bill did, even though it was originally given to him, and he was the one who gave it to me. And said, "I think this is pretty good. I think we ought to try to do it."

I took it to Vegas under my arm, and he was the first person to see it. And we took a theater, which was a common practice up there, we took a theater in the middle of the day when there was nobody in it and there were no screenings scheduled. And he brought a few people over from wherever it was, I forget where he was playing at that time. It was not the Hilton. And so we had maybe as many as ten people in the house at ten o'clock in the morning or eleven o'clock in the morning, and we showed the film. When everybody left, he was still sitting there. He went down and had sat way down in the front, like the second or third row, by himself. Watched the film. Everybody else was out. I stayed in the back and just sat there and waited for them to come back. He walked past me and said, just sort of muttered under his breath, "I just wish you had let them up." His instinct—I don't have to explain to you—as an entertainer is more for a happy ending than this flat statement. But I went with what I considered to be the material the way Hill had written it, and in terms of the fleshing that it needed, because it was, really, bare bones when we bought it from Walter Hill, or from Warners, who had purchased it from him. Just bare bones. And it needed an awful lot of flesh to make a real movie out of it. And that was the nature of the beast. I did what was there. I did not shape it, except to keep it very simple. It shaped itself.

Gaydos: You and I spoke a little about what you were thinking about in making this picture, the kind of influences you brought to the film. You had mentioned at the time the cinema that you really were attracted to and interested in was primarily European. Do you want to expand on that a little bit?

Culp: [*Hesitatingly.*] Well, yeah, that was my original background in film when I was a kid. It was immediately after the war when I was a teenager and foreign films were permitted in the United States for the first time. No one had ever seen them. There were hundreds. There were thousands of great pictures that no one in America had ever been allowed to see. They had been prohibited from being distributed here by the majors, who up until that time, until '48, until the consent decrees, controlled all of the theaters, except a few little ones here and there. And after the war was over, some independents began to bring them in. For example, Janus is a film distributor whose name you will now know, but it was brand new then. And I used to sneak out of high school and go across the Bay Bridge to San Francisco and Marin County and check out these little theaters. There were about three of them in the Bay Area that showed foreign films. And all the great ones came there, and I saw them all when I was in high school.

The point is that there is probably an oblique reference to that kind of French reality in this piece, but it's minimal. I was trying to go for something that I believed in, where I could believe the people, because I hadn't.

Not since the glossy stuff of the late thirties and eary forties had I believed anything having to do with the so-called detective fiction in film. I thought it was all bull.

Champlin: There's a definite narrative style in the film, and I don't know whether it was in Walter Hill's script or not.

Culp: No, it wasn't.

Champlin: I mean, it was a very elliptical. Is that what I want to say?

Culp: That's not Walter's style. It's my style. I try to pack as much information into a frame as I know how to do because it's necessary when it is so sparse, when the emotions of the people are being held down, just, you know, to a bare minimum.

Champlin: It also involves a certain amount of trust in the audience, too. I mean, you keep the audience working. You don't lay it out for them; they have to figure it out.

Culp: Yes. Yes. Yes. I'm still a great believer in the art of surprise. And to me the very essential notion of fiction is surprise, as it is in comedy. Surprise is comedy. Comedy is surprise. Without that, I don't think fiction is real fiction. I don't think it can hold your attention. It doesn't hold mine. And so there are a great many little tiny surprises in this picture, which I'm sure you noted some of. But you didn't see them all. It takes three or four times to see this picture to get them all.

J. Culp: I'd be curious to hear you run down, Dad, how it got cut down from the rough cut. And how long the rough cut actually was.

Culp: Well, the rough cut, for those of you who are really involved in film, the rought cut, and it was a finished cut, but it was, you know, it was still picture in track, it wasn't married. It was seventeen reels. And you have to cut that down to somewhere between ten and twelve. And so I could have shortened, Elliot, yours and my misery, probably in the making of this picture by two weeks had I known what was going to have to be cut.

Gaydos: How many weeks did you shoot?

Culp: We shot six? What? Six and half? Well, anyway we shot thirty-six days. What does that come out? Yeah, a five-day week. Thirty-six days in Los Angeles.

Audience Question: For me one of the most extraordinary scenes is the one where they talk your character into coming back to life and continuing on the case. And I was wondering how you do that as an actor and a director, because it's one long take? How do you know when it's right? And how do you trust it? How do you make the decisions on both sides of the camera?

Culp: Well, you have to be very coldly analytical. If you can't be pragmatic as hell about it, you're going to get into trouble. And so you set up what all the setups are going to be, and you keep them to an absolute rock-bottom minimum, which I did — it was really only one angle in coverage. One angle and singles. There was no right to left, and left to right, or anything like that. Otherwise, it never would have worked.

I had to keep it terrifically simple. Then I had to say, "Shoot it no matter what happens." You take your own cue to start. You'll know when it's over. And then I had to go away to prepare as an actor. Now, obviously you have to know the words.

But past that, when you set what it's going to do, you also have to kind of have, in this instance, a feel. You're an actor and you're acting in the scene, but you also have to have sort of a feel for where the lens is and where it's located.

But then you have to dismiss that and trust the fact that it's going to be OK, and the operator's not going to mess it up. And I was blessed here with three different operators I was nuts about. They were wonderful. They said, "I got it. I knew I got it." I had serious problems, which I won't go into, with the man who was director of photography, who since has become a big star — but that's not important at this point. The operators, nevertheless, always "got it." You have to trust them, however, and then go away and just cut it off and act the scene.

Schick: One thing that I would lilke to add is the fact that even though some directors consider knowing what they want to do and not leaving it all for the cutting room, having a point of view, Bob never walked in in the morning unprepared. He might have changed his mind when he had a better idea — that's fine, that's what moviemaking is all about. But he was prepared. He knew this show. He had visited every location. He had picked most of the locations. The location manager had a number of choices for him, but essentially Robert walked this territory. It was not a question of standing there and rubbing your nose, and then after lunch we'll have our first setup.

He did not waste a moment. We did not have a moment to waste. He did not need me, nor the first AD, pushing him. He came prepared to make his movie. And he took the responsibility for it. He choreographed it.

Gaydos: A friend that I was watching the picture with just now commented on references inside the picture that seemed very clear to us today — and maybe they're happenstance or maybe they're intentional — but there seems to be so much of a political nature to this film — sort of under the surface and around the corner all the time.

For instance, Moriarty and the other fellow, the tremendous actor who is the pilot and the driver — what is his name, the fellow with the glasses?

Schick: Bill Hickney. He's the stunt coordinator.

Gaydos: Bill Hickney. Yeah. Great. But you have this blond-headed guy up here in this chopper with a machine gun, blowing away brown people and black people, and my friend leaned over and said, "It's Vietnam. They got Vietnam in this movie."

And it seems like the time that this movie was made, the late sixties, early seventies, there was such a political nature to the environment in Hollywood, to the kind of filmmaking that was going on. Did that sneak into this movie? Or was that something that was consciously injected into the movie? Or was it something you see now and say, "Oh, I wonder where that came from?"

Culp: All of what you're talking about is completely accidental and had nothing to do with any form of thinking of mine, and it's your layover. Altogether this is the most apolitical film ever made, from my point of view, with the exception, of course, of poking a little friendly fun at some folks that I had spent a lot of time hanging around with in '68 and '69 who were very political in terms of black-white relationships in the United States. When I'm working on fiction, I just take it all. I don't have a point of view. I'm a very apolitical creature. From what you might call a political standpoint, which

Robert Culp

really translates more as a moral standpoint. I was resolved only because, not because there was a big hue and cry about it in the country, because I didn't care about that. Only because I didn't want to do it the same way as everybody had recently been doing it.

Mind you, this came out the same year as *Straw Dogs*. I was determined not to shed any more blood than there was in *The Maltese Falcon*, where there isn't a drop onscreen.

I had to concede one blood bag at the end, which I had planned as an enormous effect. Just one. And it was going to be, you know, twelve, fourteen frames long and that's all. It was to be an enormous effect, however.

The pan from the blood bag was to have been, I mean, it was to spread twenty feet across. Way out of proportion to reality. And that was the only one in the picture. If you will think back, there isn't another drop of blood shed on screen in the movie.

Unfortunately when the AD got there that day, he had the wrong blood bag, and we just made do. And that's why it's shot profile. That's because it was the only way we could see it. It was nothing.

I wanted to destroy machines rather than human beings. That was the only conscious thought I had.

AQ: You had the reference to Vietnam that I was actually thinking about. It wasn't as literal as the one Steven was talking about. I was thinking more about the unrepentant annihilation that goes on — nobody cares, nobody showed up, it's for nothing. And that had some relationship to the history, the period and the time, '72, less than any kind of literal Vietnam references.

Culp: No. My interpretation of the detective genre is as it was created or re-created in the United States starting in the twenties, which then became, when it was really terrific, something that we now call film noir, although nobody thought of it in those terms then. They were just trying to make down and dirty. They were trying to make simple. They were trying to make, also, poetry with images.

And all of that stuff put together has at its base a terrifically — it's beyond cynicism. This is probably a specious conversation for this evening, but at any case, yeah it was there. And it was very, very definitely there. And it was the underlying theme of the entire piece. These guys were doing a job which at that time had been gutted. It was true. That's all my rewrite. I rewrote this thing a good fifty percent.

Legislation out of Sacramento had absolutely castrated the profession of the private detective as it had been known, fictional or nonfictional, in the United States. And these guys were truly nothing but process servers who wouldn't accept the fact. That's what it was really all about. It was about nothing. And one said so, and the other kept arguing, "No, it's about money," which is fairly ironic.

AQ: I had another question which is on the more practical line, somewhat like the one Marty had. Was the schedule that you were on, and the kind of hours that you talked about working in order to accomplish this, on the kind of budget that you had? Was that an aid in any way to the kind of character that you played in the film? Somebody who always seemed to be a little high, a little tired, a little beaten up and bedraggled?

Culp: Yeah, probably it was. Probably it was.

AQ: So that was real booze in the bottle, then?

Culp: That was real booze in the bottle. You better believe it.

Champlin: You know, I'm not sure you could have made that script before 1968, although the ratings system had begun to fall apart with Otto Preminger and so on and so forth. I mean I think that you probably would've had trouble with the Hays office, production office.

Culp: I did have trouble.

Champlin: Even so? At this time you did?

Culp: I did have trouble. I don't know exactly, Charles, what you are referring to, but I certainly know that I had a terrible time trying to do that go-go dancer scene the way I wanted to do it. And I didn't want to, you know, feature frontal nudity. But the frame was a little bit wide in one place, and I wanted to use the shot. And the actress was doing a damn good job, and all of a sudden, I had to cut the scene down, and it was all I had. So, yes, nipples and stuff was a big problem.

Champlin: Well, I wasn't even thinking about that. I was thinking more of Cosby shooting the guy, although, presumably the guy was attacking him with the thing. I think that the old Hays Office might have given you some trouble over that.

Culp: I'm sure you're right about that. I remember that in 1970, mind you, this now was shot in '71 or later. In 1970, I'd done my first television show that I hadn't done in a long, long time. I remember that it was required that I punch some guy. And they said, "Oh, you can't do that." And another time I was supposed to shoot somebody, and they said, "And oh, they said you can't point the gun at the guy."

And I said, "What the hell are you talking about?" Well, all of the rules had changed. Now, that was television, but those censorial restrictions in television crept over into film very quickly, and very soon. But I got in under the wire. And yet the graphics side of it is all they really cared about. The philosophy, or anything like that, the philosophy of Bill executing this guy — nobody even blinked at that. And now look what happens in films today. It's so gratuitous that it seems ludicrous what we did have to go through.

Gaydos: One other thing that you talked about before was the editing style of this picture, which you thought was interesting. Could you elaborate on that a little bit? You had said that you felt that it was edited in a way that was fairly fresh at the time?

Culp: I throw it to you, Charles, because you're really the expert in that. It seemed to me at the time, and it still does, that I could not remember a picture which, over the entire length of it once it had begun — got underway — where so many elements were so rapidly woven together in such an abrupt manner.

Champlin: I was thinking about it earlier. You really put great demands on the viewer because you're giving him a lot of information very fast. And you know the old thing they used to say about watching a guy go into a building and go upstairs, and so and so forth. And now you just establish him going into a building and then have him upstairs. And in a sense that's the approach, what I talked about, the narrative style, the editing style of course, is that you really got things going in a big hurry. The whole long sequence before the credits I think is interesting. I mean it happens more often now, but it didn't happen much then.

Culp: Well, that replaced a sequence that Elliot and I fought over almost every day of the picture because we were getting ready to go and shoot this at the very end, which was the original bank robbery, supposedly in Pittsburgh. I think it's the best thing that Hill designed in the picture. And I loved it a lot and I wanted to shoot it. And we were going to go to Long Beach, and we had locations picked out, and we had actors picked out and everything. And by the time we shot the first week of film, I knew I was never going to shoot it because we were never going to get enough money, never going to get enough time. And I knew it was going to take me the entire thirty-six days just to shoot what we did shoot. So by the time we got to the end, I made my plea and I knew it was going to fall on deaf ears. We never did shoot the sequence. Now, that means that when you get to the cutting room and you sit down at the moviola, you have to do something that prepares the audience for the rest of the story and leaves out the beginning. It's very difficult.

So I invented all that stuff with her. And as we were going through, I said, "This is my fallback position." If I can't tell the story about how we got the money going in the first place, with the bank robbery—and I don't think I'm ever going to be able to get to it because I don't have enough money or time— then in that case, I'm going to have to figure out something that will arrest their attention.

And the thing I came up with, originally, was they dig it up from under a plant of some kind that we know has been growing there for a long time, but we saw it at the very beginning of the first few cuts. And it comes up so we know a lot of time has gone by, but the focus of this amazing little suitcase has got to carry our interest. So that's why that was designed that way is, to make up for the lack of the bank robbery.

Champlin: But it's just a wonderful area of mystification, you know, it's very intriguing. So it works.

Culp: Remember the thousand-dollar bills, Elliot? Remember the problem we had? There were no thousand-dollar bills anywhere! We had to mortgage our souls to get ten of them. And I double-cut it—medium and then very close—with the same ten to make it look like there were twenty. And the guard came, and the guard went back, and it was a federal case. They were worth much more than a thousand dollars apiece, like they were collector's items or something. No such thing. Very difficult.

Champlin: It was great to see it again. Congratulations. I think I liked it at the time I first saw it, but I don't remember. You may remember it better than I did.

Culp: Yes, oh, yes, you liked it. You liked it a lot as a matter of fact. Some of the nicest things that were ever said about the picture, Charles said.

Champlin: Thank God.

For Further Study

Books

Silver, Alain, and Elizabeth Ward. *Film Noir*. New York: Overlook Press, 1979.

Smith, Ronald L. *Cosby*. New York: St. Martin's Press, 1986.

12

DUŠAN HANÁK

AND

Pictures of the Old World

(with Kevin Thomas and Steven Gaydos)

On April 4, 1991, Slovakian director Dušan Hanák was interviewed by critics Steven Gaydos and Kevin Thomas after a screening of Hanák's 1972 documentary, *Pictures of the Old World*, and after Thomas presented the Los Angeles Film Critics Association award for best documentary of 1990. Hanák's film distributor, Pavel Cerny, of the European Film Office, translated and also participated in the discussion.

The Film

Pictures of the Old World (*Obrazy Stareho Sveta*) (1972, released in 1988). Produced by Slovak Film, Short Film Studios, Bratislava. Written and directed by Dušan Hanák. Inspired by the photographs of Martin Martincek. Director of photography, Alojz Hanusek. Music by G. F. Handel, Vaclav Halek, and Jozef Machovec. Filmed on location in the villages of the Tatra Mountains, Slovakia. Black and white, 74 minutes. U.S. distribution by East European Film Office, Los Angeles.

Synopsis: Pictures of the Old World offers a stark portrayal of Slovakian rural life and was banned on its original release for depicting a flawed society. Finally released in 1988, it won the grand prize at the Nyon Film Festival.

Remarks and Reviews

"*Pictures of the Old World* is no sentimental journey into the past. Instead, director Dušan Hanák offers us much more in his frank and poetic study of people who have lived in extreme conditions and, nearing the end of their lives, now reflect on life, love, hardship, happiness, loneliness, war, dreams. . . . There's the legless man who built his own house, the women in the market, the man who talks of space travel and his girlfriend, the fellow whose idea of paradise is grazing sheep. They don't always have answers for Hanák's questions, but the film says much about the complexity of the human spirit, its persistence, and its capacity to endure" (Laura Thielen, San Francisco Film Festival, 1990).

"The documentarian Hanák's . . . contribution confirmed the originality of the new generation from Slovakia" (Anton Liehm).

"Hardly a celebration of a disappearing world, Hanák's film instead captures the essence of humanity in the face of abject misery. This is filmmaking of the finest order" (Steven Goldman, *L.A. Weekly*).

"What emerges is not the cliché of wise old peasantry but a harsher and keener picture of people who have come to terms with deprivation as a daily fact and discover their joys and sadnesses within that austere context" (Henry Sheehan, *Hollywood Reporter*).

"Almost as astonishing as *Pictures of the Old World*, which raises the documentary to the level of poetry, is the revelation that it was banned for 16 years, apparently because its subjects could be regarded as having been neglected by the government. In any event, it is a bleak irony that so perfect a film was suppressed for showing a 'flawed' society" (Kevin Thomas, *Los Angeles Times*).

The Filmmaker

Slovakian feature director/documentarian Dušan Hanák is one of the many promising film artists whose careers were thwarted when the state became threatened by the honesty of their work. His feature debut, *322*, dealt with a man living beneath the shadow of a deadly disease, and struggling to find purpose and meaning in a life he was forced to examine for the first time.

One of the finest documentary works, *Pictures of the Old World* (1972), was kept from socialist and Western audiences because it dared to record the harsh, primal lives of aged Slovakian peasants, a reality the authorities found clashed with the image of what was supposed to be a perfect proletarian society.

Hanák made only four films between 1972 and 1989, but since the fall of Communism, Hanák's work is coming out of political exile with international screenings and awards greeting these largely unseen films. Hanák is busy at work on several new projects, and the hope is that with the switch to capitalism, and especially through commercial television, there will be more new opportunities for Hanák to resume his filmmaking career.

Dušan Hanák's Filmography

As writer and director except as noted: *322/Diagnosis 322* aka *On Disease of the Individual and Society* (1969, grand prize winner, Mannheim Film Festival); *Pictures of the Old World* (1972, best of the festival award, Festival of Documentary Film, Munich, 1989); *Rosy Dreams (Ružové Sny*, 1976); *I Love, You Love (Ja Milujem, Ty Miluješ*, 1980, special jury prize, Strasbourg, 1990; best director, International Film Festival, Berlin, 1989); *Quiet Joy (Tichá Radost*, 1985, best actress award for Magda Vašaryová, San Remo, 1986; Czechoslovak Film Critics Prize, 1985); *Private Lives (Súkromé* Životy, 1990).

Shorts: *The Artists (Artisti*, 1965); *Apprenticeship (Učenie*, 1965); *Old Shatterhand has Come to See Us (Prišiel k Nám Old Shatterhand*, 1966); *The Mass (Omša*, 1967); *To Leave an Imprint (Zanechat' Stopu*, 1970); *A Day of Happiness (Den Radosti*, 1972).

Reasons   for   Selection

I believe that Dušan Hanák's *Pictures of the Old World* is a remarkable work of art that illuminates what it means to be old better than any film I know.

—K.T.

The   Interview

Kevin Thomas: I would like to know, first of all, how Mr. Hanak was inspired to make an unusual film like this in the first place.

Dušan Hanák: In the beginning there was a series of thirty photographs by a Slovak photographer called Martin Martincek. At the beginning, I traveled to meet these old people, and I shot a short feature which was a portraiture of these old people.

It was originally produced by Slovak TV, but since it was after the Soviet occupation of 1968, the TV powers that be got scared, and they stopped it. I continued to work on this material, and I found a number of other interesting old people, and I managed to talk to the directors of the feature film department of Slovak Film to let me shoot a whole feature.

When the film was finished, it was banned immediately. Actually, even before that, I was asked to cut seven parts out of the film. I was promised that if I cut those seven parts out, I would be able to distribute the film once we edited it out. We never got it distributed, anyway. We were never able to put those seven missing pieces back.

In 1972, when this film was made, the party leadership couldn't accept any kind of truthful view, and that's why this film was not acceptable, and could not be shown.

As far as my inspiration and my experience with the old people is concerned, I was fascinated by how strong and pure they are internally. How wise and worldly they were without ever leaving that little village, or little hamlet, where they lived.

About twice when I was visiting these people, I had this very intensive experience. I had a feeling for a moment that these people are saying lines straight out of Sartre or Beckett.

It was only years later that I realized that one of the reasons that I was so attracted to them was because they really were not touched by the demoralization of the whole society. And identification with these people meant great happiness for me.

Steven Gaydos: Could Mr. Hanák talk a little bit about the nature of what it was in this film that the authorities objected to? What was the nature of their dissatisfaction?

Hanák: It's very difficult to put you in the mind of these people; it's almost impossible. They said that those people are ugly, and I'm finding joy in showing ugly old people.

Thomas: What about the sequences that were taken out that have not been restored? I would like to know about those sequences.

Hanák: I don't think, really, that they exist anymore. First, it would be very difficult to do it technically because of the negative being cut, but that's possible.

Thomas: What were they about?

Hanák: They managed to catch, by the camera, a special moment in the life of an old woman, when she got the last rites from a priest, and she was very happy and relaxed leaving this world. She talked with very beautiful words about the paradise — about the paradise she was going to enter very soon. What was very interesting was our studio director was very suspicious of all religious things because he, as a communist, secretly was attending church. I'm trying to reproduce the ending, and it's very difficult for me, already, after all these years. The original ending was the same as the beginning: It means the camera is panning between the old houses and then it enters one of the houses, into the darkness. And in that context, for me, the meaning was that either it returns into the womb or it is the darkness that waits for us at the end of our lives. They refused to allow it because they didn't want the end of this film to show old houses when during Socialism we build beautiful, modern, paneled constructions.

Thomas: Are all the subjects, all the people in the film, are they all within one community? Or several communities?

Hanák: These were about ten basic stories which were shot in two larger regions in Slovakia. Especially at the time I made these films, in each of these little villages there were people who, basically, existed on the border of civilization. But I was not looking for these people based on social keenness. What was important for me was how authentic these people's personalities were. And how rich was their internal life. So, this is what unites these people. It's not the regional place as much as their inner life.

Gaydos: Could you also talk a little bit about the reception the film has gotten since it's been released? And what led to its getting a release? The reception both in Czechoslovakia and around the world?

Hanák: In Czechoslovakia the critics and the film specialists accepted the film very well. It got a very good reception. In Western Europe the film won a number of major festivals, but a rich moviegoer has never heard about this film in Czechoslovakia. There is this very special paradox happening in Czechoslovakia which we filmmakers are facing. During the Communist regime, when a film like this came to the theaters, if it was permitted, it existed only in one print that was moving around the country. Today, again, this film is being distributed in one print only because there is no money to make another one.

Gaydos: And what led to it being shown again? What were the circumstances?

Hanák: I will try to explain it to you, but it's not easy because much of the decision-making was completely irrational. The ways people in Czechoslovakia are manipulated by the Communist system or the films and information were manipulated by the system was much more sophisticated than the 1950s old-time Communists. So, basically, the last two or three years before the 1989 changes, we all felt, and I don't know what the physical expression is, when the matter is tired? Yes, fatigue—stress fatigue—both on the side of the Communists and on the side of the population. So in the last years, just a formal agreement from the population was needed. The last Communist director of the studios in Bratislava finally decided that this film is really more about old people than against the Communist system, and in a kind of very— he's calling it diet form—very limited form of one print they permitted it to be distributed.

Audience Question: [Inaudible, a question about the old woman.]

Hanák: First of all she lived with fourteen other people in the house. And they were all dead, already, so she lived alone. And on the All Saints Day, which is customary to go and visit the graves of your family, but since she lived alone for such a long time, she was already imagining some of the things in her life. For instance, she's talking about a man who was buried there for many, many, years, and she was saying that she just met him last year, and he didn't say hello. This is already mixed up. But that village where she lives is in the center of a very pure, untouched photographic folkloristic region. And the people there still believe in the customs, which to us look already more magical than to us more real.

AQ: Thank you for a powerful film. The people seem to me to live in complete isolation—old people. Is that true? Or were there young people or other people in their lives, or did they truly live in complete isolation in their oldness?

Hanák: No. No. No. I was really interested in cases where people lived under these conditions, even if the camera wasn't there. I was sorry that some of the translation wasn't perfect. Some of the subtitles weren't very good. For instance, that first woman who's talking about living for fifty years out of what's translated, "There is the village." She doesn't live outside the village. She lives outside the community of that village. She was ostracized all of her life, and it was only when she died that she was finally accepted by the village. Many of these old people arrived at their wisdom by paying for it through their loneliness. And the village communities often didn't like them.

AQ: Two questions: What's your next film? And also I wanted to know if during some of your shots you're hiding the camera?

Hanák: In the first two sequences we used quite a bit of hidden camera. The film was a combination of many methods. We used some candid camera, but not much.

Pavel Cerny: He was talking, originally, about candid camera being used in the shots at the beginning. Maybe I should jump in for a second to make it easier. Dušan shot a number of short films besides *Pictures of the Old World* and five other features. Most of them were major prize-winning features throughout the world, usually not shown in Czechoslovakia. We are at this moment working on a complete retrospective of all of his works, which is comprised of six evenings, which is going to Chicago, Denver, and so on, and will also come to Los Angeles, hopefully, in the fall, to the Cinematheque.

So you'll have a chance to see the rest of *Old World*, because I think it's really remarkable, and it's interesting that he's one of the few filmmakers who can combine the documentary, on the one hand, and very specific hand-writing, or specific style of films, about dramatic films with actors.

Hanák: It seems that in Czechoslovakia at this moment will live a kind of documentary film. I believe that when one is working on a documentary feature, one still needs to distance from the team. And I will attempt to make a feature documentary about the experience of a typical Czechoslovakian citizen in the forty-two years of a totalitarian government, religion, and whatever, system. And what's still alive from the totalitarianism in present time.

AQ: Two questions, actually: Did you ever see the people involved in the film at a later date? Did you keep in touch with them?

Hanák: The situation is as following: As soon as the film was finished, it was screened for the Soviet counsel general, who cried throughout the film. But my only print was taken away from me, so I couldn't make the promised screening for the old people, which I promised to them. But I noted the one who survived the longest was the one who said that he was a hundred years old and lived alone with his sheep. He survived the longest of them all, but that was a long time ago.

AQ: Were the still-shot photographs that were intercut shot by someone else beside the filmmaker?

Hanák: That's an interesting question because it concerns the method [we used when] we shot the film. When I had those sturdy photographs at the

A stark portrayal of Czechoslovakian rural life in Dušan Hanák's *Pictures of the Old World*.

beginning, they were so strong that I filmed those photographs first. And those remaining shots with those three original people, I shot both with a regular film camera. And some of the scenes I prepared or arranged for the photographer who was a film photographer. It was not Martin Martincek. So I arrived at a point where the still photography at certain points was just as valid as the film.

AQ: It was so beautiful the way the peasants lived with nature, and they felt part of nature, and their religion seems to have something from prehistoric times. I wondered if that was true. And I would also like to ask if you would consider or have thought about making a film about the Gypsy people of the Slovak area.

Hanák: Good question. You must have sensed it, because my next feature after this one, which was called *Rosy Dreams*, was about Gypsies. It was a story of a Slovak "white" boy who was a postman and a mailman, and he goes into a Gypsy village to deliver. It was, as far as I know, the only film about Gypsies ever made where all the Gypsy characters were played by Gypsies. And they spoke the Romany language in between. That was completely against the official policies of the Czechoslovak government at the time, which insisted that the Romanys adopt the Czechoslovak culture and completely get soaked up by that culture, which is impossible because they are such a specific nation they will never be able to adapt so well.

A piece of folk artwork from *Pictures of the Old World*.

AQ: Did these people ever have any visitors? Did their children come to see them? Did their children find out if they were all right? Did they know whether they lived or died? Did they have any money to live on at this time? And were they always alone?

Hanák: There were very few children left who belonged to these old people. I know that the man who was walking on his knees for twenty-five years had a son, and they communicated very, very badly. I really wasn't cheating when I showed them living completely alone. They all had a little state pension plan, which is normal under Socialism. It's very minimal, but everybody in the village had it. Maybe it's absurd, but despite the minimal amount of money they were getting, most of them didn't require more. They accepted very aesthetically the reality they lived under, which doesn't mean that I'm saying these people shouldn't get better conditions to live under.

AQ: Perhaps you could tell us more about the man who had the musical instruments? Did he build them himself? Was it something he did for his pleasure? For his living? Did the other villagers appreciate it? Does it still go on? Do those people still build those things there?

Hanák: This man, actually, is a little cheat. He's not a Slovak. He was from Northern Moravia. Everybody once read an article where they were talking about what they called "pacifism," which is, basically, naïve artistic abilities by people without any kind of schooling for it.

Unfortunately, after the old man's death the things basically disappeared. And eighteen years later, when the film was rereleased and we had interest from America by several collectors who wanted to buy these pieces, it was all gone because his kids didn't have any kind of relationship toward it.

For   Further   Study

Books

Dewey, Langdon. *Outline of Czechoslovakian Cinema*. London: Informatics, 1971.

Liehm, Angon, and Mira Liehm. *The Most Important Art: Soviet and Eastern European Film after 1945*. Berkeley: University of California Press, 1977.

13

CHARLES BURNETT

AND

To Sleep with Anger

(with Harriet Robbins)

On May 16, 1991, screenwriter and director Charles Burnett was interviewed by Harriet Robbins after a screening of *To Sleep with Anger*.

Also on the panel were four actors from the film—Sy Richardson, Wonderful Smith, Carnetta Jones, and DeVaughn Nixon—along with associate producer Linda Koulisis. Richardson, Smith, and Jones all have extensive Los Angeles area stage credits. Richardson also has appeared in the films *Straight to Hell* (1987), *Colors* (1988) and *Kinjite: Forbidden Subjects* (1989), among others. Nixon was five years old when the film was made. Closing remarks were made by UCLA's Teshone Gabriel.

The Film

To Sleep with Anger (1990), an Edward R. Pressman production in association with SVS, Inc. Written and directed by Charles Burnett. Produced by Caldecot Chubb, Thomas S. Byrnes, and Darin Scott. Executive producers, Edward R. Pressman, Danny Glover, and Harris E. Tulchin. Director of photography, Walt Lloyd. Editor, Nancy Richardson. Music by Stephen James Taylor. Filmed in South Central Los Angeles.

Cast: Danny Glover (Harry Mention), Paul Butler (Gideon), Mary Alice (Suzie), Richard Brooks (Babe Brother), Sheryl Lee Ralph (Linda), Carl Lumbly (Junior), Vonetta McGee (Pat), Wonderful Smith (Preacher), Ethel Ayler (Hattie), DeVaughn Walter Nixon (Sunny), Sy Richardson (Marsh), Davis Roberts (Okra Tate), Julius Harris (Herman), Jimmy Witherspoon (Percy), Carnetta Jones (Woman in Labor), Reina King (Rhonda), Cory Curtis (Skip), Paula Bellamy (Mrs. Baker), DeForest Coven (Fred Jenkins), John Hawker (MC), Irvin Mosley Jr. (William Norwood), Marguerite Ray (Loviray Norwood), Rai Tasco (Phil), Lorrie Marlow (Cherry Bell), Christina Harlye (Nurse), James Grayer (Man at Hospital), Robin Scholer (E.R. Nurse), Mark Phelan and Robert Terry Lee (Paramedics), Greta Brown (Virginia), Sip Culler (Neighbor).

Synopsis: In South Central Los Angeles, Gideon, the retired patriarch of a contemporary middle-class family, retains an affectionate nostalgia for his southern youth. He tends a garden out back and keeps a few chickens. His wife, Suzie, functions as a midwife within the community. Their adult children—the older and wiser Junior and the young, hotheaded Babe Brother, a "Buppie," that is a black urban professional—continue their differing opinions about race, money, and life-styles. Showing up on the family doorstep with his cardboard suitcase and seemingly quaint southern ways is glad-hander Harry Mention, and old friend of Gideon's from their poor sharecropping days in the South. A seemingly mystical man, a charmer and a dandy, Harry is possessed of a dark side that manifests itself in the traditional macho ethic: card playing, boozing, and cronyism within the neighborhood. Harry is a cultural throwback in terms of African American history. The longer Harry stays in Gideon's household, the more strained the relationships become within the family, as Junior and Babe Brother argue with their wives and, eventually, with themselves.

Remarks and Reviews

"We finally have an American film that can be called flat-out wonderful. . . . droll, visionary, alarming, ironic and deeply moving, all at the same time. . . . What's wonderful . . . is the lightness of touch with which Burnett transforms his naturalistic characters and setting into the stuff of fable. . . . As thick a slice of African-American life as anybody has put on the screen, ever" (Stuart Klawans, *Nation*).

"As in his haunting 1977 *Killer of Sheep*, Burnett makes deeply personal—and refreshingly unhackneyed-images that illuminate worlds the screen has long ignored. This movie has both meat and mystery—it rumbles around in your head long after it's over" (David Ansen, *Newsweek*).

"If Spike Lee's films are the equivalent of rap music—urgent, explosive, profane—then Burnett's movie is good old urban blues. It catches both the music of black American speech and the rhythm of the inner-city working class. This picture transcends racial stereotypes . . . with an accurate evocation of the down-home ghosts that may haunt and taunt any urban family. Like Harry at his eloquent best, *To Sleep with Anger* is a spellbinder" (Richard Corliss, *Time*).

"Pungent and richly comic drama. . . . Glover gets straight down into the soul of Harry with a generous, brilliantly detailed performance" (Sheila Benson, *Los Angeles Times*).

"Many symbols and leitmotifs run through *To Sleep with Anger*. . . . Burnett renders a delicate visual and narrative counterpoint. . . . It raises questions about the politics of nostalgia, about the dangers as well as the pleasures of the past. . . . An intimate and thoughtful film" (Gabrielle J. Forman, *Magill's Survey of Cinema*).

"A rich, layered performance, quite the best Glover has been allowed to bring to the screen, worthy of recognition at Oscar time" (Jay Carr, *Boston Globe*).

"A fascination piece that proves Burnett a filmmaker of rich imagination and talent" (Daws, *Variety*).

"A very interesting, complex film, a comedy of unusual substance . . . played by Mr. Glover with great insinuating ease. . . . All the performances by the members of the large cast are quite wonderful" (Vincent Canby, *New York Times*).

The Filmmaker

When Charles Burnett's *Killer Of Sheep* (1977) was named in 1990 to the second annual group of 25 films to be added to the National Film Registry by the Library of Congress, a great many people—film aficionados among them—had never heard of the film or Burnett.

Although he later made a movie with a somewhat higher profile, *To Sleep with Anger* (1990), his films of insight, craftsmanship, and quiet poetry have yet to gain much notoriety beyond the cognoscenti. Despite the fact that *To Sleep with Anger* boasted a major star in Danny Glover and was released twice by the Samuel Goldwyn Company to many glowing reviews, it never found a broad audience. Considering that in the past decade Burnett created two of the most astute films ever made about people in Los Angeles, he is as close to Hollywood's front door as the moon.

Killer of Sheep concerned a Los Angeles slaughterhouse worker whose emotions and behavior begin to register the ill side effects of his occupation. Although that film garnered a raft of awards at film festivals, it never received a commercial release, settling for some exposure on the Public Broadcasting System. In 1981, the film won the Critic's Prize at the Berlin International Film Festival and first place at the United States Film Festival in Park City, Utah.

Burnett was born in Vicksburg, Mississippi in 1944 and was educated at Los Angeles City college and the University of California at Los Angeles. He was awarded the MacArthur Foundation Fellowship, or "genius grant," of $275,000 in 1988. He also has been the recipient of a Guggenheim Foundation Fellowship in 1981, a National Endowment for the Arts grant in 1985, and a Rockefeller Foundation Fellowship in 1988. Burnett won special awards in 1990 from both LAFCA and the New York Film Critics Circle.

Charles Burnett's Filmography

As screenwriter and director, except as noted: *Several Friends* (1969); *The Horse (1973); Killer of Sheep* (1977, also producer, director of photography, and editor); *My Brother's Wedding* (1983, also producer and director of photograhy); *Bless Their Little Hearts* (1984, screenwriter and director of photography only); *The Crocodile Conspiracy* (1985, director of photography only); *I Fresh* (1987, screenplay only); *Guests of the Hotel Astoria* (1989, director of photography only); *To Sleep with Anger* (1990).

R e a s o n s   f o r   S e l e c t i o n

Charles Burnett's innovative and perceptive films reflect the black culture in universal terms. To quote him, *To Sleep with Anger* is a film that "explores how people survive, how they treat each other and how much they can understand from the past." The title is derived from the saying "Never go to bed angry." But, as Burnett says, "The people in this film have lived with their frustrations not just for the night but for years."

This film is a powerful, poetic, and humorous drama and fully reflects Burnett's enormous talents, which have not had the opportunity to reach the wide audience that they certainly deserve.

—H.R.

T h e   I n t e r v i e w

Harriet Robbins: How did the film *To Sleep with Anger* become a reality?

Charles Burnett: It was started by wanting to do something about the black community. When I was living in South Central in the early 1950s, there was a sense of a community. And in looking back, there seems to be an absence of a lot of cultural things that I had experienced then. I wanted to do a film that sort of addressed those problems, those issues of folklore, and try to superimpose that on a situation that exists today, where if one saw the movie, he or she would ask questions about it.

Robbins: I thought it would be a good idea if each of the panel would give a little background about themselves and how they became involved in the film.

Linda Koulisis: I read the script at an early stage. Cottie [Caldecot] Chubb had been introduced to Charles through a screenwriter, Michael Tolkin [*The Rapture* (1991), *The Player* (1992)], and the script came into our office [Edward R. Pressman Film Corp.]. It was outstanding, you know. You could tell that there was a vision there. And, definitely, after I saw *My Brother's Wedding* and *Killer of Sheep*, it was just something that had to get made, and we just had to get behind it. So, we submitted it to *American Playhouse*, and we were rejected. We fought even harder to get actors aboard. We went after Danny Glover. And then, after securing him, it all fell together. So it's the power of the script.

Carnetta Jones: I became a part of this film just through auditioning and getting the part. And, after seeing it during the screening, the first screening, I was really impressed with Charles. Working with him was just a real blessing and just a lot of fun.

Wonderful Smith: My name is Wonderful Smith. I had nothing to do with naming myself. But when I came to, I just said "Amen." When I was eight years old, they cast me in a part on the stage as a minister and my preaching subject was "watch, fight, and pray." And I have been watching and fighting and praying ever since. Apparently, it carries with it a certain aura because when I walked into Mr. Burnett's office, he—without asking me my name—looked up at me and he said, "You are my preacher." So I realized that I was working with a sensitive, articulate, creative genius.

I found out that my idea was borne out by subsequently working for him and with him. And the thing that really impressed me in working with Mr. Burnett was the atmosphere on the set. After having worked with several directors, there's a lot of rough talk going on from time to time. But during the whole production of this film, I never heard one curse word. And coming on the heels of several black exploitation pictures, pimps, et cetera, et cetera, et cetera, this was quite a relief and appealed to my moral upbringing. I wish him nothing but success in the world. And, with that, I'm going to pass it on to my friend, Sy.

Sy Richardson: Charles and I go way back to 1978. In this very room [Melnitz Film Theater, UCLA], I met Charles after a student film. A lady named Winona Riley, who did a movie called *Gray Area*, said, "Sy, you have to meet this man, Charles." He said, "Hello." I said, "Hello." And that was the last time I saw him until 1983. I auditioned for him to be an extra in a film called *My Brother's Wedding*. And for the second time, I did a student film where I started as an extra and ended up getting a principal part in it. I was the father of the bride.

I've got to tell this story: A friend of mine from London also went to school here, too, Alex Cox [the director of *Repo Man* (1984) and *Sid and Nancy* (1986)]. He called me from London and said, "I read Charles's new script, *To Sleep with Anger*. There's a part in there that was written for you. It's got to be yours." I believed him. They started casting for this film. Every human being I know my age, black actor, read for this part but me. I called my agent every other day. I said, "Well, I know the man, I worked for him." He said, "Well, I sent your picture in. They don't want to see you."

I said, "OK." I was doing a play. I gave up. And I thought, "OK, I guess I'm not right for the part." And a couple of days later, I get a call from my agent, and he says, "Sy, I don't know what's going on, but there's a script on my desk, and there's an offer for you to do *To Sleep with Anger*." I said, "I'll do it." He said, "You haven't read it." I said, "Who cares? I love Charles's work." To me, Charles is the only director I know that shows us African Americans like we really are. This is one thing I enjoy. Every time I see the film I love it, even more so. I tell everyone to go see it. If anyone will let the world know what we're like, it will be Charles Burnett. And I will work with him anytime. Thank you.

Robbins: And now we'll hear from one of the youngest members of the cast. And your name is?

DeVaughn Nixon: DeVaughn.

Robbins: And how was it working on that film? How did you enjoy it?

Nixon: Good.

Robbins: What was the most fun?

Nixon: When I got those marbles and knocked Danny Glover over.

Robbins: Do you have any special thing you want to say?

Nixon: I want to say thank you to Charles and thank you for inviting me.

Audience Question: [*to Burnett*] When the film first came out, there were quite a number of articles about the problem of distribution. And several people weren't very happy with the fact that Samuel Goldwyn was distributing the film and really didn't give it the budget that it needed for publicity. And I'm wondering if you would care to comment on your view of how the press presented the issue.

Burnett: Well — may I ask — how many of you knew about the film before this evening? [*Show of hands indicates that most everyone had heard of it.*] Well, that kills my argument. I've been in places where no one knew anything about the film. But it's very difficult for me because it's hard to kick a dead horse. We've been complaining to Goldwyn a lot about what had happened. And it's unfair because they're not here to represent themselves.

But I think I'm in a position of most directors who feel that when things go wrong, the film has been poorly marketed. And I'm trying to be objective. And, I think that in this particular case, I have a lot of legitimate complaints. Because a lot of people in the black community don't even know anything about the film.

Then it was marketed in such a way where no one knew what it was about. They'd go to see the film and walk inside the theater, and they didn't know if they were going to view an art film or a regular film. And no one [at Samuel Goldwyn Company] took any advice; no one wanted to listen. For example, in New York, it opened in three theaters: The Angelica, a theater on Forty-second Street, and one on One Forty-fourth, which is all Hispanic shows. The one on Forty-second Street — no one goes to it because it's [a high-crime area]. So it was really only at the Angelica. Then, it was supported by the community down there.

The implication was that the black people don't support the film, which they did at this theater. And why is that? And then there were all these things about blacks — we don't read, and we don't go to movies, and so forth and so on. And that's what I was upset about. If the film failed because it didn't work as a film — that was one thing I could understand. But I think no one really asked the right questions. It was always — "Well, you know, you made a film with positive images and no one wants to see it. What's wrong with black people?" And that was my objection.

AQ: In regard to the distribution: I just thought it was important that it probably wasn't any accident that they released *Predator 2* with Danny [Glover] in the lead within a week or two of the time that this film came out. So there was a lot of confusion about which one to see.

As a writer myself, I would like to applaud your portrayal of our [black] traditional folk beliefs or traditions, as they are passed on here. A lot of times, when we do work about our own people and our own culture — when we talk about it in a critical way — people get the impression that we are criticizing it in a negative way. And I want you to understand that everything that I'm saying here is supportive.

I was wondering why in the portrayal of those traditions and beliefs and the different superstitions were they depicted as an evil aspect in many ways? At least to my perception, it was. For instance, when the choir came, they were looking at the leaves underneath the covers. You contrast between the modern and Christian perspective versus the folklore.

Danny Glover in his embodiment of these folklore beliefs and the other people that believed him tended, to my perception, to be portrayed in a way that this was something that people did in hiding or behind doors. And it was something that was seen in the film in conflict with their church beliefs and therefore was negative or evil as opposed to something that was well integrated in a positive way into people's belief system.

Burnett: Well, I came from a situation where you have this sort of dual situation. And the church really didn't respect it. I mean, it did look down upon it. But it did exist in my family. And I think I wasn't being negative. Danny played a trickster. That was a folk character who was basically evil. But as far as herbal medicine and so forth, I think I portrayed it in a legitimate way in conflict with religion but also in a way where they sort of equalized one another, in the sense that you experienced.

When Mr. Wonderful Smith [as the preacher] came in and said, "Well, why are you doing this with all these old-fashioned ways?" And the other guy said, "Well, let's pray." And I felt that they were both the same. You know that one was looking down. There's this whole thing about old religion and new religion, when one comes and replaces the other one, they condemn the values of the old. In my environment, they were practiced at the same time. There actually is conflict, but I wanted to show how the dynamic worked with both of them.

AQ: Can you explain, like in the beginning of the film, this symbolism behind the scene of the burning of the fruit?

Burnett: Well, two things: one, for Gideon, it's his nightmare of being in hell. And there's certain beliefs of spontaneous combustion, as well. And so it was a combination of those things. But mainly that he was in hell. And then he realizes that he lost his Toby. It foreshadows what's to come.

AQ: What was [producer] Ed Pressman's role in the production?

Koulisis: Well, I think it was his track record, that he was able to muster all the financing. He has a huge slate that he's produced [*Badlands* (1973), *True Stories* (1986), *Talk Radio* (1986), among others]. And somebody had to go out and put their name on the line because the artists weren't enough.

There had to be a producing factor. He got involved about a year and a half after the script was in. It took a while.

Robbins: When did Danny Glover get involved with the project?

Burnett: Cottie [Caldecot Chubb] had the script, and I think the whole thing took two and a half years to find the financing. Chubb moved in with Ed. And then Danny came in about two-thirds of the way, I believe. And when Danny came along, things began to roll.

AQ: I'd like to applaud you for the film and for the spiritual angle of the film. The theme of the film is the spirituality of the people involved. I just interpreted it very simply as good versus evil: Danny Glover being the devil and the other people being that way. Is that kind of something you're always dealing with?

Burnett: No, it depends on the subject. This particular film dealt with good and evil. And also the other theme is, can you learn from experience? My last film was about something else. And the one I'm planning to do is a different subject altogether.

AQ: I'd like to know if you're interested in working under any sort of Hollywood studio system? And, what do you think of Spike Lee and his body of work?

Burnett: I'm supposed to be working on a script now for Warner Brothers. I don't know how that's going to work out because I'm still doing the first draft. There are things in it that I'm worried about, that may not pass, that they may be concerned about, but I'm going to try anyway because they invited me. I didn't go to them, so I really have nothing to lose. But, as far as Spike Lee is concerned, I think Spike Lee is a very talented filmmaker. He's done a great deal for black independent filmmaking. His work speaks for itself.

AQ: I just wanted to thank you for casting Danny Glover because I worship him as an actor. I think he's a great man. I also wanted to ask you, what's swamp root [which is depicted in folklore rites in the film]?

Burnett: Well, actually, it's an herbal medicine. But Danny uses it in a sexual sense here. It sort of has an implication, but it's actually an herbal medicine. And I think you can still buy it. It's like one of those Indian chief snake oils.

AQ: I was just going to say that I did some research for a film that was supposed to take place in South Central [L.A.] last summer. I spent a lot of time down there. And it would be very difficult to get a black audience for your film because there are no theaters down there.

I'm sure that's the case across the country for a lot of the inner cities where they probably just didn't play in the neighborhoods where you would have gotten an audience. I also found that I was having trouble with my producers, almost immediately, as soon as I dropped some of the clichés about black people. When I tried to represent the area the way I found it, they very soon turned their backs on what I tried to put in that depicted the reality of the people living down there. It died a quick death. Good luck with Warner Brothers.

AQ: I had a comment prefacing a question. I found it very interesting that the Danny Glover character has a certain aura of darkness about him, but also that there was something kind of sinister and dark around the family and the relationships, especially [concerning] the younger Babe Brother's wife. There was something scary in the dynamic of the family, which I didn't see as good versus evil. And in some ways, I was kind of rooting for Harry because I felt like there was a sense that it's not a question of old ways are bad and new ways are good.

I know what I got from it. But I'd be interested in knowing whether you see it as a complex and organic struggle that's continuing or whether it's something that in the community or in your growing up that you found that says that the old ways are shunned and thought of as hayseed and just unsophisticated and uninteresting. Because I found that, in fact, Danny Glover's worldview is much more sophisticated than most of the other characters. And that's what I found very fascinating about the piece.

Burnett: Well, it wasn't about old and new. What it was about, actually, in some sense, was about cultivating the old and respecting it and using it as a foundation because the problem with the younger son was the fact that he didn't respect his family ways. So, I wanted to try to present the idea of: Can you recognize evil? Can you judge people?

Danny's character was based on the character known as the Trickster. And this particular Trickster was called Harry Man, and he robbed you of your soul. He was, basically, an evil person. But I didn't want Danny's character to be that as such. I wanted him to embody everything that was human. At the same time I wanted to feel ambivalent about his character because, like incidents involving most con artists and people, things happen, and you don't know if it's a consequence of their being there or what. You don't know. And so I didn't want to make a direct relationship with Harry and events. What I wanted was for it to appear less circumstantial.

AQ: I heard about the film by word of mouth, and unfortunately the film was gone from the theater before I got a chance to see it. I just wanted to thank you for being here. It's a beautiful film to me, particularly the aspect for traditional folk. For me, it was very refreshing to see traditional African religious or cultural expression portrayed in such a positive manner. And I think you held it in balance and tension, portraying contemporary dynamics of the black urban family, which is in turmoil and at a figurative yet actual crossroads [with the past]. I think it was really beautiful how you brought it together. You know, there are so many other things — *Angel Heart* [the 1987 Alan Parker film that portrays voodoo rituals] for one — that have a diabolical undercurrent. I wanted to say that it's a shame that this movie didn't get wider distribution.

I'd like to know: What did the production cost? And how long was the shoot? And where was the location?

Burnett: It cost $1.4 million. And it took twenty-eight days plus three second-unit days. And the location was the Adams Heights area near Grammercy and Twentieth [South Central Los Angeles], near the freeway.

AQ: The challenge that you answered with this film — which is how to present our spiritual and cultural traditions in a comprehensible way — is one that many of us are struggling with. Were there any particular methods that you used to address the fact that the audience might have such a low level of knowledge about it?

Burnett: Well, I think the thing you didn't want to do is have too much exposition. And I think you sort of have to trust the audience. I was certainly aware of what might be a lack of knowledge. But I think if I tried to explain everything, it would have been a different story. It would have been too obvious. It would have been very didactic, or pedantic. But you can't do that. The film had to have a life of its own, you know. And, I think people have to come to it and sort of work at it — rather than just giving them digested information. I think in that area you really couldn't compromise.

AQ: By seeing the commercial alone, my husband said to me: "Oh, people don't really believe that, do they?" And I said, "Let's call my grandmother." We called her on the phone. I said, "Granny, do you really believe that thing about sweeping the broom across your feet?" She gave me all the background, and she's an upstanding Christian woman. But she could spout off all of these beliefs and went on for about a half an hour telling me some of the things I had a feeling that she didn't want to let me know that she believed, but they were part of our culture and our background. And so it is being passed on to the younger generation, and it's causing — at least me — to ask questions about it.

AQ: I just wanted to make a comment kind of in keeping with what she just said. For myself, it was so refreshing to see a different aspect of black life that's not somewhere between *Good Times* and *The Cosby Show*. You know, I think that the viewing audience, period, are being so cheated out of aspects of black life that everyone could benefit from seeing this movie. My three friends and I were just reminiscing; one is from Philadelphia, and one is from St. Louis, and one is from Detroit. But we could all remember things from our childhood that kind of related to this.

And, I had a great-grandma who, if someone like Danny [Glover] had left her house, she would have thrown ammonia down the steps, and then put Borax around the cracks around the whole room, put newspaper over the window, and left it like that for weeks. I just really enjoyed it. I just can't say enough good things about your script and your direction. And I hope that more filmmakers — black filmmakers — get a chance to show some of the other aspects of black life. I really enjoyed it.

AQ: I just wanted to say amen to that, Charles. I just wanted to say amen to that.

AQ: I wanted to ask you about the aspects of traditional African culture you mentioned: the broom, the crossroads. Were these part of your observances of your family from the South? Or was there some background in studying traditional African religions?

Burnett: It was all a part of my background, actually. And it was something that you sort of come to later in life in a sense because earlier it was something that I took for granted. It was like the blues and everything else. I was sort of into rock 'n' roll and that sort of thing. And then years later, I discovered the blues. Well, let me put it this way—the best example would be [collard] greens. I used to hate greens until one day I got my own apartment and everything, and I was walking down the street. And all of a sudden, I had to have greens.

I went home and I tried to cook a pot of greens myself. It's strange how things come back to you at a certain point in life, and how important it is, and how much you need it now. A lot of things I didn't need as a child. Now I'm having the same problems trying to get my kids to eat greens. Hopefully, maybe thirty years from now, they'll turn toward them.

But I was the same way with blues. My mother used to play blues all the time, over and over and over again. You listen to everyone like Billie Holiday and Lowell Fulsom. I used to play a trumpet. But it wasn't until I had more experience that I really came to appreciate the blues. You know, the same thing—I was walking around and there's all these songs that were going through my head, and I'm trying to figure out where they came from.

Like the opening song of this picture, here, Sister Rosetta Thorpe's song, "Precious Memories." These songs kept going over and over in my mind—certain parts of it. And I started looking for it. I said, "Well, God, this is the thing." It just sort of comes back to you, you know? I guess the brain cells start to do something with it—regenerate it or something.

AQ: I wanted to ask you if you stuck to the Harry Man Trickster from the folklore, or if you changed him around after having read American Indian folklore, where the Trickster always has multiple sides to his personality. In your movie, he actually functions like the hero because he does what the hero always does: He harmonizes the universe. The family actually gets back together, over him and despite him. And as soon as his role is over, of course, he dies, which is, you know, pretty traditional stuff.

Burnett: This character, like you said, you find him in native American culture, African American tradition—everywhere—but not in industrial societies. It really depends on how the story is told, and for what purpose the Trickster functions.

AQ: Charles, do you view yourself as a filmmaker whose purpose, in some sense, is to motivate social change within the black community? I think, obviously, this first film is a major step toward that. And, if so, do you have a strategy or series of other issues that you plan in the future do deal with on film as they relate to the black community at large?

Burnett: Whew! Well, you know, I learned film in the sixties. And during that period, there was the civil rights movement. And so you were informed by that period. When I was at UCLA, I was a part of film as a means for social change. I still sort of hold those values. I like to do stories that represent my experience and the experience of black people. I don't want to be presumptuous and say that what I think and write about is absolute truth, but that's my impression. I try to be very fair about it.

Because, just by having gone to UCLA, you find that there's a wide gap in your experience and how you view and see life, as opposed to some of the kids I grew up with, kids who didn't have an opportunity. And just talking about life in general, in their options, you find that there actually isn't any common ground in a certain sense. The reason I did *Killer of Sheep* was because of that very fact.

A friend of mine was involved in a crime, and we all grew up together. It was my opinion that he was wrong. Of course, everyone else was opposed to my opinion and said, "No, no, no, he was right." I mean, he had killed a guy while he was robbing a store. I looked at it like this: Since he went in and robbed the store, and he killed a guy, he's guilty—right? And these other guys said, "No, it was self-defense because the other guy pulled a gun on him." [To them, that] sort of made everything null and void, and it was just life, you know. It was in self-defense at that point.

So having realized you know that difference, you see that. I mean, you really can't speak for anyone except for your own experience, and you hope that people share in that experience.

AQ: For young black people who are making films right now—with the exception of maybe Robert Townsend's *Five Heartbeats*—we really haven't seen black families or black experiences on a human, nonstereotypical level. It's like they don't think that something realistic and nonexploitational will sell. And it seems like they're backing and finding young black people to come forward and sort of do what they sort of methodically think will sell. Do you agree?

Burnett: Well, yeah. It's something I think about. One has to struggle against it because you find that people in the studios don't interact with people of color and know very little about other people's experience. Yet still you find people by the door in the driver's seat dictating what the public will accept.

And even this film was very difficult. Even a place like *American Playhouse* didn't want to deal with it. Even the CPB—the Corporation for Public Broadcasting—which, supposedly, one guessed, there was a place for people with a different vision, an alternate vision for Hollywood. And you find them very reactionary there. The problem has been, I guess, the fact that there really have been too few films that sort of dealt with a realistic point of view of the black family or group. Hollywood does things in terms of formula, I believe.

If something works, they keep doing it over and over again. And the thing that works for them, basically, is those action-driven films. They don't want to go below the surface to try to get at the depth of things. And when you're talking about film as a means of social change, to make a healthy society — those are not the words you use in this business. You talk about how much money you can make.

The funny thing about it is that I truly believe if I wanted to do a film tomorrow, and if I say that the movie is about a black family, that the brother's a dope dealer, the mother's on drugs and a prostitute, and there's this one son, a kid, sixteen or thirteen years old — and if I say that he's going to be rescued and saved by this white cop who's going to get him out of the ghetto and get him into college and change his life — I'll bet you I can sell that film tomorrow.

AQ: I was wondering what filmmakers or films have particularly influenced your own cinematic style?

Burnett: I think it sort of varies from film to film. I think of a story, and a theme, and it sort of evolves out of that, basically. You know there are a lot of filmmakers that I really admire — Italian filmmakers in particularly. Ermanno Olmi is a filmmaker I have a lot of respect for. Basil Wright, who was teaching documentary film when I first came to UCLA, was an influence. It was a different school then than it is now because there were very few people of color then. And then they had Royce Hall screenings, and those are the best films that UCLA did. They were films I couldn't really identify with — I come from South Central. I was really disenchanted about this whole place until I took a class with Basil Wright, who had said something about film being not necessarily made for entertainment. He also said that one thing you have to remember is that you have to treat your subject with decency.

That's the first time I ever heard someone talk like that. And I always try to keep that in mind because he did films like *Song of Ceylon* and things like that. And it was just so interesting to hear someone say that. [In England, Wright was integral, in tandem with John Grierson, to the development of the documentary film in the 1930s]. And I just wanted to make sure that if I ever did something that whoever was in it and whatever it would be, it would give all the dimensions of a person.

AQ: I have worked in advertising and marketing, and one thing I have come to believe from my years of experience is that you do have to market films to the black community in a different manner than films are traditionally marketed. And I do feel that the people that make those final decisions really have no idea how to target that particular market, and I don't know why anyone would want to put money into a film and not do their best to market it.

Robbins: Yes: Teshone Gabriel from UCLA.

Teshone Gabriel: I think one of the problems that minority filmmakers face when making a film is that if they try to do something completely different, as Charlie was saying — basing it on everyday life or memories of black people with the likelihood that it's going to have a different kind of structure, a different kind of language — it's not going to more or less fit into the old filmic language.

So one faces a problem of that kind. You want to do something new, you want to do something relevant by speaking to your own people. But at the same time, you face this category of business sales that has been created. What I found very interesting about the film, by the way, is there is a certain quality of everydayness about it. A lot of scenes, like when they're coming to the party, getting together — there's a certain earthiness about it — which I thought was really good.

It's not a film in the traditional sense, a film that tells you a story [with] the beginning, the middle, the end in a package. It's the telling of the tale that's most important in this film. It's the kind of film that allows everybody to make their own stories. Obviously, blacks were very taken with folklore or mythology.

One of the comments made earlier [concerned the idea of] characters depicting evil and good. I think that that was not really a part of this film. Every character is complex — every single one of them was complex. So to cast them as evil or good is to totally to miss the point. With black people, there is always this need for inviting the past so as to make sense of our existence. But to stick with that past consistently is dangerous. But to more or less recall it at times of need is obviously fine. So Harry was, in a sense, welcome at the beginning. But then, the longer he stayed, the more he had to be gotten rid of. So it is with that kind of obsession about the past.

Then there is another quality to the film, and that is what is actually spoken is not actually the thing that is being spoken about. Some of it is actually of the state of mind. Folklore operates in this sort of way: What's inside comes out, more or less. So there's a certain ambivalence about what's being said. For instance, the guy who said, "I'll be the first in line to marry you" — obviously it's a very strange kind of statement. I'm sure when people looked at the screen, they might say, "You know, this doesn't make sense." This kind of statement is a mixture of what goes on simultaneously in the mind and in actuality. This kind of stuff is the power of the film.

I wish Charlie would follow this area, which is very unique, which is very much steeped in a culture that most of us are not familiar with. So instead of categorizing the movie and putting it into the old sort of storytelling device, the idea is to encourage him and let him make the kind of film that he wants to make. I think that would be a major contribution to film. This film will be a classic. And this is the kind of film that people will see over and over again because it's not an exhaustible kind of film or story. Thank you very much.

Robbins: I wanted to say that Charles works with women in his crew. He has black and white people working. He is the kind of filmmaker that we have to support. And the fact that this film has had such a poor marketing approach in the sense that very few people have seen it is something that we have to remember and work on for the future. And there's just one thing I want to know from Charles: What is he working on now? And what can we look forward to for the next feature that you're making?

Burnett: I'm working on a script that's called, right now, *My Word of Honor.* And it's about a guy who killed a guy in Vietnam—a lieutenant. These two guys—one ended up in jail and the other one is an aide to the governor, in San Francisco. And the one in jail discovers this guy, and he wants to use him to try to get the governor to block his extradition because he's wanted for murder in Missouri. Then it gets out of hand, and it gets into sort of a Watergate kind of a situation. One of the themes is, who has the right to kill?

For Further Study

Videocassette

To Sleep with Anger is available on videocassette from Sony/Columbia-Tri-Star.

Periodicals

Cerone, Daniel, "Awakening to the Realities of Black Life." *Los Angeles Times*, August 12, 1989.

Dargis, Manhola. "To Live and Die in L.A.?" *Village Voice*, November 20, 1990.

Hahem, Samir. "On Location: The House of Spirits." *Village Voice*, August 22, 1989.

Hearty, Kitty Bowe. "An Everyman Called Danny." *Premiere*, February 1992.

"In from the Wilderness at Last." *Time*, June 17, 1990.

Lopate, Phillip. "Charles Burnett Does the Right Thing." *Esquire*, November 1990.

Rohter, Larry. "An All-Black Film (Except the Audience)." *New York Times*, November 20, 1990.

Sharp, S. "Charles Burnett." *Black Film Review* (Washington, D.C.), 1990.

Thompson, Anne. "Anger Strike Back: The Non-Marketing of Charles Burnett." *Los Angeles Weekly*, November 16, 1990.

Vaughn, Christopher. "Case Study: *To Sleep with Anger.*" *Hollywood Reporter*, August 7, 1990.

Wallace, David. "Burnett—Telling a Story on a Shoestring." *Los Angeles Times*, October 24, 1990.

14

WILLIAM FRIEDKIN

AND

To Live and Die in L.A.

(with Steven Gaydos)

On November 15, 1991, director William Friedkin was interviewed by critic Steven Gaydos after a screening of *To Live and Die in L.A.* They were joined in a panel discussion by Andy Klein, film critic for the *Los Angles Reader*; Gerald Petievich, author of the novel that the film was based on and cowriter of the screenplay; Officer John Petievich of the Los Angeles Police Department and brother of Gerald; and Geoff Gilmore, program director of the UCLA Film and Television Archives.

The Film

To Live and Die in L.A. (1985). an MGM/UA Entertainment release from UA of a New Century Productions, Ltd., and SLM, Inc., presentation of an Irving H. Levin production. Produced by Irving H. Levin. Executive producer, Samuel Schulman. Directed by William Friedkin. Screenplay by William Friedkin and Gerald Petievich, based on the novel by Petievich. Director of photography, Robby Muller. Editor, Bud Smith. Music by Wang Chung. Shot on location in Los Angeles. Technicolor. 116 minutes.

    Cast: William L. Petersen (Richard Chance), Willem Dafoe (Eric Masters), John Pankow (John Vukovich), Debra Feuer (Bianca Torres), John Turturro (Carl Cody), Darlanne Fluegel (Ruth Lanier), Dean Stockwell (Bob Grimes), Steve James (Jeff Rice).

Synopsis: In Los Angeles, treasury agent Richard Chance and his partner, John Vukovich, try to catch a master counterfeiter who has killed Chance's partner. On their way to ensnaring this brilliant criminal, the duo find themselves breaking the law. Vukovich, at first reluctant to be a party to the unprincipled lengths to which his partner will go, finds himself willing to match, and perhaps even surpass, his partner's zeal.

Remarks and Reviews

"*To Live and Die in L.A.* in full of flash, style and grit. What it isn't full of is even an ounce of humanity or hope. It's difficult to say whether it's a movie about cynical, pathetic people or simply a cynical, pathetic movie" (Jimmy Summers, *Boxoffice*).

"The movie has everything that money can buy, but it doesn't have its own identity. It has no reason for being" (Vincent Canby, *New York Times*).

"This is a movie that tears up your nerves: both cinematographer Robby Muller and editor Bud Smith work you over brilliantly. . . . Friedkin's L.A. . . . is a Darwinian world, clogged with trash, hard as a brick, soaked with evil. It's *film noir* blanched" (Michael Wilmington, *Los Angeles Times*).

"I've never been a fan of William Friedkin. . . . But this new thriller has such controlled technical snap that I was engrossed throughout. . . . This is far and away the best thriller of the year" (Andy Klein, *Los Angeles Reader*).

"Friedkin . . . shows more empathy for [the] villain than for any of his protagonist-cops. Yet he stays with the cops for his heroes. Maybe next time he will switch from cops to robbers. That's where his heart is" (Kirk Honeycutt, *Daily News*).

"*To Live and Die in L.A.* is a deep-set nutcase movie. You get the feeling that the filmmakers responsible for it are working out of some manic, militarized zone for which they alone hold the map" (Peter Rainer, *Los Angeles Herald-Examiner*).

"*To Live and Die in L.A.* is a sleek piece of trash with dispensable heroes thrown onto the garbage heap along with everything else" (David Denby, *New York*).

"The story is taking place around Christmastime, and . . . there is a noticeable absence of . . . Christmasy touches. If a Santa ventured into this film, he might very well — like several of the other characters here — find himself shot point-blank in the face" (Janet Maslin, *New York Times*).

"If I were forced to choose between . . . a sleazo-from-birth like Friedkin . . . and Michael Corleone for godfather of my child, I'd think about kissing the ring" (David Edelstein, *Village Voice*).

"This one's going to get some very violent reaction: some will be appalled by its rapacious violence, others will be thrilled by its searing action. Certainly, William Friedkin's *To Live and Die in L.A.* travels the meanest streets of film noir, and genre buffs will be blown away. On a visual and visceral level, *To Live and Die in L.A.* is nonstop powerful. . . . The glossy, sun-drenched L.A. scene in Friedkin's scorching drama is itself a visual correlative for the moral turpitude of fast-life L.A. Sunsets burning through smog, warning lights glimmering on oil refineries, panty hose shining on luscious legs are among the beautifully horrible images that Friedkin and director of photography Robby Muller so strikingly jar one with throughout. *To Live and Die in L.A.* is a superbly realized film" (Duane Byrge, *Hollywood Reporter*).

The Filmmaker

Since Robert Aldrich, Don Siegel, Anthony Mann, and Fritz Lang are not making Hollywood crime films anymore, can we please have a hearty round of applause and a quiet prayer for the continued good health and artistic orneriness of film director William Friedkin? With Samuel Fuller's European exile and Clint Eastwood's temporary lack of interest in the crime genre, Friedkin may be the only filmmaker in Hollywood with the skills and cinematic vision to make crime films that are thoughtful, personal, stylish, and truly disturbing.

That's disturbing, as opposed to disturbed, which describes the great glut of formulaic cops 'n' creeps thrillers that dominate the action marketplace. On the one hand you have your stock action studs, Stallone, Bruce Willis, Chuck Norris, Steven Seagal, and their brainlessly efficient action helmsmen (and women), Renny Harlin, John McTiernan, Kathryn Bigelow, Andrew Davis. And on the other hand you have Friedkin, alone and fighting forces every bit as powerful as the gangsters and goblins of his most famous films. He's fighting, as Ned Beatty explained to Peter Finch in Paddy Chayefsky's *Network*, "the primordial cash flow."

Make that loud prayer.

Friedkin's is a restless, ambitious intellect, at odds sometimes with itself and determinedly at crossed swords with the contemporary Hollywood film industry's propensity for safe fluff and empty actioners. Here is a filmmaker who started making tough social documentaries while barely out of his teens, honed his craft in the golden age of television drama, then hit the lottery for Oscars and bucks with *The French Connection* (1971) and *The Exorcist* (1973). After that he turned to making idiosyncratic, challenging films that were often erratic and just as often quite brilliant. For example, *Cruising* (1980) dared to take Al Pacino and a big budget Hollywood crime film out into the gay S & M subcuture. The results are debatable, but when most studio projects are computer-generated yawners, Friedkin's experiments and excesses always serve as a stimulating alternative.

Deal of the Century (1983) may have been a comedic misfire centered on the international arms trade, but in 1983, no one in Hollywood had the temerity to question the Reagan-era military buildup or the dizzying global arms race that resulted in the Soviet Union's economic collapse and whose aftershocks are still being felt from Somalia to America's homeless-clogged streets.

If his latest crime film, *Rampage*, is cinematographically unpleasant, full of harsh light, grainy colors, and uncosmeticized characters, it is even more narratively discomforting. But it also stands as the most serious film investigation to date of both the largely discredited slasher genre and the issue of the death penalty in America. But these films, and others, never made the kind of megabucks of his earlier hits, and most critics, busy following the grosses and rewriting studio publicity releases, never bothered to chart William Friedkin's creative progress. (From Steven Gaydos's review of *Rampage*, *Los Angeles Reader*).

William Friedkin's Filmography

As director: (*Note:* Before his work in feature films, Friedkin worked in television. By his own estimate, he worked on over a thousand television programs.) Feature films: *Good Times* (1967); *The Night They Raided Minsky's* (1968); *The Birthday Party* (1968); *The Boys in the Band* (1970); *The French Connection* (1971); *The Exorcist* (1973); *Sorcerer* (1977); *The Brink's Job* (1978); *Cruising* (1980); *Deal of the Century* (1983); *To Live and Die in L.A.* (1985); *The Guardian* (1990); *Rampage* (1992); *Blue Chips* (1994).

Reasons for Selection

To Live and Die in L.A. is a more daringly original crime film than his earlier *French Connection*, but its timing was as wrong as *Connection*'s was fortuitous. In 1971, America was sick with Vietnam and race war, and nobody bought the idea that cops and authority figures were knights in shining armor. In contrast, *Live and Die* came out in 1985, the height of Ronald Reagan's happy-face era. Dark films about official malfeasance and moral duality were not wowing the masses, and as corporate control of Hollywood tightened its grip, mavericks and auteurs were being blacklisted without the need of any messy hearings. Look back on the 1980s and try to find an American crime thriller that is as thoughtful, polished, original, or as exciting as *To Live and Die in L.A.* Good Luck.

—S.G.

The Interview

Steven Gaydos: Bill, I just read a quotation from an interview with you. You were talking about the idea of going into a picture not with a preconceived notion but going in an and learning and exploring along the way. What kinds of things did you learn during the process of making this picture?

William Friedkin: I really don't know how to answer that question, Steve. What is your next question? No, I mean I learned a great deal about how counterfeit money is made and stuff like that. Actually, as I haven't seen a picture in years—but whatever authenticity or technical background that I strived for I now realize is just sort of evaporated inside the fiction. And that very often happens to me. . . . I don't know if it happens to anybody else, but Gerry Petievich's novel *To Live and Die in L.A.* struck me as being something that had a kind of documentary realism in addition to being very incisive about a certain kinds of law-enforcement officer, the dark side of that sort individual. What I see actually happened was my own problems and hang-ups got all over the film. It's almost like taking somebody's canvas and painting over it with something else that you had in mind. I doubt seriously whether this would be the film that Gerry Petievich would have made from his own work. Gerry was a Secret Service agent for, I guess, nineteen years or so. His experiences and his observations of the people whom he worked with were very clear in the book. Then when you'd meet these people, you would see what he was talking about. I was fascinated by the kind of surrealistic life of a Secret Service agent, about which almost nothing is really known. There has never been any good fiction about it other than Gerry Petievich's. The notion that a man will be protecting the president of the United States on a given evening . . . he'll be sitting in a suite up in the Century Plaza Hotel playing poker with the president of the United States and on a very close personal basis with the president. The next day he might be chasing a guy in Watts for a $50 bad check or a credit card. And that seemed to me to be a really strange juxtaposition. It seemed like a surrealistic landscape. I guess that was what really intrigued me.

Gaydos: Would you say that your reputation for getting into the work that you are making a film about is justified?

Friedkin: No. Everything that I do is just impressionistic. It's right off the top of my head.

Gaydos: You weren't more intently involved in the research on this picture or on *The French Connection*?

Friedkin: There is a lot of research but you are not making a documentary. You know, years ago I started working on documentary films, and I found that to be very limiting because my tendency was always, for good or ill, to impose my own sensibilities on what I was seeing and experiencing. And that is not always the best way to approach a documentary. What you want to do with a certain kind of documentary film is see what's there and let it speak for itself. And I found that difficult even when I started out making documentaries. I could never let the subject speak for itself. So I was in the wrong field, clearly. But I had a lot of training in documentary that goes into a film like this. You learn how to impose the documentary style on a work of fiction. And that is what this is: a work of fiction with a documentary style imposed on it. Now, the documentary style for the most part is a very sort of improvisational acting technique. Very often I won't tell the cameraman where the actors are going. I won't tell the actors where the camera is. I'll just send everybody out there to try to find out what is going on. And that is really what happens when you go out to film documentary. You don't know if the guy is going to get up and walk over there, walk out of the room, get mad, and lean out of the frame. And I found that I could induce that technique on fiction, and that is what I have done.

Gaydos: So the exploring is not so much thematic as it is part of your filmmaking process. You are exploring in the filmmaking of the scene, not so much exploring to search for some truth in Treasury agentry.

Friedkin: I don't know if there was anything involved like a search for truth. I would never say that at all.

Gaydos: Let's use the word *authenticity.*

Friedkin: Authenticity is in the eye of the beholder. Almost anyone coming into a given story to film anybody's world will have their own idea of what is authentic and what isn't. I was always fascinated by the thin line between the policeman and the criminal. The notion that there is a great danger in having someone who is wearing a badge exposed to this kind of life every day for nineteen or twenty years — I have always been interested in what that does to the spirit. For example, a police officer who never sees people for what they are but for their stereotype, the more you go around with police officers, the more you realize how true from their standpoint the stereotype is.

Gaydos: So the transition at the end for the Vukovich character, for you just makes perfect sense.

Friedkin: Vukovich becomes Chance in a way. I don't think that was the ending to the novel. Gerry Petievich is an interesting guy, and far more interesting probably than any filmmaker you are going to meet. He is the stuff of which films are made. He was writing novels while he was in the Secret Service. Since he has left he has written a number of other novels, all of them really state of the art. I mean, the very best cime fiction is being written by people like Elmore Leonard and, I would say, Gerry Petievich. *To Live and Die in L.A.* is a story that was much closer to him and his experience than it was to me. You know, this might be interesting because Gerry and I have never really talked about this a lot. We have talked about other things. His own attitudes about the film could differ from mine to a great extent for all I know. Some guy wrote a book about me which I sort of glanced through, and Petievich had a lot of unkind things to say about me. Maybe now he can answer for them.

Gerald Petievich: Well, now I have to face the music. I would like to say one thing: The other night somebody asked me this in a class that I am teaching, and I realized that I had never told the story about how I originally got the idea for *To Live and Die in L.A.* I was working in Paris with Interpol and on a Saturday night a friend of mine in law enforcement called up and he said, "Look, I can't find anybody else, so would you go with me to the De Gaulle Airport? There are some guys flying in with a load of money and dope, and I want to arrest them and I can't find anybody else to help me." So I said, "Yeah, OK." We were driving out there, and on the way he started talking. I had known the guy for a long time and I trusted him. He says, "You know, Gerry, there is one thing about this. These guys are flying in and nobody knows they are flying in with all this money and, you know, if somebody stuck 'em up at the airport and took their money, nobody would know who it was and they wouldn't have anybody to complain to." And he says, "We have guns, so what do you think?" And I said, "Well, probably it is not really a good idea tonight." So we didn't do it. We arrested them and put them in jail, and I got home that night, and I made notes all night 'cause I thought that was the idea I had been looking for to write about.

As far as my conception of what the movie would be . . . books and movies are totally different forms. Without Billy Friedkin, I wouldn't have known what to do. Billy wrote most of the script. He instructed me on what to do and how it is a visual medium. When you write a book, it is words on a piece of paper, and you have to create a picture from words. Well, it is not like that in a film. I hadn't seen the movie in years, and tonight I am sitting here watching it, and when I look at how these shots are set up. . . . The story is still there, the basic story is cops becoming crooks. That is the story I would have told if somebody would have made me a director. That is the story I would have wanted to tell. So I have no complaints. It is not like this movie came out to be something other than what I wanted. As far as the vision of the film — I don't know that Billy would agree with this, but it is film noir. I remember sitting with some producers and some money people and Billy Friedkin. They said that you can't do this with the ending. You can't kill the hero. Billy in his very calm mannered way — told them "No. You can do it," because that is what the story is all about.

Friedkin: We told them to go fuck themselves.

G. Petievich: I am trying to be a diplomat here.

Friedkin: In a very calm way.

G. Petievich: In a very calm way.

Friedkin: No, I thought that there had to be some kind of retribution. The guy couldn't walk away from that situation that he had put himself in. I think the people who were behind the picture wanted to get a sequel and this and that. And in fact they cried so hard — they were crying, you know, and tearful and emotional — that I actually went out and shot another ending in order to appease these guys 'cause they were really nice guys. So we shot another ending that had Chance survive that bullet in the head. You see there is a television, and you see their boss Bateman on television taking credit for making this big bust. And the camera pulls back and there is Vukovich and Chance. Chance has a few bandages on, and they are sitting there watching this asshole take credit for something that he had nothing to do with. And they kind of look at each other, and the camera keeps pulling back and back. You see that they are in a very small room somewhere, and then it cuts to an exterior, and you see that they are in the middle of Nome, Alaska. They have been transferred to the Nome, Alaska, branch of the Secret Service. [*Audience laughs.*] And I feel that was pretty funny. You know, you looked at it and it was half a laugh, like you just did here. But I thought it really wasn't true to the material, so we went to this ending which was a disaster commercially because anything that anyone invests in this character is completely shot down in that moment.

Gaydos: Except that Vukovich does sort of emotionally take over that for you as a viewer. Were there any other endings considered?

Friedkin: We talked about some stuff, but nothing, really. We only talked about other endings because these guys were so panicked about killing the star after a hundred minutes of a movie about this guy. Suddenly he gets a bullet in the brain. It isn't generally done. I remember that after this picture was made, a whole bunch of guys asked me to do films for them. Like Sylvester Stallone wanted me to make a film with him. He said, "You know, I love *To Live and Die in L.A.*, but if I had been in it, you would not have killed me." I said "Well, maybe that is why you weren't in it."

Geoff Gilmore: You said before that this is a film about cops and crooks and the thin line. That is a theme that has been taken by a lot of other films. *Dirty Harry* is about a character who crosses the line between a certain kind of criminality and cops. What is different about this and *Dirty Harry* is the kind of moral ambivalence that the film has itself toward either of these characters. And it is interesting that when you talk about the hero, he is a very nonheroic figure. If anything, the ambivalence that one has toward this film is how fascinated one becomes with both the Dafoe and Peterson characters all through the film. And alternately, one's interest goes out to each of them at different points. It is constantly switching back and forth, so it is not a good guys versus bad guys film.

Friedkin: That is interesting. I think that is the thing that brought Gerry and me together. I can't speak for Gerry. He'll speak for himself, but I think that one of the things that we share is that we really don't have any heroes. Maybe we did. I mean, maybe Gerry's father is a hero to him. But I don't have any heroes, and I don't go with that stuff. I am interested in stories, and I don't know who the hero is, and I see a field of gray. I see people sometimes, very good people, doing things that you would say are horrible. Sometimes I do things myself that are so shocking to me that I can't believe it, and I would like to think of myself as a hero of myself but I am not. I mean, everybody to me is so gray. What turns me off with the films today is the generic need to have a hero with a moral center. That is interesting, but that is not my experience of life. Not at all. My experience with life is that very bad people are sometimes capable of very good things. We were talking this evening about [convicted mobster] John Gotti, who is a criminal in New York. He is one of the bosses whom I have met on a number of occasions. There is not a nicer man to meet in a social situation than this guy. Maybe it is that he has a lot of self-assurance in other ways. I don't know. I just don't happen to see the world in terms of black and white or heroes and villains.

G. Petievich: The question, of course, in the kind of stuff I write is whether the police have their morals degenerated by the work they are in or whether that came first. Actually, the egg came before the chicken. People who are policemen come to this work. You are not drafted to be in law enforcement. You pick this out of all the varieties of work there are. You decide that you go into a work where you actually put people in jail. That isn't exactly the most normal desire of most people. So I have always looked at that in those terms.

Willem Dafoe and Debra Feuer in *To Live and Die in L.A.*

Friedkin: Gerry's brother, John, is currently with the Los Angeles Police Department. John has done a couple of acting jobs for me on a couple of films and is an extraordinary guy, and there is nothing like being in that job experiencing what these gentlemen experience day after day. I have watched over the years the steady deterioration of respect for policemen to the point now that you don't know who the bad guys are anymore. I don't know. As Jack Valenti said about Lyndon Johnson, "I sleep better when Lyndon Johnson is in the White House." I sleep better because John Petievich is on the streets of Los Angeles. I thought you guys might be interested in talking about a little something other than just the filmmaking process because it fits so much with the work that I have done over the years. These are the guys that have actually experienced it. I have never experienced anything outside of 90210 area code.

Gaydos: When was the last time that you saw the picture, John?

John Petievich: I watch it about every three months.

Gaydos: That's funny because everybody that I talked to that I invited to come here tonight, has said, "Gee, I watch it all the time."

J. Petievich: Great flick.

Friedkin: These are the guys. This film is about them, in many ways, and in many ways it is about me. The moral ambivalence that Gerry introduces in his novel that is in the film, I mean, I carry to an extreme. So in that sense I don't know whether Gerry might have been better served by, let's say, Steven Spielberg, who would have put a more human face on all of this stuff. Because these guys are not all that it degenerates into in a hundred minutes. You think that all these Secret Service agents must be corrupt, or all these cops are corrupt. The fact is that the world that they are involved in on a day-to-day basis is nothing but corrupt. We were talking at dinner tonight, and both Gerry and John were saying that you can tell when a person is lying from across the room—I mean, if somebody back in the last row can spot it, and they can tell you how.

Gaydos: I'd like to ask him how.

Friedkin: Well, for example you are lying right now.

Gaydos: John, is there anything in this film that whenever you look at it, you go, "No way"? Is there anything that is cranked up so far that you think it is out of the question?

J. Petievich: Well, you couldn't do that on a daily basis. Billy used a lot of real policemen in the movie for bit parts, and I think that helped. Like *The Godfather*—I think that the character actors in that really helped it. And in this too. Not going into the story itself, but different factions of the film were pretty real.

Gaydos: Bill, did this book come to you, or did you find it?

Friedkin: I get sent a lot of stuff all the time from publishers, agents, and friends. And somebody passed me the manuscript of this book. Most of this stuff is not only not authentic, it's unreadable, or it is so false you can spot it. But this rang true. I started reading it and I couldn't believe it was just right on. It had to do with a lot of people that I had met over twenty years of knowing police officers in a number of different cities—sheriffs, people in various different branches of law enforcement. This seemed to be to me to be true in general of the characters and nature of the people that I had met.

Gaydos: Would you say that is the most striking thing about good crime fiction?

Friedkin: There is not a lot of good crime fiction to me, frankly. Gerry's work and Elmore Leonard's work—they just stick out of there. There are a lot of guys trying it and stuff and pumping it up. This stuff is really exceptional. It is as close as I have seen to what happens in the street. It is as close as you can get. It has to have a kind of fictional wrap around it; otherwise you couldn't read it. You couldn't experience it if it wasn't fictionalized in some way. For example, I made a film of *The French Connection* case, and the film has almost nothing to do with the French Connection case, although everyone thinks it does. But that was a case that took place over eight or nine months' time. A lot of it was boring police procedure, the kind of thing that John and Gerry can tell you goes on in their life all the time. The real police work has a lot of the boredom contingent. So you pump it up for the sake of a one-hundred-minute movie. Like John says, you couldn't live like this every day.

Gaydos: When you were talking about shades of gray and characters with moral ambiguity—I wonder if in your career there was a time that it was easier or more acceptable to make that kind of movie? Has that changed over the past two or three decades?

Friedkin: No. I haven't seen *Cape Fear*, but I understand that the guy at the center of that is as morally decadent as it gets. If you make a good film about a bad guy, it has got to be very interesting. When it is well done, it has a kind of my mythical or biblical overview—good and evil—and the evil character in fiction, for me, very often is much more interesting. The kind of fiction that lasts, a work like *Othello*, for God's sake, where there is goodness in him but also he is a murderer—there are many examples of that. The classic fiction has at its center really evil people.

Gaydos: So in terms of getting a film financed that deals with this sort of thing, it is no more difficult or no more easy than it was thirty years.

Friedkin: It isn't that easy for me, but it is easy for other people. A good story that comes along that has a morally ambivalent tone will always work when it is well done. What your point is, I think, is that there is not a lot of stuff well done, but I think that is true in almost any genre or any field. There aren't a lot of good comedy films around for adults. It is amazing the paucity of good fiction and good motion pictures when you really come to think about it. It is all subjective. The kind of thing that holds my interest is where none of the characters are limited to some preconceived notion of what they should be. That is why I cannot watch these guys on television—it is so false.

Gaydos: Is that something that keeps drawing you to do films about crime and cops?

Friedkin: I don't know. I may be played out on that subject, for good or ill, I mean, between *To Die in L.A.* and *The French Connection*, there is not a lot more that I really care to say about policemen and criminals. I would be just pounding out the same thing over again, which I have done to some degree. I've tried variations on that. You know, I made a film called *Cruising*, which is a deep, dark variation of a cop gone over, and it is not totally successful. Perhaps that's because I was never able to get Al Pacino to committ totally to the limits of where that character should've gone.

Gilmore: Regarding the Cody material in the film . . . I was wondering if there had been another ending at one point because all the stuff with John Turturro is great. But by the end, there is no real payoff on that in a plot sense. Was that something that was missing?

Friedkin: No, I don't think it was meant to be. He was a minor role player who struts and frets his role upon the stage and then is seen no more. We didn't feel that we had to resolve his character. You know, he was a guy who came in for three or four weeks and then went back to New York. He was on the call sheet for three weeks, and we gave him a ham sandwich, and we sent him back home.

I mean, this guy is genuinely funny. He was a real card. Gerry Petievich created all these characters, but a lot of what went into his role, for example, is improvisation of his own zaniness. He is the kind of guy you just let go to a certain extent. They are letting him go a lot more today than I wish they would. But he is an interesting, funny guy. Always was.

Gilmore: Also, the sequence at the beginning where we see how to counterfeit: Is that pretty much all down-the-line, state-of-the-art at that point?

Friedkin: We had a counterfeiter who was the technical adviser on that. I think it led to Gerry's early retirement from the Secret Service. I mean, we found a guy to counterfeit money. I passed that stuff for about a year after we made the film.

I would stick one of those twenties in a roll of real twenties, and I would go around and tip shoeshine guys twenty dollars. You know, it is as good as real money. I mean, what's the difference? Here is a very talented guy, an artist who can make this money. So why in the world of free enterprise . . . this isn't Communist China, for God's sake. I always felt that guy's was as good looking and sometimes better, and for years, from time to time I would light a cigar with a twenty at a party and people were really impressed. They'd think, Jesus, movie directors make a lot of bread that they can waste it like that. It was real money, and it was a primer on counterfeiting, if you knew what you were doing.

Gaydos: One of the things you started talking about when Gerry came up here was the way you guys worked together doing this screenplay.

G. Petievich: I can say there was one scene that I thought would have brought out more of Vukovich's character. It was a scene where he meets with someone in his family. He doesn't like the things that are going on, and he is very vague on it. It was kind of a boring scene, and I don't think there is anything in the movie that is boring. I remember mentioning that to Billy. I wrote the scene, and he looked at it, and we talked about it for a couple of weeks, but it just didn't fit with the rest of the film. Other than that, most of these scenes and the impetus for these scenes really were Billy's.

Friedkin: Well, I wrote that out of a book. I wrote the script, and then I would give to Gerry. He would make certain changes, and he wrote some scenes and put them in. It was a very impressionistic collabaoration. There is no doubt in my mind that this was his story. The first thing that I said to Gerry was that I would want him to be happy with the picture more than anyone else. Once it comes out, it may not be cast exactly as he would like, but I hoped that he would be happy with it. I told him if he was happy with it, then I thought it would probably be pretty good.

Gilmore: Were you happy with the cast?

Friedkin: I wouldn't cast the picture any differently today if I could have Mel Gibson or the biggest stars in the world. I don't know how Gerry feels about it.

G. Petievich: Well, it is evident that the people in this are good actors. They have all been successful, including Willem Dafoe and everyone else, so I would agree.

Gaydos: Maybe John can answer this or also Gerry. In the police community, what sort of feedback did you get about the picture?

J. Petievich: That was probably the most popular picture in all the prisons in the state of California and in the police departments. The cops loved it, and all the convicts that we talked to. They were playing it in Folsom, and they really liked it. And the cops still rent it out all the time and watch it and watch it over again and over again.

Friedkin: You see — I get a lousy review from Vincent Canby, but Charles Manson loves me. I am Charles Manson's favorite director, and then I turn around, and I am Jeffrey Dahmer's favorite director, you know. The guy is sitting up in Milwaukee, cutting up people and watching *The Exorcist.*

Gaydos: What would you say is the reason for the appeal? Is it entertainment, or is there something more there?

Friedkin: It is the fine line between police work and the criminal. I think that it draws the interest in both sides and the public.

G. Petievich: Policemen are part of the underworld. The criminals came first, then the policeman came. In this underworld everybody thinks the same. When you arrest criminals, particularly [when you are in] the Secret Service, you are arresting everyone for a felony crime.

These are people who make their living who have never held employment, and they just live by crime. When I went on the Secret Service I arrested a counterfeiter the first week, and I arrested the same counterfeiter two weeks before I left, fifteen years later. And he had been in and out of prison all the time. He knew me, and I knew him, and we talked the same language, and he understood me, and I understood him. This kind of understanding and this kind of undercurrent that cops and criminals know about is something that I really do think is brought out in the film and I think, more than any other film that I know about.

Gaydos: Could this story take place in any other city than L.A.? Is there something that either of you feel is distinctively Los Angeles about the film or the story?

G. Petievich: There was one scene that we had at Reflection Lake, but it didn't work. But you know, L.A. is Reflection Lake. Everything is counterfeit. Every gas station attendant has a script, and every waitress wants to be an actress, and everybody who is in business wants to be Michael Milken. So it is a very strange place. This is the land where all the counterfeiting of the world takes place. Strangely enough, in other towns it is done by organized crime. Here in L.A. it is always done by amateurs. Over my fifteen years in the Secret Service there were at least fifteen to twenty times we would go to Disneyland because someone had passed one counterfeit bill. You would say, "Do you have any other counterfeit bills?" and they would say, "No, I don't." And you would say, "Fine." And so you would sit there in Disneyland, and you would wait until midnight, when everyone had left, and there would be one car left in the parking lot. That would be the car the guy came in that you had arrested. And you would go out and open the trunk, and there would be a million dollars in the trunk of the car. I personally have done that. These are amateurs that think that L.A. is the place that you make it big. That is why I think L.A. added a lot to the movie.

Gaydos: It seems like you avoid the standard L.A. locales here. There are almost no famous locations here, no kitschy Tail of the Pup restaurants or any of that.

Friedkin: Except for the chase scene, which is shot in areas that people are familiar with, around the Seventh Street Bridge downtown, most of the rest of the film was shot in Wilmington and San Pedro. I don't know what the famous L.A. landmarks are. I don't really get around here that often. I stay at home a lot and read books and listen to music, and I really don't know. There is no Empire State Building here, or what would be a famous L.A. landmark.

Gilmore: It would be the Tail of the Pup.

Friedkin: I remember that once I saw Jayne Mansfield's heart-shaped swimming pool. If we could've shot something there, I would have loved it.

Gilmore: Is there really a Shipwrecked John's Cabaret?

Friedkin: Yeah, it's all out in San Pedro. San Pedro is a very interesting area.

Audience Question: All the movies are so predictable that you always know what is going to happen and what the good guys are going to do. I went to see *Sorcerer* again last week, and it had a similar ending. And for me, I always tell people to wait for the ending.

Friedkin: You are sort of a member of a minority in that what we hear from the studio most of the time is that "we can't root for this guy." Every time I come in with a story, they say, "Geez, but we can't root for this guy." I don't know what the fuck they are talking about. Root for what? Why do you need to root? You cannot root for Richard III, you know. But it is one of the greatest things that I have ever seen. It is outstanding. I mean if a guy brought it in today, as a screenplay, to Touchstone Pictures. . . "We can't root for this guy," and guess what. . . They would change it. He would change it. I am sure that Shakespeare, being a professional, would adapt his great talents to the genius of the people who run the studio today.

AQ: I have seen this film seven or eight times. I love it. Nonetheless, I did find myself rooting for the character of Chance. The first time I saw it, I was shocked that he was killed. I kept thinking that somehow he was going to make it back at the end. I was wondering if you gave any thought to the effect of killing his character because I found it to be emotionally frustrating.

Friedkin: Well, look, if you are so emotionally overwrought about it, give me your address, and I will send you the other ending I shot, and you can run it on your TV set, and the guy is alive. I have this ending, and I know exactly where it is in storage. Leave your address, and I will send it to you. Seriously, though, I can't look at it—it was so lacking in commitment from me as a director. I had a chance to resurrect the character that I killed, and I couldn't pull it off. But I would love to send it to you, seriously.

AQ: I would just want to pick up on the same theme a little bit more. I hadn't seen the picture before, and I think it is very strong and even artistic. Don't blush.

Friedkin: I'm sorry to hear that. I really hate it when anyone can smell art. I know that I have failed.

AQ: It is a beautiful movie. I did have a problem along the lines suggested. I wasn't upset that the so-called hero didn't make it through. As you said, he wasn't the full hero. My concern was that the picture isn't gray. I think that would be fine.

Friedkin: It is gray.

AQ: The picture isn't gray, it's black. In the end I came away with the feeling that not only does this kind of corruption affect police—we have seen that from Kingsley's *Detective Story*, and that is done very well—but you get the sense that everybody is corrupt and everything is black, and at the end I felt almost like I wanted to go home and take a shower.

Friedkin: I think that is fair. It is a dark vision. And insofar as it remains truthful to a dark vision, I appreciate it. Where it isn't and where I failed to accomplish that for one reason or another, of compromise or weakness or whatever, that is where the picture bothers me. It is a dark vision. It is set out to be. Everyone in it is corrupt. The chief of the Secret Service is a jerk. There are other kinds of pictures to get the opposite effect. Like *E.T.*, nobody is corrupt. I am not saying that in a bad way because I think that is a great movie and probably a perfect film. I couldn't do it. I don't see it. I love it when someone else does it. But it was not meant to show both sides of something. It starts out as a dark vision and ends up that way. Like T. S. Eliot's poems, I am

William Friedkin

sure you have read "The Wasteland." For God's sake, this is a dark vision. Or
Allen Ginsberg's "Howl." And not to compare this to that, but the work that
impresses me in other media are pieces like Francis Bacon's paintings. I must
tell you that I come away from those things feeling enriched. When I see a truly
dark vision, something that specifically portrays evil and you can see it and it
is labeled and it is out there, I find it exhilarating.

AQ: I have always felt that this movie was a lot closer to Genet than to
Hollywood. Before I forget to ask, in the backstage scene in the nightclub, isn't
there a male body double that is used when he goes up and, like, kisses her?

Friedkin: Yeah.

AQ: And it seems like there is a whole lot of homoeroticism in this movie to me and the only relationships that sort of have any integrity are single-sex relationships of one kind or another.

Friedkin: Yeah, I am probably a closet homosexual.

AQ: I was just wondering if it was a real conscious titillation factor.

Friedkin: Like anybody else, I am interested in sex and all forms of sex. I am interested in it. It doesn't mean to say that I have experienced everything.

AQ: Did when you put that male body double in that, was it a conscious sort of tweak or something?

Friedkin: Yeah, that was a visual joke. In all seriousness, I am not interested so much in tweaking the audience about homosexuality or heterosexuality. It was a visual joke. The audience thinks, "Here comes this guy," and then he turns around and takes off a wig. That really is part of the counterfeit theme. That's in there for that reason. The movie is about, as Gerry said, the counterfeit nature of life in Los Angeles.

You know, a large part—and I want you to take this in context—a large part of homosexual love involves a kind of counterfeit relationship in terms of, let's say, what the Judeo-Christian ethic is of a normal relationship.

AQ: In this movie it goes through Christmas, and there is no reference to Christmas at all, either.

Friedkin: Yeah, that is all conscious. But the whole tweak at homoeroticism is the male pretending to be a female. The female who is masculine. There are any number of conscious levels where there is this counterfeit notion.

Gaydos: One of the things that I read which may or may not be true, that there was a bit of discussion between you and Gerry about raising the stakes in the sexuality in this and increasing the sexuality.

Friedkin: Gerry is a lot more uptight about that stuff than I am. He was a cop, for God's sake. You know, he was a cop for nineteen years, from a family of policemen—like Vukovich in the film—and, you know, old country, Catholic. You don't raise those subjects all the time. You might see them in the street, but you don't raise that. But I always thought that it was always there. Probably the main difference was in my concept of Masters from the book. I saw the guy as a really interesting, warped character. The notion of him of being a failed artist is original to the film.

In Gerry's novel you don't know what Masters does. He is a counterfeiter, and he is a kind of low-life thief/counterfeiter. And I thought about, who is this guy really? And I started thinking about Hitler, the notion of Hitler as a failed painter, and I sort of went from there.

AQ: I was curious about the ending, where Masters is waiting, sitting down, before the warehouse goes up in flames. Is that in the book?

Friedkin: No, it's lame. The ending is very lame. When I see it now I don't know why he is sitting there. I couldn't figure it out.

AQ: I couldn't either.

Friedkin: I don't know the answer to that. The book has Chance getting shot in the street in the book, right? The ending in the book is much better than the ending in the film. I don't know why I changed it. I was going toward some metaphysical horseshit that didn't come off.

AQ: I would like to know what is the significance of that Muslim guy blowing himself up?

Friedkin: The significance of the Muslim guy blowing himself up is he is a Muslim guy blowing himself up. That was done after the whole picture was shot. That scene is not in the novel, and it was not in the original film. And after we finished the picture, I started to think more and more. The idea that intrigued me about this story had not been fulfilled in what we had, in what I said to you at the outset about the surrealistic role of a Secret Service man who one day is protecting the president and the next day out in the street chasing a guy for a bad $50 check or a counterfeit credit card. So we started to think, "Well, let's show this guy protecting the president, for God's sake," 'cause we didn't have that in the book or in the film as it was shot.

So then Gerry and I sat down and wrote a scene that would introduce Chance and his original partner on the job, protecting the president of the United States today. Of course, because it was a prologue, it had to have an impact. It had to be kind of a short story in itself that would introduce one of the main characters and would introduce him in a way that would heighten the surrealistic nature of the job of a Secret Service man. Like, first you meet this guy coming out of a room with the president of the United States, who is going back after he made a speech and playing cards. And the terrorist is up there trying to bomb the president of the United States. And at that time there was a great deal of that sort of Middle East terrorism, so we took that and used that as an incident, meaning he could have been of any particular nationality. The fact that he was a Muslim—a Shiite in that sense—was just arbitrary. It was no comment against Shiites or anybody else. It was right out of the newspaper.

AQ: When you put a picture together you deal a lot with attorneys.

Friedkin: Unfortunately.

AQ: I work for a law office myself. I was wondering, from the attorneys you deal with, did they have any favorable comments regarding the film?

Friedkin: I agree with *Henry IV, Part I,* "First, let's kill all the lawyers." Most of the films you'll see of mine will have something bad to say about lawyers and psychiatrists in general.

I don't like to label people as a group, but Watergate was lawyers, right? What can I tell you? They were all lawyers, every one of them. John Mitchell, Richard Nixon, every single one of them.

G. Petievich: In the real world of law enforcement, policemen hate lawyers more than they do crooks. And the crooks hate lawyers more than they do cops.

AQ: Another facet of the movie I'm sure everybody here likes is the Wang Chung score. I am wondering if you can tell me the background of that.

Friedkin: That is an interesting point. To get into filmmaking a little bit, the score for *Sorcerer* and the score for this picture were done in the same way and came to me in the same sort of fashion.

Many years ago I was in Munich and I heard a group called Tangerine Dream. It was at 3:00 A.M. in the Black Forest outside Munich; these three guys were sitting in an abandoned church playing the most outstanding long tonal incredible sonorities that I had ever heard. I didn't show them the picture because I didn't want them to write a score that would ape the images of the film. I wanted it to contrast to what was going on. So I simply sent the script and told them the story, and they then went out into this abandoned church out there, and they laid down some tracks and mailed them to me. Sure enough there was a symbiosis there, and I just took the tracks and fit them to the picture. With *To Live and Die in L.A.*, I had heard this group called Wang Chung in England. It is two guys who did all the tracks, the vocals and instrumentals. I had heard them in England at an obscure kind of a theater in a place called Twickenham, and I thought "This is really an interesting, hip sound. It isn't really rock 'n' roll. I can't really put my finger on it." It was some kind of bizarre take on modern music. Same thing was true. I went to these two guys and said that I would like to have them do a score for this picture, but I wasn't going to show them the movie. They went back and just laid down a whole bunch of stuff and sent it through the mail, and I listened to it, and sure enough I just found stuff and used it. The one thing I said was, "Do not write a song called 'To Live and Die in LA.' I do not want to hear a fucking song with that lyric." And after we had made the whole picture, we were sitting around, and we were talking about this new scene. One day Jack Hughes, who was sort of the head guy of Wang Chung, he said, "You are going to hate me, but I have written a song called 'To Live and Die in L.A.'" I said, "I don't want to hear it." But I listened to it. It was just as interesting and haunting. I needed something to stick over the opening, so I just put it in there. It is a funky sort of lyric. It doesn't make any sense, but then I thought that this will work because the picture doesn't make a lot of sense either, so in that sense they're very compatible.

AQ: What inspired the bungee jumping in the opening?

Friedkin: That character is true to the character Gerry created. The bridge jumping is in the book. If we were making the film today, it would be more about the vulnerability and the weakness of the guy rather than the macho pose which that is. The more I think about these guys, the more I think that they act more out of fear and weakness than anything else. I think that I would try to emphasize that today more than anything. [*To Gerry.*] Did you know a guy who was doing that, or is that total fiction?

G. Petievich: When I was writing the book I was trying to think of a way of creating a character of a macho guy who was going to go wrong. And there actually was a federal agent who ripped off some money during a case, and he was a base jumper and subsequently jumped off of El Capitan up in Yosemite, and the parachute didn't open.

Friedkin: Let this film be a dedication to him.

AQ: Could you talk about how your film changes during the editing stage?

Friedkin: Editing is a wonderful thing where you try stuff out and it works or doesn't work. It is a whole different art form. Anything is possible with editing. And sometimes I probably go a little too crazy with it because I am so enamored of the process, of what you can do—the notion that you can show a man's thoughts when that actor might not have been thinking anything like what was going on there. It is an invention that is peculiar to film to be able to do it that way, although most of my filmmaking technique, in fact the bulk of it, comes from Proust's *Remembrance of Things Past*, which I read over and over and over again. It is like a quarry of cinematic ideas. I would be very hard put to give you specifics, but Proust's sentences are filled with little moments that just intrude. Two words intrude on a sentence, and that takes that sentence off into a whole other direction.

AQ: I have always liked this film since it first came out, but there is one thing that I have always wondered about. The plot keeps turning on these very drastic mistakes that the characters make. Is this a realistic level of ineptitude? In other words, do federal agents fall asleep on stakeouts? Do prisoners try to kill other prisoners in front of dozens of guards and in broad daylight, and so forth?

G. Petievich: There is a great difficulty when you have actually been in a field like law enforcement in writing about it because truth is actually stranger than fiction. People who are in prison are almost always psychopaths or sociopaths, and their goal in life is to kill themselves. That is the end of the road for them. That is what their life is aiming toward, so they do things like that. People in law enforcement that are on stakeouts or whatever do this every day, and sometimes you do this for thirty of forty days straight. After a while it is unimportant to you, and you become desensitized, and you hate all the criminals, and you are sitting there watching some jerk across the street while he mows his lawn or sits on his porch and drinks beer, and you are there twelve, fifteen, or eighteen hours, and so you might fall asleep. So those things do happen. The reason the story is created that way is because it is a story. It is noir. People are reaching their fate.

AQ: When you are in preproduction, how much planning is there in shot lists and script preparation? And also that same question applies to when you get into post, and how much supervising of editing you do. Are you doing the editing yourself?

Friedkin: Pretty much, yeah. I work with an editor, but I basically mark the frame. Not just because I am a control freak, which I am. But, yeah, I make out shot lists. One hundred percent of everything is preplanned. Here is what that does for you: I make out the shot lists. I know exactly what I want to do. When I go to the set, everybody on the set knows what we are going to do. They know that we are going to be here, and then we are going to be there, and then we are going to do this. They know everything we are going to do in a day's work. But I have so much freedom because I have planned this and that, so I can really feel free to change it if I want to. You don't feel free enough to change it and take a chance on something when you don't know what you are doing. There are a lot of very good filmmakers who will go to the set unprepared, waiting for inspiration, and very often it works for them a lot. My own nature works best when I can be so planned that I can be open to someone saying, "Why don't you do it this other way?" I can hear that and immediately find a way that this very good idea might fit into to my plan.

Whereas if I don't have a plan, I am not open to good ideas. I am just trying to get through the day. Without a plan on a big-budget movie, you are trying to get through that damn day. There is a lot of pressure. And very often when you are trying to get through the day, you will be closed off to inspiration. To me inspiration is the most important thing that can happen on a movie set. The whole script is there, everything is there. *The French Connection* was almost one hundred percent inspiration. You could actually call it an improvised movie. But it was so planned. The actors knew well in advance who they were and how they would react to a situation—how the real officers involved reacted—that they could go out there and create.

AQ: There is a question I have always wanted to ask about that sequence.

Friedkin: I know what's coming.

AQ: You know what it is?

Friedkin: Why are the cars going the wrong way? Well, just to add to the disorientation. The scene is about disorientation, and that scene just sort of adds to it.

AQ: It just didn't get flopped in the lab?

Friedkin: No, no, we didn't flop anything in the lab. I had them drive on the wrong side of the street because I figured that the whole picture at that moment has to take on a crazy dimension. You know, that was the intention anyway. There was a guy who used to teach around here, and his name was, believe it or not, Slavko Vorkapich. Have you ever heard of him? Vorkapich was a great film theorist. He was primarily an editor, and I used to sit in on his classes. His idea of filmmaking had a lot to do with the notion of deep immersion. If you get the audience involved in a sequence, then all this other bullshit about "left to right" and this guy has to be looking screen right and this guy screen left and all of that, he said is limiting and doesn't mean a goddamn thing. If the audience is involved in the picture, you can and must break every cinematic rule, and that will draw them in even further. When I first heard that from Vorkapitch, it was very liberating. So I tried that in a number of films. The first thing I went out and tried that on was in *The Exorcist*. There is a scene where the priest is talking to the little girl, who is in bed, and she is like a demon, and he has a tape recorder. The audience is very much involved in the film at that point, and in one shot you see him reach down in a long shot with his right hand to turn on the tape recorder. Then I made a close-up, and I had him bring his left hand toward it and turn the button on with his left hand. The actor said, "Why am I doing this?" and I said, "Trust me. Don't worry about it." Then when we were mixing the sound track over and over again, the mixer saw this fifty times, and at one point I said, "Does anyone see anything wrong in this scene? Does anything bother you?" No one ever caught it. I am sure to this day no one has ever caught it. I put that in strictly to illustrate Vorkapitch's theory of deep immersion. And, you know, it was one small step along that line.

Basically what I was leading toward was to do a lot more of that, where you break the kind of standardized thing that people are used to watching on television. Over the shoulder, left to right — everything is so damn boring. Look at Antonioni's films, if you get a chance — *La Notte*, *L'Avventura*, *L'Eclisse*, *The Passenger* — the films move laterally. There is nothing predictable in them. He never does anything like over-the-shoulder single-two shot — boom — matching sizes. Every single frame stands on its own and moves on to the next frame and moves on to the next. So there is no conventional anything in it. That has always been the sort of thing that I could do more of in films — break the conventions, help find a way toward a new language of filmmaking. Which I think that anyone who is making a film owes to the next people who come along.

For Further Study

Books

Blatty, William Peter. *William Peter Blatty on "The Exorcist" from Novel to Film*. New York: Bantam Books, 1974.

Loeb, Anthony. *Filmmakers in Conversation*. Chicago: Columbia College Film Department, 1980.

Segaloff, Nat. *Hurricane Billy*. New York: William Morrow and Company, 1990.

Wood, Robin. *Hollywood from Vietnam to Reagan*. New York: Columbia University Press, 1986.

15

ROBERT ALTMAN
AND
The Long Goodbye
(with Michael Wilmington)

On December 5, 1991, director Robert Altman was interviewed by Michael Wilmington after a screening of *The Long Goodbye*.

T h e   F i l m

The Long Goodbye (1973), a United Artists release. Directed by Robert Altman. Screenplay by Leigh Brackett. Based on the novel *The Long Goodbye*, by Raymond Chandler. Produced by Jerry Bick. Director of photography, Vilmos Zsigmond. Editor, Lou Lombardo. Music by John Williams. Filmed in Los Angeles, California.

Cast: Elliott Gould (Philip Marlowe), Nina van Pallandt (Eileen Wade), Sterling Hayden (Roger Wade), Mark Rydell (Marty Augustine) Henry Gibson (Dr. Verringer), Jim Bouton (Terry Lennox), David Arkin (Harry), Warren Berlinger (Morgan), Jo Ann Brody (Jo Ann Eggenweiler), Jack Knight (Hood), Pepe Callahan (Pepe), Rutanya Alda and Tammy Shaw (Marlowe's Neighbors), Vince Palmieri and Arnold Strong [Schwarzenegger] (Hoods), Jack Reilly, Ken Swansom, Danny Goldman, Sybil Scotford, Steve Colt, Tracy Harris, Jerry Jones, Rodney Moss, Pancho Cordoba, Enrique Lucero, John Davies, Herb Kerns.

Synopsis: Los Angeles private investigator Philip Marlowe helps and old pal, Terry Lennox, get to Tijuana. He then learns that Terry might have murdered his wife, and Marlowe is grilled by the police for aiding and abetting a fugitive. After police are told that Terry committed suicide in Mexico and Marlowe is released, an alcoholic novelist's wife, Eileen Wade, hires Marlowe to find her writer-husband. He does, in a sanitorium. Meanwhile, racketeer Marty Augustine demands that Marlowe pay back the money that Terry Lennox stole from him. Wade supposedly commits suicide by drowning himself.

Suspicious, and tracking connections between Wade and Terry's dead wife and between Eileen and Augustine, Marlowe returns to Mexico to find Terry.

Remarks   and   Reviews

"In *The Long Goodbye*, Robert Altman, a brilliant director whose films sometimes seem like death wishes, attempts the impossible and pulls it off. . . . [This is] Altman's most entertaining, most richly complex film since *M*A*S*H* and *McCabe and Mrs. Miller*. It's so good that I don't know where to begin" (Vincent Canby, *New York Times*).

"The rambling plot is no more than an excuse for Altman to muse wickedly on the corrupting sleaze of a drug-hazy '70s L.A., which he can't resist lyricizing even as he savages it. As always, Altman directs as if thinking out loud—the film feels as if it's been going on for hours before we get there—but he's also a sly entertainer whose perfectly timed shock tactics . . . jerk you into realizing you're witnessing a hateful world even the unflappable private eye can't escape" (Ella Taylor, *L.A. Weekly*, 1993).

"Robert Altman's heady, whirling sideshow of a movie . . . Altman kisses off the private eye form as gracefully as *Beat the Devil* parodied the international intrigue thriller. . . . This picture is just about as funny, though quicker witted and dreamier. . . . Gould gives a loose and woolly, strikingly original performance" (Pauline Kael, *5,001 Nights at the Movies*).

"The writer and his wife are played with really fine style by Sterling Hayden and Nina van Pallandt. . . . Gould has enough of the paranoid in his acting style to really put over Altman's revised view of the private eye" (Roger Ebert, *Roger Ebert's Movie Home Companion*).

The   Filmmaker

Robert Altman is one of the American cinema's most innovative mavericks and one of the most high-profile filmmaking talents to emerge in the 1970s. He was nominated for Academy Awards for directing *M*A*S*H* (1970), *Nashville* (1975), and *The Player* (1992).

A prolific television director through the 1960s on such series as *Combat* and *Bonanza*, Altman progressed to feature films with *Countdown* (1968) and made an auspicious international showing with the antiwar satire *M*A*S*H*, which was named best film of the year by the National Society of Film Critics and received the Golden Palm at the 1970 Cannes Film Festival. For the next six years, he was one of the most critically admired filmmakers in the world, delivering such extraordinary films as *McCabe and Mrs. Miller* (1971), *Images* (1972), *The Long Goodbye* (1973), and *Thieves Like Us* (1974).

His reputation peaked with *Nashville*, a multileveled look at the country music industry. *Nashville* was named best picture of the year and Altman was selected as best director by both the National Society of Film Critics and the New York Film Critics Circle.

Afterwards Altman's career took a few dives and spins. While he could still reap critical appreciation for *Three Women* (1977) and *A Wedding* (1978), most of his films in the late seventies and early eighties failed to find a wide audience. In fact, his two films with Paul Newman, *Buffalo Bill and the Indians or Sitting Bull's History Lesson* (1976) and *Quintet* (1979), were box-office flops.

Through the eighties, Altman turned to the stage for material and filmed several critically appreciated but narrowly distributed films, including *Come Back to the Five and Dime, Jimmy Dean, Jimmy Dean* (1982), *Streamers* (1983), and *Secret Honor* (1984). He also returned to television, where his political satire, *Tanner '88* (1988), was widely regarded as one of the best programs of the year. Altman's late-career television work also includes *The Laundromat* (1984), *The Caine Mutiny Court Martial* (1987), *The Dumb Waiter* (1987), and *The Room* (1987).

The success of *The Player*, an outstanding satire of the manipulations behind the operations of a major Hollywood studio, returned Altman to front-rank prominence. It was named best picture of the year, and Altman was selected as best director by the New York Film Critics Circle.

Altman's use of mobile cameras and his ability to elicit extemporaneous performances from a wide variety of actors and to imbue his best films with a quirky sense of irony have made him one of the most distinguished postwar American directors. His best films expose the sham of American institutions and subvert hypocrisy on a general basis.

Robert Altman's Filmography

As director, except where noted: *Bodyguard* (1948, story only); *The Delinquents* (1957, also producer, screenwriter), *The James Dean Story* (1957, documentary, also producer, editor); *Countdown* (1968); *That Cold Day in the Park* (1969); *Brewster McCloud* (1970); *Events* (1970, actor only); *M*A*S*H* (1970); *McCabe and Mrs. Miller* (1971, also screenwriter with Brian Mackay, based on the novel *McCabe*, by Edmund Naughton); *Images* (1972, also screenwriter); *The Long Goodbye* (1973); *California Split* (1974, also producer); *Thieves Like Us* (1974, also screenwriter with Calder Willingham and Joan Tewkesbury, based on the novel by Edward Anderson); *Nashville* (1975, also producer); *Buffalo Bill and The Indians or Sitting Bull's History Lesson* (1976, also producer and screenwriter with Alan Rudolph, based on the play *Indians*, by Arthur Kopit); *Welcome to L.A.* (1976, producer only); *The Late Show* (1976, producer only); *Three Women* (1977, also producer, screenwriter); *Remember My Name* (1978, producer only); *A Wedding* (1978, also producer, screenwriter); *A Perfect Couple* (1979, also producer and screenwriter, with John Considine, Patricia Resnick, and Allan Nicholls); *Quintet* (1979, also producer and screenwriter, with Frank Barhydt and Patricia Resnick); *Rich Kids* (1979, executive producer only); *Health* (1980, also producer and screenwriter with Frank Barhydt and Paul Dooley); *Popeye* (1980); *Endless Love* (1981, actor only); *Before the Nickelodeon: The Early Cinéma of Edwin S. Porter* (1982, interviewee only); *Come Back to the Five and Dime, Jimmy Dean, Jimmy Dean* (1982); *Streamers* (1983, also producer); *Secret Honor* (1984, also producer); *Fool for Love* (1985); *Jatszani Kell* (1985, associate producer only); *Aria* (1987, "Les Boreades" segment only; also screenwriter); *Beyond Therapy* (1987, also screenwriter, from the play by Christopher Durang); *O.C. and Stiggs* (1987, also producer); *The Moderns* (1988, "assistance" only); *Hollywood Mavericks* (1990, documentary, interviewee only); *Vincent and Theo* (1990); *The Player* (1992); *Short Cuts* (1993); *Pret-à-Porter* (1994).

Reasons for Selection

Robert Altman is one of the most important and creative figures of the 1970s and, indeed, of right now. Like many of the best directors who emerged in the seventies, Altman had a problem making it through the eighties. How does a creative or innovative or audacious or offbeat or off-center American director make it through a period when his kinds of films are not appreciated, not sponsored, not encouraged, and when, in fact, the basic emphasis was on the mass audience's simple emotion, on simple stories, and on glowing technical expertise?

Altman always stood for something different. He stood for going out there, for exploring — more specifically, for going out there in terms of how the actors were handled, of the spontaneity of his ensemble performances, and of how the camera was handled. One of the aspects discussed with *The Long Goodbye* is a kind of major visual innovation that Altman started with this specific film: a floating kind of camera work.

The Long Goodbye is, of course, based on the Raymond Chandler novel. The film was regarded in its time as scandalous simply because the whole Chandler milieu was updated to southern California in the 1970s and because Elliott Gould was seen as an eccentric Philip Marlowe, which indeed he is. The screenwriter, however, is Leigh Brackett, who, along with William Faulkner, adapted what has turned out to be the most highly regarded of all the previous Marlowe adaptations, Howard Hawks's *Big Sleep* (1946, with Humphrey Bogart).

In both using Brackett and then in casting somebody like Elliott Gould and the rest of a typically eccentric cast, Altman was both making a statement on the genre and on how that genre collides with the reality of the time. There are lots of levels to *The Long Goodbye*; there are lots of ways to appreciate it. And it is a film that, to a certain degree, you have to work to get into. Maybe that is why it was not as appreciated in its time as it should have been, but why its reputation has held up.

—M.W.

T h e   I n t e r v i e w

Michael Wilmington: I just wanted to mention some of the people in that ensemble because it is kind of a very strange cast. Jim Bouton, who plays Terry Lennox, some of you might not remember, was basically known at the time as a pitcher for the New York Yankees and author of a book called *Ball Four*, a tell-all book. And Nina van Pallandt was — what association did she have with Clifford Irving?

Robert Altman: Clifford Irving was the guy who wrote the fake Howard Hughes biography and went to jail for it. And she was his girlfriend, and she got in the news quite a bit. She had been a folksinger before that in Europe. I saw her on *The Tonight Show* when she was being interviewed by Johnny Carson because of that Clifford Irving scandal, and she was considered sort of a femme fatale. And Bouton was considered sort of a rat because of this book he wrote. He made some money and ratted on all his friends. Anyway, this was the first film for both of them.

Wilmington: Now, Mark Rydell, who does a great job as Marty Augustine, is better known as a film director. He directed *On Golden Pond*, *The Rose*, and *For the Boys*. Henry Gibson, who plays Dr. Verringer, was a comedian out of *Laugh-In*, and he also does a great bit in *Nashville*.

Altman: Dan Blocker was going to play the Roger Wade part, and he died from what was known as one of those botched operations. Dan was also a very, very close friend of mine. And I abandoned the picture at that point. I was in Europe, and I said I wasn't going to go through with it. Then Sterling Hayden came up as an idea. Sterling was sort of a character living in Europe then, and he couldn't come back in this country because he owed so many taxes. Or he could get into the country, but he couldn't work. So we had to kind of pay him surreptitiously, and we had a lot of intrigue. And you might have recognized Arnold Schwarzenegger in that. I think that was the first film he ever made. I don't think he talks about this film very much. He didn't talk in this film very much, but he had almost as much to say as he does in most of his films.

Wilmington: Actually, I think he may have done one other film before this. I think he did a film called *Hercules Goes Bananas* [aka *Hercules in New York*, 1970], in which he was billed as Arnold Strong.

Altman: Yeah, he was Arnold Strong. He was introduced to me as Arnold Strong in this.

Wilmington: I'd also like to say a few words about the technical people behind this film because with Altman there's always an ensemble — whether it's the actors or the crew people. And recently I was a few days on the set of his current film, *The Player*, which is a terrific film. It's probably one of the best backstage Hollywood movies I've ever seen. It'll be out sometime next year. And I watched it through a lot of the preparations. But in this particular film there's kind of an ensemble going that was associated with Bob [Altman] from his early days—people like Tommy Thompson, Vilmos Zsigmond, who was also the cinematographer on *McCabe and Mrs. Miller*, which is often described as one of the great color films of the seventies. [Vilmos Zsigmond was named best cinematographer of the year by the National Society of Film Critics for his work on *The Long Goodbye*.] Lou Lombardo, who is the editor, was associated with Bob for a long time, and he's really one of the great editors. He did *The Wild Bunch*.

Altman: Alan Rudolph was the second AD [assistant director] on [*The Long Goodbye*].

Wilmington: This is a film which really conveys the atmosphere of its time and its period better than very few [*sic*] that I've seen. It's kind of a double-period piece because Marlowe comes out of this Southern California of the forties that Chandler was talking about, but the milieu that he's in is the Southern California of the seventies. And there's sort of a collision between the two, and that's one of the basic, primary things in the film. And I wondered if you can talk about that and how you developed the whole idea?

Altman: The approach we decided to use was to make the book. I don't know if any of you read *The Long Goodbye*, but it's almost impossible to comprehend. I honestly never finished it. But I became fascinated with the way in which Chandler used these plots in stories not for the story's sake but to hang a bunch of thumbnail essays about this city, the time. And that's really what my feeling is about the basis of what his writing was. There was a book that was at the time called *Raymond Chandler Speaking* [edited by Dorothy Gardiner and Kathrine Sorley Walker], which was a small volume of his essays and letters and just writings of his. And I gave that book to everybody who worked on the film. I said, "Don't worry about reading *The Long Goodbye*, but read this about Raymond Chandler." And Leigh Brackett, who had written the screenplay, made certain changes—liberal changes from the book—and I tried to reflect more on Raymond Chandler than on his story. The character of Roger Wade to me represented Raymond Chandler. In the book I think he got murdered. I don't think he committed suicide. I had him commit suicide because Chandler tried to commit suicide, but he didn't have the guts to shoot himself. He couldn't stand the thought of it, so he went into the shower and shot the gun off five times, hoping the ricochet would get him. But all it did was alert the neighbors, and they called the police. And he never succeeded in that. So he just waited and died, you know, another suicide like the rest of us. I said, "Let's take this guy out of the forties because there's no such thing as these private eyes. They don't exist as such." And we put him in 1973. We called him Rip Van Marlowe. He was still in the forties, but suddenly he was in this period. And we made that the main kind of texture we were trying to deal with. And also we wanted everybody to know it was a movie.

Wilmington: Well, there's also a kind of a critique of macho in the film,

Elliott Gould

too, or machismo, in a variety of the characters, going straight through from Marlowe to Wade — who's kind of Hemingwayesque, too — as well as Chandler. And then Marty Augustine, of course, who's completely off the wall. And how's that character in the book?

Altman: There wasn't much. He had not much character to him in the book, as I remember. He was more of a plot device. He was a name. He was, you know, the gangster.

Wilmington: Well, how did you develop that character with Mark Rydell?

Altman: Mark and Johnny Williams, who did the music for this, they had finished a film with John Wayne, *The Cowboys* [1972] or something, and here we were all in Europe at this time. And so I asked Mark to play this. Then, I remember, we were at my house, and we decided to go down to the beach and have dinner, and we went to some place. And this girl who played Jo Ann—the girl who got the Coke bottle—was waiting on us. And I noticed this profile in the light, and I said, "Look at this girl." I think we were drinking a little bit—probably. And I said, "Look at that nose." And I said, "Here's what we ought to do." And we kind of came up with this Coke bottle thing at the time.

So I asked her, and I said, "Listen, this is going to sound funny to you, but we're making a film, and we'd like to put you in this movie." She says, "OK, bud, move on." And we said, "No, no." We finally convinced her, and then it turned out that none of us had any money or any credit cards, so she didn't believe us, but anyway we did put her in the film, and this was her first film.

Wilmington: So you kind of worked out that character with Mark?

Altman: With Mark, and everybody collaborated. I mean, Elliott particularly was real helpful.

Wilmington: Now, where did you get the idea of casting Elliott as Philip Marlowe? Because that actually was the one thing at the time that critics jumped on. Elliott Gould had a very familiar persona. He was sort of lovable, dopey, and a nebbish at the time. And when he was cast as Philip Marlowe, a lot of people really couldn't look past that.

Altman: Well, I think, however, that most of the people who objected, they weren't talking about Chandler's Philip Marlowe. I think they were talking about Humphrey Bogart or Hawks's Philip Marlowe.

Wilmington: Who's very, very different from the book—Hawks's Philip Marlowe.

Altman: Yeah, he is as well. So, but Gould—I didn't want to make this picture. I had just finished a film called *Images*. I made *M*A*S*H* and *Brewster McCloud* and this little film, *Images*, in Ireland. And these guys who had the rights to this—Jerry Bick and Elliott Kastner—who kept pushing me, would I do this? And would I do that? And I said no. Then I read Leigh Brackett's script, and there was this thing that she had put in this script where Marlowe kills his friend, which, again, also wasn't in the book. That was interesting to me. And they said, "Well, we're going to change that, of course." And I said, "OK, I'll do this on one condition: That you don't change that ending and that we don't cast Robert Mitchum"—who was, at that time, I guess, the ideal Marlowe. And I love Mitchum, I think he's wonderful. Gould had worked for me in *M*A*S*H*, and he just seemed right. They went for it to get the picture made, I guess.

Wilmington: Looking at him this time, he seemed a lot more like a forties character than I remember thinking of him at the time.

Altman: Well, we put him the forties, you know. He smoked all those cigarettes. By all means he should be dead now, but he's not.

Wilmington: What about the stream-of-consciousness cracks that he's using?

Altman: A lot of that was improvised, and he came up with that phrase "It's OK with me." And we sort of used that as the key thing with all of these things that were happening. If you remember, in the early seventies there were quite a lot of social changes going on.

Wilmington: Do you want to talk about that for a second? Because this is a film that's very, very saturated in its time.

Altman: I had a really nice trip down memory lane. I haven't seen this film for over ten years. I don't think things are any different, but they seem to be, I guess.

Wilmington: One of the reasons why I was excited about showing the film is that you were telling me about certain various camera techniques that you developed in this film that you hadn't used before.

Altman: Well, in the first place, this print is fading. This film's not twenty years old yet. It's eighteen years old or something like that. It's gone. And I'm just thinking about how many others have the color gone from the negative. At this time, it would have cost them $9,000 to make a color separation, and they just wouldn't do it. And so this film is gone. I don't know what held it up, but it finally came out on cassette just recently. I think it's available now some places, but most people don't know about it.

But I had done a thing in a few scenes in *Images*, this film I had just finished before *The Long Goodbye*, in which I had used the camera going counter to what the action was. And the idea struck me. I had liked it so much in *Images* I thought, God, we could do a whole film this way because it puts the audience in a little different position. And the idea was that the camera was always moving laterally, in and out, just in different directions, but never where it should have been necessarily. The cuts aren't clean. We weren't getting good framing. And we weren't trying for it. If the close-up is on the line, it should be — if it came on his back or somebody's blocking him, that was OK, we did it. And the idea is that it puts the audience in a position of, well — we're telling you that we're not going to serve this up to you. You better pay attention and watch it and follow it because you may miss the most important things. And we dealt with the dialogue that way. We dealt with the plot that way. And it frustrated a lot of people. A lot of people don't like this film at all. If this were a regular paid audience, half of them would have been gone, I think. Half of you would have been gone. But that was the idea of putting a little tension back into the audience. It's just that simple thing: You gotta pay attention or you're going to miss it.

Wilmington: Well, everything you're talking about implies that this movie, in addition to being a Hollywood genre project, which is the way it starts out, is a very experimental film. And obviously that experimentation comes out of the period. There was a period in American studio moviemaking from the late sixties through the mid seventies—maybe *Jaws* and Steven Spielberg helped to kill it off—when there was a lot more experimentation in subject matter and acting techniques and in camera techniques. Could you talk a little bit about that period?

Altman: Well, no. What we were trying to do is say, "C'mon, how many of these can you see? How many private eyes, the blonde?" And, I mean, in every one of these films, the plots are the same, the suspense is the same. Everything is just pressing buttons that we know that work, get you to cry, or frighten you. And it's not hard to frighten you. You can jump at somebody, and they respond. So I was trying to always approach these kinds of stories differently. I saw no point in making this story. This story was meaningless, I felt. I felt that Chandler was not meaningless. And I felt that the film was almost an essay, an education, to the audience, to say, "Stop looking at everything exactly the same way." And the fun of films for me is the discovery in seeing things. It's not in necessarily getting caught up in how believable this is, but to make fun of ourselves. So we constantly made references. And told the audience, "Gosh, this is a movie. This is just a movie. Another lousy movie."

Wilmington: Was that a reference to *The Third Man* there at the end, when he goes through the trees?

Altman: I don't recall what a lot of the references were, but anything that would occur to me that reminded me of films, I would just use it. I mean, we just did it. It wasn't really thought out in great detail. It wasn't the preparation. There was not an art director on this film. We would just pick these locations and arrive and move the stuff around. And so it was not finely crafted, as all of the films that we see today are. One of the best things that you can say about many films is, "Boy, they're sure made well." But so what?

Wilmington: You talked about the fact that the film is about Chandler and you had his ruminations given to everybody in the cast. Could you describe your take on the core of Raymond Chandler, since he's become almost a bigger cultural figure now than he was in the forties?

Altman: I feel what Chandler did was use the detective story or the private-eye pulp stories to hold the audience there. And while he had them there, he gave them all these little thumbnail essays that he kept hanging up on the line. Probably in one of the best passages I feel in *The Long Goodbye* was Chandler's first description of the Eileen Wade character, of Chandler's blonde. And I was more interested in the casting. I was more interested in getting Chandler's blonde than I was in getting some actress that could cry and work her way through those things. I mean, I wasn't looking for a skilled actress, although Nina turned out to be just wonderful. And I think Chandler did this. And I think I was doing the same thing. And that's where I felt my affinity to Raymond Chandler. So the whole thing kind of fit together.

By this time, I had made not very many movies, but I had made a few, and

I had made a lot of television shows. And when I used to make television shows, I would look at these scripts and I would think, "Jesus, I've got to stop this. I can't do this." And I would try to think of some old movie, and I'd say, "OK, this will be the secret agent, or this will be this kind of movie." And with all those television shows I would do, I would try to put references in to tell the audience, "This is just another lousy movie." And [*The Long Goodbye*] just afforded the opportunity for me. And it just fit.

Audience Question: I've noticed that if you have any singular trademark, it's the ability to have a lot of characters talking all at the same time. And yet you still get certain things that they're saying that the audience should be hearing. I wondered how you came out with that concept, and whether it evolved or was just something you came up with for *M*A*S*H* and then just did with other films?

Altman: No. In many of the Howard Hawks films, overlapping dialogue was used. Jack Warner fired me one time. I made a picture called *Countdown*. He was out of the country, and he came back, and he saw it, and he threw me off the lot. I mean he literally locked me off the lot and would not allow me back in. And he said, "That fool has actors talking at the same time." And— my feeling is—of course, movies come from theater and theater is based on words because those people are always quite a distance away from you. So the structure of the words is very important. And in our lives we don't hear everything. We hear what we want to. We don't have to. We make our own minds up. We hear a smattering of a conversation, and we kind of get it, and that's really all we need. And I feel that once an audience has to work to help make the story by the way they perceive it, and they're picking things out— their own clues out on the way—that it becomes more enjoyable for them. They become a participant. You come and meet the screen halfway. And so, it's just trying to further that. I mean, I think it's dreadful what they do on television now, or have been for twenty or thirty years, which is, they say they got to repeat the line, and they got to be sure the audience gets everything. Well, the audience gets everything. But when you're told, and everything is underlined, you stop working. You sit back, and you don't really care. How many television shows, or even films that you now put on the VCR, can you get up in the middle of, walk out and come back in, and you never miss anything. I mean, you can pick it up—you weren't there when he said, "Oh, so-and-so killed her." You come back in and say, "What happened?" And he says, "I don't know, what do you think?" "Well, she probably killed him." You go right along with it because you're doing this. Well, I just tried to do the same thing and put that same thing to work in the films.

Wilmington: But there are specific devices that you also used to get overlapping conversations, like multitrack [sound recording].

Altman: I made *Thieves Like Us* after this with it. Anyway, this was shot with just a regular single microphone and boom and that sort of thing. But in

California Split I actually had built for us eight-track machines because that's the way they were doing music then, and so I could separate on microphones. And we don't even put looping clauses in the contracts with actors anymore. On most films today, the actors will come back in, and they sit there and every line, eighty percent of the lines are redone because the producers—they want clarity, they want to be sure that everybody understands. I think there are various ways to get it.

AQ: How did you approach the filming of Los Angeles in this film? How do you think about the role of the city in it?

Altman: I didn't pay much attention to it. I wasn't trying to do very much. The beach. You know, we did the Malibu thing, and up in the Hollywood Hills. I didn't pay a great deal of attention to it, I'm sorry to say.

AQ: Mr. Altman, I remembered when this film first came out that you had a heck of a time getting it into theaters. I think it was released and then it was withdrawn, and then there was a new ad campaign or something about that. Could you comment on that?

Altman: United Artists—they didn't like the film very much. They opened it in Los Angeles and in Chicago and a few other cities. They did not open it in New York, and their ad campaign showed Elliott Gould with a forty-five looking like Mitchum, and people went in to see a real honest-to-God thriller, and they didn't like this. They thought this was silly and they left. So I had big arguments with the distributors. And I said, "You know, you've got to let people know that this is a comedy, or this is a satire, or something. You got to tell them the kind of film it is. Not the kind of film that it isn't." I'm probably going to have this same argument next month on the film I just finished [*The Player*]. I mean, nothing's ever changed. But then we went ahead and *Mad* magazine did a kind of an ad for us.

Wilmington: Jack Davis.

Altman: Jack Davis did some [artwork]. We opened in New York, and this picture became a big, big hit in New York. And had that been the original opening, the film, we feel, would have gone through the country and would have been a big moneymaker. But it was too late because these other markets had already been dissipated.

AQ: You did a movie [inaudible].

Wilmington: OK, I'll repeat the question. A question about *O.C. and Stiggs*, a long-shelved teenage movie. What happened to it? And a question about Tina Louise.

Altman: Tina Louise? Oh, I thought she was wonderful. We did a film six years ago called *O.C. and Stiggs* [in which Tina Louise played the sexy school nurse]. And it was during the time when a lot of these teenage exploitation films became a big marketing thing. And this film came up, and I thought, well, good, I'll make this film. And it was a spinoff from *Mad* magazine, but I made it. And it was really a satire on teenage exploitation films, and what it really was, was an adult exploitation film. And, so, immediately, test marketing had just then become the cat's pajamas. And, so, they took this film to four hundred kids from Canoga Park and asked them about it. And, of course, it didn't test well, and so they never released the film. That picture was simply never released.

AQ: The magnificent movie *Three Women*—has that been restored? And will it ever be on video?

Altman: You know, what they put on video goes in direct relationship to what the marketing did. The picture that made the most money and the most people saw is what they make the most prints of and what they push. It should be the other way. But nobody does that.

Wilmington: Talking about *Three Women*—Bob has a lot of great stories. My personal favorite is about how he conceived the story of *Three Women*.

Altman: Well, *Three Women* was a dream, literally. I didn't dream the movie, but I dreamed I was making it. It was during the time I was going to make the film *Easy and Hard Ways Out*, with Peter Falk. And it was a comedy. It was a book about guys working in a computer manufacturing business, and it was a big comedy. I think it was the David Geffen Company that was going to pay for it, and they wanted me to direct. There were some airplanes in it. And this movie was made later, I think, with Eddie Murphy.

Wilmington: *Best Defense* [1984].

Altman: I said, "OK, these airplanes that crash." I said, "I wanted that done in the Six Day War," which had just happened about that time in Egypt and Israel. And they said, "Oh, no, you can't do that." So, I just said, "I'm not going to do this. You guys are trying to manufacture this thing away from what it is." And so I quit. I was kind of in trouble because I didn't have a job, and my wife was very sick at the time. Very sick. But she's become fine. And I was living at Malibu. And I didn't know what I was going to do. I'd lost this picture. I had a lot of people working for me at the time, and I was, literally, out of money. And I was quite worried. I went to bed. My wife was in the hospital—an emergency hospital. My son, Matthew, came and got in bed with me, and I had this dream. I dreamed the title for *Three Women*. I dreamed of the people: Shelley Duvall and Sissy Spacek. I dreamed that it was a film about personality theft, and I would wake up in the middle of the night, and I'd take a pad from the side of my bed, and I'd write down this thing. Then Bob Eggenweiler and Tommy Thompson would come into my bedroom, and I'd say, "We want to shoot this thing in the desert, so why don't you guys go down and look for a location like this?" Then I would go back to sleep, and I would come back up and write more notes, and then finally in the morning I woke up. Of course, I didn't write anything in the middle of the night. There's no note pad at my bed. But my bed was full of sand from Matthew sleeping in the bed because it came out of his ears. And I dreamed that I was just making this film, and I got up and I became very depressed. So I called Scotty Bushnell, who worked with me, still. I said, "Listen, I read a short story last night, and I think it's pretty good. How does this sound to you?" And I kind of vamped this thing. They said, "Can you get the rights to it?" And I said, "You bet." And I really developed it. Nine days later we had a deal, and we were on our way to Palm Springs. That's how *Three Women* was born.

AQ: Can you talk about postflashing in *The Long Goodbye*, and the lighting perhaps?

Altman: Postflashing, which we did in *The Long Goodbye*, is when you take the negative of the film and you expose it to light before it's shot. And you expose it to certain percentages. We had done a little bit of that before. And what it does is it cuts the contrast down and it fogs the film, actually. We did it in order to get this kind of glare that I wanted from Los Angeles in this. It was ignorant, I later decided. And we fogged this film one hundred percent, and we shot all of it that way. And I'm sure that it also helps the deterioration of the negative. I think we advanced it about ten years ourselves.

AQ: Isn't that a scary thing to do?

Altman: Yeah, but it's pretty much controlled. And, again, so what? What can go wrong? I mean, you saw the scratches on this film. You know, when we're making the thing, and if you saw scratches like this, we'd shoot ourselves. You'd say, "We can't release the film." But the prints are out in theaters for only five days and they're looking like this. You take a chance and so what? So what goes wrong? As I say, it's just another lousy movie.

AQ: Were you influenced by any particular European filmmakers during the making of your films in the early seventies?

Altman: Yes, I was influenced to make *Images*, for instance. I never would have made it had Bergman not made *Persona* [1966]. Fellini was an influence. I could name lots of filmmakers that I like. But I think probably, in retrospect, that the most influence of other filmmakers that I've had are bad ones. And you learn and you say, "I'm never going to do that." So you eliminate a lot of stuff that traps. My feeling about this kind of art—or all art—is that you pick up all this information. You pick up information that you don't even know you have. And if you trust it, it'll come there for your use when you want to use it. So I don't really know when I can consciously say I'm going to make this just like something I saw—then I try to avoid that. My feeling is to really go by the instincts and dreams in sleep. I mean, many times we've had a problem about, "What are we really going to do tomorrow?" And I'll just say, "Tomorrow? When it comes time that we'll have to do it, we'll think of something." And I've never been really stuck. When something does happen, and I think a lot of times you just giggle and give in and let what information you have in your head, in your computer, fight its own way out instead of being so methodical and so careful. They make these films now—and I'm not criticizing—I mean, I don't think I can make the films like *Batman* with this kind of technical expertise. I think I'd fall asleep. It takes so long to make everything so perfect. And when it's all so perfect, what is it? I mean, I found that in all of this art, what I'm looking for the most are errors and mistakes. If I shoot two hundred thousand feet of film and I cut it down to a two-hour film, what stays in the film are the mistakes — all the little things where the actor stumbles or somebody does something interesting. Shelley Duvall in *Three Women* closed the door and her skirt stuck out the door, and we said, "Do that every time." You know, things go wrong because that's human, and the audience identifies with that. I just feel if you get too clever and too smart and everything is calculated, it comes out that way. It comes out very rigid and you know, it's a yawn.

AQ: Given your feelings about underlining things for the audience and also given the rather loose improvisational style of your movies, how would you respond to people who find that your own style in its own way is rather manipulative, especially in the use of your zoom lens?

Altman: Well, it *is* manipulative and, you know, may not even be very attractive to some people. I promise you that everybody is not going to like this picture or any film — I mean, any film I've made or anybody else has made, because if you don't tune into it, if you don't go with it, why should you like it? I think that. And, of course, it's manipulative. Sometimes, I wished it was not. I see things that I think, "God, I hit that too hard." But I feel that in making all these pictures you've got a big frozen pond of thin ice, and I've got to walk from one side to another, and it takes a hundred steps. As long as I don't step too hard in any of the hundred steps, I'm OK. But if in one place you go too hard, the whole thing's gone. So, the zoom lens, the attention to it, the moving in — many times I'm doing that to show you that I'm doing that, so that I know that you know that that's what I'm doing. And, again, I come back to the thing of *so what?* I mean, I'm not trying to create those other kinds of films. That's not to say that if everybody made films this way it would be dreadful. Filmmakers are like painters. You can like this painter and not like that painter. You can admire this painter and not be moved by them. You can say, "God, the craft in this is wonderful." All of these things are open to you. There's no right or wrong.

Sometimes — usually, generally — I try to take the position of, where do I want to put the audience? I say, "OK, this is where the camera is." And I'll sit there and shoot the scene. I'll shoot it maybe six, seven times, and always I shoot the entire scene. I don't stop and do one close-up for three lines — and any time I say always, that's a lie. There are always exceptions to that. And I sit there and I try to say: "This is where the audience is. This is where I'm going to look at it from." And I try to almost create an even and then shoot it the best I can from that position. I'm hoping that the audience falls in tune with me and goes with it. Most of them don't.

Wilmington: Given that you're talking about the camera style, there is something really unique about your working relationship with your cinematographer and your camera operator on the film. I'm wondering if you can describe that a little because there's kind of a documentary aspect to it as well.

Altman: Yeah, there is a documentary aspect to it because I'm not trying to deny the fact that the camera is there. I'm not trying to carry you. I just don't make those kinds of films. For the last ten years, I've been working with two Canadian cameramen, Pierre Mignot and Jean Lapine. I shot a film called *Fool for Love*, on which Robby Muller was the cameraman because these guys weren't available at the time and I had to start. And he's a great cameraman. I mean, really a great cameraman. And we got down to New Mexico and started shooting, and suddenly I'm seeing these beautiful pictures, but I don't know how to make this kind of movie. And I stopped after nine days, and I said, "You know, we have to get divorced." I said, "You're making a beautiful movie. I don't want a beautiful movie." And by that time, Pierre was finished, and he came down and shot it. And it's a terrible thing to happen. But there was no communication about what we both wanted. We were just making two kinds of movies.

So I tell Pierre or Jean or whoever the cameraman would happen to be, and I let him go. And I say, "If you find something interesting, shoot it." I know what I need to cut to make the movie, what I need to have. But when he's shooting, if he sees an actor doing something or something's happened, he can go for that. He does not have to go where we said it's going to go. That's why my lighting isn't as good. Real good artistic cameramen don't like to work with me too much because they've got to have the room lit for two hundred seventy degrees — at least one eighty. And mostly when they light for a position where the camera doesn't move — I mean, you can do just beautiful stuff. But the minute you move this far, the lighting is atrocious. So the lighting has to be general so it can cover my moving from one side to another. And all these things come to bear on it. It's just a matter, again, of choice. It's not a matter that one way is better than another. It's just different.

AQ: If you were starting out now, how would you go about making the films that you wanted to make?

Altman: I don't know how to answer that question. I just show up and go to work and follow my instincts. That's what I did on the last film I did, and that's what I did on the first film.

AQ: I'm wondering, how do you now — and in the period of *The Long Goodbye* — keep track of what the cameraman is shooting? Do you or have you ever used a video?

Altman: I use now a video assist. I give one to the sound. Black and white. Very small video assist. I have one that is very mobile, one close to me. I don't record on it because I don't want people to look at it and run back and see what it was. And all that does is tell me what framing he has, so I don't have to go up and say, "Did you get it when she smiled?" or "Where was your lens when this happened?"

I'm looking through the camera all the time. I watch the actors live, usually. But I always have the reference of what the shot is. When we do the next take, I'll say, "Do it the same way, except when you come to the close-up, don't go for the close-up. Go over to this other person." Or something like that.

AQ: How would you start a film like that, that's not a mainstream Hollywood film, as far as money and so forth?

Altman: It's just a matter of persistence. In other words, there are certain films I don't make because I feel I don't want to and I couldn't. I think I would fail. So I have a very hard time making films. I came back from Europe a year and a half ago with a script from Raymond Carver. I bought a bunch of Raymond Carver short stories, and I put together a script, and I wanted to make a film called *L.A. Short Cuts* [which was released in 1993 as, simply, *Short Cuts*] based on those—it has about twenty-seven characters in it. I've got a terrific cast for it. I'm very happy with the script. But I can't get anybody to put any money in it because they read it and they say, "Oh, well, this is kind of depressing." And I said, "Well, it's not going to be depressing. I mean, it's a comedy." And they said, "Yeah, but there's too many people in it." And it's very difficult. So I have to just hold out. And I made another film, *The Player*, while I'm waiting to get this one done. And I'm starting back again on *L.A. Short Cuts*, and I'm going to keep trying to do it. I may never get it done. But it's just a matter of persistence. You know, you gotta go with your hat in your hand, and you've gotta get down on your knees, and you gotta be nice to a lot of people that you don't want to be nice to. It's difficult.

AQ: You gotta compromise, in other words?

Altman: Well, either that or you gotta lie a lot. You don't have to compromise. You compromise it a little bit. Compromise is all right. It doesn't make any difference. A lot of these things don't make any difference whether this happens or that happens. It's the idea that you just have to stay with what it is that you feel is right because if you do something that you don't feel is right, you won't do it well anyway. I think the worst thing that could happen today—wasn't so twenty years ago—but the worst thing that is happening today is that a lot of first directors are getting shots. I mean, there's a lot of pictures being made. I'd say an extraordinary percentage of people making films are making their first films. And they are $35 million films. And that's a great break for those people. But, boy, if that film fails—not if they fail—if the film fails, they may just as well go back to being a box boy because they're not going to get another shot. And at least in my time, with the television and all of the kind of work with the number of films that I've done, there's at least a backlog that people—no matter whether they like my films or not—they know I can get one finished. So you gotta be kind of careful not to just accept a film just in order to have a film because if that film fails, you've really nailed your own coffin. I just think it's a matter of being persistent to do what you want to do, what you feel. And that's what you'll do. Then you'll do something that's correct that you're able to do.

Wilmington: One of the things you told me when you were taking *L.A. Short Cuts* around [to studios] was that certain executives would tell you that there wasn't enough hope in the film.

Altman: Well, they said, "There's no hope in this film." I said, "Listen, none of these women know each other, so why don't we call all the women Hope." And the minute I said it, I knew I'd made a grave error. But that source is not interested in my film.

AQ: Is there something that can be done so at least the negative in its present state can be kept from further deteriorating? Or is there some way that someone can sort of rescue the negative a bit? And question number two: How did you work the cat [in *The Long Goodbye*]? Because that was amazing.

Altman: I didn't; the cat trainer did. But that was five or six cats, different cats that they'd trained to do different things and they'd respond to certain things. The cat was good, though, wasn't he?

But you know if that were written into a script—that scene—it's ten minutes. He's dealing with that cat for ten minutes. If that were written into a script and you took it to any studio executive and said, "This is the first scene," they'd throw you out because you can't do that sort of thing.

Marty Scorsese is doing the most active work about saving these films. Every time he makes a deal with a major company, part of the deal that goes along with it is that he grabs a couple of films and gets a real pristine print out of it. They get them on nondeteriorating stock. They're saving a lot of them.

With *McCabe and Mrs. Miller*, Scorsese did that. I saw him a year or so ago on a plane, and he said he's just gotten this print of *McCabe* which is just great and it is beautiful. And now they're going to laser disc. And *McCabe* is now on laser disc, wide-screen format, letter box, and it looks quite beautiful. So they can all be saved. Then again, you have to watch out because it's like Congress when they make a law about what films that they'll have: a committee will tell you what films can't be colorized. Well, the committee is a bunch of box-office people that would look at the selection, and *Top Gun* will be designated a classic because it made more money than *To Sleep with Anger*. It all goes back to money. It all goes back to commerce. And these people who own these companies and run these companies, they do not care. And this isn't to say they're bad people. They're in the business. But they don't understand. And I don't think they're capable of understanding that people take the work they do seriously. And the audience also takes the work to heart. A lot of the audience takes this work very, very seriously. You know, there's this wonderful stuff out there. And forty years from now this film won't exist.

Wilmington: What about the negative of this film, though? Do you know that the color is deteriorating?

Altman: I have no idea. I don't know where it is. United Artists has broken up. God knows who owns the negative of this film, even. I just know that most of the films, the prints that I've seen, had the colors gone from them. And I assume that the negative is in better shape. But it's very expensive for them to take that film out—find it in the first place—take it out of the vault, get some people to work on it. Suddenly, there's somebody who has to sign that check and they say, "What are we doing this for? This film is worthless. It didn't make any money the first time out. What do we want with this?"

AQ: All the actors are really great in the film, and Sterling Hayden was the best. Was he hard or easy to work with?

Altman: Oh, he was great. Sterling was wonderful. And his wardrobe, as he came walking up to my house—because he had to come into California illegally or something—it was some weird stuff. And those were his own clothes. And I said, "OK, well, that's your wardrobe. Try to wear it every day." He was terrific.

AQ: My question is, do you just want to make films? Or do you want something to last? And I say that not necessarily about film preservation, but when you say things like, you know, "It's just another lousy movie."

Altman: Well, when I say, "Just another lousy movie," I don't mean that. I'm saying I don't put a great deal of weight in these things. They mean a great deal to me. I mean, I love all the films I make. When people ask what's your favorite film, I really can't answer that because each one of them is a success. I've not made a film yet that I do not consider a success. By that I'm talking about the collaboration of the people who made it. These films are what we set out to make. People may say, "I hate that *Quintet*. I don't get that." *Quintet*? I love *Quintet*. And I can find five people who agree with me. I say this because I don't think there's a lot I can do about it. But the real personal treasure that comes from this, the real personal pleasure, is the process of doing this. The finished product is great. And an evening like this is very moving to me. I mean, I'm very thrilled. I could, you know, be in tears if somebody says a catch word because this just brings back all kinds of—it's my life. So I treasure these things very, very much. But if they were all gone and disappeared, I don't think, it's a big deal. But I think if the memory of that process were eliminated from my brain, it would be a great loss. There are more important things.

Geoff Gilmore: I did want to thank you very much for coming tonight. I did want to mention that the preservation officer of the [Academy of Motion Picture Arts and Sciences] is here, and the preservation officer of the UCLA Film and Television Archive. I think they're both interested in talking to you about preservation of this film. So, again, thank you very, very much for coming. Thank you very much, Michael.

Wilmington: Thank you.

For Further Study

Videocassette

The Long Goodbye is available from MGM/UA Home Video.

Books

Boorman, John, and Walter Donohoe. *Projections 2: A Forum for Filmmakers*. London and Boston: Faber and Faber, 1993.

Chandler, Raymond. *The Long Goodbye*. Boston: Houghton Mifflin Company, 1954.

Clark, Al. *Raymond Chandler in Hollywood*. London and New York: Proteus, 1982.

Feineman, Neil. *Persistence of Vision: The Films of Robert Altman*. Manchester, N.H.: Ayer Co., 1978.

Gardiner, Dorothy, and Kathrine Sorley Walker. *Raymond Chandler Speaking*. Boston: Houghton Mifflin Company, 1977.

Jacobs, Diane. *Hollywood Renaissance*. New Jersey: A.S. Barnes, 1977.

Kagan, Norman. *American Skeptic: Robert Altman's Genre-Commentary Films*. Ann Arbor, Mich.: Popular Culture, 1982.

Karp, Alan. *The Films of Robert Altman*. Metuchen, N.J., and London: Scarecrow Press, 1981.

Kass, Judith. *Robert Altman: American Innovator*. New York: Popular Library, 1978.

Keyssar, Helene. *Robert Altman's America*. New York and Oxford: Oxford University Press, 1991.

Kolker, Robert Phillip. *A Cinema of Loneliness: Penn, Kubrick, Coppola, Scorsese, Altman*. New York and Oxford: Oxford University Press, 1980.

Luhr, William. *Raymond Chandler and Film*. New York: Frederick Ungar Publishing Co., 1982.

McGilligan, Patrick. *Robert Altman: Jumping off the Cliff. A Biography of the Great American Director*. New York: St. Martin's Press, 1989.

Peary, Danny. *Cult Movies*. New York: Delacorte Press, 1981.

Pendo, Stephen. *Raymond Chandler on Screen: His Novels into Film*. Metuchen, N.J.: Scarecrow Press, 1976.

Plecki, Gerard. *Robert Altman*. Boston: Twayne Publishers, 1985.

Scavullo, Francesco. *Scavullo on Men*. New York: Random House, 1977.

Wexman, Virginia Wright, and Gretchen Bisplinghoff. *Robert Altman: A Guide to References and Resources*. Boston: G. K. Hall and Co., 1984.

Periodicals

Brackett, Leigh. "From *The Big Sleep* to *The Long Goodbye* and More or Less How We Got There." *Take One* (Montreal), January 1974.

Dawson, Jan. "Robert Altman Speaking." *Film Comment*, March/April 1974.

Gregory, Charles. "Knight without Meaning?" *Sight and Sound*, summer 1973.

Lipnick, Edward. "Creative Post-Flashing Technique for *The Long Goodbye*." *American Cinematographer*, March 1973.

Oliver, Bill. "*The Long Goodbye* and *Chinatown*: Debunking the Private Eye Tradition." *Literature/Film Quarterly* (Salisbury, Md.), summer 1975.

Powers, John. "Marlowe's Long Goodbye: Chandler's Legacy in Film and Television." *L.A. Style*, June 1986.

Stewart, Garrett. "*The Long Goodbye* from *Chinatown*." *Film Quarterly*, winter 1974–75.

16

ROY SCHEIDER

AND

52 Pick-Up

(with Kirk Honeycutt)

On January 23, 1992, actor Roy Scheider was interviewed by Kirk Honeycutt after a screening of *52 Pick-Up*.

The Film

52 Pick-Up (1986), a Cannon Films release. Directed by John Frankenheimer. Screenplay by Elmore Leonard and John Steppling. Based on the novel *52 Pick-Up*, by Elmore Leonard. Produced by Menahem Golan and Yorum Globus. Director of photography, Jost Vacano. Editor, Robert F. Shugrue. Music by Gary Chang. Filmed in Los Angeles, California.

Cast: Roy Scheider (Harry Mitchell), Ann-Margret (Barbara Mitchell), Vanity (Doreen), John Glover (Alan Raimy), Robert Trebor (Leo Franks), Clarence Williams III (Bobby Shy), Kelly Preston (Cini), Lonny Chapman (Jim O'Boyle), Doug McClure (Mark Averson), Alex Henteloff, Michelle Walker, Philip Bartko, Robin Bronfman, Debra Burger, Laisa Carrie, Blackie Dammett, Barbara Ferris, John Frances, Conroy Gedeon, Bill Gratton, Jai M. Jefferson, Lenora Logan, Mark M. Mayuga, William J. Murphy, Anthony Palmer, Frank Sivero, Amber Lynn, Sharon Mitchell, Tom Byron, Harvey Cowen, Ron Jeremy Hyatt, Ines Ochoa, Allyson Palmeter, Katherine Poland, Debra Satell, Shirley Thompson, Amy White, Charles Bowden, Marc Castenada, Mike Caruso, Steven Clawson, Christopher Cory, Maurice Jenkins, John Kahnen, Bobby Ponce, Ray Vela, Lorrie Lovett, Sandra Perron, Barbara Summers, Arlin Miller, Ted Grossman.

Synopsis: Industrialist Harry Mitchell is blackmailed by three second-rate hoods involved in the pornography trade. They demand $105,000 from him for a videotape, a secret recording of his affair with a stripper. He has no choice but to tell his wife, Barbara, an aspiring local politician, about his seedy affair, which could jeopardize her career. But instead of paying the blackmail money, he shows his ledgers to the ringleader, Raimy, who reduces the payment to $52,000. Harry then cunningly plays off one hood against the other, hoping to rattle them. Raimy eventually kills the other two conspirators and shows Harry a snuff film he made depicting the brutal murder of the stripper who had been Harry's mistress. Raimy wants to collect all of the money at an arranged drop in San Pedro.

Remarks and Reviews

"It's fast-paced, lurid, exploitative and loaded with malevolent energy. John Frankenheimer . . . hasn't done anything this darkly entertaining since *Black Sunday*. . . . Roy Scheider gives a leathery, tough-guy performance . . . exactly right for these surroundings" (Janet Maslin, *New York Times*).

"Frankenheimer's utterly implausible but consistently tense and downright sleazy adaptation of Elmore Leonard's novel . . . Scheider is strong as the beleaguered blackmailee . . . but the real show here belongs to three of the weirdest, sickest (to say nothing of clumsiest) villains ever seen on the screen, vividly brought to lowlife by Glover, Trebor and Williams" (*The Phantom's Ultimate Video Guide*).

"John Frankenheimer's best work in years. . . . *52 Pick-Up* blind-sided me" (Roger Ebert, *Chicago Sun-Times*).

"Robust in its sleaziness, John Frankenheimer's *52 Pick-Up* is the ultimate guilty husband movie" (J. Hoberman, *Village Voice*).

"The sturdy, underrated Scheider is in fine form. . . . A trio of unforgettable slimeballs, played with great theatrical relish, . . . inspires shudders one minute, laughs the next" (David Ansen, *Newsweek*).

"Fleshing out this stringent tale are the solid, well-realized performances of Roy Scheider and Ann-Margret. Low-key but with a hard, feral energy, Scheider is perfect as the driven protagonist, while Ann-Margret is appropriately both warm and alluring" (Duane Byrge, *Hollywood Reporter*).

"Since [Frankenheimer] avoids any real sense of the 'designer' violence of *The Hitcher* or *Manhunter*, he's created a film that's much more deeply disturbing. He elicits performances that are so frighteningly real you believe everything—John Glover, Clarence Williams III and Robert Trebor are exemplary nasties, and Scheider and Ann-Margret are their usual captivating selves" (Michael Dare, *L.A. Weekly*).

The Filmmaker

Roy Scheider was nominated for Academy Awards for his performances in *The French Connection* (1971) and *All That Jazz* (1979). His status as an action star rose with the outstanding success of Steven Spielberg's *Jaws* (1975), in which he played police Chief Brody. His multifaceted performance as a Broadway director in Bob Fosse's auobiographical *All That Jazz* earned Scheider wide acclaim.

His second-lead performances in the espionage thrillers *Marathon Man*

(1976) and *The Russia House* (1990) were also roundly praised. Often cast as a reluctant man of action battling both the system and outlaw forces, Scheider has played many characters who exhibit tension, determination, and intelligence under pressure.

Scheider was born in Orange, New Jersey, and graduated from Franklin and Marshall College in 1955 with a bachelor's degree in history. He served in the U.S. Air Force, then made his stage debut in 1963 and his film debut, billed as Roy R. Scheider, a year later in the horror film *The Curse of the Living Corpse*. After a few small parts, he played major supporting characters to the two Oscar-winning lead actors of 1971: as Jane Fonda's pimp in *Klute* and as Gene Hackman's detective partner in *The French Connection*.

Although none of his films eclipsed the success of *Jaws* and none of his performances to date brought the kind of personal acclaim that he received for *All That Jazz*, his career choices have continued to be eclectic and include thrillers, big hardware pictures like *Blue Thunder* (1982) and *2010* (1984), John Frankenheimer's *Fourth War* (1990) and the adaptation of William S. Burroughs's *Naked Lunch* (1991).

The actor's made-for-television movies include *Assignment: Munich* (1972); *Jacobo Timerman: Prisoner without a Name, Cell without a Number* (1983); *Tiger Town* (1983); *Someone Has to Shoot the Picture* (1990); *Leopold and Leob* (1991); and *Barr Sinister* (1992). He also starred in the Steven Spielberg–produced undersea adventure series *seaQuest*.

Roy Scheider's Filmography

As actor, except where noted: *The Curse of the Living Corpse* (1964); *Paper Lion* (1968); *Star!* (1968); *Stiletto* (1969); *Loving* (1970); *Puzzle of a Downfall Child* (1970); *The French Connection* (1971); *Klute* (1971); *L'attentat* (1972); *Un Homme Est Morte* (1973); *The Seven Ups* (1973); *Jaws* (1975); *Sheila Levine Is Dead and Living in New York* (1975); *Marathon Man* (1976); *Sorcerer* (1977); *Jaws 2* (1978); *All That Jazz* (1979); *Last Embrace* (1979); *Still of the Night* (1982); *Blue Thunder* (1983); *2010* (1984); *In Our Hands* (1984, documentary); *Mishima: A Life in Four Chapters* (1985, narrator only); *52 Pick-Up* (1986); *The Men's Club* (1986); *Cohen and Tate* (1988); *Listen to Me* (1989); *Night Game* (1989); *The Fourth War* (1990); *The Russia House* (1990); *Naked Lunch* (1991).

Reasons for Selection

52 Pick-Up is a thriller lover's wet dream: John Frankenheimer, a master at white-knuckle tension, tackles an Elmore Leonard crime novel with a host of irrepressibly colorful and nasty characters. The result is one of the best and, unfortunately, least appreciated thrillers of the 1980s. The interplay of personalities and plot turns keep twisting the knot in your stomach tighter and tighter.

—K.H.

The Interview

Kirk Honeycutt: Thank you for coming. This film combines two of my favorite entertainers: Elmore Leonard, the novelist who began as a writer of Westerns but now writes some of the best urban crime fiction in America, and John Frankenheimer, who is arguably one of the best makers of thrillers in America, who did such things as *The Manchurian Candidate*, *Black Sunday*, and *Seven Days in May* and brought this story to the screen.

Previous Elmore Leonard stories have not been well translated to the screen. They usually are sort of lame star vehicles, like *Mr. Majestyk* with Charlie Bronson and *Stick* with Burt Reynolds. This is the first film that I felt got it right in regard to Leonard's tone and style. I've read a number of his books, and there's a real nice sense of B-movie pace, real malevolent action, and some very sly wit. And it really captures the kind of gritty and tough urban environment that Elmore Leonard writes about. It's usually in Detroit, but for budgetary reasons, *52 Pick-Up* was set in Los Angeles. Nothing's been lost by that, and I think the film really captures that ominous atmosphere that you get in Elmore Leonard. And certainly the villains are quite wonderful in this. In fact, the problem was in keeping them from running away with the film, John Frankenheimer told me.

John tells me that Roy was very instrumental in shaping the script as they were moving toward production on this back in 1986. So let's get to the movie. Thank you.

[*Movie.*]

Honeycutt: First of all, before Roy Scheider gets here, I would like to say that I really got into this movie all over again. It's a very uncompromising movie, and I think the best of John Frankenheimer's films are both political and philosophical. And he brings a sense of his own moral justice to his films and here you have, brilliantly played by Roy Scheider, a man who's kind of like an Everyman. He could be you or me or anybody who makes one mistake and pays dearly for it. The film is all about his seeking redemption through the action of the melodrama.

It's kind of interesting that this film anticipates *Fatal Attraction*. And it has a little bit of *Bad Influence* in it, what with the videotaping sequence. *Fatal Attraction* was a lot more successful than this was commercially, and we'll explore some of the reasons for that as we go along.

But what I really like about this film is the way the script makes you live the experience as it happens to those characters, just from the tension that he was able to build right from that opening scene where—it's innocuous and seemingly nothing is happening—a man is leaving home. A wife is watching. But you know something is wrong here with that marriage already.

Frankenheimer was going to be here but he got called away to France. *The Year of the Gun*, the film he just made last year, is opening in France this week, and he promised the distributor that he would help open it. He was very disappointed he couldn't come here, but it was just a case of bad timing. And I did speak to him about it, and one of the things he mentioned to me—I really was noticing it this time—is how he tried to make the film a black-and-white film. If you'll notice the decor and the costumes and everything, even the cat is black and white. And I think it's a usage of those certain images that you get in the B movies of the forties and the fifties. The three bad guys, too, are just extraordinary, and I'm not quite sure what the relationships are among them and the sexual tensions that are there. But there's one real thing you know—that what their real high is, what their real kick is, is crime.

The only thing I don't like about the film, the one misstep, I think, is Ann-Margret and the lack of precaution in that swimming scene where she knows there's somebody after them, and it seems like nothing has been done in that estate to secure it, and I don't know why that is. It just seems like it's a setup for a woman in jeopardy, and it doesn't quite pay off for me.

The film was shot on a very low budget, $7.5 million. It was shot in fifty-four days, all on locations. There's no studio footage there. And John tells me that Cannon left him alone. They didn't do a thing to him. What they didn't do was promote it. They only spent $2 million to promote it. And you can't do that to open a film. And, even in '86, you couldn't do that.

The cinematographer was Jost Vacano—he was the cinematographer for *Das Boot*—a German cinematographer, and you may have noticed that influence in the way the camera roams around space and gives you a sense of an environment closing in on you. He also did some wonderful shots, exterior shots. This is really before Steadi-Cam had been used a lot. They were just developing it when this picture was made, and he apparently got an Arriflex and used a Chapman crane on a gyroscope, which explains all those swooping shots in the desert where [Scheider's Harry Mitchell] is being set up as a man who knows explosives. But even the shots of the house give you a sense of the environment. It's a brilliantly shot film and a brilliantly designed film for a very inexpensive film. The production designer was Phillip Harrison.

Scheider is a classical actor. I don't know how many of you know it, but he did a lot of classical work in theater for the first ten years of his career. He was Mercutio for Joseph Papp in the early days of Papp's Shakespeare in the Park productions. And his first important film role was in *Klute*. He was Jane Fonda's procurer, and he went on to be the partner of Gene Hackman in *The French Connection*, and, of course, the sheriff in *Jaws*. And through these performances there's a certain quiet authority, and he kind of functions, interestingly, as an Everyman kind of character. I think that's how John Frankenheimer used him here.

John said that when he got the rights to the book, it was his thought to use Roy Scheider. Roy called him and said that he wanted to do the role very much. And after the first few drafts of the script, neither John nor Roy were too happy with it, and Roy started working with John on the screenplay. Then they sent it off to Elmore Leonard, who lives in Michigan, and he took some passes at it. So, I'll be very interested in how they shaped it for the film. But many times — and I can tell you this from having read Elmore Leonard's stuff — the dialogue was straight out of the book, things like, "Yeah, I gotta talk to the man." That kind of thing is exactly the way Elmore Leonard writes movie dialogue. Instead of saying: "What are you talking about?" he's saying, "You talking about, man?" He uses very short — staccato-short — sentences. And he's so good at low-life characters, such as he has in here. And a lot of that is straight out of the book. Just like *The Maltese Falcon*, they shot the book.

This seamlessness in Roy Scheider's performances, I think, has made him an underrated actor in many respects. I think he's one of the finest actors we have in the American cinema.

And I think John Frankenheimer's very underrated too. He had a period of time where he was not getting good projects, and this is the first thing that made me think he was back. He was back to the things he did with *Black Sunday*. And his films since this have been very good, but they have not been seen for a variety of reasons. Even *Black Sunday* was hurt by bad luck. It came out the same time as a film called *Two-Minute Warning*, which was also about a terrorist action at a football game, and audiences got mixed up about which one was which and one was awful and one was brilliant. So, he's had a lot of bad luck. It was suggested by Michael Wilmington in the *Los Angeles Times* that perhaps the moral sleaziness, the atmosphere of [*52 Pick-Up*], turned off people. But I don't think people saw it because it didn't have the promotion behind it.

Audience Question: [Inaudible].

Honeycutt: This is a question about filming Elmore Leonard novels and what their plans in the future are. I know that John Frankenheimer wants to do *La Brava*. There are usually options. They're trickier to adapt than I think they might seem because there's not a lot of action. It's a lot of character-driven stuff. And it seems to be a great idea for a movie, but I think considering it and really getting those characters right is trickier than it looks. There have been a lot that have been attempted, as you know, but unfortunately they haven't been terribly successful. Some of his Westerns, including *Valdez Is Coming*, did pretty well.

And I see our guest of honor has arrived.

Roy Scheider: Good evening.

Harry (Roy Scheider) in pursuit of his blackmailers enters the projection booth of an adult movie house in *52 Pick-Up*.

Honeycutt: We were talking about your involvement with the script itself, because I understand that you worked on it with John.

Scheider: Some of it, yes. The blowing up of the car was my idea.

Honeycutt: Oh, really? Because it was a briefcase in the book, I believe.

Scheider: That's right. It was a briefcase in the book. And I just thought we needed something a little more dramatic, especially since such a relationship was growing up between myself and the antagonist. And so I thought that we'd do something with the car, and we wrote into the script the businesss about him always playing and touching the car. He really liked the car. So that when the phone call comes at the end, I plant the idea of throwing the car into the deal. Then you see him go to the garage, and he tampers with the car, and he produces that ending.

Honeycutt: It's interesting how you plant something in the first act and pay it off in the third act. A film I otherwise liked, a Wolfgang Petersen film earlier this year, *Shattered*, played with that where you had a scene where the character talks about his car and how much he loves it and restores it, and in the very next scene it's totaled so, the payoff—you're set up for it too quickly, and you think, well, we knew what was going to happen. In this one you've almost forgotten about it by the time you get to it so that—and there's real money in there, so your mind is not on that at all—and yet it pays off perfectly. It's a perfect plant and a perfect payoff on that. What was it that attracted you to this role? Are you an Elmore Leonard fan?

Scheider: I'm an Elmore Leonard fan, and I've read almost everything he's written, and he's not been done justice in films. This is probably the only film of his that he can tolerate—so far. He has a lot of other wonderful projects if they ever get done. For instance, there's one called *La Brava*. It's a wonderful story. And the book just before the last one, called *Get Shorty*, is about Hollywood. It's about a sort of a gangster who collects people's debts, and he comes to Hollywood to collect a debt and winds up becoming a filmmaker. It's hilarious.

So anyway, I read all of his stuff. And when I heard that John was involved in this, we got together, and we decided we would try to do one good Elmore Leonard project if we could.

Honeycutt: Is there anything about the character itself that grabbed you?

Scheider: Well, at the time, I was going through a rough relationship in my own life concerning an outside attraction, and some of that was interesting. But I think the most important thing is a guy who is trying to live his life the best he can and then some very vicious and beastly people come into it. This movie took a lot of flak because of the murder scene of the young girl.

Honeycutt: It is tough.

Scheider: Unfortunatley, the movie for the most part got very, very good reviews, but the scene of killing her was usually examined in the first paragraph of most reviews. The moviegoer was so put off by the description of it that a lot of people thought the movie was about that kind of brutality. It's not. The scene itself is quite frightening, and it was meant to be frightening to show how brutal these guys were. But a lot of feminists felt that it was another example of, you know, showing women in dire straights and a director having a good time torturing them. I don't think that's what John had in mind.

Honeycutt: No, in fact, you have a very strong character played by Ann-Margret, and I think most people associate her with Las Vegas, and it's been a long time since *Carnal Knowledge*.

Scheider: There were problems. I mean, every project has its problems. One of the problems with Elmore Leonard is that he writes his antagonists— makes his bad guys—so attractive. They're so perversely comic, so ridiculously macho. You can't stop being attracted to them. And in this film, in looking at it—Monday-morning quarterbacking—we realize how much screen time these undesirable guys get in this project. And, perhaps, we should have had more screen time devloping the difficult relationship between Ann-Margret and my character. It might have helped the picture a little bit more.

Honeycutt: I think the scenes that are there, especially the coffee-table scene where you're separated by that enormous glass coffee table, and the tension in that scene—I've seen this picture three or four times now—that's actually the most violent scene in the movie in many respects.

Scheider: It is in many ways. It's a good scene. And I always felt we needed more of those. A few of those wouldn't have hurt.

Honeycutt: No, probably not. One thing I understand happened is that you had a couple of weeks rehearsal before shooting it. Were these the areas you worked on?

Scheider: Yeah, that scene in particular was very, very important in their relationship. If she was going to move to his side in the story, which she does after Bobby Shy attacks that night — she kind of moves over on his side — if that was going to happen, he at least would have to have the guts to come and tell her exactly what was going on. And so he starts off rather mealymouthed and unable to express himself in that scene, but at least he's making an effort to be honest. And, although she feels that he doesn't have any idea of the pain that he's causing, at least he's got enough guts to be honest with his wife.

Honeycutt: What were the problems in the adaptation?

Scheider: Mostly dealing with that relationship. Trying to hone down the attractiveness of the bad guys and then coming up with a climax that was a little bit more cinematic and a little more visual than the book. Other than that, it was a very enjoyable set to be on. Interesting thing, John is [Alcoholics Anonymous] — he makes no bones about talking about it. Ann-Margret is AA. Doug McClure is AA.

Honeycutt: And so is Elmore Leonard, isn't he?

Scheider: Yeah, and Elmore Leonard is AA. So, I felt we were in a clinic.

Honeycutt: And all that drinking you did on the set.

Scheider: All coffee.

Honeycutt: What is John like as a director? You made a subsequent film with him, *The Fourth War*.

Scheider: What can I say about him? He's very possessed with obsessions. He likes stories where people are obsessed. And if you look back at his pictures — *The Train*, *Birdman of Alcatraz*, *The Manchurian Candidate* — those are all about people who are obsessed with ideas. This film is about a guy who was obsessed with revenge and ridding his life of these leeches. So John brings that enthusiasm to his projects. He's a bit of a martinet. He's very demanding of his staff and his crew, and he expects the actors to be on time and be enthusiastic.

As you know, he comes from the Golden Age of Television, when himself and Sydney Pollack and Sidney Lumet and a lot of directors that we know and respect today earned their spurs by doing live television in New York. So nothing surprises them. I mean, they're used to having some dreadful things happen live on television, so not many things throw them. But they're very hard workers, and they are used to making the most of the time that's available.

Honeycutt: John's films are very kinetic, too. I was kind of interested in how he works with actors because it seems like there's such an emphasis on visuals, and yet the acting is always superb in his films. Does he work closely with you, or does he let you go about your business?

Scheider: He likes actors very much. And the actors that he chooses are the ones that he feels have the qualities that he wants for this particular picture. So, he encourages you to use those qualities, to bring those qualities out, and to serve his picture and his story. I mean, he used Burt Lancaster many times because he liked that kind of energetic obsessiveness that Lancaster has. And some of that I have too, I think.

Honeycutt: I think so. Do you prepare for a role physically as well as learning the script? I mean, is there a physical preparation that goes into it?

Scheider: Well, my training is mostly from the theater. And I've never considered myself to be a particularly intellectual actor, so the physical aspects of any character is where I start. Until I know how the guy sits in a chair and talks to people—whether he leans back or forward when he talks to people—until I feel that, I'm not really comfortable with the character. It's only then that I can really start to think about his psychology. So, in a strange way, my method is to begin from the outside and work in. But every actor has his own personal method. That's what I've found.

Honeycutt: What did you discover about this character? How does he behave physically?

Scheider: Well, you don't get that much of his background. But you know that he's been in positions of responsibility and positions of command. He likes running his company. He likes running his company the way he wants to run it. He's been in the Air Force. He's a fighter pilot, so he likes responsibility, and he likes being alone in the responsibility. Except for her cooperation, he goes about without the police to solve the problem that faces him. And he likes that. And that's also a part of the American mythology of *The Lone Ranger*. I always think it's interesting that the pioneer or the American frontiersman—all of the qualities that he possesses that we admire and we love so much in our movies are all qualities that he stole from the American Indian. He's quiet. He's self-organized. He goes by his instincts. He does all of the things that the Indian does naturally. So, I feel that most of our heroes adopt their ways from the American Indian.

Honeycutt: You mentioned the reviews. I actually pulled the file from the Academy [of Motion Picture Arts and Sciences] library, and the reviews are pretty good on this film. And it certainly has its cult reputation now. But I know Cannon didn't really back it the way they should have. But do you feel anything else might have hindered it from reaching an audience? Do you have any sense of it?

Scheider: No. I think the material, for what it is, could not have been done much better than it's been done. But it's not a high-concept movie, nor is it about any great world-shaking theme or philosophy. It's a slice of life, kind of a street movie about some of the ugliness that faces everybody in their daily life, especially in this society that we live in. I don't think it's an important movie. I think it's a good movie. I think it's a very exciting movie. I think it's a good thriller, and it provides something to hold on to for an evening. So I don't think it could have received important reviews. It's a good piece of work by a good filmmaker. I think it would have helped if Cannon had more money at the time to publicize it and to give it more publicity. But they didn't, and that's the way it is.

AQ: *52 Pick-Up* was obviously a little bit out of the mainstream. The characters are very dark. Obviously, it was low-budget. My question is, was it the studio's choice to not . . . drop the rating on it from R to a PG or something to make it more mainstream and to open it up to larger audiences?

Scheider: John Frankenheimer wanted to do the book. He wanted to do a film that was faithful to Elmore Leonard's writing, and his writing is definitely R-rated.

AQ: Would you have made the same choice?

Scheider: Yes. I would have made it pretty much the same way. I would have maybe taken some of the rough edges off the scene in which the girl is killed, and I would have maybe insisted on making more of a romance between myself and Ann-Margret. I would have done a little commercial manipulating, but its main thrust is his relationship with these scumbags.

For Further Study

Videocassette

52 Pick-Up is available on videocassette from Media Home Entertainment.

Books

Leonard, Elmore. *52 Pick-Up*. New York: Avon, 1983.

Pratley, Gerald. *The Cinema of John Frankenheimer*. New York: A. S. Barnes and Co., 1969.

Periodicals

Byrge, Duane. "Frankenheimer Filming Cannon's *52 Pick-Up*." *Hollywood Reporter*, June 9, 1986.

Galligan, David. "Roy Scheider." *Drama-Logue* (Los Angeles), November 6–12, 1986.

Mann, Roderick. "A Career Picks Up with *52 Pick-Up*." *Los Angeles Times*, June 8, 1986.

Roberts, Jerry. "Frankenheimer Says Casting Is the Key." *Daily Breeze* (Torrance, Calif.), November 18, 1986.

17

SLOBODON ŠIJAN

AND

Who's Singing Over There?

(with Harriet Robbins)

On May 26, 1992, director Slobodan Šijan was interviewed by film critic Harriet Robbins after a screening of *Who's Singing Over There?* They were joined in the discussion by critic Michael Wilmington, who at the time wrote for the *Los Angeles Times* and is now film critic for the *Chicago Tribune*.

The Film

Who's Singing Over There? (Ko To Tamo Peva) (1980), a Centar Film release. Directed by Slobodan Šijan. Screenplay by Dusan Kovacesic. Director of photography, Bozidar Nikolic. Edited by Lana Vukobratovic. Music by Vojislav Kostic. Filmed on location in Yugoslavia. Color. 83 minutes. In Serbo-Croatian with English subtitles.

Cast: Paule Vujisic (Krstic), Aleksander Bercek (Misko), Dragan Nicolic (Seducer), Danilo Stojkovic (Fat Fascist), Miodrag and Nenad Kostic (Gypsy Singers), Neda Arneric (Bride), Slavko Stimac (Bridegroom), Millvoje Tomic (Old Soldier).

Synopsis: April 5, 1941, somewhere in Serbia, a rickety old bus crammed with a motley group of passengers tries to make it to Belgrade before the Nazis arrive and World War II breaks out in Yugoslavia. The passengers who create this ensemble piece include an egotistical singer, an accident-prone hunter, two sexually ravenous newlyweds, and a pair of Gypsies who sing of the scenario unfolding before our eyes.

Remarks and Reviews

"No sooner have we accepted the passengers as a microcosmic depiction of prewar Yugoslavia than Šijan begins breaking the rules by pushing petty character defects into undisguised malevolence, getting uneasy comic effects taking us one step further into chaos than we expected" (Dan Sallitt, *Los Angeles Reader*).

"Part Steinbeck's *The Wayward Bus*, part Thornton Wilder's *The Bridge of San Luis Rey*, this film is about a group of people boarding a bus bound for Belgrade—in the middle of the Nazi bombing of the city. They represent willfully blind human folly in its infinite variety as they mindlessly careen toward destruction" (Kevin Thomas, *Los Angeles Times*).

"*Who's Singing Over There?* is a little classic; wry, trenchant, moving and absolutely hilarious—with the kind of laughter that stings deepest, stings like blood, like acid and tears. In a year especially blessed by excellent movie comedies from abroad—such as *The Gods Must Be Crazy* and *Les Compères*—*Who's Singing Over There?* is the funniest of all, and the one you'll probably remember longest." (Michael Wilmington, *L.A. Weekly*).

"Šijan . . . has the graphic flair of a world-class satirical cartoonist. His genius is a distinctive sense of space that makes simple settings seem surreal and transforms faces into living caricatures" (David Chute, *Los Angeles Herald-Examiner*).

The Filmmaker

Yugoslavian director Slobodon Šijan burst onto the international film scene in 1982 with his debut feature, *Who's Singing Over There?* a major festival hit and multiple award winner. The film is so well known in the former Yugoslavia that the movie's title has become part of the vernacular. His second feature, *The Marathon Family*, was also a sizable international hit, but Šijan's early dazzling promise is yet to be fully realized, and the fragmentation and destruction of his homeland cannot have helped his professional situation. One look at any of his films should be enough to convince producers in search of a director with a distinctive, humanistic, and blackly humorous vision of mankind that the world needs another Šijan film, *Who's Listening Out There?*

Slobodan Šijan's Filmography

Who's Singing Over There? (1982) (special jury prize, Montreal Film Festival, Georges Sadoul Award for best foreign film to play in France); *The Marathon Family* (1984); *How I Was Systematically Destroyed by Idiots* (1985); *Strangler vs. Strangler* (1986).

Reasons for Selection

Who's Singing Over There? is a film that will endure. A stylish, manic, picaresque black comedy, this tale of a rickety old bus and its passengers works as a microcosm of humanity, revealed in comic tones.

H.R.

The Interview

Harriet Robbins: Where specifically was the film shot? Is it in Serbia?

Slobodan Šijan: It was shot about fifty kilometers north of Belgrade. It's a strange region which is not typical, really, for the landscape of Yugoslavia. It's kind of California-like landscape a little.

Robbins: And I was also curioius where you got the Gypsy actors.

Šijan: I got them on an obligatory military exercise. It was an exercise that lasted ten days. They brought a folksinger, a famous lady that was singing folk songs, and a harmonica player. He was very excited to be able to follow her on a harmonica, and he started singing also. And I just remembered his Frankie Laine kind of voice. Since I already did some work with Gypsies before, I remember that it wasn't that easy to find Gypsies. You know, there is always this legend that they are great singers. They are great in singing their songs, but they're not so great if you write something specially for the movie, like this song was written. So I just said that maybe I will need this guy one day, and then after two years we were preparing this film, and I was looking for singers, and I just remembered the guy and succeeded in locating him. The kid is his younger cousin. He doesn't sing originally in the film. There is another voice that we used.

Michael Wilmington: Could you talk a little about the genesis of the film?

Šijan: The project was offered to me as a TV project, for a forty-minute TV film, and it was quite different from what you saw. It was a contemporary story about the old man going to the city to buy a winter coat, and he takes a city bus, and there are some strange weird characters in the bus. They quarrel, and then they move on, and then he gets to the city and then he finds out it is Sunday and the shops are closed so he cannot buy a coat. That was the story. We started from that story and then the screenplay was written by one of the greatest comedy writers in Serbia, Dusan Kovacevic, and the TV script was written by him also. And you know, I talked to him and I said, "Listen, I like very much the comedy and the characters in the bus. But there is the chance for me to make my first film. It has a simple structure and it can be done cheaply. Do you have any ideas to expand the story?" And he said, "Yeah, I thought of some ideas. Let's work on it." We talked a lot. He wrote several drafts, but we still didn't have the story happening on the eve of the Second World War. So it came out as a solution from the formal requests. I kept bugging him. We had kind of a structure of a lot of small, crazy situations. In order to end the film we needed something that is crazier than everything. So one day he came up and said, "Listen, I had that idea, but I was afraid to mention. If it happens just the day before the war starts and the bomb hits the bus..." And I said, "Well, great."

Robbins: Now, everybody in Yugoslavia knows that that's the day the war was going to start, right?

Šijan: Yes. On April sixth the Germans bombed Belgrade, and that was like the official beginning of the war. And then we worked back when we made that decision, and we went back and suddenly everything worked. Characters started speaking for themselves in that situation. You start building that special psychosis. So it really went well from then on.

Robbins: This is your first feature film, right?

Šijan: This is my first theatrical feature film. Before this film I directed five TV feature films which were ranging from fifty to sixty-five minutes. So that was not my first dramatical feature, but it was my first for theatrical release.

Robbins: What was the actual budget was for this film?

Šijan: This film was done for about for $150,000. It was shot in twenty-two or twenty-three days, I think.

Robbins: What were the steps before you became a filmmaker? You had another career which I think might be of interest.

Šijan: I studied painting first and then after that I enrolled in film school and became a film director. So I finished two art schools. We call it film art also. So anyway, I was a painter. I had some exhibitions even, but somehow I felt that the work was for a limited audience. You work for people that have enough money to pay for your paintings. And that is like a selected audience. I always liked popular culture, and I wanted to do films for general audiences. This film was a big hit in Yugoslavia. It was maybe one of the most commercial films there. So that is why I moved to films. I wanted to make something that everybody can see by paying just a simple ticket. And I started working on it, and then I liked it more and more.

Wilmington: I'll sketch in something quickly for you here. . . . After this film Šijan directed another film with many of the same actors called *The Marathon Family*, which was another comedy. It probably had even more extreme comic elements. It was about a family of crazy undertakers in a series of feuds in a small town. His third film is actually a really daring political film for Yugoslavia. It was called *How I Was Systematically Destroyed by Idiots*, and its central character was played by the actor who played Mr. Mustache in this film. How would you describe him?

Šijan: I would describe it as a story about a little big guy. It's about a little man that thinks about himself as being a big and important person.

Wilmington: He regards himself as the only politically correct individual in all of Yugoslavia. That's sort of his attitude. His fourth film is a hard comedy called *Strangler vs. Strangler*. He has directed one English language film which hasn't been released yet. It's a good English-language chase comedy shot in Yugoslavia. That brings you up to date on what he has done since then. *Who's Singing Over There?* as Slobodan remarked, was an outstanding hit in Yugoslavia, and it also won a number of international awards at the time.

Šijan: It was screened in a lot of countries, and it made the international theaters, which is very hard for Yugoslavian films to do.

Wilmington: You also told me that it put the phrase into the language, and for years afterward people would do little kind of plays on *Who's Singing Over There?* in headlines and titles.

Šijan: We were not sure about the title of the film, but in Serbo-Croatian, it's like a very catchy title. It turned out to be a title that was used in news headlines for more than a decade. Even when war started in Yugoslavia, I saw a headline, *Who's Shooting Over There?* It kept on going.

Robbins: Could you tell us something about the filmmaking process in Yugoslavia when it was functioning? Because right now things are in disarray.

Šijan: I could not answer that question properly even when Yugoslavia existed. It's even harder now. As it was, at the time when this film was made, it was quite different from republic to republic. Generally, people mystify things too much. My theory is, that you have sources of money and you have to convince people who are deciding where that money goes to give that money to you to make a film. So that is the same approximately everywhere. It's just over there, it was either the Central Committee. In the Soviet Union and in Yugoslavia there were production company's art committees. Every company had its own so-called artist committee made out of important personalities—some politicians, some artists. Then you had to come there with the project, and then they have to approve it. Just to demonstrate the process: When I was making my third film, *How I Was Systematically Destroyed by Idiots*, I had big problems because one of the leading film critics in one of the Serbian main newspapers—he had been on the scene and in politics for thirty years—he was in a committee, and he said that it is unspeakable that I have that main character who is a kind of a bum pretending to be Che Guevara and is sleeping with a Russian woman who was hanging around in Yugoslavia like some kind of a bum also. He said, "You know, you are having this Soviet woman sleep with this crazy guy, and it is just offending the Soviet Union, and we cannot tolerate that." And I said, "Well aren't we supposed to be a nonallied country?" That was the ideological thing in Yugoslavia, that we were neither East nor West.

And I just saw a film where somebody said that Americans are idiots. So we can at least have a Soviet woman making love to somebody. He said, "Well yes, but you know in the United States of America everyone can criticize their president, and over here we respect that, and so we also are critical. But in the Soviet Union you cannot do that, so we respect that." That was his explanation.

Audience Question: Are any of your films available on video anywhere?

Šijan: Two of my films were released on video here by International Home Cinema, the distributors of this film at that time. But I think that was quite a limited release, and I don't think that it is available anymore.

Wilmington: There are some copies. International Home Cinema is in Santa Monica, and they are listed in the phone book.

Šijan: Maybe some little stores have them, but only those that handle rarities.

Wilmington: You can probably only get them through International Home Cinema right now, and you can call them. The films that are available are *Who's Singing Over There?*, *The Marathon Family*, and *Strangler vs. Strangler*.

Šijan: It was dubbed in English, and it was shown on the Movie Channel, I think several times.

AQ: Everyone noticed that they were using the Gypsy as the scapegoat. This is happening all over Eastern Europe now, and it happens in Western Europe too.

Šijan: The ethnic diversity in Yugoslavia basically became a hot issue several years ago. Before it was there and the official theory was that ethnic problems were solved, you would really be politically punished or arrested as a nationalist or whatever at the time. So ethnic issues were not really issues to be discussed publicly too much at the time of the strong Communist rule. So the same thing is with the Gypsies. They were a part of the society. They were never organized as a compact ethnic group if you compare it to other ethnic groups in Yugoslavia that had more politically organized structures. Gypsies were more organized around cultural societies, like Gypsy theater or some kind of music and some literary societies trying to revive the language. Some of them were present in some structures of society. You had some good writers, and you had some good famous people. But I'm not sure how many of them really made political careers. I don't remember too many of them being in politics, to be honest with you.

AQ: I believe they had their newspapers and everything in Yugoslavia.

Šijan: They did because that was the official policy in every Communist country. You had a strong official policy of giving newspapers to every minority. Giving a lot of other things. They were state subsidized. They existed so every single national group in Yugoslavia, even the very tiny ones, had a paper in their language or something like that. That was taken care of. My experience with Gypsies is just an experience of living in a city where you communicate with them when you just live with them. From the childhood they were there all the time in different place. But they were not a group that had an organized movement at the time. The thing about Yugoslavia is, now you say that you are from Yugoslavia, and suddenly everybody is explaining to me what's happening in Yugoslavia. And it is really a ridiculous situation because it is such a complex country, and I think what is happening now is very hard to explain. It is such a complicated set of events, but how we started to talk about it is that I grew up on American popular culture. On rock and roll, on American films, but we were a European country also, so you also grew up with European films with all the European culture that you have there. But, at that time being a Socialist country, Western culture was kind of looked down upon, and films had to have some essence and value in terms of content. Since I enjoyed a lot great American classic movies at the time, I tended to talk a lot about American

Slobodan Šijan directs Miodrag Kostic in *Who's Singing Over There?*

films. So I have a reputation for being one of the people over there who likes American cinéma. I was a big fan of John Ford, Hitchcock, and Howard Hawks, but my emphasizing that came out of the situation where American cinema was not really respected that way.

Wilmington: Were you thinking of *Stagecoach* at all when you did this?

Šijan: Absolutely. But there is another Ford film which I think is maybe even more similar to this: *Wagon Master*. That's a travelogue through a desolate terrain with strange groups of people appearing along the way.

Wilmington: It's a little more grotesque and lyrical than *Stagecoach*.

Robbins: It doesn't have the comical overtones that you have.

AQ: You seem to have such a cohesive acting ensemble. How much rehearsal time did you have before the actual filming of the movie? Also, could you talk about the casting?

Šijan: Well, no rehearsal time at all. The thing is that I really succeed in assembling a group of excellent actors. Especially the older guy, who is the father of the driver of the bus. He was in more than three hundred feature films made in Yugoslavia. He is the veteran actor, our Jean Gabin. The thing is, I had excellent actors, and they were different kinds of actors. So my main job was to make their acting styles and acting fashions get together so that they don't stand out in different ways. I think I succeeded in it, but I think that's because the script was excellent and gave them a lot of opportunity for character development. And I also take a lot of care in casting, picking the right looks, right characters for the right roles, and so that is important. It is seventy percent of the director's job sometimes.

AQ: I was trying very hard to think of some film that this reminded me of. The only one I thought of is the Luis Buñuel film that in this country is known as *Mexican Bus Ride*.

Šijan: There is a whole genre of films with buses. All of them are good, so it pays to make another one. A lot of it works. There is another film that I also liked a lot and that I thought of when I was making this film and that was the John Huston film *Beat the Devil*. You know, it has something in the atmosphere.

AQ: Yeah, black comedy.

Šijan: Hidden craziness.

AQ: I was really interested in your talking about the influence of Hollywood movies in Yugoslavia. Are the people able to see them? Have they always been able to see them?

Šijan: They were always able to see them. There was maybe a period of three years after the Second World War when it was not simple. Otherwise, they were always there. The main influence of American films on me was, like in this film, I was not using too many close-ups, which was sometimes fashionable. I went for some two shots, three shots, and only used a close-up when it was really important.

AQ: Just in terms of the structure of your film, what was your motivation behind having the Gypsies singing to the camera and then going off? In terms of pace of the film, how did that contribute to it?

Šijan: It was a structure that we developed while working on those different versions of the screenplay. The Gypsy characters evolved from the original story, where we had a group of musicians and two thieves. Then we had two Gypsies that were really stealing the wallet. Then we worked on it and we said, "Why do we need musicians and Gypsies? They can be musicians!" And then finally the crucial thing was that we decided that they basically should not steal the wallet. That was the whole point of the story at the end and the moral of the story. At the same time, I did one TV feature before in which I had a group of Gypsies singing. As a matter of fact, I have to say that it was not my device, there were several Yugoslav films made before where Gypsies were already used in that fashion. Like *The End of the World Will Come Soon*, where a group of fabulous Gypsies commented along the way with songs. And also some other things were made using that device. I was not thinking of using it as something too original. I was more trying to connect with something that was already done, some tradition that existed in using the Gypsies in that fashion. I did one feature film for TV where I had just a band of Gypsies, but only intercut in the action, having nothing to do with the film. They just appear in certain points and command the story, and they are not in the movie after that. In this film, when we were working on these Gypsy characters, I thought that it would be interesting to try to develop a structure in which they would command the story but at the same time be a part of it—to make them like people that are above the events because the mythology about Gypsies is that they know more. That may be a cliché, but there is something that is kind of following them as characters, and that's how I tried to use it.

AQ: In a year that has been filled with $70 million films and $40 million films that are pompous nothingnesses, I applaud you for your work, and I look forward to more of it. And I thank Mike Wilmington and Harriet Robbins for introducing your work to me.

Šijan: Thank you.

AQ: It's very hard to explain to the American people what this movie actually means. This is not just a regular movie, and it was not a regular movie in Yugoslavia. This is part of our youth, a part of our culture. This movie represents everything that is going on. I strongly believe that if it wasn't for Mr. Šijan that our film industry would not be where it is, and I really appreciate your work, and I thank you very much.

Šijan: Thanks. But I also have to say that I haven't been able to raise money for films in Yugoslavia for the past four years.

AQ: Could you talk a little about the Yugoslavian film industry? The country has been in a state of flux, but what was it like then? What happened? What were some of the specific, different problems?

Šijan: The interesting thing about the Yugoslav film industry is that basically it was developed as a systematical organization and something that is really an industry only under Communist rule. Before the Second World War, in the old kingdom of Yugoslavia, the film industry existed, but those were real desperadoes. They were people who ruined everything that they had in order to make a film. So I wonder what will happen now that Communism collapsed.

AQ: What is the situation right now?

Šijan: The state has to give money over there for films, and there is not a big market there, although there exists an interesting theory in Yugoslavian cinema in the 1980s, and I can say that I was a big part of it, as were some of my colleagues from my generation as well, where Yugoslav films were really commercial. And also good films. That period lasted about five, six years and not more. It is an interesting question as to why that happened and why that trend did not succeed because usually American films are at the top of the list, and at that time you had two or three Yugoslav films first, and then you had big hits like *Star War* and *Jaws.*

AQ: Was there a specific political reason why it stopped?

Šijan: I don't know, really. It is a hard thing to explain. It was just maybe the atmosphere and the movie-going community or the films that they were making or maybe the distribution policy at the time. I still cannot explain why that happened. Although that wave was not celebrated by some critics—they wanted sometimes more critical films and all that. It is kind of a combination of different things. After six or seven years, films just stopped bringing audiences into the theaters.

AQ: Do you think that this is the moment in Yugoslavia that people can enjoy seeing the movie and seeing what was happening like forty, fifty years ago, because of similar things happening over and over?

Šijan: I think the story of this movie is that evil exists in very ordinary and little people, as we call them. And that's where it starts, and how it starts is by not looking at yourself but at trying to find the guilty one in another one. That's how it develops basically. You are always looking for somebody else to be the guilty one, and when that process multiplies, you start killing each other. That's how it develops. I think that was the story that interested me in this film, and it is not even funny anymore for me because the events just made it too close to the truth.

For Further Study

Book

Goulding, Daniel J. *Liberated Cinema: The Yugoslavian Experience.* Bloomington: Indiana University Press, 1985.

Periodical

Mosier, John, and Andrew Horton. "Buses, Undertakers and the Belgrade Strangler: Slobodan Šijan on Comedy." *New Orleans Review*, summer 1985.

INDEX

Abbott, Bud 58
Abrahams, Jim 62–63
Aguilar, Claire 4
Air America 69, 78
Airplane! 62
Albeck, Andreas 29–30
Aldrich, Robert 232
Alice, Mary 215
All Night Long 31
All Quiet on the Western Front 90, 152
All That Jazz 276, 277
All the President's Men 144
Allen, Woody 46
Altman, Robert, 11 253–273
Amazon Women on the Moon 51 61, 109
An American Werewolf in London 54
Angel Heart 223
Ann-Margret 275, 279, 282, 283, 285
Annabella, 177
Another Woman 46
Ansen, David 25, 42, 68, 127, 216, 276
Anthony, Joseph, 155, 156, 158, 159, 160–161, 168, 170
Antonioni, Michaelangelo 252
Arkin, Alan 69, 75
Arkin, David 253
Arkoff, Samuel Z. 195
Arkush, Allan 51, 54–55
Attenborough, Richard 93
Aurthur, Robert Alan 162
Aykroyd, Dan 151

Baby, the Rain Must Fall 157, 164
Bacon, Francis 246
Bad Influence 278

Badlands 221
Bail, Chuck 67, 80
Bakunas, A.J. 67, 74
The Ballad of Cable Hogue 96, 97, 98–99
Bang the Drum Slowly 195
Barry, John 194
Bartel, Paul 56, 63
Batman 81, 266
Beat the Devil 254, 294
Beatty, Ned 233
Bellamy, Ralph 173
Bellin, Olga 155, 156, 158, 159, 161
Benson, Sheila 172, 216
Benton, Robert 113
Berenger, Tom 133
Beresford, Bruce 168
Berghoff, Herbert 159
Bergman, Ingmar 266
Berlinger, Warren 253
Best Defense 265
Betty, Sass 103
Beverly Hills Cop 151
Beyond the Valley of the Dolls 107–131
Bick, Jerry 253, 260
Bickford, Charles 157
The Big Sleep (1946) 256, 273
Bigelow, Kathryn 233
Bird, Laurie 7, 12, 14
Birdman of Alcatraz 283
Bite the Bullet 174, 188
Black Sunday 276, 278, 280
Blackboard Jungle 174, 180
Blackmur, R.P. 163
Blade Runner 32
Blake, Robert 180
Blatty, William Peter 252
The Blob (1988) 63

Blocker, Dan 257
Blodgett, Michael 107, 113–114, 117, 119, 130, 131
Blue Thunder 277
Bluhdorn, Charles 183
Bogart, Humphrey 185, 256, 260
Bonnie and Clyde 113
Boone, Richard 157
Boorman, John 272
Das Boot 279
Born on the Fourth of July 4, 133–154
Bottin, Rob 49, 50, 54, 60, 65
Bouton, Jim 253, 257
Boyle, Richard 144
Brackett, Leigh 253, 256, 258, 260, 273
Brando, Marlon 157
Breakthrough 102
Brewster McCloud 255, 260
A Bridge Too Far, A 93
Bridges, Jeff 3, 23, 24, 26, 27, 28–29, 31, 33, 39
Bring Me the Head of Alfredo Garcia 86, 91
Brodeur, Paul 67, 71, 82
Brodkin, Herbert 158
Brody, Jo Ann 253, 260
Bronson, Charles 37, 278
Brooks, Richard (actor) 215
Brooks, Richard (writer/director) 4, 173–190
Brown, David 124, 125, 127
Brute Force 187
Buffalo Bill and the Indians or Sitting Bull's History Lesson 255
Buñuel, Luis 294
The 'Burbs 51, 58–60, 61
Burnett, Charles 215–230
Burns, Ken 157, 166
Burroughs, William S. 277
Burrows, Abe 111
Bush, George 145
Bushnell, Scott 266
Butch Cassidy and the Sundance Kid 125
Butler, Paul 215
Butler, Terence 87
Byrge, Duane 135, 232, 276, 285

Caan, James 37, 69, 75

California Split 255, 264
Cameron, James 52–53
Canby, Vincent 29, 37, 134, 153, 217, 232, 243, 254
Cannel, Stephen J. 187
Cape Fear (1991) 241
Capote, Truman 180–181
Capp, Andy 112, 129
Capra, Frank 141
Cardinale, Claudia 173
Carnal Knowledge 282
Carr, Jay 216
Carradine, John 49, 128
Carroll, Kathleen 68
Carson, Johnny 257
Carter, Jimmy 142
Carver, Raymond 269
Cassavetes, John 20
Cat on a Hot Tin Roof 174
Cerny, Pavel 205, 210
Chamberlain, Jeff 180
Champlin, Charles 4, 5, 82, 173–190, 191–204
Chandler, Raymond 253, 256, 258, 259, 260, 262, 272
The Chase 157, 163, 164
Chayefsky, Paddy 162, 233
Cherry, Harry and Raquel 109, 118, 126
Chinatown 273
Chopra, Joyce 166
Chubb, Caldecot 215, 218, 222
Churchill, Winston 181–183
Coburn, James 85–106
Cocks, Jay 8
Cohan, George M. 152
Coleman, Cliff 105
Color of Night 69
Colors 215
Come Back to the Five and Dime, Jimmy Dean, Jimmy Dean 255, 256
Connery, Sean 69, 78
Conrad, Joseph 186
Convicts 158, 162, 166, 167
Coppola, Francis Ford 9, 11, 32, 184, 272
Corliss, Richard 154, 216
Corman, Roger 3, 9, 50, 51, 55, 56–57, 63
Corry, Will 7, 17, 22
Cosby, Bill 191, 192, 193, 194, 196, 197, 203, 204

Costello, Lou 58
Countdown 254, 255, 263
The Cowboys 259–260
Cowie, Peter 48
Cox, Alex 219
Crimes and Misdemeanors 46
Crisis 179–180
Crist, Judith 68, 189
Cronenweth, Jordan 23, 32–33, 34
Cross of Iron 3, 85–106
Cruise, Tom 133, 134, 139, 147, 154
Cruising 233, 234, 241
Culp, Jason 191, 197, 199
Culp, Robert 85, 87, 90–92, 98, 99,
   103, 105, 191–204
Curse of the Living Corpse 277
Cutter's Way 3, 11, 23–39

Dafoe, Willem, 133, 231, 238, 239,
   243
Dante, Joe 3, 9, 49–65
Dare, Michael 5, 107–131, 276
Davis, Andrew 233
Davis, Jack 264
Day for Night 71
The Dead 169
Deal of the Century 233, 234
De Carlo, Yvonne 128
De Mille, Agnes 170
Denby, David 25, 232
De Niro, Robert 14, 25
Detective Story 245
Diary of a Mad Housewife 12
Diller, Barry 183
Dirty Harry 238
*Dr. Strangelove: or How I Learned to
   Stop Worrying and Love the
   Bomb* 148
The Doors 136, 143, 144
Dornan, Bob K. 140
Douglas, Kirk 113
Douglas, Michael 72
Dreyfuss, Richard 27–28
Duvall, Robert 155, 156, 158, 159, 160,
   161–162, 166, 167
Duvall, Shelley 265, 267

Eastwood, Clint 233
Easy Rider 11–12, 13, 15, 20, 36

Ebert, Roger 107–131, 254, 276
Eggenweiler, Bob 265
Ehrenstein, David 5, 49–65, 82
Eichhorn, Lisa 23, 27, 31 33–34
Elliot, T.S. 245–246
Elmer Gantry, 174, 175, 186, 188–189
Emerson, Jim 5, 41–48
*The End of the World Will Come
   Soon* 294
E.T., the Extra-Terrestrial 82, 245
Eve and the Handy Man 108, 112
The Exorcist 233, 234, 252

Falk, Peter 265
Faster, Pussy Cat! Kill! Kill! 109, 112,
   114
Fatal Attraction 278
Faulkner, William 155, 156, 157, 158,
   159, 168–169, 170, 171, 172, 256
Fellini, Federico 266
Ferrer, Jose 179, 180
Ferriol, Caroline 76
Feuer, Debra 231, 239
Feury, Peggy 167–168
Fever Pitch 174
52 Pick-Up 275–285
Finch, Peter 233
Finnell, Mike 63
Fiskin, Jeffrey Alan 23, 29, 35
Five Easy Pieces 13
The Five Heartbeats 226
Fleming, Charles 82
Fluegel, Darlanne 231
Fonda, Henry 113
Fonda, Jane 157, 277, 279
Fonda, Peter 11
Fool for Love 256, 268
Foote, Hallie 157
Foote, Horton 4, 155–172
Foote, Lillian 157, 161
Foote, Shelby 170
For the Boys 257
Ford, John 6, 293
Forman, Milos 12, 25, 35
Fosse, Bob 276
Foster, Jodie 58
The Fourth War 277, 283
Fraker, William A. 188
Frankenheimer, John 157, 275, 276,
   277, 278, 280, 281, 283–284, 285

Freebie and the Bean 69, 72, 75, 76, 79

Freedman, Samuel G. 164, 166, 172

The French Connection 233, 234, 235, 241, 251, 276, 277, 279

Freund, Karl 178

Friedkin, William 138

Frontiere, Dominic 76

Full Metal Jacket 148

Fuller, Sam 232–233

Fulsom, Lowell 225

Gable, Clark 178

Gabriel, Teshone 215, 227–228

Gardenia, Vincent 191, 195

Gardens of Stone 32

Garfield, Allen *see* Goorwitz, Allen

Geffen, David 265

Genet, Jean 246

The Getaway (1972) 86, 91, 104

Getting Straight 69, 71

Ghostbusters 151

Gibson, Henry 253, 257

Gibson, Mel 69, 78, 243

Gilliatt, Penelope 105

Gilmore, Geoffrey 4, 7, 19, 21, 231, 238, 242, 243, 244, 271

Ginsberg, Allen 246

Gish, Lillian 163, 168

Globus, Yorum 275

Glover, Danny 215, 216, 217, 218, 220, 221 222, 223, 224, 229

Glover, John 275, 276

The Godfather 195, 240

The Godfather, Part III 183–184

Golan, Menahem 275

Goorwitz, Allen (a.k.a. Allen Garfield) 67, 74

Gotti, John 238

Gould, Elliott 69, 253, 254, 256, 259, 260, 264

Graham, Martha 170

Grand Illusion 152

Grand Theft Auto 50, 51

Grant, Cary 179–180

The Grapes of Wrath 143

Gray Area 219

Gremlins 50, 52, 53, 54, 63, 64

Gremlins 2: The New Batch 51, 53, 54

Grierson, John 227

Guber, Peter 71

Gurian, David 107, 117, 119

Gurian, Paul 28–29

Haas, Charlie 53

Haber, Katy 4, 85, 87, 90, 92, 93, 94, 97, 98, 101, 102, 105

Hackman, Gene 26, 31, 188, 277, 279

Haji 107, 114–115

Hall, Conrad 32, 173, 174, 187–188

Hall, Jon 176, 177

Hanak, Dusan 205–213

Hanks, Tom 59

Harlin, Renny 233

Harmon, Jack 131

Harrison, Philip 279

Hartwig, Wolf 85, 90, 92, 93, 94, 102

Hawks, Howard 256, 260, 263, 293

Hayden, Sterling 157, 253, 254, 257, 271

Heard, John 23, 24, 27, 28, 33, 34

Heaven and Earth 136

Heaven's Gate 3, 28, 31

Hellinger, Mark 188

Hellman, Lillian 157, 164, 168

Hellman, Monte 4, 5, 7–22

Hello Dolly! 117

Hellzapoppin 54

Henry: Portrait of a Serial Killer 151

Hercules Goes Bananas 257

Hershey, Barbara 67, 74

Hickey and Boggs 191–204

Hickney, Bill 200

Hill, Walter 193, 198, 203

The Hired Hand 12

Hitchcock, Alfred 293

The Hitcher 276

Hoberman, J. 25, 39, 50, 276

Hoffman, Abbie 133

Hoffman, Dustin 103

Hofstra, Jack 76

Holiday, Billie 225

Hollywood Boulevard 50, 54, 55, 57, 61, 63

Honeycutt, Kirk 6, 232, 275–285

Hooper 72

Hopper, Dennis 11

Houston, Pernelope 174

How I Was Systematically Destroyed by Idiots 288, 290, 291
Howard, Ron 50
The Howling 49–65
Hudson, Rock 181–182
Hughes, Howard 257
Hughes, Jack 249
Hurry Sundown 157
Huston, John 169, 174, 178, 184–185, 294

I Am a Fugitive from a Chain Gang 143
Images 254, 255, 260, 261, 266
The Immoral Mr. Teas 108, 111, 113
In Cold Blood 174, 180–181
The Incredible Shrinking Woman 63
Innerspace 50, 51, 57, 58
Intimate Lighting 11, 25, 26, 37
Irving, Clifford 257
It's a Wonderful Life 63

Jaffe, Herb 195
James, Steve 231
Jameson, Richard T. 24, 39
Jarmusch, Jim 21, 151
Jarre, Maurice 173, 176
Jaws 262, 276, 277, 279, 295
JFK 135
Jones, Carnetta 215, 218
Jones, James 101
Jones, James Earl 166
Jones, Tommy Lee 157
Junior Bonner 86, 99

Kael, Pauline 49, 68, 137, 173, 254
Kanin, Garson 120
Kaplan, Jonathan 63
Kastner, Elliott 260
Kauffmann, Stanley 135
Kawin, Bruce F. 65, 156, 171
Kelley, Walter 94, 101
Kenyatta, Jomo 181–182
Key Largo 174, 178
Kieslowski, Krzysztof 47
The Killer Elite 86, 91, 137
Killer of Sheep 217, 218, 226
The Killers (1946) 187
King Kong (1976) 105

The King of Marvin Gardens 13
Kingsley, Sidney 245
Kinjite: Forbidden Subjects 215
Klawans, Stuart 135, 216
Klein, Andy 231, 232
Klute 127, 277, 279
Knight, Arthur 68
Koch, Howard 179
Koenekamp, Fred J. 107, 128
Komorowska, Maja 45
Koulisis, Linda 215, 218, 221–222
Kovacevic, Dusan 287, 289
Kovic, Ron 133–154
Kroeger, Berry 127–128
Krohn, Bill 4, 7, 12, 21–22
Kubrick, Stanley 148, 272
Kurasawa, Akira 37
Kurtz, Gary 14

Lancaster, Burt 173, 174, 186, 187, 284
Landis, John 51, 54, 64
Lang, Fritz 232
Lapine, Jean 268
The Last Movie 12
The Last Temptation of Christ 110
Lawson, Tony 85, 93, 100
LaZar, John 107, 116–117, 119, 130
Leakey, Dr. Louis B. 181
Lee, Harper 157, 163, 169
Lee, Spike 151, 216, 222
Leonard, Elmore 240, 275, 276, 277, 278, 280, 281, 282, 283, 285
Lewis, Jerry 58
Lewis, Sinclair 186–187
List, Doug 23, 30, 36
Little Man Tate 59
Lloyd, Walt 215
Lombardo, Lou 253, 258
The Long Goodbye 253–273
Looking for Mr. Goodbar 174, 175, 180, 183
Lord Jim 174, 186
Lorna 109, 112
Louise, Tina 264
Love, Andrew 176
Lovelady, Stephen 112
Lucas, George 9, 11
Lumbly, Carl 215
Lumet, Sidney 283
Lynch, David 112

McBride, Joseph 83
McCabe and Mrs. Miller 254, 255, 258, 270
McCarthy, Kevin 49
McCarthy, Todd 65, 131
McCloud, Duncan 131
McClure, Doug 275, 283
McGee, Vonetta 215
McGilligan, Patrick 190, 272
McNaughton, John 151
Macnee, Patrick 49
McQueen, Steve 164
McTiernan, John 233
The Maltese Falcon 201, 280
Maltin, Leonard 86, 156
Maltz, Albert 188
The Manchurian Candidate 278, 283
Manhunter 276
Mann, Anthony 232
Mann, Roderick 83, 285
Mannix, Eddie 182
Manson, Charles 111, 243
The Marathon Family 288, 290, 292
Marathon Man 276
Marcus, Lawrence, B. 67, 71, 75
Martin, Dean 58
Martin, Dick 114
Martin, Dolly Read *see* Read Martin, Dolly
Martincek, Martin 207, 211
Marvin, Lee 173–174, 184
*M*A*S*H* 125, 254, 255, 260, 263
Mask, Johnny 155, 160
Maslin, Janet 154, 232, 276
Mason, James 85, 100
Masterson, Peter 155, 166, 167, 168
Maugham, W. Somerset 182
Maunder, Wayne 128
Mayer, Louis B. 178–179
Mayer, Roger 182–183
Mayer, Vivian 4
Mazursky, Paul 192
Meisner, Sanford 161
Mengers, Sue 31
Meredith, Burgess 113
Metz, Rex 196
Mexican Bus Ride 294
Meyer, Russ 107–131
Meyers, Peter 124
Midnight Express 135, 136
Mignot, Pierre 268

Milius, John 145
Miller, Dick 49, 56, 57
Miller, George 51, 64
Missing 151
Mississippi Burning 143
Mr. Majestyk 278
Mr. T 187
Mitchelson, Marvin 184
Mitchum, Robert 6, 260, 264
Monaco, James 86
Mondo Topless 109, 112
Montalban, Ricardo 179
Montez, Maria 176, 177
Moriarty, Michael 191, 195, 200
Morrison, Jim 143, 144
Morrissey, Paul 11 20
Morrow, Vic 64
Mosel, Tad 162
Motor Psycho! 109, 111–112
Mud Honey! 109, 112, 124–125
Muller, Robby 231, 232, 268
Mulligan, Robert 161, 162, 163
Murphy, Eddie 151, 265
My Brother's Wedding 217, 218, 219
My Word of Honor 229
Myers, Cynthia 107, 114, 119, 130
Myra Breckinridge 108, 125
Mystery Street 178

Naked Lunch 277
Napier, Charles 107, 117, 118–119, 125, 126, 130
Nashville 254, 255, 257
Natural Born Killers 136
New York Stories 62
Newman, David 113
Newman, Paul 180–181
Nicholson, Al 196
Nicholson, Jack 9, 10, 69
Nielsen, Leslie 62–63
Night Moves 26, 71
1918 162
Nitzsche, Jack 35
Nixon, DeVaughn 215, 219–220
Norris, Chuck 233
Novarro, Ramon 180

Oakie, Jack 55
Oates, Warren 7, 10, 16
O.C. and Stiggs 256, 264–265

Olmi, Ermanno 227
On Golden Pond 257
On Valentine's Day 157, 158, 162
One Flew Over the Cuckoo's Nest 35,
    72
O'Rourke, Frank 173, 175
The Orphans Home Cycle 156, 167,
    168
O'Toole, Peter 67, 68, 69, 70, 73, 74,
    78, 81, 82, 83
Ozu, Yasujiro 37, 147

Pacino, Al 14, 233, 241
Page, Geraldine 157, 168
Pakula, Alan J. 144, 163
Palance, Jack 173, 188
Pankow, John 231
Papp, Joe 27, 279
Parker, Alan 223
The Passenger 252
Passer, Ivan 11, 23–39
Pat Garrett and Billy the Kid 86, 102
Paths of Glory 148
Patton 125
Patton, Gen. George S. Jr. 119–121
Pearlman, Gilbert 155, 159, 160
Peary, Danny 108, 272
Peck, Gregory 163
Peckinpah, Sam 3, 10, 85–106, 137,
    192
Peggy Sue Got Married 32
Penn, Arthur 26, 71, 157, 272
Persona 266
Petersen, William L. 231, 238
Petersen, Wolfgang 281
Petievich, Gerald 231, 234–235,
    236–237, 238, 239, 240, 242–243,
    244, 247, 248, 249–250
Petievich, John 231, 239, 240, 243
Pickens, Slim 49, 104
Pictures of the Old World 205–213
Piranha 50, 52, 57
Plan 9 from Outer Space 109
Platoon 135, 136, 145, 146, 149–150,
    152
The Player 218, 254, 255, 257, 264,
    269–270
Poitier, Sidney 181–182
Pollack, Sydney 283
Power, Tyrone 177

Powers, John 273
Predator 2 220
Preminger, Otto 202
Pressman, Edward R. 215, 221
Preston, Kelly 275
Pretty Woman 70
The Professionals 4, 173–190
Proust, Marcel 250
Puzo, Mario 183

Quintet 255, 271

Raging Bull 151
Railsback, Steve 67, 70, 73
Rainer, Peter 68, 232
Ralph, Sheryl Lee 215
Rampage 233, 234
The Rapture 218
Read Martin, Dolly 107, 114, 117–118,
    119, 126, 130
Reagan, Ronald 145
Rear Window 59
Redford, Robert 157
Renoir, Jean 153
Repo Man 219
Reversal of Fortune 136
Reynolds, Burt 72, 278
Richardson, Robert 148
Richardson, Sy 215, 219
Ride the High Country 86, 90, 96
Riley, Winona 219
Robbins, Harriet 6, 215–230, 287–296
Roberts, Julia 192
Robinson, Edward G. 185
Roebling, Paul 155, 159
Roland, Gilbert 180
Roland, Henry 131
A Room with a View 151
Roos, Fred 14
The Rose 257
Rosen, Robert 1–2, 107, 110–111
Rosy Dreams 207, 211
Rotten, Johnny 123
Ruark, Robert 181
Rudolph, Alan 258
Rush, Richard 3, 67–83
The Russia House 277
Ruthless People 62
Ryan, Jim 120–121, 127

Ryan, Robert 173, 176
Rydell, Mark 253, 257, 259–260

Sabu 176, 177
Safford, Tony 7, 13, 15, 16, 20
Said, Fouad 193–194, 195, 196
Salvador 136, 144, 150
Sands, Julian 47
Sarrazin, Michael 14
Sarris, Andrew 25
Sayles, John 49, 51, 65
Scarface (1983) 136, 145
Scheider, Roy 4, 275–285
Schell, Maximilian 85, 95, 101, 103,
   104
Schick, Elliot 191, 194, 195, 196, 199,
   200, 203, 204
Schwarzenegger, Arnold 253, 257
Scorsese, Martin 9, 270
Seagal, Steven 233
Secret Honor 255, 256
Sedgwick, Kyra 133
Selleck, Tom 128
Serling, Rod 64, 162
Seven Days in May 278
The Seven Minutes 127
sex, lies, and videotape 151
Seydor, Paul 106
Shattered 281
Shaw, Tom 188
Sheehan, Henry 4, 206
Sheen, Charlie 146
Short Cuts 256, 269
A Short Film About a Killing 47
Sid and Nancy 151, 219
Siegel, Don 86, 232
Sijan, Slobodon 287–296
Simmons, Garner 106
Simon, Melvin 67, 72–73, 76, 81
Siskel, Gene 42, 126
Sitting Pretty (1933) 55
Smith, Bud 231, 232
Smith, Wonderful 215, 218–219, 221
Soderbergh, Steven 151
Something of Value, 181–183
Song of Ceylon 227
Sorcerer 234, 244, 249
Soutendijk, Rene 47
Spacek, Sissy 265
Spiegel, Sam 163

Spielberg, Steven 11, 50, 51, 64, 262,
   276, 277
Spottiswoode, Roger 69, 78
Sragow, Michael 68, 83
Stagecoach 293
Stallone, Sylvester 233
Stanley, Kim 157, 161
Star Wars 82, 295
State of Grace 33
Stick 278
Stockwell, Dean 231
Stone, Oliver 133–154
Storaro, Vittorio 148
Storm Fear 157, 162
Straight to Hell 215
Strangler vs. Strangler 288, 290, 292
Straw Dogs 86, 91, 97, 103, 195, 201
Streamers 255, 256
Streisand, Barbra 31
Strode, Woody 173, 187
Strong, Arnold *see* Schwarzenegger
The Stunt Man 67–83
Suez 177
Super Vixens 109, 118, 122, 124–125
Superman (1978) 105
Susann, Jacqueline 125
Sweet Bird of Youth 174

Taking Off 12
Talk Radio 136, 221
Tangerine Dream 249
Tannen, Ned 12, 15
Tarantino, Quentin 10
Tarkovsky, Andrei 46
Taylor, Ella 254
Taylor, James 12, 13, 14
Tender Mercies 156, 157, 161, 162, 167,
   171
That Cold Day in the Park 255
Thieves Like Us 254, 255, 263
The Third Man 262
This Island Earth 64
Thomas, Kevin 6, 205–213, 288
Thompson, Anne 229
Thompson, Tommy 258, 265
Thomson, David 8, 9, 22
Thornburg, Newton 23, 29, 36, 38
Three Women 255, 265–266, 267
To Kill a Mockingbird 156, 157, 161,
   162, 163, 171

To Live and Die in L.A. 231–252
To Sleep with Anger 215–230, 270
Tobey, Kenneth 49
Tolkin, Michael 218
Tomlin, Lily 63
Tomorrow 155–172
Top Gun 270
Top Secret! 62
Townsend, Robert 226
The Train 283
Travolta, John 184
Trebor, Robert 275, 276
Triola (Marvin), Michelle 184
The Trip to Bountiful 156, 157, 162,
    163, 167, 168, 171
The True Glory 120
True Stories 221
Truffaut, François 71, 147
Turan, Kenneth 6, 50, 65, 67–83, 131
Turner, Ted 160
Turturro, John 231, 242
Twilight Zone — The Movie 51, 64–65
Two-Lane Blacktop 4, 7–22
Two-Minute Warning 280

Vacano, Jost 275, 279
Valdez Is Coming 280
Valenti, Jack 240
Valley of the Dolls 113
Van Pallandt, Nina 23, 253, 254, 257
Vanity 275
Vicious, Sid 123
Visciglia, Robert 85, 87, 92–93, 94,
    96, 98–99, 100, 104
Voight, Jon 14
Vorkapitch, Slavko 251–252

Waggner, George 176
Wagon Master 293
Wall Street 136, 145, 147
Wallace, Dee 49
Wallace, Irving 127
Wang Chung 231, 249
Warhol, Andy 112
Warner, David 85, 87, 93, 96–98, 100,
    103–104, 106
Warner, Jack L. 263
Wasserman, Lew 12
Waters, John 122

Wayne, John 259
Webb, Jack 179
A Wedding 255
Weddle, David 86, 106
Welles, Orson 87
Who's Singing Over There? 287–296
Wilborn, Charles 99
Wild at Heart 112
The Wild Bunch 86, 88, 96, 103, 105,
    195, 258
Wilde, Cornel 162
Williams, Clarence III 275, 276
Williams, Edy 107, 108, 110, 114,
    115–116, 127, 128, 130
Williams, Elmo 127
Williams, John 253, 259
Williams, Tennessee 175, 180
Willis, Bruce 69, 233
Wilmington, Michael 4, 6, 42,
    133–154, 232, 253–273, 280, 287,
    288, 289, 290, 291, 292, 293,
    295
Wilson, Dennis 13, 14
Wilson, Scott 41–48, 180
The Witches of Eastwick 64
Witherspoon, Jimmy 215
Wolf, William 83, 156
Wolfe, Tom 126
Wood, Robin 252
Woods, James 191, 195
Woronov, Mary 56
Wright, Basil 227
Wrong Is Right 174
Wurlitzer, Rudy 7, 17, 22

Yankee Doddle Dandy 152
Year of the Dragon 136
The Year of the Gun 279
A Year of the Quiet Sun 4, 41–48
Young Guns II 48
Young Mr. Lincoln 144

Zandy's Bride 32
Zanuck, Darryl F. 111, 143
Zanuck, Richard 111, 124, 127
Zanussi, Krzysztof 41–48
Zsigmond, Vilmos 253, 258
Zucker, David 62–63
Zucker, Jerry 62–63